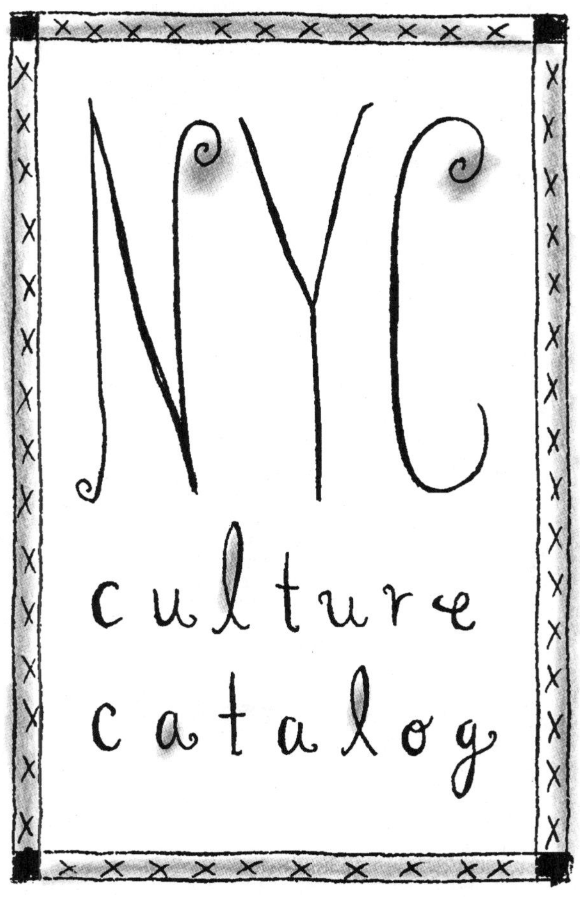

A GUIDE TO NEW YORK CIT

THEATERS, ZOOS, LIB

BOTANICAL GARDENS, CONCERT HALLS

AND HISTORIC HOUSES

HARRY N. ABRAMS, INC., PUBLISHERS
IN ASSOCIATION WITH
ALLIANCE FOR THE ARTS

FOR ALLIANCE FOR THE ARTS

Writer and Editorial Consultant
William L. Beavers

General Editor
Randall Bourscheidt

Associate Editor
Sarah S. Peterson

Editorial/Research Assistants
Jason Childers
Peter Cury
Francine Goldenhar
Christopher Macdougall
Barbara Mateer
Susan Peterson

DESIGN

Patterson Wood
Peg Patterson
Caroline Kavanagh
Michael Graziolo

FOR HARRY N. ABRAMS, INC.

Project Manager
Margaret Rennolds Chace

Editor
Kate Norment

NEW YORK CITY CULTURE CATALOG is produced by the Alliance for the Arts, a nonprofit organization dedicated to policy research, information services and advocacy for the arts in New York City.

ALLIANCE FOR THE ARTS
330 West 42nd Street
New York, New York 10036

Library of Congress Cataloging-in-Publication Data

New York City Culture Catalog: a guide to New York City's museums, theaters, zoos, libraries, botanical gardens, concert halls and historic houses.
p. cm.
Includes index.
ISBN 0-8109-2578-8
1. New York (N.Y.)—Guidebooks.
2. Family recreation—New York (N.Y.)—Guidebooks.
I. Alliance for the Arts (New York, N.Y.)
F128.18.N386 1994
917.4'710443—dc20 93-34782

Published in 1994 by Harry N. Abrams, Incorporated, New York. A Times Mirror Company.

Printed and bound in the United States of America

In memory of Robert F. Wagner, Jr., true son of New York

As a major supporter of the arts for 35 years, Philip Morris is proud to underwrite this comprehensive guide to New York City institutions.

Though Philip Morris is a global company with facilities throughout the world, New York City is our home, with some 2,000 employees in this area. We believe that helping to create a strong cultural environment where our employees live and work makes for a dynamic and responsive community that benefits us all.

We hope that this publication will inspire New Yorkers and visitors alike to become more familiar with and to utilize the resources of the excellent museums, performing arts centers, libraries, zoos, botanical gardens and cultural institutions found here.

Stephanie French
Vice President, Corporate Contributions
and Cultural Affairs
PHILIP MORRIS COMPANIES INC.

This publication is funded in part by Philip Morris Companies Inc.

The Alliance for the Arts gratefully acknowledges the following foundations and corporations for their generous support of the NEW YORK CITY CULTURE CATALOG:

The J.M. Kaplan Fund, *Principal Sponsor;* New York State Council on the Arts; Loews Foundation; The Samuel H. Kress Foundation; New York Telephone.

Additional funding was provided by the Tourism Grant Program administered by the New York City Policy and Marketing Group.

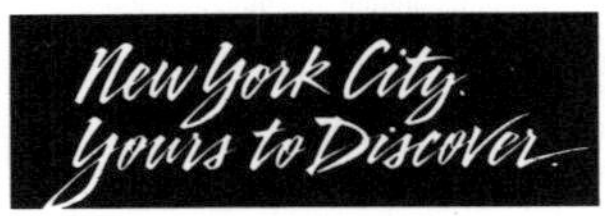

Contents

5 Introduction

6 How to Use This Guide

10 The Bronx

24 Brooklyn

44 Manhattan

172 Queens

190 Staten Island

204 Appendixes

213 Alphabetical Index

216 Subject Index

219 Acknowledgments

Introduction

n all my years as an arts advocate and administrator, this is the first guidebook I have come across that gives the reader a truly comprehensive overview of all the cultural resources New York City has to offer.

Both New York residents and visitors to the city usually have a sense of the highly visible mega-institutions they want to visit. These are astonishing resources that have put New York City on the cultural map and they have become a source of immense pride for New Yorkers.

There exists, however, a host of other cultural institutions in the city—virtually all with outstanding resources of their own. The public needs to be reminded that they are out there, ripe for the picking. Hence, this wonderful guide.

New York City is an extraordinary cultural resource of immense diversity attracting millions of visitors every year. Its buildings represent the most concentrated aggregation of architectural styles in America. Its many early houses reflect the city's Dutch beginnings. Its museums are encyclopedic and represent the best America has to offer. It boasts symphony orchestras, dance troupes, dozens of galleries, science and natural history museums, libraries, zoological parks and historic sites.

I believe the **NEW YORK CITY CULTURE CATALOG** will have a long life and be enormously popular with readers who want to delve into this rich and varied concentration of cultural institutions. Use it as your own personal key to the city.

Kitty Carlisle Hart
Chairman, New York State Council on the Arts

How to Use This Guide

The **NEW YORK CITY CULTURE CATALOG**—the most comprehesive guidebook of its kind—was written to help visitors and New Yorkers alike make better use of the amazing number of cultural institutions operating throughout the city's five boroughs.

The Manhattan section of this guidebook contains descriptions of 167 cultural institutions, large and small. In the Bronx, Brooklyn, Queens and Staten Island sections you will find 71 more. All entries include information about exhibition programs or live performance offerings; permanent collections, if any; educational activities, such as lectures and workshops; and, when pertinent, interesting historical and architectural details.

The **NEW YORK CITY CULTURE CATALOG** is arranged in alphabetical order by New York City borough: the Bronx, Brooklyn, Manhattan, Queens and Staten Island. Each borough section is preceded by a map—three maps for Manhattan—indicating the location of every institution described in the section.

Each entry begins with the institution's formal name, address, nearest cross street and telephone number. Below this basic information there may be up to six symbols, which, if present, indicate the availability at that institution of a giftshop, food service, library or archive, full disability asscess, parking and landmark status (see Symbol Key).

The introductory information and symbols (if present) are followed by a brief narrative of the cultural organization's activities, focusing primarily on its exhibition or live performance offerings. Note that the exhibitions or performances referred to are, in most cases, not current; they are mentioned only to give the reader an idea of the scope of a particular institution's programming.

For listings of current exhibits or performances refer to periodicals such as The New York Times, New York magazine, The Daily News, The New York Post, New York Newsday, The Amsterdam News, The New Yorker, The Village Voice, El Diario and Museums New York. Listings of current theater, dance or music offerings can also be obtained by calling the TDF Arts Information Phone Line (New York City On Stage) at 212-768-1818.

The general information section following the narrative will augment the symbols by providing more detail on giftshops, food service, libraries or archives, disability access, parking and landmark status. It will also indicate hours of operation; admission charges, if any; public transportation directions and—for all boroughs except Manhattan, where commercial garages are abundant—suggestions for parking.

Limited space has made the inclusion of automobile directions impossible. It is suggested that you write or telephone ahead in sufficient time to receive these by mail or fax. In most instances, you will find public transportation to be the most efficient, least expensive mode of moving about the city.

SYMBOL KEY

Institutional Giftshop

On-Site Food Service

On-Site Library or Archive

Full Accessibility

On-Site Parking

Listing on The National Register of Historic Places or Designation as a New York City Landmark

Almost all institutions described in the **NEW YORK CITY CULTURE CATALOG** provide extensive education programs for everyone from school-age children to adults. These activities frequently include lectures, artists' talks, workshops, courses of instruction, roundtables, panel discussions, and film and video screenings. Readers interested in education should call the institution for information or ask for it when visiting.

Strictly commercial venues—such as on and off Broadway theaters, rock and jazz clubs, retrospective movie houses, galleries, etc.—are not described in the **NEW YORK CITY CULTURE CATALOG**. However, many of these venues are listed in the supplemental appendixes at the back of the book. Ads and schedules in daily newspapers and magazines are a good source of information about current attractions at these establishments.

Also in the back of the book you will find an index listing all institutions alphabetically, regardless of city borough. There is also an index grouping all organizations by type (i.e., science museums, theaters, libraries, botanical gardens, etc.) to help you choose from a range of offerings in any given subject area.

A final thought to keep in mind when using this guidebook. The Greek philosopher Heraclitus wrote that "nothing endures but change." While this publication has been meticulously researched for accuracy and timeliness of information, institutional changes are inevitable. Hours of operation will change, admission fees will fluctuate and occasionally an institution will relocate or cease operation altogether. The prudent reader will avoid inconvenience by telephoning ahead to confirm particulars.

ALLIANCE FOR THE ARTS

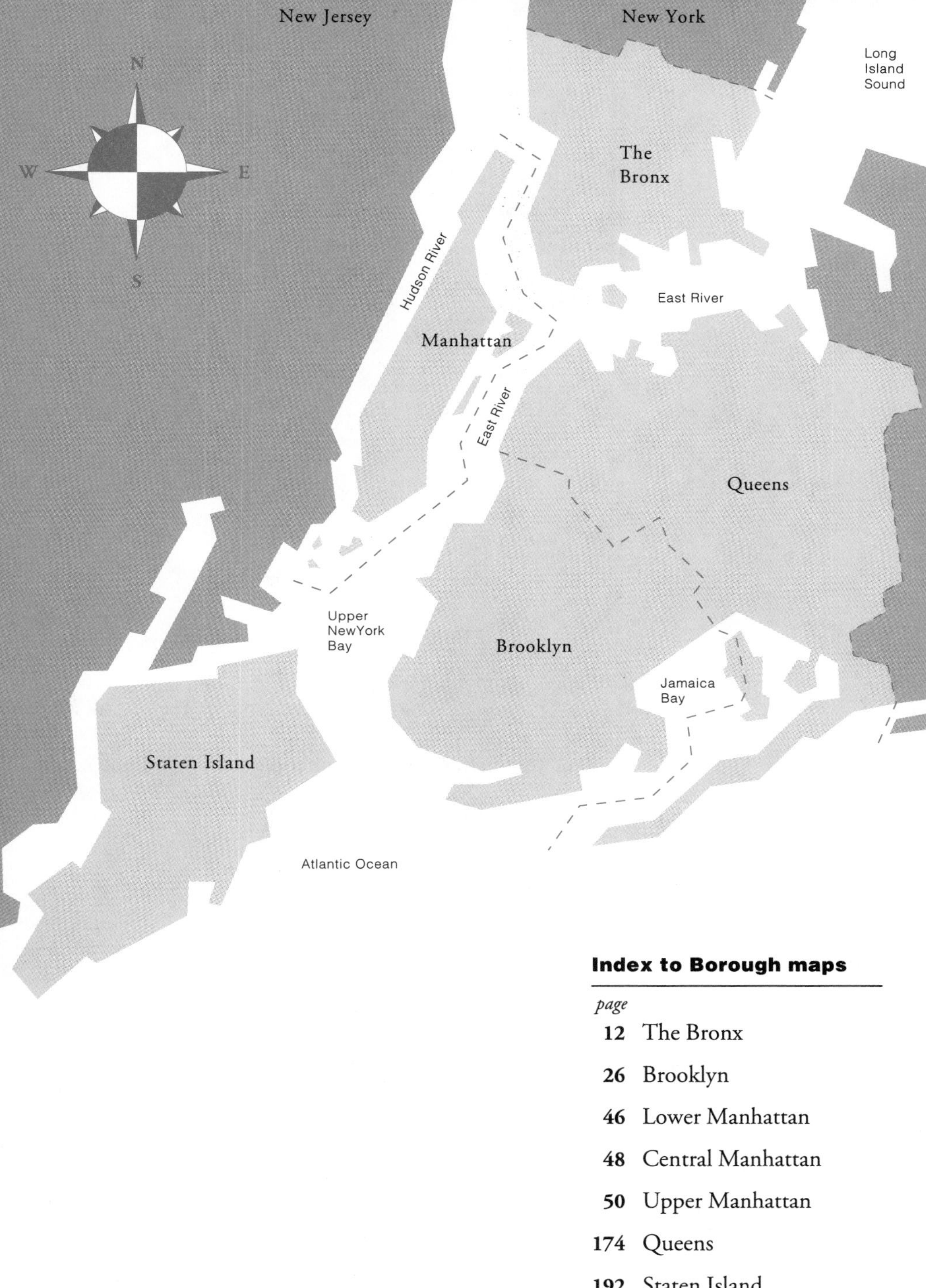

Index to Borough maps

page

12 The Bronx

26 Brooklyn

46 Lower Manhattan

48 Central Manhattan

50 Upper Manhattan

174 Queens

192 Staten Island

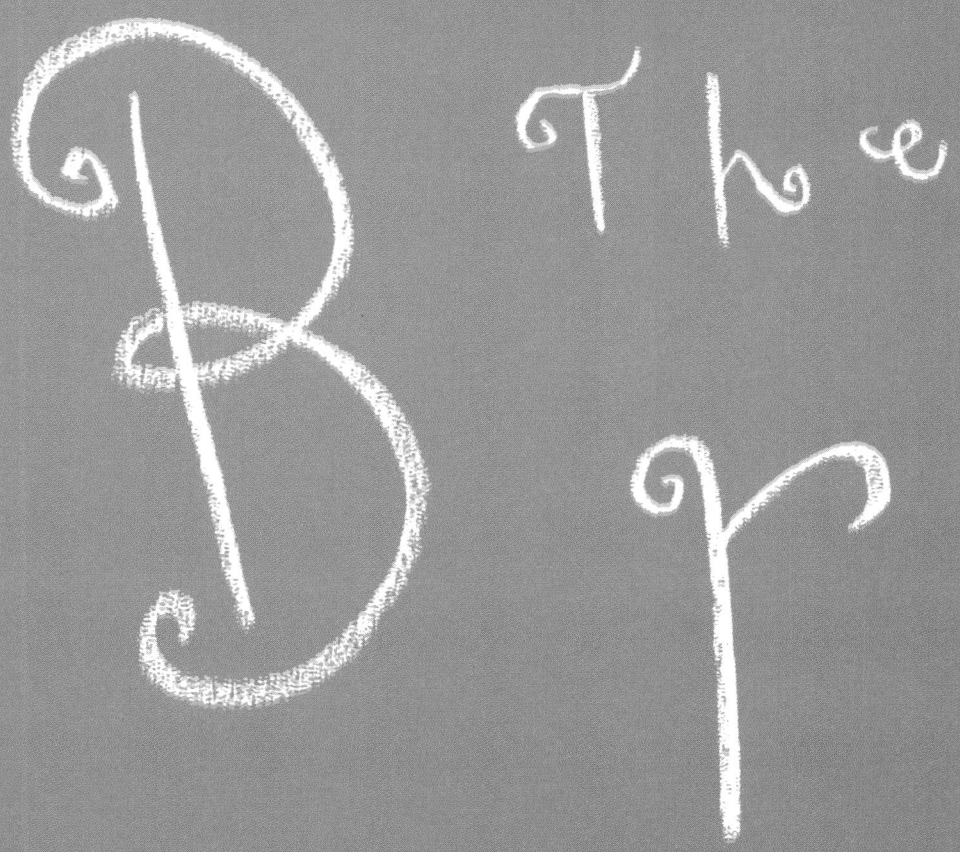

The Bronx is the only mainland borough of New York City. It was named after Scandinavian farmer Jonas Bronck, the first European to settle the area in 1639. After the British occupation during the Revolutionary War, most of the territory was divided between the Morris and Van Cortlandt families. During the 19th century the Bronx was known for its farms and market villages—protean commuter towns of country estates and rural pleasures.

The lower Bronx was annexed by New York City in 1874, bringing bridge-building, mass-transit extensions, industry and many more people. The rest of the borough joined the city under the Greater New York Charter of 1898. Thanks to Frederick Law Olmsted's 1883 design, about one-fifth of the borough's

landscape has been kept as parkland, which contains two of New York's greatest cultural attractions: the New York Botanical Garden and the Bronx Zoo.

In the late 1800s Irish and German immigrants were among the very first large communities of new Americans to settle in the Bronx. When the city's famous elevated trains reached the borough at the turn of the century, the borough became home to immigrants from Eastern and Southern Europe. After World War II these groups were largely replaced by a vibrant Latino and African-American population. Such ethnic flux and diversification that has always characterized New York City, especially the Bronx. Today the 42-square-mile borough is home to 1.2 million people of myriad cultural backgrounds residing in both new and long-established communities.

The Bronx

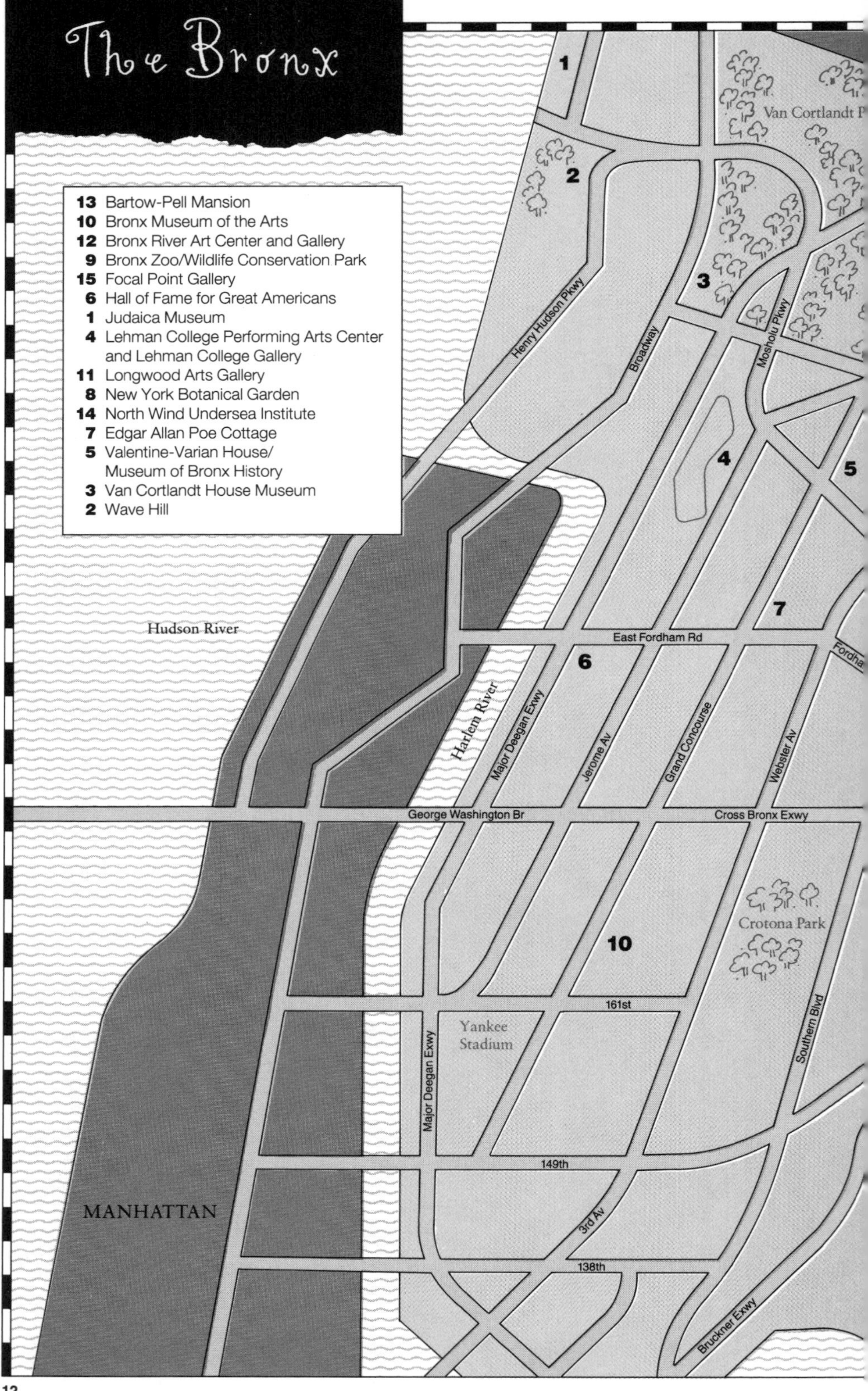

13 Bartow-Pell Mansion
10 Bronx Museum of the Arts
12 Bronx River Art Center and Gallery
9 Bronx Zoo/Wildlife Conservation Park
15 Focal Point Gallery
6 Hall of Fame for Great Americans
1 Judaica Museum
4 Lehman College Performing Arts Center and Lehman College Gallery
11 Longwood Arts Gallery
8 New York Botanical Garden
14 North Wind Undersea Institute
7 Edgar Allan Poe Cottage
5 Valentine-Varian House/ Museum of Bronx History
3 Van Cortlandt House Museum
2 Wave Hill
Hudson River
Harlem River
MANHATTAN
Henry Hudson Pkwy
Broadway
Mosholu Pkwy
East Fordham Rd
Major Deegan Exwy
Jerome Av
Grand Concourse
Webster Av
George Washington Br
Cross Bronx Exwy
Crotona Park
161st
Yankee Stadium
Southern Blvd
149th
3rd Av
138th
Bruckner Exwy

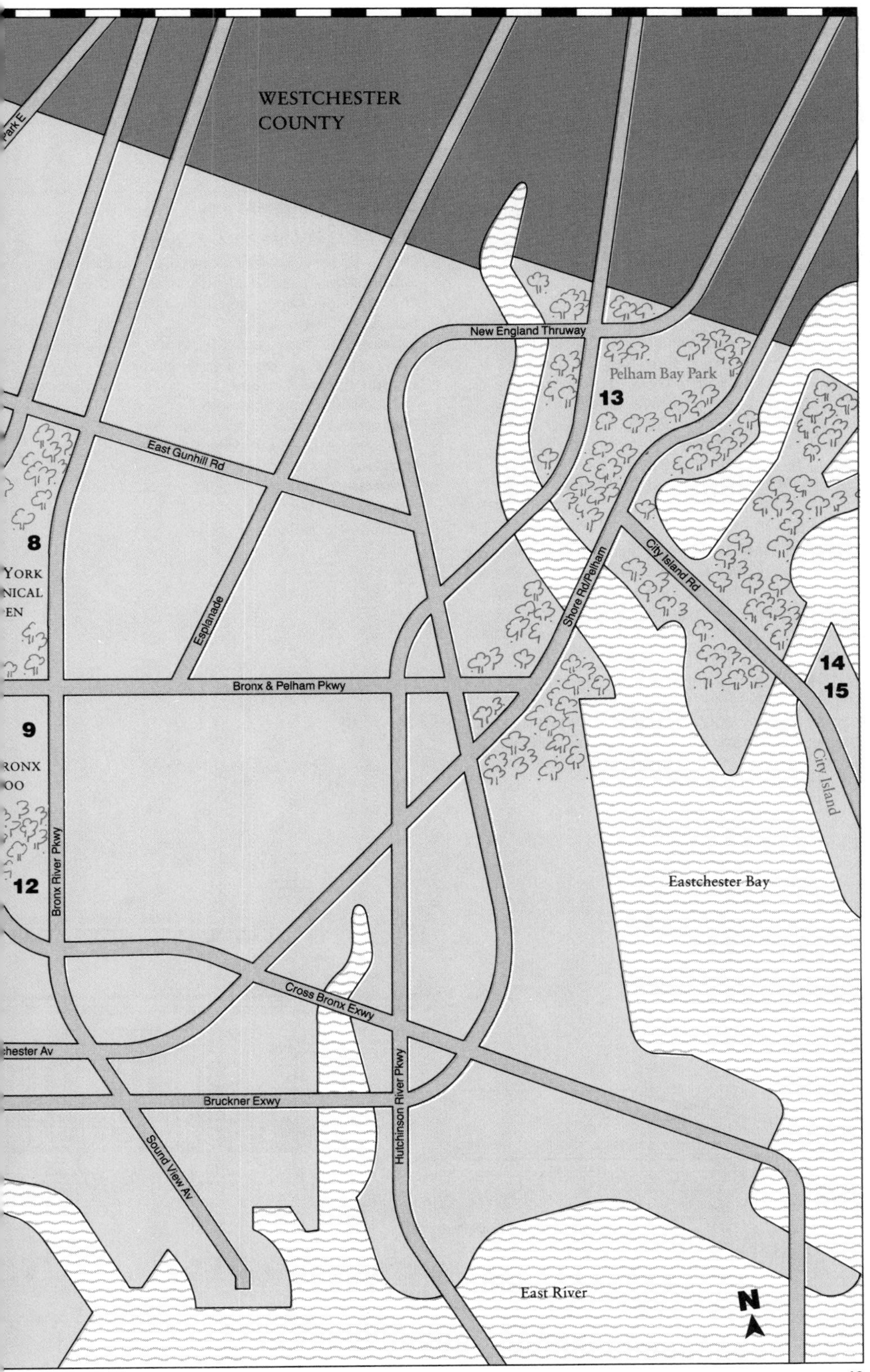
WESTCHESTER COUNTY
Park E
New England Thruway
Pelham Bay Park
13
East Gunhill Rd
8
YORK
NICAL
EN
Esplanade
Shore Rd/Pelham
City Island Rd
14
15
Bronx & Pelham Pkwy
9
RONX
OO
City Island
12
Bronx River Pkwy
Eastchester Bay
Cross Bronx Exwy
chester Av
Hutchinson River Pkwy
Bruckner Exwy
Sound View Av
East River
N

Bartow-Pell Mansion Museum

Shore Road North
Pelham Bay Park
Bronx, NY 10464

718-885-1461

Inside the entrance to the Bartow-Pell Mansion Museum, an unusual freestanding staircase rises in a grand spiral. The two main floors have been decorated with Empire furniture, and decorative plaster illuminates the expansive, high-ceilinged double parlor. On the second floor, one bedroom features a crowned mahogany sleigh bed hung in crimson silk, and floor-to-ceiling windows open onto black wrought-iron balconies. From here you can see the nearby conservatory, which shelters fruit trees and a statue of Venus.

The adjacent 1840s stone carriage house serves as an exhibition center for the museum. The main house and grounds—which include formal terraces, a fountain, and herb and perennial gardens that offer stunning views of Long Island Sound—have been maintained by the International Garden Club since 1914.

In 1654 Connecticut physician Thomas Pell purchased land from the Siwanoy Indians upon which the mansion would eventually be built. A manor house was constructed in 1675 and served several generations of Pells before being burned during the Revolutionary War. Pell descendant Robert Bartow built his mansion here in 1842. New York City bought the estate in 1888 as part of its parks program. The last of many mansions that once graced the Pelham Bay Park area, the house was used by Mayor Fiorello La Guardia as a summer office in 1936. The architect is unknown.

GENERAL INFORMATION

Hours Wed, Sat, Sun 12–4 pm; closed Mon, Tues, Thurs, Fri; carriage house closed Dec–March
Admission Adults $2.50, seniors and students $1.25, children under 12 free; free admission to all on the first Sunday of the month
Library 200 volumes containing archival material on the house and gardens; open by appointment only
Handicapped Access Carriage house and grounds are accessible, mansion is not
Directions Subway: 6 to Pelham Bay; Bus: No.45 Westchester Bee-Line bus to gates (except Sun)
Parking On-site lot
Landmark Status National Register of Historic Places, New York City Landmark
City-owned, privately operated

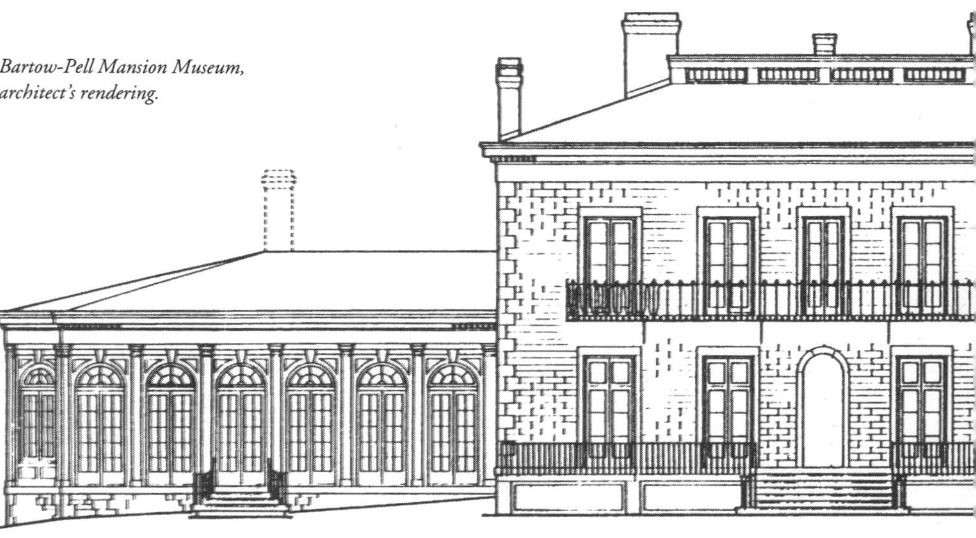

Bartow-Pell Mansion Museum, architect's rendering.

The Bronx Museum of the Arts

1040 Grand Concourse
Bronx, NY 10456

718-681-6000

The Bronx Museum of the Arts, founded in 1971, mounts exhibitions of modern and contemporary art by both established artists and new talents. About a third of the museum's changing exhibitions focus on the work of Bronx artists or works relating to the Bronx. Exhibitions have included "Chicano Art: Resistance and Affirmation, 1965–1985," "El Taller Torres-García: The School of the South and Its Legacy" and "Contemporary Painting and Calligraphy from Japan."

In 1986 the museum began developing a permanent collection, focusing on 20th-century works on paper by artists from Africa, Latin America and Asia, as well as American artists whose ancestors are descendants from these areas. To date, it has accumulated 200 works by artists such as Romare Bearden, Luís Jiménez, Marisól and others, which are exhibited regularly.

Housed since 1982 in a converted synagogue, the 33,000-square-foot museum contains four galleries, four classrooms, a computer lab for youngsters and a three-story, glass-enclosed atrium with lobby and lounge. The museum also mounts exhibitions at three satellite galleries: the Hebrew Hospital Home, the Jerry Clifford Community Gallery and the Bronx Borough President's Office.

GENERAL INFORMATION

Hours Wed–Fri 10 am–5 pm; Sat, Sun 1–6 pm; closed Mon, Tues
Admission Adults $3, students $2, seniors $1, children under 12 free
Giftshop Posters, T-shirts, exhibition-related materials, gift items
Disability Access Fully accessible; restrooms and telephones available
Directions Subway: CC to 161st St–River Ave; 4 to 161st St–Yankee Stadium; D to 161st St–River Ave or 167th St–Grand Concourse; Bus: BX1, BX2, BX6, BXM4 to 165th St and Grand Concourse
Parking On public streets and at garage on 165th St, across from museum

City-owned, privately operated

Bronx River Art Center and Gallery

1087 East Tremont Avenue
(at 177th Street)
Bronx, NY 10460

718-589-5819

The Bronx River Art Center and Gallery was established in 1985. Located near the Bronx Zoo (see separate entry), it overlooks the scenic Bronx River. The center's gallery is housed in a former 1920s dress factory and presents artworks by contemporary artists from the Bronx and the metropolitan New York area in six to seven exhibitions a year. Exhibits feature the work of individual artists and groups in a range of disciplines with culturally diverse themes. An outdoor sculpture garden contains larger works. Guest artists frequently lecture on the arts. An annual festival and open house celebrate student work, and introductory workshops, exhibitions, concerts and special programs are offered. Workshops are conducted by artists-in-residence.

GENERAL INFORMATION

Hours Tues–Thurs 3–6 p.m; closed Fri–Mon
Admission Free
Disability Access Street-level gallery; restrooms, telephones and water fountains available
Directions Subway: 2 or 5 to East Tremont Ave–Boston Rd; Bus: BX9, BX21, BX26, BX36, BX40, BX44 to West Farms Sq
Parking On public streets

Bronx Zoo– Wildlife Conservation Park

Bronx River Parkway
at Fordham Road
Bronx, NY 10460

718-367-1010

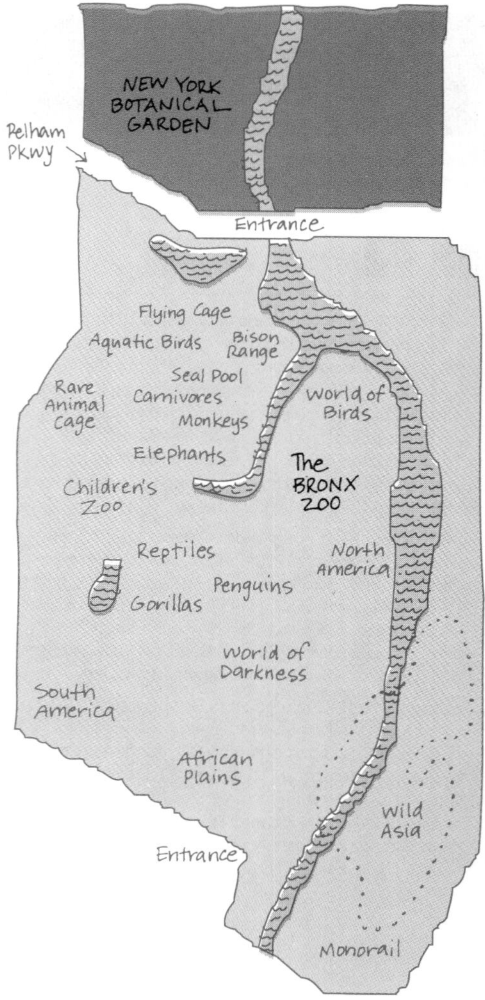

Sharing Bronx Park with the New York Botanical Garden is the Bronx Zoo, the largest urban zoo in the United States. Its woods, streams and parklands cover 265 acres. Within this enclave live more than 4,300 animals representing 674 species.

Visitors view animals in spacious, naturalistic habitats. The Bengali Express monorail carries visitors on a two-mile journey through Wild Asia, where Siberian tigers, Asian elephants, Indian rhinoceroses and rare sika deer roam. The Zoo Shuttle, the Skyfari aerial tramway and camel rides offer other means of transportation. The Himalayan Highlands Habitat recreates the lofty terrain that is home to snow leopards, white-naped cranes and other species. The Sea Lion Pool is a freshwater environment simulating the rocky beaches of California.

Major interior exhibits include Jungle World, a tropical rain forest for Asian wildlife with waterfalls, ravines and exotic plants; the World of Darkness, home to dozens of nocturnal species; and the Reptile House, where crocodiles, snakes, turtles and a reptile nursery are displayed.

The Bronx Zoo also features the Lion House, the Monkey House, the World of Birds, the Giraffe Building, the Aquatic Bird House, the Great Apes House and the new Mouse House. In the Children's Zoo, youngsters learn about animals by crawling through prairie dog tunnels, climbing spiderwebs and listening to sound through simulated fox ears.

The Bronx Zoo opened in 1899. Since 1941, when the first naturalistic habitats appeared, it has been a major international attraction. The zoo is managed by New York Zoological Society/The Wildlife Conservation Society, which also operates the Queens Zoo, the Central Park Zoo, the New York Aquarium and the St. Catherines Wildlife Conservation Center in Georgia. The society supervises some 150 wildlife conservation projects in 40 nations.

GENERAL INFORMATION

Hours April–Oct: Mon–Fri 10 am–5 pm; Sat, Sun, holidays 10 am–5:30 pm; Nov–March: 10 am–4:30 pm daily
Admission April–Oct: adults $5.75, seniors and children under 12, $2; Nov–March: adults $2.50, seniors and children under 12, $1; every Wed admission is free; children under 2 always free
Giftshop Stands selling books, animal souvenirs, T-shirts, toys
Food Service Four main eateries: Lakeside Cafe, Zoo Terrace, Africa Market and Flamingo Pub; refreshment stands throughout zoo; tables available
Disability Access Fully accessible; parking and restrooms available; call 718-220-5188 to reserve an adult stroller. Special tours arranged through Friends of Wildlife Conservation: 718-220-5141
Directions Subway: 2 to Pelham Pkwy, then walk west to Bronxdale entrance; Bus: BX9, BX19 to Southern Blvd entrance; BX12 to corner of Fordham Rd and Southern Blvd, then walk east on Fordham Rd to Rainey Gate; Q44 to 180th St and Boston Rd, then walk north to Asia entrance; Liberty Lines BXM11 from mid-Manhattan, call 718-652-8400 for information
Parking On-site lot
Landmark Status New York City Landmark

City-owned, privately operated by New York Zoological Society/The Wildlife Conservation Society

Focal Point Gallery

321 City Island Avenue
(between Fordham and
Hawkins Streets)
Bronx, NY 10464

718-885-1403

Focal Point Gallery was founded in 1974 by photographer Ron Terner. It serves as an alternative exhibition space for exceptional but largely unknown artists unable to gain recognition elsewhere. It is the only art gallery on City Island and it mounts eight exhibitions a year. The work displayed is primarily photography, which ranges in style from ultra-realistic to impressionistic, from classical portraiture to expressionistic photomontage. Techniques and subject matter embraced by photographers have included Florida landscapes, pinhole and computer images, and photographic wall sculptures.

GENERAL INFORMATION

Hours Tues–Thurs, Sun 12–7 pm; Fri, Sat 12–9 pm; closed Mon
Admission Free
Giftshop Photographs, paintings, handcrafted jewelry
Food Service Numerous seafood restaurants nearby
Disability Access None
Directions Subway: 6 to Pelham Bay, take City Island bus from subway; Bus: City Island bus to City Island Ave at Fordham St
Parking On public streets

The Hall of Fame for Great Americans

Bronx Community College
of the City University of New York
University Avenue and
West 181st Street
Bronx, NY 10453

718-220-6003

Since 1900 the Hall of Fame for Great Americans has honored prominent citizens who have had a significant impact on human advancement. Ninety-seven busts of presidents, statesmen, scientists, inventors, artists and humanitarians stand side by side in the Colonnade, designed by Stanford White, which overlooks a magnificent view stretching from the Harlem River to the Cloisters in Fort Tryon Park.

Those honored include Alexander Graham Bell, who patented the telephone, writers Edgar Allan Poe and Walt Whitman, Red Cross founder Clara Barton, painter John James Audubon, educator Booker T. Washington and aviation pioneers Wilbur and Orville Wright. Each great American is commemorated with a bronze bust and tablet bearing a summary of his or her accomplishments. Elections to the hall are held every three years by an assembly of 100 distinguished Americans.

Bronx Community College manages this architectural treasure. Renovated in the 1980s, the hall now contains lecture and performance spaces to complement its education and group tour programs. Adjacent Gould Memorial Library—modeled after the Pantheon in Rome and one of White's greatest accomplishments—mounts exhibitions about historical achievements in the arts and sciences.

GENERAL INFORMATION

Hours 10 am–5 pm daily
Admission Free
Food Service Cafeteria on campus; catering can be arranged for large groups
Library Gould Memorial Library is not an active library
Disability Access None
Directions Subway: 4 to Burnside Ave; Bus: BX3 to University Ave; BX36 to University and Tremont Aves; BX40 to Burnside and University Aves
Parking On-site lot
Landmark Status National Register of Historic Places, New York City Landmark

City-owned

The Hall of Fame for Great Americans.

The Judaica Museum of the Hebrew Home for the Aged at Riverdale

5961 Palisade Avenue
(at 261st Street)
Bronx, NY 10471

718-548-1006

The Judaica Museum houses the Ralph and Leuba Baum Collection of over 800 Jewish ceremonial objects. This collection acquaints the visitor with the customs and ceremonies of European and Oriental Jewry over the last three centuries. It includes delicately fashioned objects in silver, gold, pewter, brass, ivory, wood and rare embroidered textiles, as well as paintings and an extensive amulet collection. In addition to the permanent collection, there are temporary exhibitions twice a year on Jewish art and culture. The museum also offers guided tours, education programs, exhibit-related lectures, hands-on workshops and senior citizen programs.

GENERAL INFORMATION

Hours Mon–Thurs 1–4:30 pm; Sun 1–5 pm; closed Fri, Sat
Admission Free
Food Service Coffee shop on campus
Disability Access Fully accessible
Directions Subway: 1/9 to 231st St, then take bus; Bus: BX7 or BX10 to Riverdale Ave and West 261st St
Parking On-site lot

"Torah Crown" by Bernard Bernstein, 1963

Lehman Center for the Performing Arts and Lehman College Art Gallery

250 Bedford Park Boulevard West
Bronx, NY 10468

718-960-8833
Box Office
718-960-8732
Art Gallery

Lehman Center for the Performing Arts, founded in 1980, is the first fully professional performing arts facility to be built in the Bronx. The center presents world-class artists at below standard admission costs, with many programs offered free. The center presents both traditional ethnic art forms and mainstream popular and classical performances.

Artists appearing at the center over the years have included: the Dance Theatre of Harlem, the Chieftains, violinist Isaac Stern, the Hungarian State Folk Ensemble, the Odori Festival of Japan, Latin Pianos in Concert, the Balinese-American Fusion Theatre, the Red Army Chorus and Dance Ensemble, the American Indian Dance Theatre and the National Dance Company of Senegal. Facilities for these events include a 2,300-seat concert hall and the 500-seat Lovinger Theater.

Community outreach efforts target those with limited means, providing them with free tickets to performances and transportation to and from the center. Every year, Bronx schoolchildren by the thousands attend the Young People's Series of free performances.

Lehman College Art Gallery emphasizes contemporary art in its large, main exhibition space and smaller graphics gallery. Shows range from one-artist shows by major innovators—such as Romare Bearden, Christo and Robert Wilson—to surveys honoring established and emerging Bronx artists. Thematic exhibitions have included "Landscape in the Age of Anxiety," nontraditional treatments of a familiar genre; "Convergences/ *Convergencias*," American artists whose work reflects their Latin American or Caribbean heritage; and "Black Printmakers and the Work Projects Administration."

The gallery also offers education programs that engage thousands of students each year. There are regular lectures, film and video screenings, and talks by prominent artists. The gallery is located in the Fine Arts Building on the Lehman College campus. The structure was designed by the renowned architect Marcel Breuer, who also created the Whitney Museum of American Art (see separate entry).

The Lehman College Campus

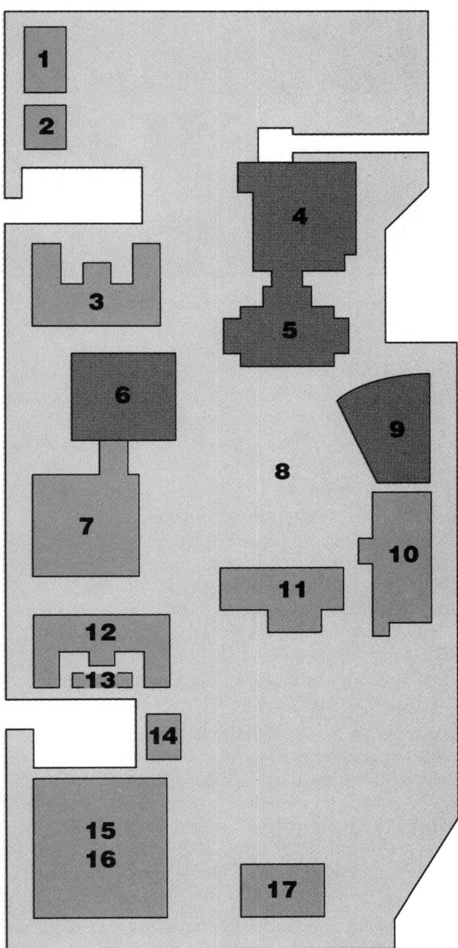

1 Student Health Center
2 Computer Center
3 Gillet Hall
4 Theatres/Speech & Theatre Building
5 Music Building/ Cafeterias
6 Fine Arts Building/ Art Gallery
7 Shuster Hall
8 Plaza
9 Concert Hall
10 Library
11 New Gymnasium
12 Davis Hall
13 Greenhouse
14 Bookstore
15 Carman Hall
16 Academic Computer Center
17 Student Life Center

GENERAL INFORMATION

Center Hours Box Office: Mon, Tues, Thurs, Fri 9 am–5 pm; closed Wed, Sat, Sun
Gallery Hours Sept–May: Tues–Sat 10 am–4 pm; closed Sun, Mon; June–Aug: Mon–Thurs 10 am–4 pm; closed Fri–Sun
Center Admission Various ticket prices; 10 percent discount for groups of 25 or more
Gallery Admission Free
Disability Access Both facilities fully accessible
Directions Subway: 4, C or D to Bedford Park Blvd; Bus: BX10 to Bedford Park Blvd–Goulden Ave; BX1, BX28 to Paul Ave and 205th St; BX3 to Sedgewick Ave and Perot St; BX24 to 231st St and Bailey Ave; BX26 to Bedford Park and Jerome Ave; BX34 to Valentine Ave and 199th St
Parking On public streets and at lot across Goulden Ave
City-owned

Longwood Arts Gallery at P.S. 39

965 Longwood Avenue
Bronx, NY 10459
718-842-5659

Established in 1981 by the Bronx Council on the Arts, Longwood Arts Gallery mounts contemporary art exhibitions throughout the year. Both individual and thematic group shows are featured. Exhibitions have included "Female Body Parts," in which women artists employed feminist and psychoanalytic approaches to depict the female body; "Here and Now: Now and Then," works by artists of Vietnamese descent; "Real Life Comics," serious artistic expression in a deceptively superficial format; and "Maps and Madness," works by 13 artists who use maps to portray political situations, ecological dilemmas and the inner self. The gallery is located in Longwood, one of the Bronx's last surviving historic brownstone districts. Once a public school, the gallery also houses several artists' studios.

GENERAL INFORMATION

Hours Thurs, Fri 12–5 pm; Sat 12–4 pm; and by appointment
Admission Free
Disability Access None
Directions Subway: 6 to Longwood Ave; 2 or 5 to Prospect Ave; Bus: BX19 to Longwood Ave; BX4 to Westchester Ave and East 161st St
Parking On public streets
City-owned, privately operated

The New York Botanical Garden

200th Street and
Southern Boulevard
Bronx, NY 10458

718-817-8500

Sharing Bronx Park with the Bronx Zoo is the New York Botanical Garden, one of the foremost gardens in the world. The 250-acre garden has beautiful natural terrain, with dramatic rock outcroppings, a river and cascading waterfall, undulating hills, wetlands, ponds and 40 acres of virgin forest.

The New York Botanical Garden contains 16 specialty gardens, including the Peggy Rockefeller Rose Garden, a perennial collection, a large rock garden containing tens of thousands of flowers from mountainous regions around the world, a native-plant garden displaying flora of the northeastern United States, and a garden where children plant and cultivate vegetables and flowers.

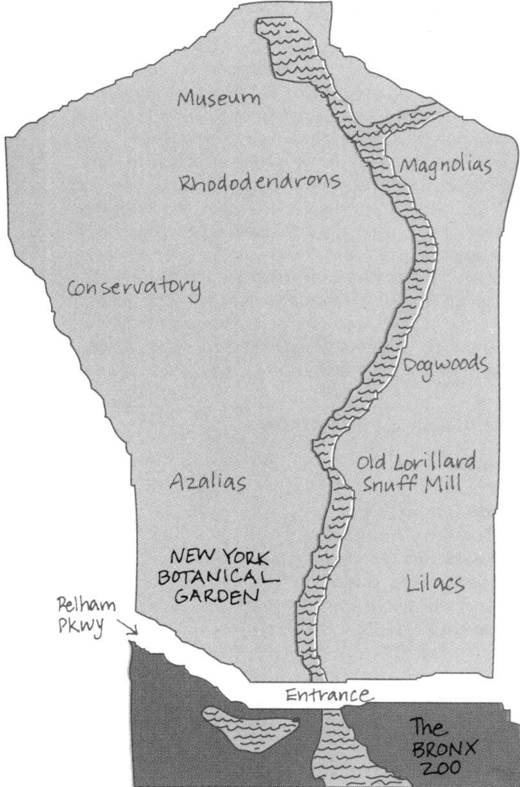

The Enid A. Haupt Conservatory (closed for renovations until 1995)

The Enid A. Haupt Conservatory is the garden's architectural gem. Built in 1902, this soaring Victorian crystal palace is based on the greenhouses of the Royal Botanic Garden at Kew, England. Its 11 glass pavilions house tropical plants, palm trees, desert flora, a fern forest and various seasonal exhibits.

The Education Department offers courses, tours, certificate programs and college-level study for adults, in addition to programs for children and school groups. Other offerings include symposiums, lectures, a speakers' bureau and foreign tours. The garden's library is one of the country's largest botanical repositories, and the herbarium, a cataloged collection of more than five million dried plant specimens, is an essential resource for scientists.

In addition to sponsoring horticulture and education programs, the garden is a leader in environmental research. The institution's scientists perform research in systematic and economic botany, using the extraordinary collections of the herbarium, library and living plant collections. At the garden's Institute of Ecosystem Studies at the Mary Flagler Cary Arboretum in Millbrook, New York, long-term ecological studies are conducted.

Much of the garden's land belonged to the Lorillard family, tobacconists in the early 1800s. The property was acquired by New York City in 1884, and in 1891 the New York Botanical Garden was established.

GENERAL INFORMATION

Hours April–Oct: Tues–Sun 10 am–6 pm; closed Mon
Nov–March: Tues–Sun 10 am–4 pm; closed Mon
Admission Suggested contribution: adults $3, seniors, students and children $2
Giftshop Plants, plant supplies, botanical gifts and garden books; open Tues–Fri 10 am–5 pm, Sat, Sun 10 am–6 pm
Food Service Snuff Mill River Terrace Cafe, a restaurant overlooking the Bronx River, open 10 am–5 pm, 12 months a year; Tulip Tree Cafe, offering lighter fare, open 11 am–5 pm, April–Oct
Library Open Tues–Thurs 12–6 pm; Sat, Sun 12–4 pm

Disability Access Fully accessible; ramps, elevators, restrooms, telephones and parking available; visitors with special needs contact Security, 718-817-8664; TDD: 718-817-8596
Directions Subway: D or 4 to Bedford Park Blvd, then take BX26 bus; Bus: BX12, BX19, Bx26, BX41. Also, on weekends a shuttle runs between the American Museum of Natural History, the Museum of Modern Art and the garden; call 718-817-8700 for reservations
Parking On-site lot, entrance at 200th St and Southern Blvd
Landmark Status National Register of Historic Places, New York City Landmark
City-owned, privately operated

North Wind Undersea Institute

610 City Island Avenue
Bronx, NY 10464
718-885-0701

Once you cross the small City Island bridge it's hard to believe you're still in New York City, until you see the Empire State Building across Long Island Sound. You may be reminded more of a small fishing village on the shore. The slender island is home to the North Wind Undersea Institute, a museum and research center committed to educating the public, especially children, about the need to preserve marine life and habitat.

The institute is housed in a renovated Victorian mansion and adjoining 100-year-old tugboat, the *Jacques Guillet.* Anchors, an 18th-century cannon, a two-man submarine, diving bells and a life-size, 20-foot model of a killer whale are on display in the front courtyard. Inside is a large collection of scrimshaw, towering models and skeletons of whales, whaling artifacts and model boats, diving gear, navigational instruments and rare seashells. The Treasure Exhibit includes formerly sunken booty from the *Capitan Arubi* Spanish treasure fleet, which was swamped off the Florida Keys in 1733.

Live exhibits include the Undersea World of the Bronx, with local fish and other marine life, and a touch tank, where visitors can hold horseshoe crabs, sea stars and the like. The education program offers guided tours, pollution workshops, wilderness excursions and other activities. The institute also presents diving demonstrations with seals and a seal-recovery simulation in which visitors participate. North Wind was cofounded in 1976 by Executive Director Michael Sandlofer and the singer-songwriter Richie Havens.

GENERAL INFORMATION

Hours Mon–Fri 10 am–5 pm; Sat, Sun 12–5 pm
Admission Adults $3, children and senior citizens $2
Giftshop Marine-related items and souvenirs
Disability Access Limited wheelchair access; no access to restrooms
Directions Subway: 6 to Pelham Bay Station, then take BX29 bus to City Island; Bus: BX29 to City Island
Parking On public streets

Edgar Allan Poe Cottage

Grand Concourse and
East Kingsbridge Road
Bronx, NY 10458
718-881-8900

This residence, built in 1812, is where Edgar Allan Poe —one of America's literary masters—wrote "Annabel Lee," "Ulalume," "The Bells" and "Eureka." It has been kept much as it was when he lived there, a simply furnished cottage that was his final home.

In 1846 Poe left the crowded New York City he had come to dislike and moved with his dying wife to this wooden cottage in the village of Fordham. She died within the year. Poe's death occurred, suddenly, three years later. By 1895 the first apartment houses were encroaching on the site and the cottage was threatened with demolition. The New York Shakespeare Society worked to preserve it. In 1902 New York City created Poe Park across the street from the cottage. The house itself was moved there in 1913.

Three period rooms—a kitchen, parlor and bedroom—are filled with furnishings from the 1840s, including Poe's own rocking chair and bed. Even the paint on the walls is the same color Poe saw during his lifetime. A screening room offers films about Poe and a history of the house. There is also a small gallery where paintings, photographs and drawings from the 1840s are on view. Poe Cottage was converted into a museum in 1917.

GENERAL INFORMATION

Hours Sat 10 am–4 pm; Sun 1–5 pm; closed Mon–Fri
Admission $2
Giftshop Publications and Poe memorabilia
Library The Bronx County Historical Society's headquarters, 3309 Bainbridge Ave, contains the Poe Research Collection; open by appointment Mon–Fri 9 am–5 pm
Disability Access House not accessible; with advance notice slide presentation for hearing-impaired
Directions Subway: D or 4 to Kingsbridge Rd; Bus: BX1, BX2, BX32 to Kingsbridge Rd; BX12, BX24 to Grand Concourse; BX15, BX17 to Fordham Plaza; BX9, BX26, BX28, BX34 to 194th St
Parking On public streets
Landmark Status National Register of Historic Places, New York City Landmark
City-owned, privately operated by the Bronx County Historical Society

Valentine-Varian House/ Museum of Bronx History

3266 Bainbridge Avenue
(at East 208th Street)
Bronx, NY 10467
718-881-8900

During the Revolutionary War, the Bronx was the site of frequent skirmishes between American and British troops. The Valentine-Varian House (1758), sitting on the main thoroughfare between New York and Boston, became an object of constant territorial dispute. Ultimately, in 1777, the house was captured by British Colonel Robert Rogers, who used it as his headquarters for the rest of the war.

The restored fieldstone house is designed in a symmetrical Georgian vernacular style, with evenly placed windows and identical chimneys at either end. Inside rooms mirror each other across a central hallway. Sections of the house retain original floorboards, handforged nails and homemade mortar used by the builder and first owner, blacksmith Isaac Valentine. In 1792 Valentine sold the house and surrounding 260 acres to butcher and farmer Isaac Varian, whose family kept it until 1964. Period plantings, an herb garden, an outdoor seating area and the Bronx River Soldier Monument embellish the gardens surrounding the house.

Today the Valentine-Varian House serves as the Museum of Bronx History. Exhibitions focus on the Bronx since its establishment in the 17th century. Two rooms contain changing exhibitions, while the front parlor has a permanent display about the development of the area, from the Indian and Dutch periods through the Revolution. The museum also offers monthly lectures, educational programs and tours.

GENERAL INFORMATION

Hours Sat 10 am–4 pm; Sun 1–5 pm; open for groups on weekdays by appointment
Admission $2
Giftshop Merchandise related to the Bronx County Historical Society's collections and programs
Library The Bronx County Historical Society Research Library (3309 Bainbridge Ave) contains books, photographs, manuscripts, etc., related to Bronx history; open by appointment Mon–Fri 9 am–5 pm
Disability Access Limited wheelchair access
Directions Subway: D to 205th St; 4 to Mosholu Pkwy; Bus: BX10, BX16, BX28, BX30, BX34 to Bainbridge Ave and 208th St
Parking On public streets
Landmark Status National Register of Historic Places, New York City Landmark

Van Cortlandt House Museum

Broadway at 246th Street
Bronx, NY 10471
718-543-3344

The Van Cortlandt Mansion is a fine example of vernacular Georgian architecture and the oldest surviving residence in the Bronx. Built in 1748 by Frederick Van Cortlandt, it was once the core of a lucrative wheat plantation that in the 18th century spread across much of the borough. During the Revolutionary War, George Washington camped on its grounds and lighted campfires on a nearby hill to fool the British into believing the rebels awaited them. Meanwhile his troops moved to Yorktown for the war's final battle.

Located on the edge of Van Cortlandt Park, the mansion is built of rough-hewn stone and brick. Grotesque faces carved in stone serve as keystones above the exterior windows; these were common in Europe at the

time but rare in Colonial America. Inside, commodious formal rooms and bedchambers are furnished with 18th-century antiques. The kitchen has a huge fireplace, cauldrons and a shovel oven. America's oldest doll-house and child's sled are among the mansion's many treasures. Group tours, concerts, lectures and special programs are offered occasionally.

GENERAL INFORMATION

Hours Tues–Fri 10 am–3 pm; Sat, Sun 11 am–4 pm; closed Mon
Admission Adults $2, students and seniors $1.50, children under 14 free
Giftshop Books, cards, gifts and toys
Disability Access None
Directions Subway: 1/9 to 242 St; Bus: BX9 to 244th St; Liberty Lines BXM3 to 244th St
Parking On public streets
Landmark Status National Register of Historic Places, New York City Landmark

City-owned, privately operated

Wave Hill

675 West 252nd Street
and Independence Avenue
Bronx, NY 10471

718-549-3200

Wave Hill is located in Riverdale, a residential neighborhood in the Bronx. It features flower, aquatic and wild gardens, manicured lawns, woodlands and spectacular views of the Hudson River and the Palisades. Adirondack chairs dot Wave Hill's 28 acres, and a stroll over gravel paths reveals greenhouses with tropical and succulent plants and a beautifully sculpted landscape.

Two restored houses function as a cultural center. The annual concert series attracts audiences for chamber music and jazz performances. Exhibitions have concentrated on the work of painters of garden scenes, photographers and the work of American landscape designers.

The outdoor sculpture series has featured works by Archipenko, Moore and Nevelson, as well as site-specific works by contemporary sculptors. A popular summer dance series sets music and movement into the landscape. There is also an extensive program of educational offerings, particularly strong in environmental studies.

Originally built in 1844 for lawyer William Lewis Morris, Wave Hill has served as a residence for such luminaries as Mark Twain, Theodore Roosevelt and Arturo Toscanini. In 1960 the family of George W. Perkins, who bought the estate in 1903, gave a portion of it to the City of New York. The main Wave Hill house has gone through several architectural transformations over the years and now has a fieldstone facade. Inside is a parlor featuring Victorian teak paneling and the Armor Hall, which has been converted into an airy concert hall with a vaulted ceiling.

GENERAL INFORMATION

Hours Mid–May through mid–Oct: Tues–Sun 9 am–5:30 pm; Wed until dusk; Mid–Oct through mid–May: Tues–Sun 9 am–4:30 pm; closed Mon
Admission Free weekdays; weekends and holidays $4 adults, $2 seniors and students, children under 6 free
Giftshop Nature-related books, gift items, gardening tools
Food Service Cafe open Tues–Sun 11 am–4:30 pm (weekends only, Oct–March)
Library The Catalog of Landscape Records in the U.S. is the cumulative index to all documentation on landscapes, past and present; for information call and ask for the Catalog
Disability Access Grounds are accessible, houses are not
Directions Subway: 1/9 to 231 St or A to 207th St, then take BX7 bus to 252nd St; Bus: BX7, BX10, BX24 to 252nd St
Parking On-site lot
Landmark Status National Register of Historic Places, New York City Landmark

City-owned, privately operated

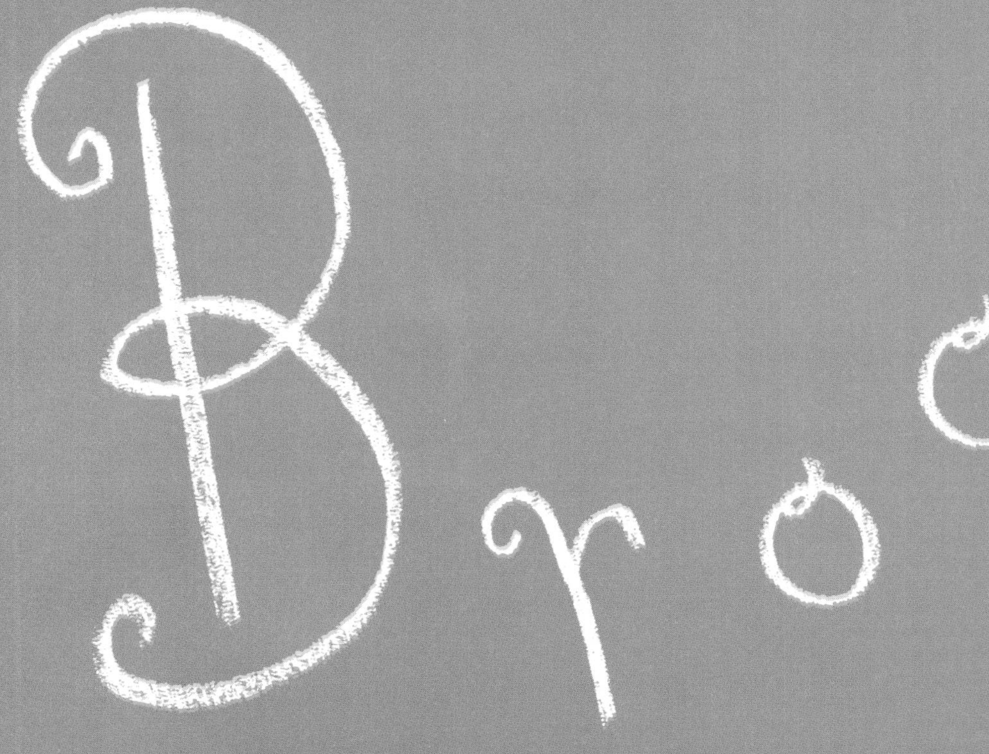

The 71 square miles that make up Brooklyn still contain the six villages founded by Dutch settlers in the 17th century. One of them, Breuckelen, meaning "broken land," was incorporated as a city in 1834 and had absorbed all the others by 1898, when it merged with the City of New York and was officially designated the borough of Brooklyn. (It is also Kings County, a name bestowed by the British when they occupied the area in the 18th century).

Residents are quick to point out that if the borough were independent it would be America's fifth largest city, with a population of 2.3 million—it is the city's most populated borough—and its own impressive cultural offerings. Demographers estimate there are over 100 separate ethnic communities in Brooklyn, including the Hassidic Jewish enclave of Crown Heights, the Russian-American community in Brighton Beach

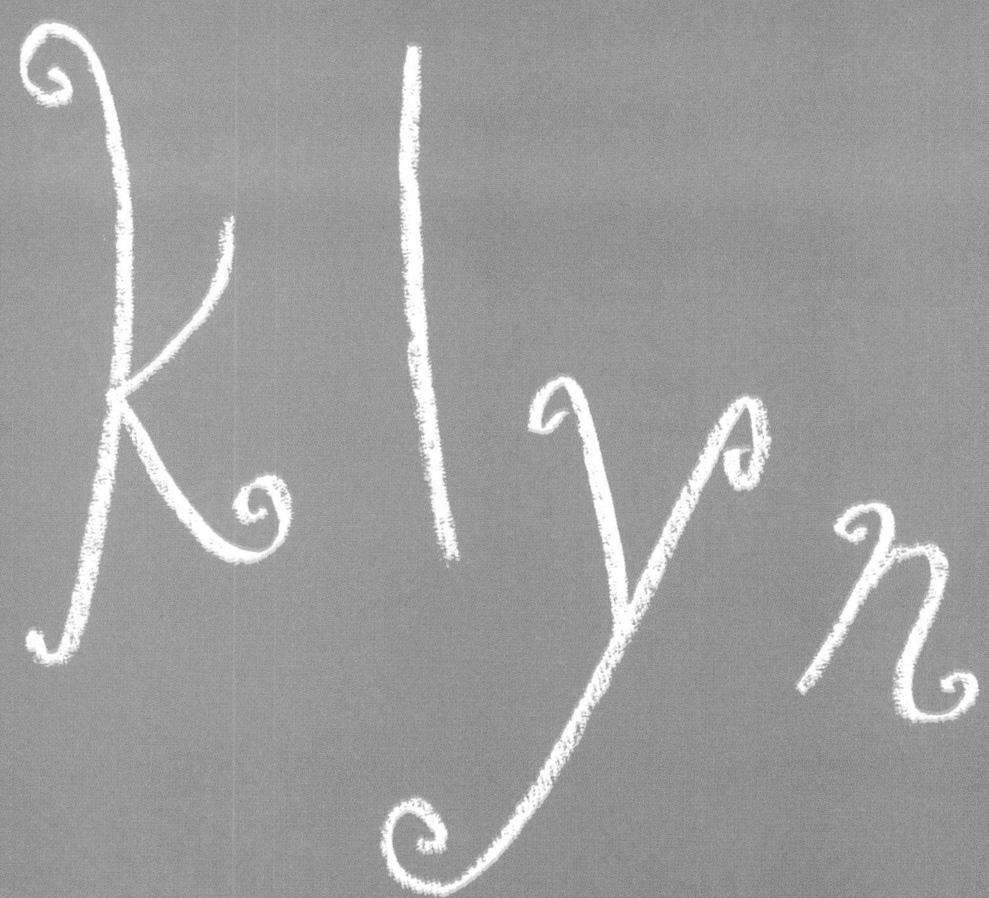

and, in Bedford-Stuyvesant, New York City's largest African-American population. Such broad diversity makes the borough one of the world's most fascinating human crossroads and pays rich dividends to the visitor, not only in terms of visiting cultural institutions, but sightseeing and dining as well.

In many neighborhoods, Brooklyn retains the appearance of the 19th century in its tree-shaded streets, lined with handsome row houses and religious buildings. Its cultural institutions—like the Brooklyn Academy of Music, the Brooklyn Museum and the Brooklyn Botanic Garden—are among the nation's most venerable and important. Newer institutions, such as the Center for Art and Culture of Bedford-Stuyvesant, reflect the rich cultural traditions of Brooklyn's African-American and Latino residents.

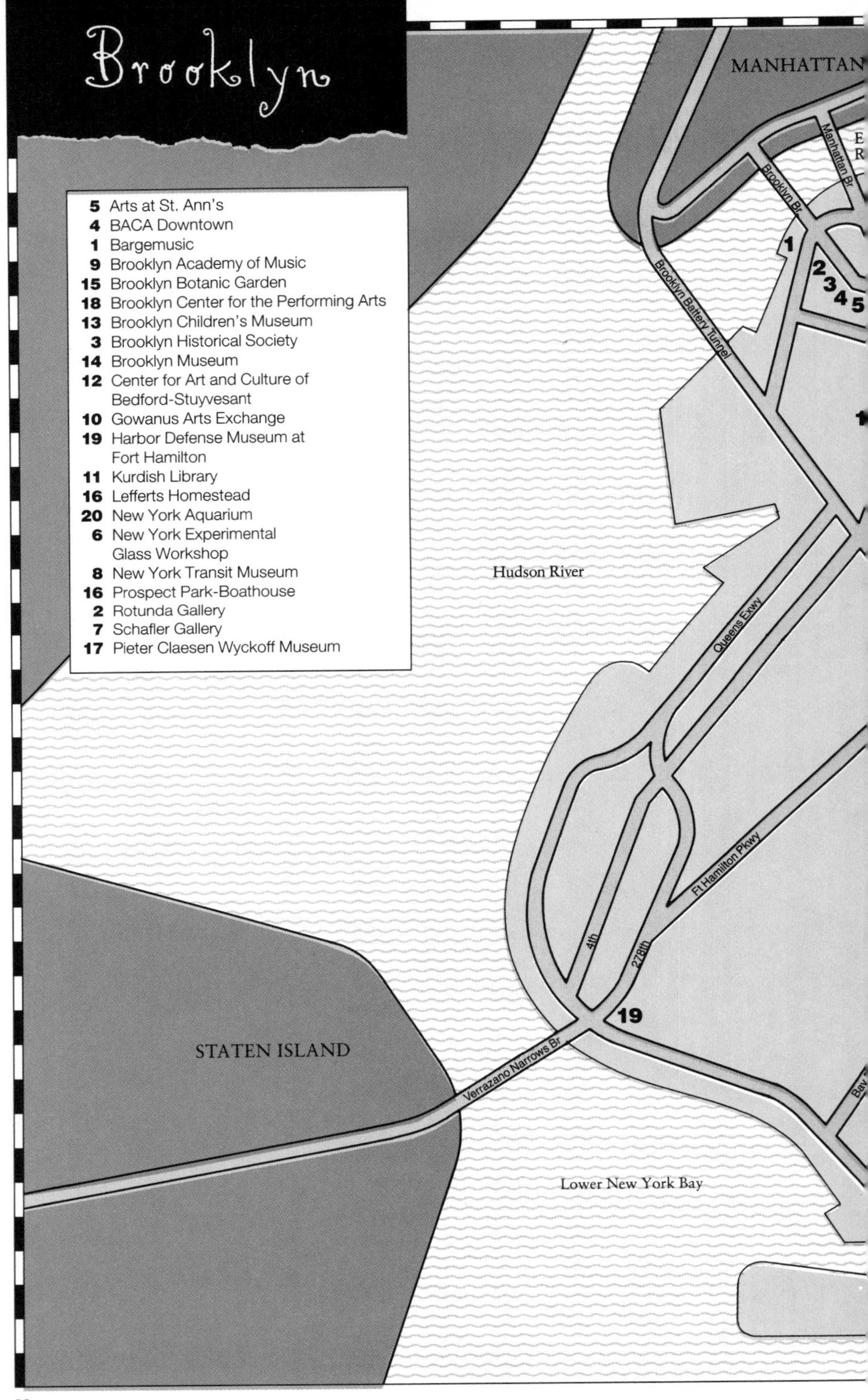

Brooklyn
5 Arts at St. Ann's
4 BACA Downtown
1 Bargemusic
9 Brooklyn Academy of Music
15 Brooklyn Botanic Garden
18 Brooklyn Center for the Performing Arts
13 Brooklyn Children's Museum
3 Brooklyn Historical Society
14 Brooklyn Museum
12 Center for Art and Culture of Bedford-Stuyvesant
10 Gowanus Arts Exchange
19 Harbor Defense Museum at Fort Hamilton
11 Kurdish Library
16 Lefferts Homestead
20 New York Aquarium
6 New York Experimental Glass Workshop
8 New York Transit Museum
16 Prospect Park-Boathouse
2 Rotunda Gallery
7 Schafler Gallery
17 Pieter Claesen Wyckoff Museum
MANHATTAN
Manhattan Br
Brooklyn Br
Brooklyn Battery Tunnel
1
2
3
4
5
Hudson River
Queens Exwy
Ft Hamilton Pkwy
4th
278th
19
STATEN ISLAND
Verrazano Narrows Br
Lower New York Bay

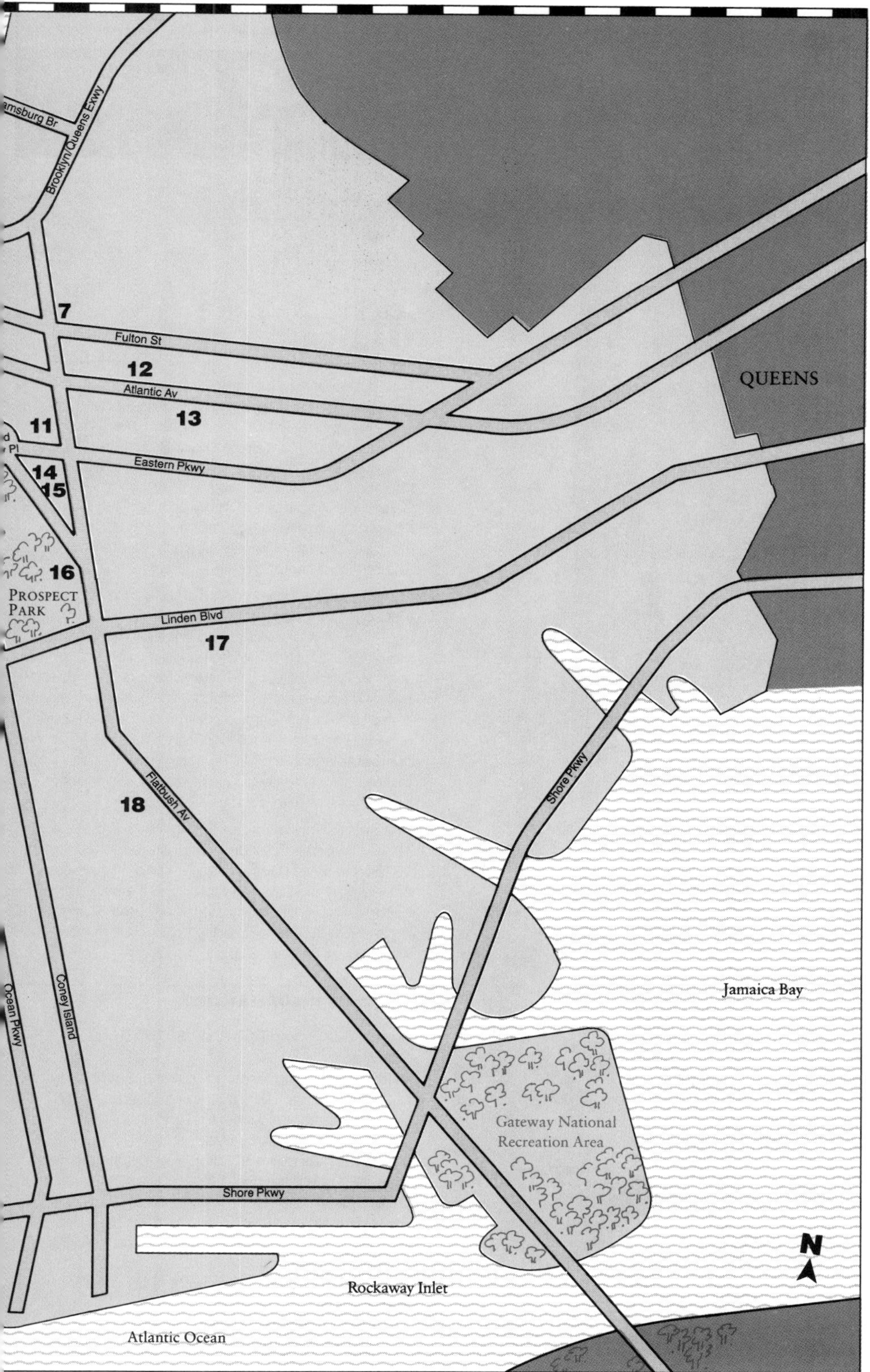

amsburg Br
Brooklyn/Queens Exwy
7
Fulton St
12
Atlantic Av
13
11
Pl
Eastern Pkwy
14
15
16
PROSPECT
PARK
Linden Blvd
17
18
Flatbush Av
Shore Pkwy
QUEENS
Jamaica Bay
Gateway National
Recreation Area
Ocean Pkwy
Coney Island
Shore Pkwy
N
Rockaway Inlet
Atlantic Ocean

St. Ann and the Holy Trinity, home of the Arts at St. Ann's.

Museum of the City of New York

Arts at St. Ann's

The St. Ann Center for Restoration and the Arts
157 Montague Street
(at Clinton Street)
Brooklyn, NY 11201

718-858-2424
Box Office

The Arts at St. Ann's presents musical performances in a range of formats: blues, jazz, musical theater, rock and chamber music. Started in 1980, the program has included performances by David Byrne, the St. Luke's Chamber Ensemble, Dr. John, Junior Lockwood, Marianne Faithful, Lou Reed, Richard Thompson, John Cale, Katie Webster and many others. There is also a series of literary readings and monologues, some with musical accompaniment, which has featured novelist Richard Price, among others.

St. Ann and the Holy Trinity, the Gothic Revival church that houses the arts program, was built between 1844 and 1848. It is an enchanting coalescence of architectural subtlety, from its flamboyant tracery to its soaring vaulted ceiling. The structure is distinguished by 7,000 square feet of stained-glass windows, designed in the 1840s by William Jay Bolton, which have been hailed by architectural historians as national treasures comparable to those of Chartres. The exterior is considered an unusually pure example of 19th-century brownstone construction.

St. Ann's fell into disrepair during the late 1950s and 1960s. After the Episcopal Diocese reopened it in the 1970s, the small parish, overwhelmed by the needs of the damaged structure, turned to the New York Landmarks Conservancy, which adopted St. Ann's for restoration. It functions today as a house of worship as well as a performance space.

GENERAL INFORMATION

Hours Box Office: Tues–Sat 12–6 pm; closed Sun, Mon

Admission Various, call for ticket prices and performance schedule; TDF vouchers accepted; WNYC Arts Card accepted; discounts to high school and college students, seniors and groups

Disability Access Building is wheelchair accessible, restrooms are not

Directions Subway 2, 3, 4, N or R to Court St–Borough Hall; A or F to Jay St–Borough Hall; Bus: B38, B51, B52 to Cadman Plaza and Johnson Ave; B25, B41 to Court and Montague Sts

Parking On public streets or lot at Clinton and Pierrepont Sts

Landmark Status National Register of Historic Places, New York City Landmark

California sea otter

Aquarium for Wildlife Conservation

NYZS/Wildlife Conservation Society 718-265-3474
West 8th Street and Surf Avenue
Brooklyn, NY 11224

Giant sea turtles, sandtiger sharks, baby beluga whales, blue lobsters, sea coral and 10,000 other exotic and colorful marine creatures live at the New York Aquarium. The aquarium has 100 tanks stationed throughout its 14-acre campus, which is located next to the boardwalk of Brooklyn's famous Coney Island.

The Aquatheater features California sea lions balancing balls and jumping through hoops. Beluga whales demonstrate their "breaching" capabilities by splashing audience members in the front rows. And don't forget the giant octopus. Nearby, the African Rift Lake displays the world's most colorful freshwater fish.

Discovery Cove is an exhibit complex where visitors learn about the aquarium's Coral Reef Initiative and stand under a 400-gallon tidal wave, crashing overhead every 30 seconds. Here youngsters can touch sea urchins, sea stars and other sea creatures. The Bermuda Triangle teems with eels, sea turtles and colorful fish from the Caribbean.

The new Sea Cliffs exhibit is a state-of-the-art naturalistic environment that roughly doubles visitor space at the aquarium. Recreating the rocky Pacific coast, Sea Cliffs represents the first time that pinnipeds (seals and walruses) and penguins have been exhibited with invertebrates, fish and kelp in a naturally mixed-species ecosystem. Featuring above- and below-water viewing, both indoors and outdoors, it is the largest walrus exhibit on the East Coast. Sea Cliffs is augmented by interactive graphics and displays.

An integral part of the aquarium is the Osborn Laboratories of Marine Sciences, which undertake research projects in fish pathology and genetics, marine pollution, aquaculture, toxicology, pharmacology and marine zoology. The New York Aquarium is managed by New York Zoological Society/The Wildlife Conservation Society, which also operates the Bronx Zoo, the Queens Zoo, the Central Park Zoo (see separate entries) and the St. Catherines Wildlife Conservation Center in Georgia. The society supervises some 150 wildlife conservation projects in 40 nations.

GENERAL INFORMATION

Hours Open 10 am–5 pm daily; summer weekends and holidays open until 7 pm
Admission Adult $5.75, seniors and children under 12, $2
Giftshop Aquarium souvenirs and books
Disability Access Fully accessible, except for cafeteria; parking and restrooms available
Directions Subway: F or D to West 8th St (Brooklyn); Bus: B36, B68 to West 8th St and Surf Ave
Parking On-site lot

City-owned, privately operated by New York Zoological Society/The Wildlife Conservation Society

BACA/The Brooklyn Arts Council

195 Cadman Plaza West
(between Hillary and
Pineapple Streets)
Brooklyn, NY 11201
718-625-0080

BACA/The Brooklyn Arts Council is dedicated to the advancement of the arts, particularly as they touch the lives of Brooklyn residents. Both its gallery and theater are located in the Brooklyn War Memorial Building on Cadman Plaza West in Brooklyn Heights.

BACA stages scores of exhibitions each year. Its most prominent shows occur twice yearly on the Brooklyn Heights Promenade. It also mounts indoor exhibits at its BACA Downtown Gallery, which presents about ten group exhibitions a year intended to introduce Brooklyn artists to the larger public. Popular installations have included Susan Share's free-wheeling wall paintings and a Matisse-like panel created by students of the Brooklyn Friends School.

The all-new BACA Downtown Theater facility offers dramatic performances and film screenings throughout the year. This professionally equipped facility presents artists in solo performances, dance competitions and plays. There is an annual film festival held in the theater featuring the work of independent filmmakers.

BACA's Folk Arts Series encourages Brooklyn's many ethnic communities to share their artistic heritage with the larger public. The annual summer series presents high-quality opera, jazz, salsa and other musical forms, as well as theater pieces, magic acts, dance and storytelling, at parks throughout the borough.

GENERAL INFORMATION

Hours Theater: various, call for hours; gallery: by appointment only
Admission Theater: adults $12, seniors and students $8; gallery free
Library Information on Brooklyn Arts Council grants, programs, etc.; open Mon–Fri 10 am–5 pm
Disability Access Limited access
Directions Subway: R or N to Court St; 2 or 3 to Clark St; A or C to High St.; Bus: B25, B52, B75 to Cadman Plaza West
Parking On public streets and lot adjacent to theater

Bargemusic

Fulton Ferry Landing
(at the foot of Furman Street)
Brooklyn, NY 11201
718-624-4061

This is interesting: a 102-foot coffee barge that has been converted into a floating concert hall for chamber music. Olga Bloom is the visionary behind Bargemusic, which she founded in 1977. Ms. Bloom, a musician herself, and her artistic director, Ik-Hwan Bae, have been able to assemble a pool of 90 or so players with international reputations who return to Bargemusic regularly to perform. Seating capacity is limited to about 130 people, which contributes to the intimacy of the performances. There are two concerts, 52 weeks a year, on Thursday and Sunday, with an additional concert on Friday during the summer months. Musicians

appearing at Bargemusic have included violist Steven Tenenbom; cellist Carter Brey; pianists Edward Auer, Christopher O'Riley and Paul Schoenfield; violinist Pamela Frank; and flutist Ramson Wilson. A typical program might consist of sonatas by Mozart and Brahms and a piano trio by Mendelssohn. Bargemusic is docked on the East River near the Brooklyn Bridge, next to the River Cafe and the Brooklyn Maritime Museum.

GENERAL INFORMATION

Hours Performances weekly: Sun 4 pm, Thurs 7:30 pm; an additional Fri concert during summer 7:30 pm
Admission Tickets: Sun $23, Thurs $20 ($6 less if multiples purchased); students and seniors always $15; TDF vouchers accepted
Disability Access None
Directions Subway: 2 or 3 to Clark St; A or C to High St.; Bus: B25, B41 terminate in front of Bargemusic
Parking On public streets

Brooklyn Academy of Music

30 Lafayette Avenue
(between St. Felix Street
and Ashland Place)
Brooklyn, NY 11217

718-636-4100

The Brooklyn Academy of Music (BAM) is America's oldest performing arts center. Since opening in 1861, it has presented the finest in traditional and contemporary performing arts. Today BAM's mission is twofold: to present artists of international stature who have a cutting-edge artistic vision; and to serve Brooklyn's ethnically diverse population. BAM accomplishes these goals through numerous innovative offerings.

The Next Wave Festival—BAM's fall flagship event—focuses on artists probing new and emerging areas of the performing arts. Since beginning in 1983, it has been the nation's showcase for contemporary performing arts. Performers have ranged from emerging artists to established legends and have included Robert Wilson, Bill T. Jones/Arnie Zane Dance Company, Philip Glass, Pina Bausch's Tanztheater Wupertal and many others.

BAM Opera started in 1989 to promote innovation in opera and musical theater. Notable productions have included "Nixon in China" and "The Death of Klinghoffer," both collaborations by composer John Adams, director Peter Sellars and choreographer Mark Morris; and Lully's "Atys," performed by the Paris ensemble Les Arts Florissants.

Each spring DanceAfrica, a week-long celebration of African-American dance, music and culture, features companies such as the African Heritage Drummers and Dancers, Chuck Davis Dance Company and the Dinizulu African Dancers, Drummers and Singers. BAM also features the popular "Performing Arts Program for Young People" and regular concerts by the Brooklyn Philharmonic Orchestra.

Many renowned performers have appeared at BAM since its opening, including Isadora Duncan, Enrico Caruso, Sarah Bernhardt and Arturo Toscanini. In its early years BAM was also an important lecture site, bringing in Booker T. Washington, Mark Twain and Henry Stanley, with his account of the discovery of Dr. Livingston, among others. Today its programs fill four performance spaces: the Opera House, the Carey Playhouse, Lepercq Space and the nearby Majestic Theater, an unusual converted movie house located at 651 Fulton Street.

GENERAL INFORMATION

Hours Box Office: Mon–Fri 10 am–5:30 pm; no performances July–Sept
Admission Various ticket prices; discounts for seniors, youths (21 and under), group sales and TDF
Giftshop Open during performances: CDs, programs, BAM T-shirts, mugs, etc.
Food Service Simple fare, sandwiches and snacks offered during performances
Disability Access Fully accessible
Directions Subway: B, Q, N, R or M to Dekalb Ave; A or C to Lafayette Ave; G to Fulton St; 2, 3, 4, 5, D, Q or M to Atlantic Ave; B, N or R to Pacific St; Bus: B25, B52 to Fulton St and Fort Green Place; B26 to Fulton St and Ashland Place; B45 to Flatbush Ave and Livingston St; B38 to Fulton St and Lafayette Ave; B41 to Flatbush Ave and Lafayette Ave; B37 to Third Ave and Schermerhorn St; BAM Bus for Opera House and Majestic Theater events only: leaves for BAM from East 51st St and Lexington Ave (Manhattan); after performance BAM Bus makes return stops in Greenwich Village, Midtown, Upper East and Upper West Sides, to 86th St ($4 one way)
Parking On-site lot, across Lafayette Ave
Landmark Status National Register of Historic Places, New York City Landmark

City-owned, privately operated

Courtesy of BAM

BAM Opera House

Brooklyn Botanic Garden

1000 Washington Avenue
Brooklyn, NY 11225
718-622-4433

The Brooklyn Botanic Garden is located just behind the Brooklyn Museum and on the perimeter of Prospect Park (see separate entries). Its 52 acres contain more than 12,000 living plant varieties from all over the world. A Systematic Collection—arranged by taxonomic order—is combined here with formal and informal gardens to create an engaging visual and environmental experience.

The Local Flora Section of the garden exhibits trees, shrubs and wildflowers—native to within a 100-mile radius—in eight miniature ecosystems. The Japanese Hill-and-Pond Garden, constructed in 1914, is one of the finest representations of this garden style outside of Japan. The Fragrance Garden provides significant encounters for both visually impaired and sighted visitors. The Herb Garden—with medicinal, culinary, fragrant and ornamental herbs—features a 16th-century Elizabethan-knot design. The Rock Garden, Shakespeare Garden and Osborne Section offer yet more opportunities to discover gardening at its best.

The Steinhardt Conservatory, completed in 1988, has expanded the garden's capacity to display plants from

Seasonal Garden Highlights

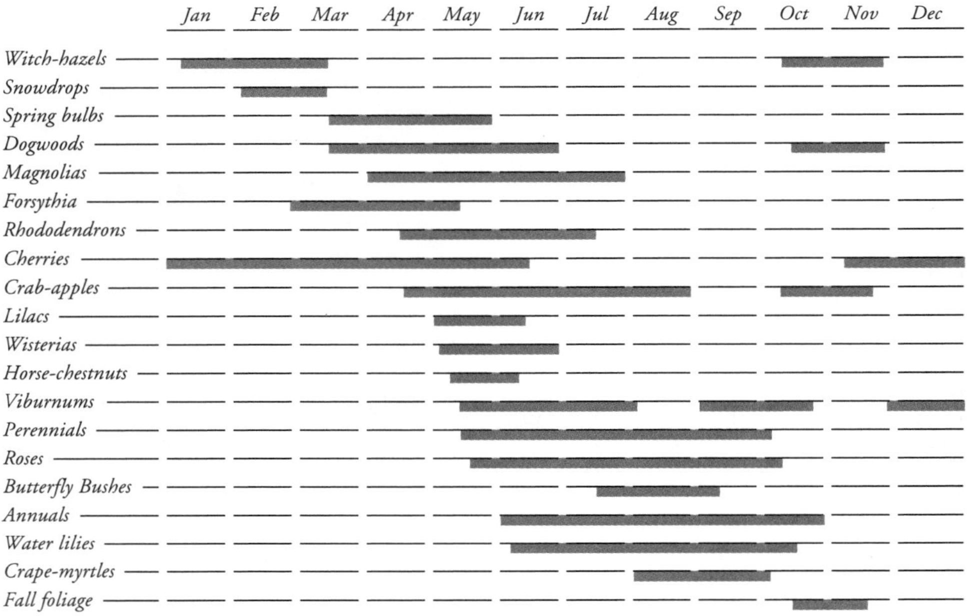

	Jan	*Feb*	*Mar*	*Apr*	*May*	*Jun*	*Jul*	*Aug*	*Sep*	*Oct*	*Nov*	*Dec*
Witch-hazels	■	■	■							■	■	
Snowdrops		■	■									
Spring bulbs			■	■	■							
Dogwoods			■	■	■	■				■	■	
Magnolias				■	■	■	■					
Forsythia			■	■	■							
Rhododendrons				■	■	■	■					
Cherries	■	■	■	■	■	■					■	■
Crab-apples				■	■	■	■	■		■	■	
Lilacs					■	■						
Wisterias					■	■						
Horse-chestnuts					■	■						
Viburnums					■	■	■	■	■	■		■
Perennials					■	■	■	■	■	■		
Roses					■	■	■	■	■	■		
Butterfly Bushes							■	■	■			
Annuals						■	■	■	■	■		
Water lilies						■	■	■	■	■		
Crape-myrtles								■	■			
Fall foliage										■	■	

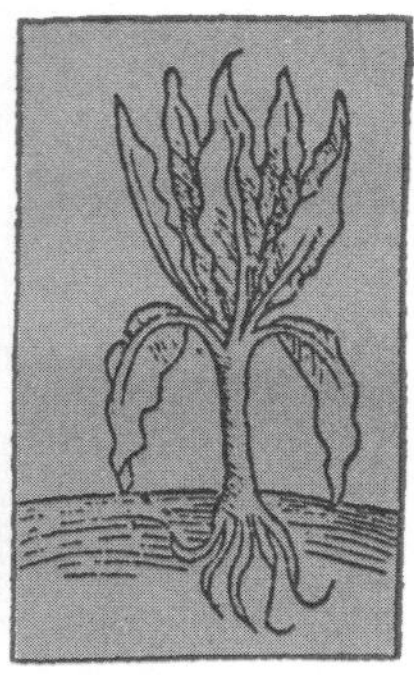

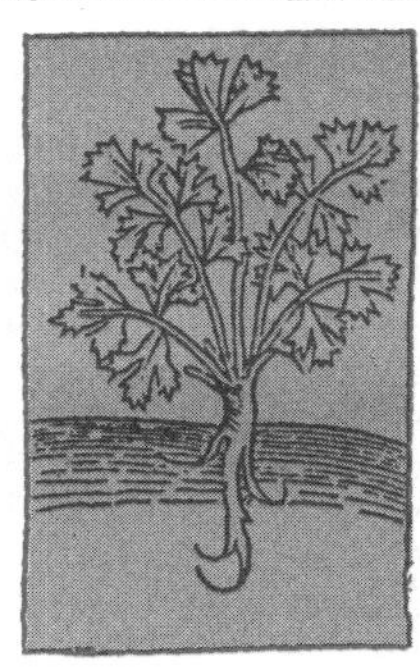

around the globe. Visitors can stroll through desert, tropical rain forest and warm temperate environments in three attractive pavilions. The C. V. Starr Bonsai Museum houses a world-renowned collection. Orchids and tropical aquatics are exhibited all year. And the exceptional Trail of Evolution traces development in the natural world over three and a half billion years.

GENERAL INFORMATION

Hours April–Sept: Tues–Fri 8 am–6 pm; Sat, Sun 10 am–6 pm; closed Mon
Oct-March: Tues–Fri 8 am–4:30 pm; Sat, Sun 10 am–4:30 pm; closed Mon
Admission Free
Giftshop Plants, gardening tools, books, seeds, T-shirts, posters
Library 55,000 volumes on horticulture and botany, open to scholars and members by appointment only
Disability Access Fully accessible, wheelchairs provided; fragrance gardens have elevated beds and braille signage
Directions Subway: 2 or 3 to Eastern Pkwy; D to Prospect Park; Bus: B41, B47, B48, B71 to Washington Ave
Parking Attended lot at 900 Washington Ave
City-owned, privately operated

Brooklyn Center for the Performing Arts

Brooklyn College of the
City University of New York
Campus Road and Hillel Place
Brooklyn, NY 11210

718-951-4500
Box Office

The Brooklyn Center for the Performing Arts at Brooklyn College (BCBC) has presented internationally known artists, ensembles and dance companies to a devout, largely Brooklyn-based following since 1954. Over 100,000 people a year attend BCBC events in the center's 2,500-seat Walt Whitman Hall.

Memorable performances have been given over the years by such notables as Vladimir Horowitz, Ray Charles, Luciano Pavarotti, Victor Borge, Suzanne Farrell and Peter Martins, Harry Belafonte and many more. Over 30 dance companies have made their New York City debuts at BCBC, including France's Ballet du Nord, the Miami City Ballet, Italy's Aterballetto and the Washington, Chicago, Atlanta, Cincinnati, Tulsa and Oakland ballets, many of them performing new works.

The ShowTime series features comics and stars of Broadway such as John Raitt and Jerry Lewis. A special SchoolTime series presents five or six matinee performances a week for schoolchildren. FamilyTime offers shows—illusionists, mimes, acrobats and jugglers—geared to appeal to everyone from toddlers to adults.

GENERAL INFORMATION

Hours Box Office: Tues–Sat 1–6 pm and one hour prior to performances
Admission Various, call for ticket prices and performance schedule; discounts for students, seniors and groups of 20 or more
Giftshop Souvenirs in the Boutique
Disability Access Fully accessible
Directions Subway: 2 to last stop at Flatbush and Nostrand Aves; Bus: B6, B11 to Bedford Ave and Campus Rd
Parking On-site lot

The Brooklyn Children's Museum

145 Brooklyn Avenue
(at St. Mark's Avenue)
Brooklyn, NY 11213

718-735-4400

There are no QUIET or DO NOT TOUCH signs in the Brooklyn Children's Museum. Here children are encouraged to freely indulge the full range of their senses. Designed to make youngsters feel comfortable exploring the relationships between human culture, technology and the environment, the museum's vast range of displays and activities provide an exciting learning experience.

Permanent exhibits include a light show, colorful aquariums and a flowing stream that children divert with gates and sluices. In the Music Studio, youngsters sound notes of a piano by bouncing on massive keys in the floor; the interactive Night Journeys exhibit allows them to try beds from other cultures and hear lullabies from around the world. In the Animal Diner, children push buttons and various animals light up, disclosing their diets. And the Greenhouse teaches youngsters about botany, ecology and horticulture.

Drop-in workshops and crafts events — geared to all ages—are held throughout the museum and include storytelling, science projects and sign-language instruction. In addition to workshops, films and field trips, youngsters enjoy the unique "portable collections" program, which allows them to borrow small objects or instruments, taking the fun of learning beyond the museum's walls.

The Brooklyn Institute of Arts and Science, parent of the museum, was founded in 1823. In 1899 the Brooklyn Children's Museum was established as the nation's first such institution designed expressly for children. It was redesigned by the firm Hardy Holzman Pfeiffer and reopened in 1977.

GENERAL INFORMATION

Hours Wed–Fri 2–5 pm; Sat, Sun, most school holidays 12–5 pm; closed Mon, Tues
Admission Suggested contribution $3
Library In the Children's Resource Library youngsters use print and nonprint resources, including computers, to research favorite subjects
Disability Access Fully accessible; restrooms, telephones available; TDD 718-735-4402
Directions Subway: 3 to Kingston Ave; Bus: B25, B45, B65 to Brooklyn Ave; B47 to St. Marks Ave
Parking On public streets
City-owned, privately operated

The Brooklyn Historical Society

128 Pierrepont Street
(at Clinton Street)
Brooklyn, NY 11201

718-624-0890

There are five permanent exhibits in the Brooklyn Historical Society's gallery which give viewers an overview of Brooklyn's history and achievements. Brooklyn Dodgers retraces baseball's early roots in the borough and recalls the great team of 1955; Brooklyn Bridge shows how this world-famous span spurred neighborhood growth; Coney Island resurrects some of the great seaside hotels and shows viewers what the old boardwalk was like; Brooklyn Navy Yard describes the borough's unique role during World War II; and Brooklynites expands upon the borough's incredible history of cultural diversity.

In addition, the gallery mounts temporary exhibitions that are more narrowly focused. Installations have included "*¿Por Qué Brooklyn*? Our Borough's Latino Voices," "Brooklyn's Historic Black Churches" and exhibitions on the Chinese community and Crown Heights neighborhood. Lectures and programs for schoolchildren and families are offered throughout the year. Walking tours are conducted to sites and structures of architectural or historic significance, which abound in Brooklyn.

The society's landmark building, designed by George B. Post, opened in 1881 and was the first structure in New York to make extensive use of terra-cotta in exterior design. Its second-floor library, which contains the largest collection of Brooklyn-related research materials in the world, has been designated an interior landmark.

GENERAL INFORMATION

Hours Tues–Sat 12–5 pm; closed Sun, Mon
Admission Adults $2.50, seniors and children $1; free Wed
Library Brooklyn historical materials, open Tues–Sat 12–4:45 pm; $5 user fee
Disability Access Fully accessible; restrooms available
Directions Subway: 2, 3, 4 or 5 to Borough Hall; A or F to Jay St; R or M to Court St; Bus: B25, B26, B37, B41, B45, B52, B61 to stop nearest Borough Hall
Parking On-site lot, diagonally across Pierpont St
Landmark Status National Register of Historic Places, New York City Landmark

City-owned, privately operated

The Brooklyn Museum

200 Eastern Parkway
Brooklyn, NY 11238
718-638-5000

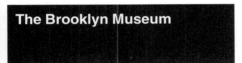

Containing 1.5 million artworks, the Brooklyn Museum is one of the nation's premier art institutions. The museum's collections, housed in a neoclassical structure designed in 1893 by the renowned firm of McKim, Mead & White, encompass virtually the entire history of art.

The art of China, Japan, Korea, Southeast Asia and the Islamic world—from ancient times to the present—is represented in numerous ceramics, sculptures and paintings. The world-famous Egyptian collection, filling ten galleries and covering 5,000 years of Egyptian art, was redesigned in 1993. The museum also has a fine assemblage of works from Greek and Roman antiquity.

The museum contains 28 period rooms covering a historical span from a 17th-century Brooklyn Dutch house to an Art Deco study, all complemented with pieces of matching furniture, glass and metalware. The costumes and textiles collection encompasses a range of styles from 14th-century ecclesiastical lace accessories to 19th-century ball gowns.

The painting and sculpture collection contains works from the 14th century to the present, including a substantial number of 19th-century French works, a large number of Spanish Colonial paintings and one of the country's most comprehensive collections of 19th-century American painting and sculpture. The museum's 20th-century American holdings include works by Willem de Kooning, Marsden Hartley, Georgia O'Keeffe, Richard Diebenkorn and others. An ongoing series in the main lobby highlights new work by contemporary artists.

Holdings in the prints, drawings and photographs department include major groups of works by John Singer Sargent, Winslow Homer, John Singleton Copley and Thomas Eakins. There are notable drawings by Dürer, Goya, Rembrandt and Toulouse-Lautrec. The print collection contains works by Bonnard, Denis, Redon and Vuillard, as well as many German Expressionist images. Photographic masters such as Lewis Hine and Edward Steichen are well represented.

In 1923 the Brooklyn Museum was the first in the United States to exhibit African objects as art rather than artifacts, and since then many rare and historically significant works have been acquired. During this period a fine collection of Native American objects was also assembled. Ancient American artistic traditions are represented by Peruvian textiles, Central American gold and Mexican sculpture. The Oceanic collection includes sculpture from Papua, New Guinea, the Solomon Islands and New Zealand.

The museum has now implemented a large portion of its master construction plan, the result of an international design competition won by architects Arata Isozaki and James Stewart Polshek. The entire West

The Brooklyn Museum Eastern Parkway facade.

Wing, for decades home to an art school, has been redesigned and completely renovated, creating three floors of new gallery space, one of the most beautiful settings for viewing art in the city.

GENERAL INFORMATION

Hours Wed–Sun 10 am–5 pm; closed Mon, Tues
Admission Suggested contribution: adults $4, students $2, senior citizens $1.50, children under 12 free
Giftshop Posters, books, reproductions, etc.; open Wed–Sun 10:30 am–5:30 pm
Food Service Museum Cafe features breakfast, deli sandwiches, hot entrées and a salad bar; open Wed–Sun 10:30am–4:30pm
Library Two libraries: the Art Reference Library contains titles on African, American and Native American art, and 19th-century costumes and textiles; the Wilbour Egyptology Library is one of the most comprehensive repositories of its kind in the world; both are open by appointment only
Disability Access Fully accessible; TDD 718-738-6501
Directions Subway: 2 or 3 to Eastern Pkwy/Brooklyn Museum; or take 4 or 5 to Nevins St and cross platform to 2 or 3; Bus: B41, B48, B69, B71 to Eastern Pkwy
Parking On-site lot at rear of museum
Landmark Status National Register of Historic Places, New York City Landmark

City-owned, privately operated

The Center for Art and Culture of Bedford-Stuyvesant

1368 Fulton Street 718-636-6948
(at Marcy Avenue)
Brooklyn, NY 11216

Housed in a former milk-bottling plant, this spacious exhibition space offers valuable public exposure to talented artists from one of the city's great African-American communities and beyond. Designed by the illustrious architect I. M. Pei, the main gallery rises 40 feet to an elaborate skylight.

Individual and group shows change every four weeks, a regular theme being the politics and culture of the Third World. The work of prison inmates is also shown frequently. Workshops and classes offer artists technical assistance in painting, drawing, silkscreening and printmaking.

In 1967 the Bedford-Stuyvesant Restoration Corporation was founded to promote economic revitalization. The center was opened as part of the program in 1970.

GENERAL INFORMATION

Hours Mon–Fri 10 am–6 pm; Sat 1–5 pm; closed Sun
Admission Suggested contribution $2
Giftshop Fine art and prints
Disability Access Fully accessible
Directions Subway: A or C to Nostrand Ave, then walk two blocks east; LIRR to Nostrand Ave; Bus: B25 to Nostrand Ave; B44 to Fulton St
Parking On-site lot

Gowanus Arts Exchange

295 Douglass Street 718-596-5250
(between Third and Fourth Avenues)
Brooklyn, NY 11217

Located in the Gowanus section of Brooklyn, on the western edge of Park Slope, the Gowanus Arts Exchange occupies the third floor of a former soap factory. It is a modest organization with two studios, the largest being 37 by 40 feet, but in these spaces a broad range of activities occurs.

"The Outback Series for New Dance and Performance" presents the work of emerging and seasoned artists once a month. The "Groundhog Performance Series for Young Audiences" introduces youngsters to dance, music and storytelling in an audience-participation environment on Sundays during winter. The "Special Productions" series brings excellent dance, theater, comedy, music and political satire to the theater in two- or three-night runs. "Kids Outback" is a special showcase for works created and performed only by young artists, ages 8 to 18.

Gowanus Arts Exchange is home to several dance and theater companies, including the American Dance Theater for the Deaf. There are classes for all ages in dance, theater and performance.

GENERAL INFORMATION

Hours Various, call for hours
Admission Various, call for ticket prices and performance schedule
Disability Access None
Directions Subway: N or R to Union St; 2, 3, 4, 5, D or Q to Atlantic Ave; N, R, B or M to Pacific St; Bus: B71 to Fourth Ave; B37 to Union St
Parking On public streets

The Harbor Defense Museum at Fort Hamilton

Fort Hamilton
Brooklyn, NY 11252

718-630-4349

Fort Hamilton, the earliest granite fortification built in New York Harbor, is today the official United States Army Museum of the City of New York. The caponier, or flank battery, where the museum is housed, is a wedge-shaped, granite-and-brick structure with its original 19th-century sod roof and whitewashed walls. It is the best preserved part of the original 1825–31 construction. The main fort, which lost its seaward wall to new armament at the turn of the century, was further modified during its conversion to an officers' club in the 1930s.

Permanent displays tell the story of the generations of guns, mines, airplanes and missiles that have protected the harbor. Two temporary exhibitions mounted every year focus on the fort and U.S. military history. Exhibits have addressed the 50th anniversary of Pearl Harbor and the Persian Gulf War. An interesting self-guided tour of the fort and related sites in the surrounding neighborhood takes about 90 minutes.

GENERAL INFORMATION

Hours Mon–Fri 1–4 pm; closed Sat, Sun
Admission Free
Giftshop Booklets, photo reproductions and souvenirs related to exhibits
Library Newly dedicated research center, open by appointment only
Disability Access Fully accessible; ramps, restrooms available
Directions Subway: R to 95th St, walk to 101st St; Bus: B63 to 99th St and 4th Ave; B16 to 4th Ave and Shore Rd, walk to 101st St
Parking On-site lot
Landmark Status National Register of Historic Places, New York City Landmark

Self-Guided Neighborhood Tour

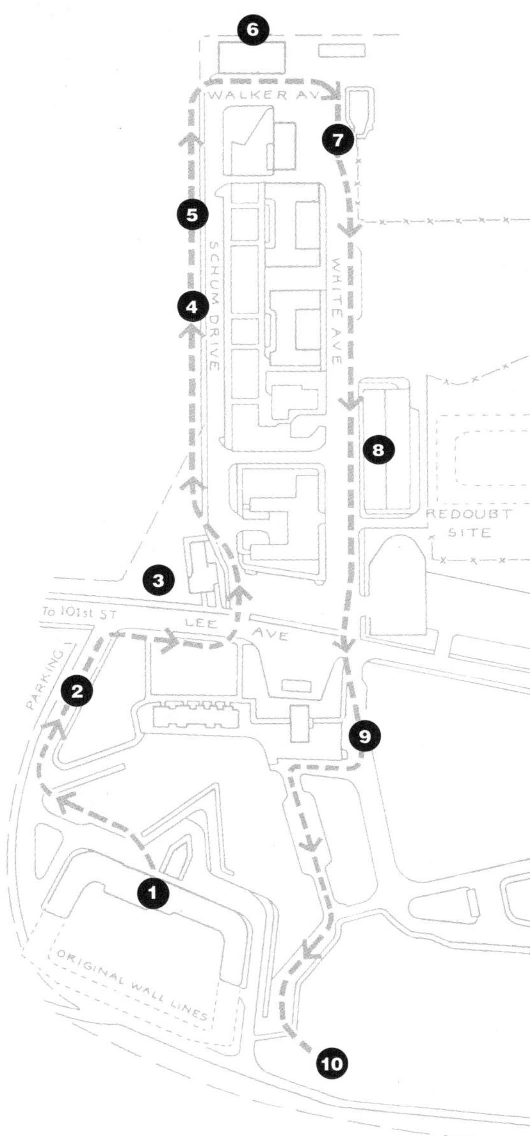

1 Harbor Defense Museum

2 Cannon Walk—artillery and row houses built 1911 as officer quarters

3 Robert E. Lee's house

4 Barrack, built 1908-10, and polo field

5 17th century Indian longhouse commemorative tablet and 4½-inch Civil War-era seige rifle

6 Former Fort Hamilton Commissary, built 1896

7 Quartermaster stables

8 Fort Hamilton's redoubts—first landward defense

9 Officer quarters, built 1892

10 Historic site and artifacts

The Kurdish Library and Museum

144 Underhill Avenue
(corner of Park Place)
Brooklyn, NY 11238
718-783-7930

The Kurdish Library and Museum is located in a privately owned brownstone on Park Place in Brooklyn. It contains over 2,000 volumes on Kurdish history and culture, many of which were smuggled out of the Middle East at great risk to those carrying them. Some sacred books have even been dropped anonymously on the doorstep because the donors fear for the safety of their families abroad should their names become public.

Sharaf Khan Bitlisi, historian and author of "Sharafnameh", late 16th century.

Many of the books are written in Kurdish; the remainder are in 15 other languages, among them English, French and German. Titles include a rare history of the Kurds, classics such as Austen H. Layard's "Nineveh and Babylon" and "Ma Vie de Kurde" by Noureddine Zaza. The collection also contains periodicals, newspapers and maps, as well as video and audio materials.

The reading room, featuring attractive stained-glass windows, is adorned with numerous artifacts of this threatened culture, including unique musical instruments, kilim rugs, hand-loomed scarves and crocheted silk slippers. Mannequins in traditional dress wear pantaloons, brocade jackets, skirts of hand-loomed goat hair from Turkey and velvet dresses from Iran and Iraq. Large color photographs of the Kurds themselves and the Kurdistan landscape decorate the walls.

GENERAL INFORMATION

Hours Mon–Thurs 10 am–3 pm, appointment advised; closed Fri–Sun
Admission Free
Library See narrative above
Disability Access None
Directions Subway: D or Q to 7th Ave; 2 or 3 to Grand Army Plaza; Bus: None
Parking On public streets

Lefferts Homestead Children's Historic House Museum

Prospect Park–Willink Entrance
Flatbush Avenue and
Empire Boulevard
Brooklyn, NY 11215
718-965-6505

Lefferts Homestead in Prospect Park is one of the few surviving Dutch farmhouses in Brooklyn. The house combines Dutch Colonial architecture with Federal details. A bell-shaped gambrel roof creates sloping eaves which, as they extend over the front and back porches, are supported by slender columns. Carved woodwork and circle-and-diamond-pattern transom windows adorn the Dutch-style split front door.

A large *kas*, or Dutch cupboard, a four-poster bed, Bibles and a grandfather clock belonging to the Lefferts family are exhibited in period rooms furnished to reflect daily life in the 1820s. Demonstrations of early American crafts, hands-on workshops and other adult education programs are offered by the Prospect Park Alliance, which operates the house. Exhibitions explore life in Kings County in the 1820s, when the freeing of slaves and the opening of the Erie Canal had profound significance for local farmers. Herb and vegetable gardens are a seasonal attraction.

Peter Lefferts built the house between 1777 and 1783 to replace an earlier family home burned during the battle of Long Island (1776). At the time, Flatbush was a farming village, surrounded by woodlands, with about 1,000 residents. Lefferts was one of the richest men in Kings County, with 240 acres of land, heading a large household of eight family members and twelve slaves. He was a lieutenant in the Colonial Army and became a judge of the County Court. In 1788 he was a delegate to the state convention in Poughkeepsie when New York ratified the United States Constitution.

GENERAL INFORMATION

Hours March–July, Sept–Dec: Sat, Sun 12–4 pm; closed Mon–Fri
Admission Free
Giftshop Historical memorabilia and toys
Library Reference materials about Brooklyn history and Lefferts family, open to public
Disability Access None
Directions Subway: D, Q or S to Prospect Park; Bus: B33, B41, B47, B48 to Empire Blvd–Flatbush Ave
Parking On-site lot at Wollman Rink
Landmark Status National Register of Historic Places, New York City Landmark

City-owned, privately operated

New York Experimental Glass Workshop

Robert Lehman Gallery
647 Fulton Street
(enter on Rockwell Place)
Brooklyn, NY 11217

718-625-3685

The New York Experimental Glass Workshop is dedicated to the expressive art of glass-making. Six to eight exhibitions are mounted a year in the Robert Lehman Gallery, featuring glass work ranging from the traditional to the experimental by contemporary masters of the medium and emerging artists. Works on display vary from large-scale sculpture, conceptual art and installation work to functional crafts, furniture and decorative art. A windowed reception area allows visitors to view artists as they work with their molten materials. The workshop also offers beginning to advanced courses in glass-making and free slide lectures provide an opportunity to hear artists discuss their work.

GENERAL INFORMATION

Hours Sun, Mon 10 am–6 pm; closed Tues–Sat
Admission Free
Giftshop Some works on display are for sale
Library Slide library, open by appointment only
Disability Access Fully accessible; elevators, restrooms available
Directions Subway: D, Q, M, N or R to DeKalb Ave; 2, 3, 4 or 5 to Nevins St; Bus: B25, B26, B52 to Fulton St; B38 on DeKalb Ave to Rockwell Place
Parking On public streets

New York Transit Museum

Corner of Boerum Place
and Schermerhorn Street
Brooklyn, NY 11201

718-330-3060

The New York Transit Museum—home to 100 years of transit lore and memorabilia—occupies the platforms and mezzanine of a decommissioned 1930s subway station. The museum houses 19 completely restored vintage subway and elevated cars dating from 1904 through 1967, a working signal tower and other artifacts demonstrating the vital role mass transit has played in the city's development. Permanent exhibits include Architectural Drawings, which display detailed designs for the first Inter-Borough Rapid Transit line; and City Beautiful, Its Beginnings Underground, focusing on the tile mosaics for which subway stations are famous.

Periodically the museum rolls out its collection of antique buses. Also on view: bas-reliefs, a surface transit exhibit and an assortment of turnstiles used over the past 85 years. The museum's archive is one of the most significant public transit historical records in the country. Public programming also features lectures, walking tours and demonstrations of emergency rescue and crime-fighting equipment. Take the subway (or bus) to get there.

New York Transit Museum Archives, Brooklyn

Third Avenue Elevated Railroad, circa 1880s.

GENERAL INFORMATION

Hours Tues–Fri 10 am–4 pm; Sat, Sun 11 am–4 pm; closed Mon
Admission Adults $3, seniors and children under 18, $1.50
Giftshop Transit-related books, toys, T-shirts and other gifts
Library Access to archive by appointment only, call 718-694-1068
Disability Access None
Directions Subway: 2, 3, 4 or 5 to Borough Hall; F to Jay St; M, N or R to Court St; A, C or G to Hoyt–Schermerhorn St; Bus: B25, B26, B37, B41, B45, B52, B61 to Boerum Place and Schermerhorn St
Parking On public streets

Top of a subway exit kiosk, New York City, circa 1902-3.

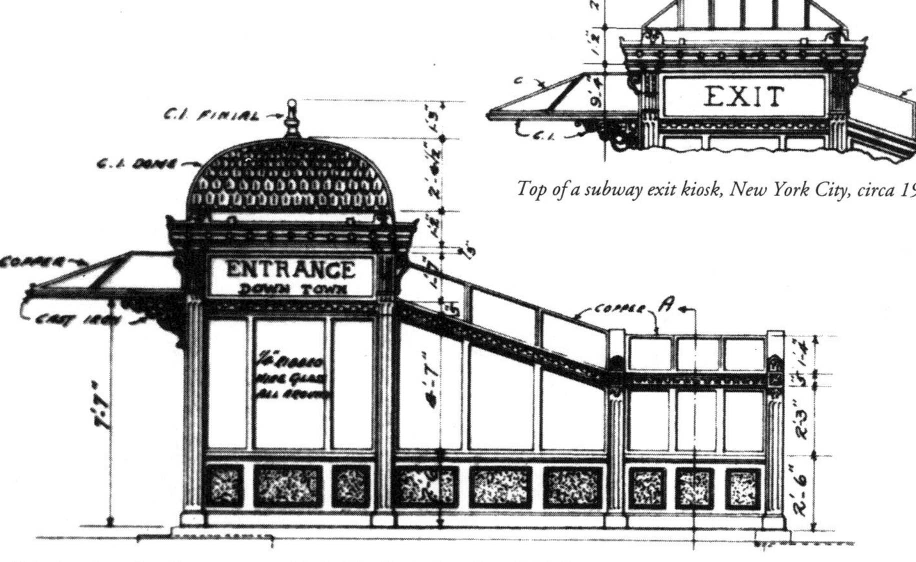

Side elevation of a subway entrance kiosk, New York City, circa 1902-3.

Kiosk drawings courtesy of the New York Transit Museum Archives, Brooklyn

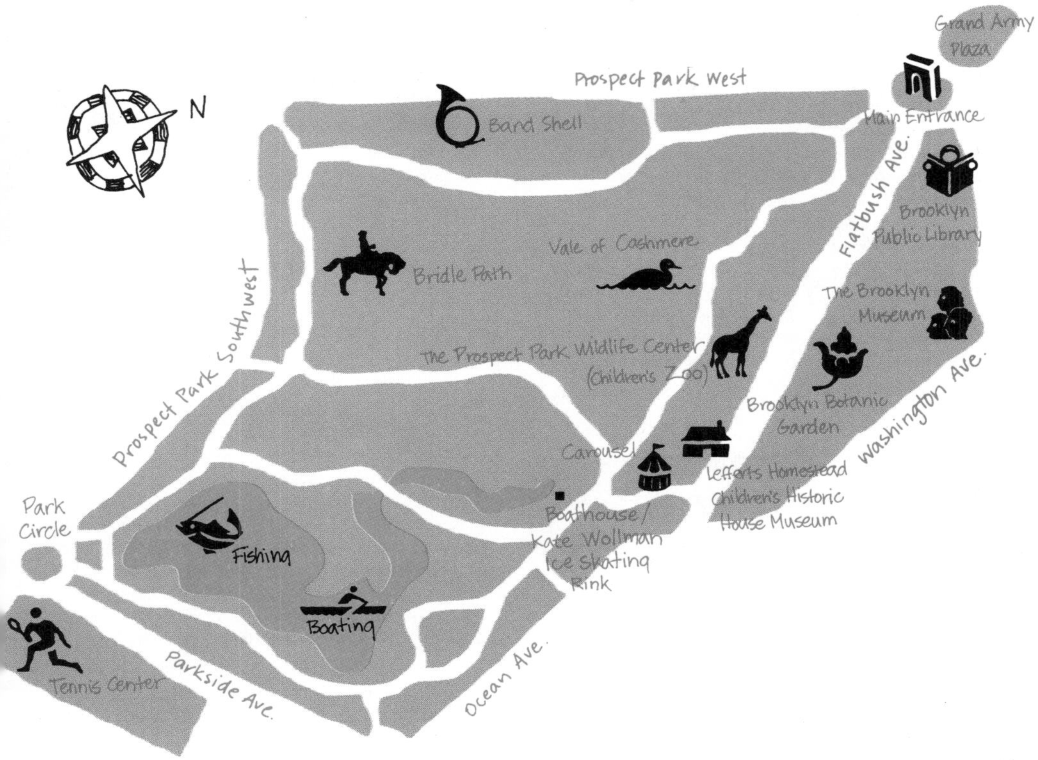

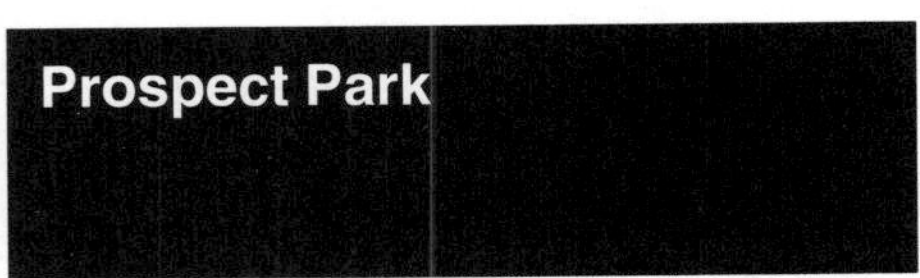

Prospect Park

Bordered by Flatbush Avenue, Ocean Avenue, Parkside Avenue, Prospect Park Southwest and Prospect Park West
Brooklyn, NY 11215

718-965-8999

Prospect Park is one of the finest creations of the landscape architects Frederick Law Olmsted and Calvert Vaux, whose other notable achievements include Central Park (see separate entry), the National Zoo in Washington, DC, and the Emerald Necklace in Boston. The 526-acre park, begun in 1866, has a 60-acre lake on its east side, the 90-acre Long Meadow on the west, and Brooklyn's last remaining woodlands in between. Prospect Park is the site of one of the Revolutionary Wars' fiercest battles.

The park bandshell is home to theater, music and dance performances during the temperate months. Performances have been given here by Taj Mahal, Ray Barretto with the Brooklyn Philharmonic Orchestra, DanceBrazil and Hugh Masekela.

The boathouse is an architectural treasure. Designed in the Italian Renaissance style and constructed in 1905, it is meticulously crafted with exterior aquatic motifs that include dolphins and swans. Inside is informative free literature that enhances enjoyment of the park and its many cultural offerings. The boathouse also occasionally houses exhibitions.

Other park attractions include the Picnic House, overlooking Long Meadow, home of the "New Prospects" performance series; the Kate Wollman Ice Skating Rink; the Memorial Arch at Grand Army Plaza, site of indoor art exhibitions; Lefferts Homestead and the nearby Brooklyn Botanic Garden and Brooklyn Museum (see separate entries).

The **Prospect Park Zoo**, the newest addition to the park, has just undergone a $36 million restoration to become the country's largest children's zoo. It is operated by New York Zoological Society /The Wildlife Conservation Society, which also manages the Central Park Zoo, the Bronx Zoo and the Aquarium for Wildlife Conservation.

GENERAL INFORMATION

Hours Park: dawn to dusk daily; Boathouse Visitors Center: Sat, Sun 11 am–5 pm throughout the year; also open Fri 11 am–5 pm during summer
Admission Free
Giftshop Park T-shirts and publications in boathouse
Food Service In boathouse
Library Archival materials housed in the Arsenal, Central Park, Manhattan
Disability Access Boathouse and carousel fully accessible; most park paths accessible
Directions Subway: D, Q or S to Prospect Park; Bus: B33, B41, B47, B48 to Empire Blvd–Flatbush Ave
Parking On-site lot at Wollman Rink
Landmark Status National Register of Historic Places, New York City Landmark

The Rotunda Gallery

33 Clinton Street (at Pierrepont Plaza) Brooklyn, NY 11201 — 718-875-4047

The Rotunda Gallery mounts eight to ten exhibitions a year, including group, thematic and individual artist shows focusing on painting, sculpture, photography, site-specific installations and video. Exhibiting artists have included Judy Pfaff, Robert Longo, Alex Katz and more than 400 of the borough's emerging talents. The Rotunda Gallery also sponsors art in public spaces throughout Brooklyn, such as the installation of outdoor sculptures in Cadman Plaza Park and the Artists' Garden Competition. In 1983, during the Brooklyn Bridge's centennial celebration, the gallery mounted an outdoor showing of 25 sculptures on the theme of bridges. A Brooklyn–artists' slide registry and education programs for schoolchildren are an important part of the gallery's activities. The rotunda referred to is the central lobby of nearby Brooklyn Borough Hall, the original site of the gallery and itself a space well worth seeing.

GENERAL INFORMATION

Hours Tues–Fri 12–5 pm; Sat 11 am–4 pm; closed Sun, Mon
Admission Free
Disability Access Fully accessible; restrooms available
Directions Subway: 2, 3, 4, 5, M, N or R to Court St–Borough Hall; A or C to High St; Bus: B25, B38, B41, B51, B52 to Pierrepont St
Parking Lot near gallery and on public streets

Schafler Gallery

Pratt Institute
Chemistry Building, First Floor
200 Willoughby Avenue
(between Hall Street and Classon Avenue)
Brooklyn, NY 11205
718-636-3517

Established in 1985 by Pratt Institute, the Schafler Gallery mounts faculty and student exhibitions as well as thematic shows featuring the work of unaffiliated artists. These displays are also mounted at the Pratt Manhattan Center Gallery in the Puck Building on Lafayette Street. Shows go beyond the fine arts of painting and sculpture to include the applied arts of graphic and interior design. Exhibits have included "Fantasists," focusing on fantasy art; "Silent Sell," a look at contemporary package design; and "A Painter's Brooklyn." There are periodic lectures relating to the exhibits and to issues in art and design.

Founded in 1887, Pratt Institute started as a trade school. Today it is considered one of New York City's foremost academies, offering numerous programs in the humanities, architecture, design and engineering.

GENERAL INFORMATION

Hours Mon–Fri 9 am–5 pm; closed Sat, Sun
Admission Free
Disability Access Limited wheelchair access
Directions Subway: G to Clinton St–Washington Ave; Bus: B38 to St. James St and Lafayette Ave
Parking On public streets
Landmark Status National Register of Historic Places

Pieter Claesen Wyckoff House Museum

Clarendon Road and Ralph Avenue 718-629-5400
Brooklyn, NY 11203

This wood-shingled Dutch Colonial farmhouse, buillt about 1652, is probably the oldest home in New York City. It stands on land that is believed to have been purchased in 1636 from the Canarsie Indians by Van Twiller, the first Director General of New Netherland.

A modest structure with wide pine floorboards, a shingled exterior and a gable roof with flared "spring" eaves, it is typical of its time. The oldest section, the kitchen, has a low ceiling designed to retain heat in winter. In several rooms, stripped walls show the original construction of wooden slats filled with handmade brick and mud for insulation and covered in plaster.

On display are original mauve and white ceramic fireplace tiles imported from Holland in the 1660s, as well as a *kas*, or Dutch cupboard, a spinning wheel and a 17th-century pistol. A kitchen garden contains plants popular during colonial times. Occasionally the museum mounts small exhibits, such as "Domestic Life in Colonial Brooklyn." There are demonstrations of period crafts and children's programs are also offered.

Pieter Claesen Wyckoff, who built the house, arrived in New Netherland in 1637 as an illiterate indentured servant. He eventually became a magistrate, a successful farmer and the wealthiest citizen of New Amersfoort, which later became the town of Flatlands. His descendants occupied the house until 1902. In 1970 the City of New York came into possession of the property.

GENERAL INFORMATION

Hours May 15–Nov 30: Thurs–Sat 12–5 pm, closed Sun–Wed; Dec–May 14: Thurs, Fri 12–4 pm, closed Sat–Wed
Admission Adults $2, seniors and children $1
Disability Access Grounds fully accessible; house reached through kitchen door with assistance
Directions Subway: D to Newkirk Ave; Bus: B6 to Glenwood Rd and Ralph Ave; B7 to Kings Highway and Clarendon Rd; B8 to East 79th St and Beverly Rd; B78 to Clarendon Rd and Ralph Ave
Parking On public streets
Landmark Status National Register of Historic Places
City-owned, privately operated

The island of Manhattan gets its name from the indigenous people who, as late as the 17th century, lived on its northernmost reaches. The Dutch bought it in 1626. Since then the 23-square-mile island has evolved through Dutch, English and American hands into one of the world's great cities.

Manhattan has been the site of several cultural zeniths, including the period of great institution-building in the late 19th century,

a t t a n

which produced the American Museum of Natural History, the Metropolitan Museum of Art, the Metropolitan Opera and Central Park; the Harlem Renaissance of the 1920s, a legendary period of African-American creativity in the arts; the Abstract Expressionist school of painting in the 1950s; and, from the 1930s through the 1980s, world leadership in dance through the work of Martha Graham, George Balanchine and others.

Today Manhattan is the nation's center for commerce, communication and the arts. Its 1.5 million residents—and the millions it attracts daily to work and recreation—have access to an astonishing assortment of activities. Manhattan possesses an unparalleled wealth of cultural resources, as reflected in the definitive collections of its museums, the great theater on Broadway and off, the experimental work at numerous alternative spaces, its preeminent opera and dance companies, the richness of one of the world's great architectural troves, its encyclopedic libraries, numerous concert halls, and great monuments like the Empire State Building, Rockefeller Center and the Statue of Liberty.

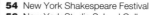

Lower Manhattan

36 Alternative Museum
53 American Indian Community House
41 Anthology Film Archives
66 American Institute of Graphic Arts
65 Aperture Foundation/Burden Gallery
26 Artists Space
14 Asian American Arts Centre
63 Baruch College/Sydney Mishkin Gallery
24 Castillo Cultural Center
3 Castle Clinton National Monument
37 Center for Book Arts
47 Charas, Inc.
17 Chinatown History Museum
35 Cinque Gallery
20 Clocktower Gallery
60 Con Edison Energy Museum
43 Cooper Union for the Advancement of Science & Art
67 Dance Theater Workshop
31 Dia Center for the Arts–Mercer St.
70 Dia Center for the Arts–22nd St.
40 Dixon Place
44 Downtown Art Co.
27 Drawing Center
16 Educational Alliance, Inc.
2 Ellis Island Immigration Museum
34 Exit Art/The First World
71 Fashion Institue of Technology
8 Federal Hall National Memorial
59 Forbes Magazine Galleries
32 14 Sculptors Gallery
19 Franklin Furnace Archive
6 Fraunces Tavern Museum
12 Governor's Room at City Hall
55 Greenwich House Pottery
29 Guggenheim Museum SoHo
72 Guinness World of Records Exhibition
17 Henry Street Settlement
73 Japan Society
52 Joseph Gallery
68 Joyce Theater
39 Kampo Cultural and Multi-Media Center
22 Kenkeleba House
69 Kitchen Center for Video, Music, Dance, Performance, Film and Literature
45 La Mama E. T. C.
21 Lower East Side Tenement Museum
16 Midtown Y Photography Gallery
15 Mulberry Street Theater
13 Municipal Archives of New York City
33 Museum for African Art
4 Museum of American Financial History
5 National Museum of the American Indian
30 New Museum of Contemporary Art
25 New York City Fire Museum

54 New York Shakespeare Festival
56 New York Studio School Gallery
51 New York University
42 Old Merchant's House
46 P.S. 122
11 Pace Downtown Theater
57 Pen and Brush, Inc.
73 Pierpont Morgan Library
61 Police Academy Museum
38 Pratt Manhattan Gallery
64 Theodore Roosevelt Birthplace
23 Roulette
58 Salmagundi Club
9 South Street Seaport Museum
48 St. Mark's Church in-the-Bowery
1 Statue of Liberty
28 Synchronicity Space
18 Tribeca Performing Arts Center
7 Trinity Museum at Trinity Church
49 Ukrainian Museum
62 Visual Arts Museum
50 White Columns
10 Winter Garden

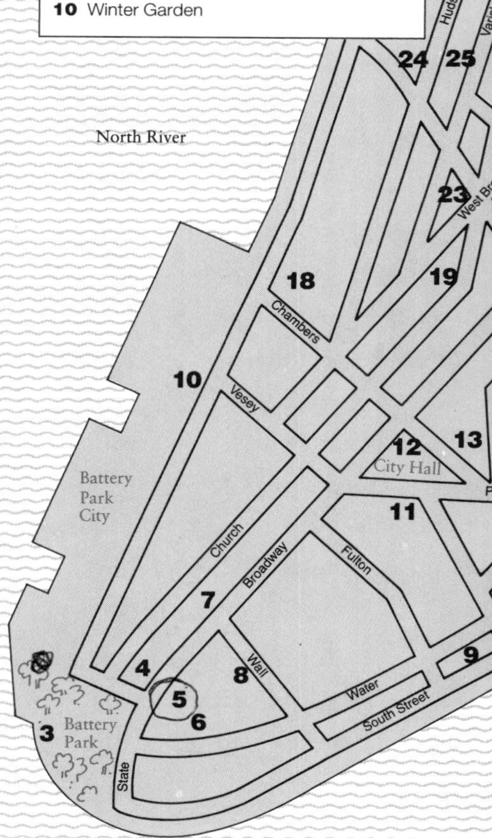

1

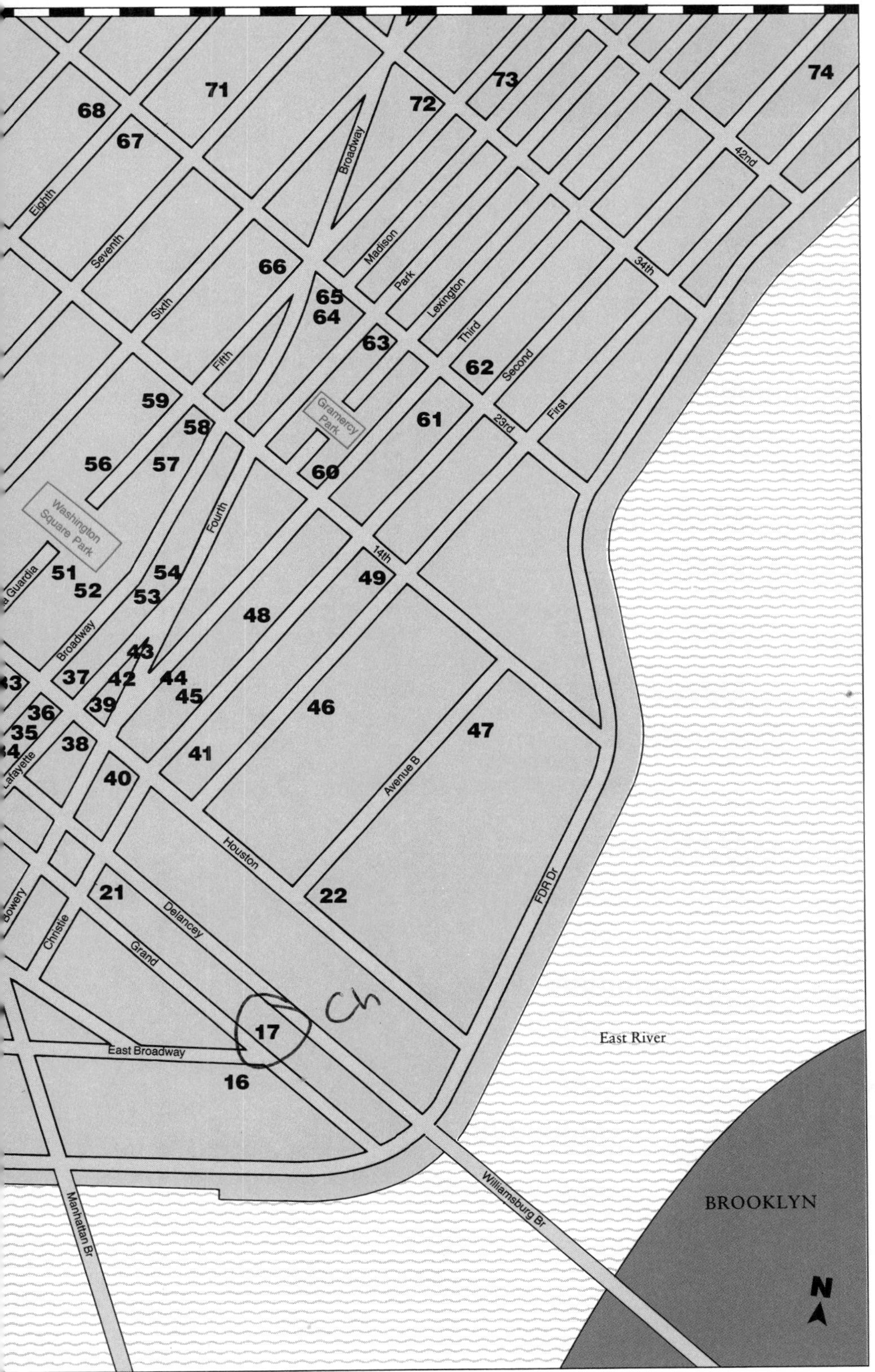

74
73
72
71
68
67
42nd
Broadway
Eighth
Seventh
Madison
66
34th
Park
65
64
Lexington
Sixth
63
Third
62
Second
Fifth
59
58
Gramercy Park
61
23rd
First
56
57
60
Washington Square Park
Fourth
14th
51
54
49
La Guardia
52
53
48
Broadway
43
37
42
44
45
46
39
47
36
35
38
41
Lafayette
40
Avenue B
Houston
21
22
Bowery
Delancey
FDR Dr
Christie
Grand
Ch
17
East Broadway
East River
16
Williamsburg Br
BROOKLYN
Manhattan Br
N

Central Manhattan

21 ACA Exhibition Space
31 Abigail Adams Smith Museum
12 American Craft Museum
54 American Museum of Natural History
44 Americas Society
11 Archives of American Art
25 Art Students League of New York Gallery
41 Asia Society
15 Austrian Cultural Institute
62 Bard Graduate Center for Studies in the Decorative Arts
74 Black Fashion Museum
5 Caribbean Cultural Center
24 Carnegie Hall
73 Cathedral of St. John the Divine
59 Central Park
38 Central Park Zoo
60 Children's Museum of Manhattan
36 China Institute in America
23 City Center
65 Cooper-Hewitt Museum
9 Equitable Center and Gallery
34 French Institute/Alliance Française
45 Frick Collection
32 Gallery 62
4 Gallery 1199
57 Goethe House New York—German Cultural Center
46 Gracie Mansion
28 Grand Central Art Galleries
33 Grolier Club
63 Solomon R. Guggenheim Museum
27 Horticultural Society of New York
29 IBM Gallery of Science and Art
3 INTAR Hispanic American Arts Center
7 International Center of Photography Midtown
67 International Center of Photography
1 Intrepid Sea Air Space Museum
2 Irish Arts Center
19 Elsa Mott Ives Gallery
66 Jewish Museum
42 Sylvia and Danny Kaye Playhouse
30 Korean Cultural Service
39 Kosciuszko Foundation
49 Lincoln Center for the Performing Arts
51 Merkin Concert Hall
56 Metropolitan Museum of Art
70 Museo del Barrio
48 Museum of American Folk Art
35 Museum of American Illustration
22 Museum of Modern Art
13 Museum of Television & Radio
26 Museum of the American Piano
69 Museum of the City of New York
64 National Academy of Design
37 New York Academy of Sciences
8 New York Public Library
50 New York Public Library for the Performing Arts
20 New York School of Interior Design Gallery
55 New York Shakespeare Festival/ Delacorte Theater
53 New-York Historical Society
14 Nikon House
68 92nd Street Y
10 PaineWebber Art Gallery
17 Park Avenue Atrium
72 Nicholas Roerich Museum
40 Sculpture Center Gallery
18 Seagram Gallery
43 Spanish Institute
75 Studio Museum in Harlem
52 Swiss Institute
61 Symphony Space
71 Taller Boricua Gallery
5 Town Hall
16 Urban Center Galleries
47 Whitney Museum of American Art
58 YIVO Institute for Jewish Research

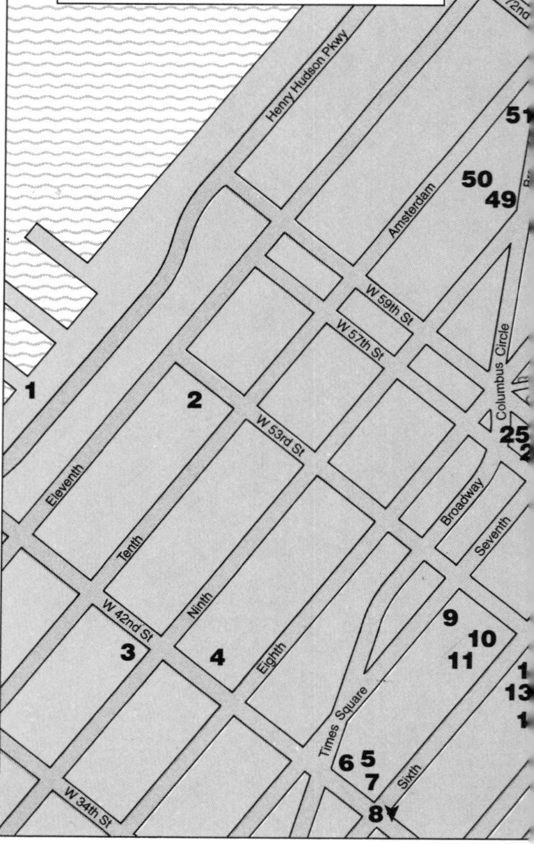

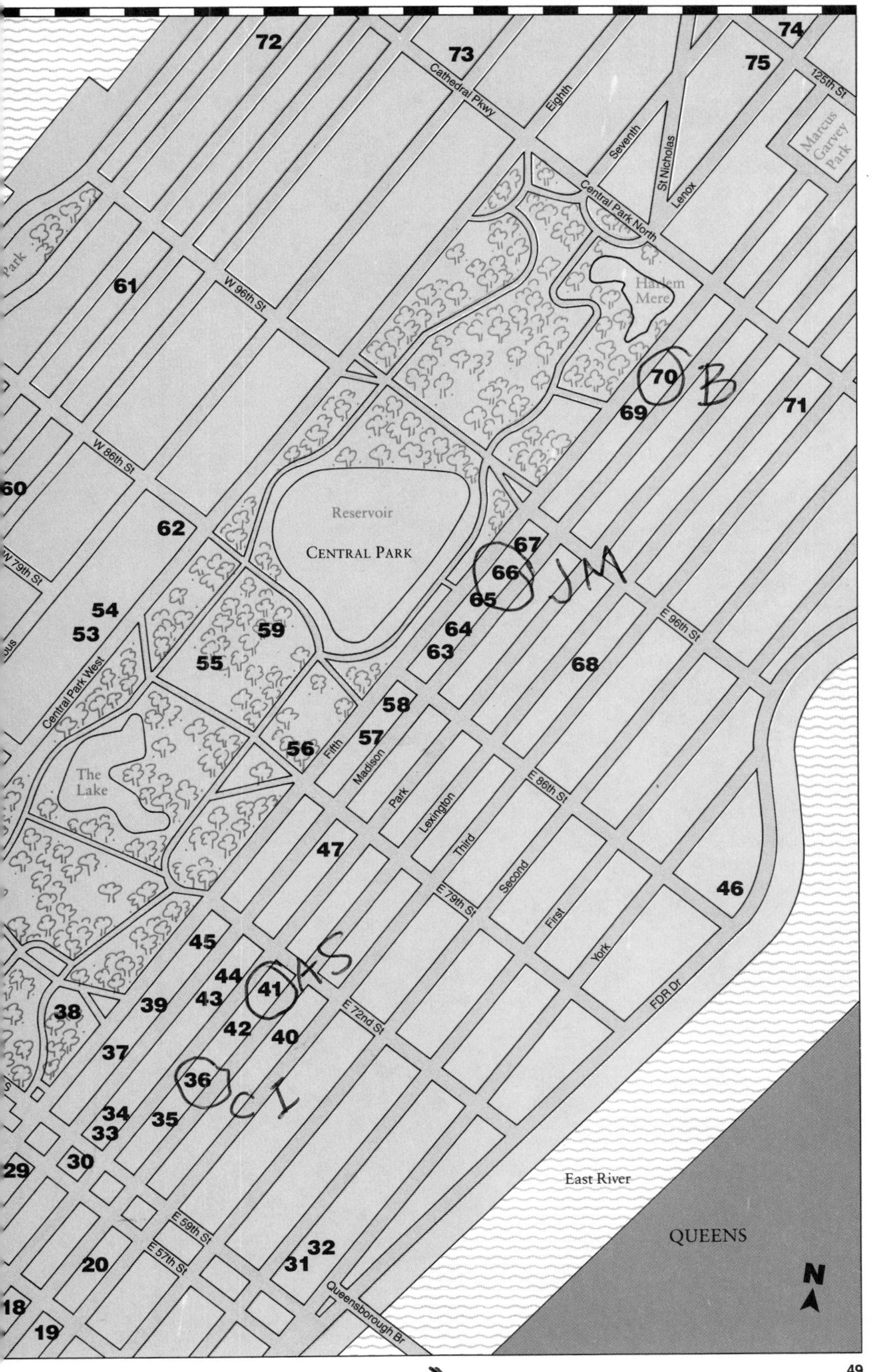
72
73
74
75
Cathedral Pkwy
Eighth
Seventh
St Nicholas
Lenox
125th St
Marcus Garvey Park
Central Park North
Harlem Mere
Park
61
W 96th St
70
69
71
W 86th St
60
Reservoir
CENTRAL PARK
62
67
66
65
64
63
W 79th St
54
53
59
55
Central Park West
68
E 96th St
58
57
56
Fifth
Madison
Park
Lexington
E 86th St
The Lake
47
Third
Second
E 79th St
First
46
45
44
41
43
39
42
40
E 72nd St
York
FDR Dr
38
37
36
34
35
33
30
29
E 59th St
E 57th St
20
32
31
East River
QUEENS
18
19
Queensborough Br
N

Upper Manhattan

4 African Arts Cultural Center
9 American Academy of Arts and Letters
8 American Numismatic Society
6 Children's Museum of the Native American
12 Cloisters
1 Columbia University
3 Aaron Davis Hall for the Performing Arts
13 Dyckman House Museum
2 General Grant National Memorial
7 Hispanic Society of America
10 Morris-Jumel Mansion
5 Schomburg Center for Research in Black Culture
11 Yeshiva University Museum

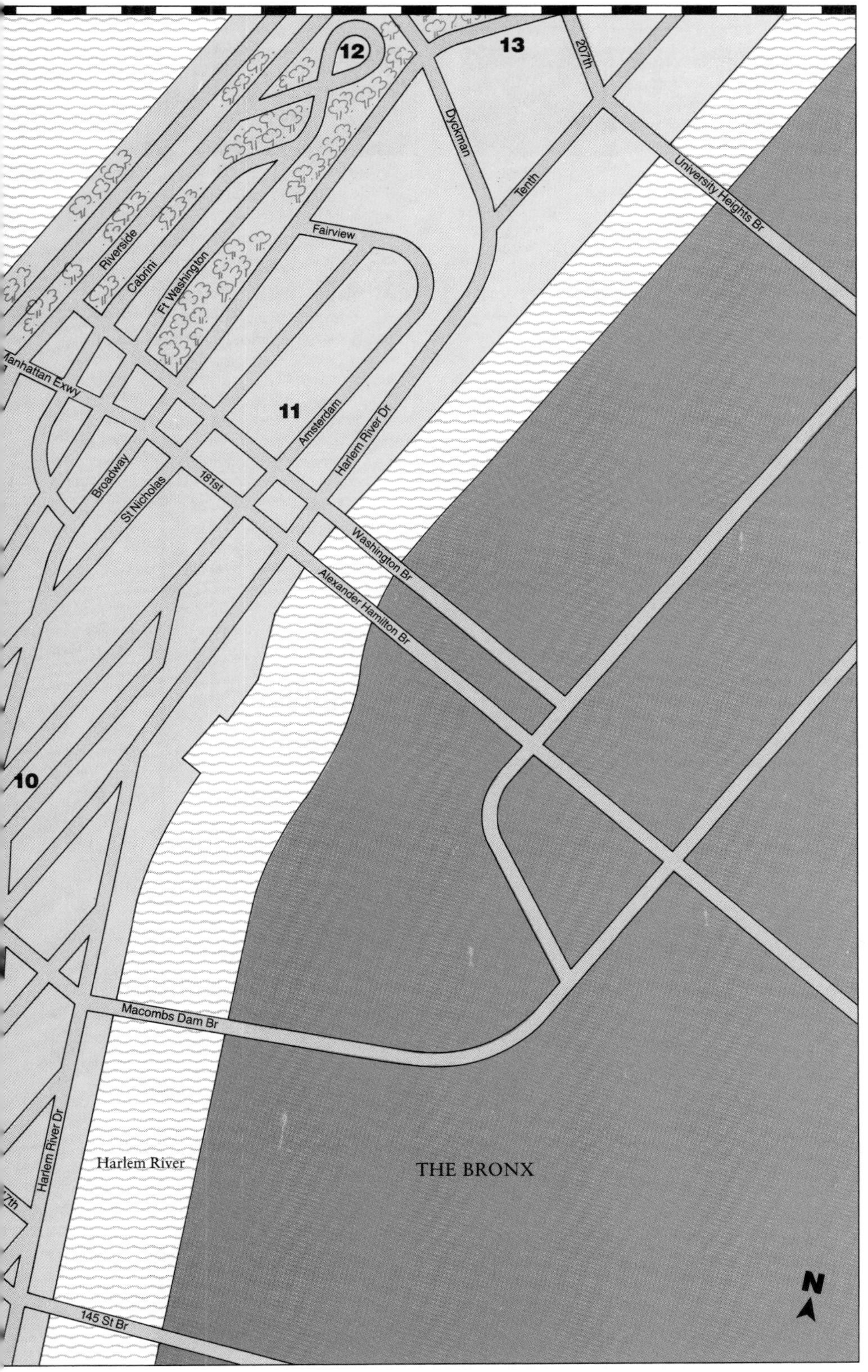
12
13
207th
Dyckman
Tenth
University Heights Br
Fairview
Riverside
Cabrini
Ft Washington
Manhattan Exwy
11
Amsterdam
Harlem River Dr
Broadway
St Nicholas
181st
Washington Br
Alexander Hamilton Br
10
Macombs Dam Br
Harlem River Dr
Harlem River
THE BRONX
N
145 St Br

ACA Exhibition Space

One East 53rd Street 212-223-2787
(between Fifth and Madison Avenues)
New York, NY 10022

ACA Exhibition Space, one of Manhattan's newest galleries, is dedicated solely to showcasing the art of students from the elementary through graduate levels. Exhibitions have included children's art from "Dream Makers," a national elementary art education program, and various collaborative works. The gallery also sponsors the annual "Summer Seminar," which teaches gifted high school juniors college-level visual arts skills in drawing and painting skills. ACA Exhibition Space is located in the Arts Consortium Building at One East 53rd Street.

GENERAL INFORMATION

Hours Mon–Fri 8 am–8 pm, Sat 8 am–6 pm; closed Sun
Admission Free
Disability Access Fully accessible
Directions Subway: E or F to 5th Ave–53rd St; B, D, F or Q to 47th–50th St; Bus: M27, M50 to 5th Ave; M1, M2, M3, M4, M5 to 53rd St
Landmark Status New York City Landmark

The Abigail Adams Smith House Museum

421 East 61st Street 212-838-6878
(between First and York Avenues)
New York, NY 10021

The Abigail Adams Smith House Museum was constructed in 1799 as the carriage house for the country estate of Abigail Adams Smith, daughter of President John Adams, and her husband Colonel William Smith. Colonel Smith had served under George Washington and named the estate Mount Vernon in honor of the general's Virginia home. The estate was one of a number of fashionable country residences lining the East River in the early 1800s.

As the Mount Vernon Hotel, the main house became a country resort popular with city residents and famous for its turtle soup. After the main house burned in 1826, the carriage house was converted into a hotel. Greek Revival mantels, cornices and staircases were added at this time. As the rural landscape gave way to industrialization, the building—a fine example of

The Abigail Adams Smith House Museum

Drawing: C. Fraser & W. Klein

Federal-style stonework—became, successively, a private residence, a gas company and an antique shop. The Colonial Dames of America opened it as a museum in 1939 to coincide with the New York World's Fair.

GENERAL INFORMATION

Hours Mon–Fri 10 am–12 pm (groups only), 12–4 pm; June–July additional hours Tues 5:30–8 pm; Sept–May additional hours Sun 1–5 pm; closed Aug
Admission Adults $3, seniors and students $2, children under 12 free
Giftshop Books, postcards, posters, historic memorabilia
Library Historical and genealogical reference materials; open by appointment
Disability Access Limited; auditorium accessible
Directions Subway: N or R to Lexington Ave; 4, 5 or 6 to 59th St, then walk three blocks east; Bus: M15, M31 to 61st St; M58 to 61st St and York Ave
Landmark Status National Register of Historic Places, New York City Landmark

African Arts Cultural Center

2191 Adam Clayton Powell Jr. Boulevard (at 125th Street)
New York, NY 10027
212-996-3333
212-749-0827

The African Arts Cultural Center in Harlem organizes educational and community service programs. Its permanent collection contains more than 2,000 African artifacts and 1,000 paintings and sculptures, which the gallery exhibits on a rotating basis. The center sponsors science and engineering workshops in conjunction with nearby Columbia University to encourage young African-Americans to enter these fields. The goal of the cultural/educational center is to teach young people pride in their African-American heritage. The center is now planning an African university that will occupy several city blocks.

GENERAL INFORMATION

Hours 9 am–5 pm daily
Admission Free; charge for large groups
Disability Access Fully accessible
Directions Subway: 2, 3, A, B, C or D to 125th St; Bus: M2 to 125th St; M100, M101, BX15 to Adam Clayton Powell Jr. Blvd
Landmark Status New York City Landmark

Alternative Museum

594 Broadway, Suite 402
(between Houston and Prince Streets)
New York, NY 10012
212-966-4444

Its founders created the Alternative Museum in 1975 to compensate for what they perceived as the segregation of the art world along racial lines. From its inception, the museum has presented exhibitions on pressing cultural issues that explore the definitions and boundaries of art. Exhibitions have focused on issues such as homelessness, media manipulation, the environment, and ethnic and gender stereotypes. Solo shows have included many of today's outstanding artists; early in their careers Andres Serrano, David Hammonds and Nancy Spero exhibited here. The museum presents between six and 12 exhibitions each year, as well as a program of new music and jazz.

GENERAL INFORMATION

Hours Tues–Sat 11 am–6 pm; closed Sun, Mon
Admission Suggested contribution: $3
Giftshop Exhibition catalogs and prints
Library Resource File Library has slides and other documents on exhibiting artists
Disability Access Fully accessible
Directions Subway: N or R to Prince St; B, D, F or Q to Broadway–Lafayette St; 6 to Spring St; Bus: M1, M6 to Prince St; M21 to Broadway
Landmark Status National Register of Historic Places, New York City Landmark

Symbol Key

 *Institutional Giftshop*

 *On-Site Food Services*

 *On-Site Library or Archive*

 *Full Accessibility*

 *On-Site Parking*

 *National Register of Historic Places and/or New York City Landmark*

American Academy of Arts and Letters

633 West 155th Street (at Broadway) New York, NY 10032 212-368-5900

The American Academy of Arts and Letters was founded to recognize achievement in the arts. Artists admitted to the academy are selected by their peers; most artists consider admission one of the highest honors they can achieve.

Current members include Christo, Allen Ginsberg, Jasper Johns, Philip Johnson, Toni Morrison, Stephen Sondheim and Susan Sontag. Among past members are Duke Ellington, William Faulkner, Dizzy Gillespie, Henry James, John Steinbeck, Mark Twain and Frank Lloyd Wright.

The academy's galleries mount three exhibitions a year on the arts and literature, drawing on the works and experiences of its members and award recipients, some of America's greatest composers, painters, architects and writers. The academy's permanent collection includes 18,000 books and 2,000 original manuscripts, paintings and photographs illuminating the lives and work of members.

The academy shares its location with the Hispanic Society, the American Numismatic Society and Boricua College. All are located at Audubon Terrace, the former estate of the American artist John James Audubon. Archer Milton Huntington, the railroad and steamship magnate, financed these handsome neoclassical buildings, which were designed by McKim, Mead & White and by Cass Gilbert and built in the 1920s.

GENERAL INFORMATION

Hours During exhibitions: Tues–Sun 1–4 pm; closed Mon
Admission Free
Library Manuscripts, correspondence, photographs, first editions, music scores, notebooks, etc. related to members; open to students and researchers by appointment
Disability Access Limited access
Directions Subway: 1/9 to 157th St; A or B to 155th St; Bus: M4, M5 to 155th St; M100, M101 to 155th St; BX6 to Broadway
Landmark Status National Register of Historic Places, New York City Landmark

American Craft Museum

40 West 53rd Street (between Fifth and Sixth Avenues) New York, NY 10019 212-956-3535

The forms of the many beautiful objects within the American Craft Museum originate in their functionality. There are numerous familiar objects here—baskets, quilts, tableware, vessels, clothing, chairs, teapots, etc.—in clay, fiber, glass, metal, wood and various exotic materials. In the museum's soaring atrium and intimate galleries, the work of American masters as well as emerging artists is exhibited. Thematic exhibitions reveal trends and styles in everything from hand-crafted jewelry to tableware. Many exhibitions have been firsts, including "Made with Paper," "American Glass Now" and "Plastic as Plastic."

"Large Bowl," Gertrude and Otto Natzler, turquoise crater glaze, 1956.

Eva Heyd/American Craft Museum

Established by the American Craft Council in 1956, the museum is dedicated to collecting, exhibiting and interpreting the finest craft pieces. The institution opened new galleries in 1986, designed to display everything from the smallest brooch to the most monumental tapestry. There are educational activities for everyone from young children to adults, including lectures, hands-on workshops, docent-led tours and symposiums.

GENERAL INFORMATION

Hours Tues 10 am–8 pm; Wed–Sun 10 am–5 pm; closed Mon
Admission Adults $4.50, seniors and students $2, children under 12 free
Giftshop Contemporary craft items
Disability Access Fully accessible
Directions Subway: E or F to Fifth Ave and 53rd St; 1/9 to 50th St; B, D, F or Q to 47th–50th St ; Bus: M2, M3, M5, M7, M104 to 53rd St

American Indian Community House

708 Broadway (between Astor Place and 4th Street)
New York, NY 10003
212-598-0100

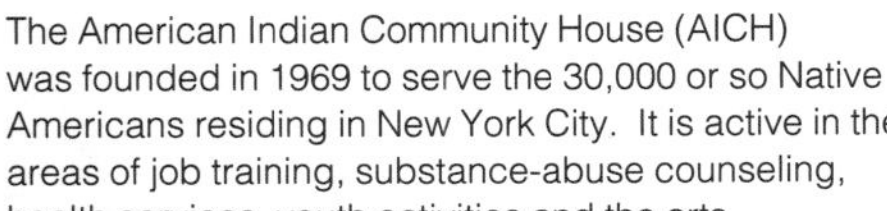

The American Indian Community House (AICH) was founded in 1969 to serve the 30,000 or so Native Americans residing in New York City. It is active in the areas of job training, substance-abuse counseling, health services, youth activities and the arts.

The AICH has the only Indian-owned and operated art gallery in New York; it exhibits the work of both emerging and established painters, sculptors and photographers of Native American descent. At least five exhibitions are mounted each year. Related lectures and forums are also offered. During the holiday season, the gallery hosts its annual Indian Market crafts fair.

Performing arts groups present 15 to 20 events a year at AICH, including dramatic productions, concerts, storytelling events, powwows, lectures, forums and conferences. The organization produces contemporary Native American theater works, furthering the creative development of Indian actors, playwrights, composers, directors, designers and producers. It also serves as a booking agency for American Indian actors and actresses, provides rehearsal space and technical assistance to performing artists and presents the annual Native American Actors Showcase.

Photograph courtesy of Smithsonian Institution

Native American storytellers, Vira and Hortensia Colorado.

GENERAL INFORMATION

Hours Tues–Sat 12–6 pm; closed Sun, Mon
Admission Free
Giftshop Books and traditional Native American crafts and jewelry
Library Extensive collection of plays by Native American playwrights
Disability Access Fully accessible; restrooms available
Directions Subway: 4, 5 or 6 to Astor Place; N or R to 8th St; Bus: M1, M6 to Broadway and Waverly St; M1 to Lafayette St; M2 to East 8th and Mercer Sts; M5 to Broadway and West 3rd St; M101, M102 to Cooper Sq and East 6th St

The American Institute of Graphic Arts

164 Fifth Avenue
(at 21st Street)
New York, NY 10010
212-752-0813

The American Institute of Graphic Arts advances excellence in professional graphic design through exhibitions, competitions, publications, seminars and educational activities. The AIGA exhibition series is considered among the finest in the field. While AIGA has no permanent collection, its gallery presents several shows each year, many the result of national and international competitions, which show winning examples of books, as well as print advertisements, promotional materials, labels and packaging. Exhibits have included “Design for the Public Good,” “Charts, Maps and Diagrams,” “One Color/Two Color,” “Just Type” and “Political Art.”

GENERAL INFORMATION

Hours During exhibitions: Mon–Fri 9:30 am–4:30 pm; closed Sat, Sun
Admission Free
Library 1,000 books, periodicals and guides relating to graphic design and production
Disability Access Limited access
Directions Subway: N, R or F to 23rd St; Bus: M23 to 5th Ave; M1, M2, M3, M4, M5 to 23rd St

American Museum of Natural History

Including Hayden Planetarium 212-769-5100
Central Park West at 79th Street
New York, NY 10024

Anthropology, astronomy, ichthyology, ornithology, vertebrate paleontology and related disciplines are explored at the American Museum of Natural History. Exhibits in the institution's 40 galleries draw from a collection of 35 million artifacts and specimens. Shows range from fossilized dinosaur skeletons (the largest collection in the world) to dioramas depicting North American, Asian and African animals in their natural habitats.

The new permanent Hall of Human Biology and Evolution explores the place of humans in the natural world. Geological specimens tell the story of the earth's origins. The 34-ton Ahnighito meteor (the largest ever retrieved from the earth) is the centerpiece of a large meteorite collection. The museum's outstanding gem collection includes the Brazilian Princess Topaz (21,005 carats), one of the world's largest cut gems, and the Star of India sapphire (563 carats).

Other permanent exhibits are located in the Hall of Asian Peoples, the Hall of Man in Africa, the Hall of Mexico and Central America, and the Hall of Ocean Life, which contains a replica of a 94-foot blue whale, believed to be the largest animal ever to live on earth.

The Naturemax Theater houses a four-story IMAX-format movie screen, the city's largest, and 6-channel sound to immerse the viewer in the sights and sounds of the planet. For children there is the Discovery Room, where there are hands-on displays. The museum also offers educational opportunities for adults, including lectures and demonstrations.

Hayden Planetarium, on the north side of the museum compound, features its daily Sky Shows, which are augmented by two floors of astronomical exhibits. The Wonderful Sky show for preschoolers features the Muppets, and the Robots in Space show, narrated by mechanized characters from the film "Star Wars," is geared to children 7–12. There are many courses for adults covering subjects from basic astronomy to advanced navigation.

American Museum of Natural History, West 77th Street facade.

Lynton Gardiner

Kwakiutal Mask, North America, Northwest Coast, 19th Century.

The museum was founded in 1869 during a period of intense interest in the natural sciences spurred by the theories of Darwin, Huxley and other Victorian scientists. Spanning four city blocks, the museum now consists of 23 interconnected buildings. The first wing dates from 1872 and is based on a design by Calvert Vaux (co-designer of Central Park) and J. Wrey Mould. Critics generally agree that the Romanesque Revival exposure facing West 77th Street is among the most architecturally successful elements of the structure; its two turrets, arcade of seven arches and central granite stairway were designed by J. C. Cady & Co. in 1892.

GENERAL INFORMATION

Hours Museum: Sun–Thurs 10 am–5:45 pm; Fri, Sat 10 am–8:45 pm
Planetarium: Oct–June: Mon–Fri 12:30–4:45 pm, Sat 10 am–5:45 pm, Sun 12–5:45 pm; July–Sept: Mon–Fri 12:30–4:45 pm, Sat and Sun 12–4:45 pm
Admission Museum: suggested contribution: adults $5, seniors and students $2.50
Planetarium: suggested contribution: adults $7, seniors and students $6, children 2–12, $4
Giftshop Museum: three shops offering fine jewelry, books, gift items and children's items related to collections and exhibitions; Planetarium: astronomical publications and space-related gifts
Food Service Garden Cafe, offering fine dining; Dinersaurus, a cafeteria; Whales Lair, cocktails and snacks
Library 440,000 volumes, largest natural history library in the Western Hemisphere; open Tues–Fri 11 am–4 pm; 212-769-5400
Disability Access Museum: fully accessible; telephones and restrooms available
Planetarium: fully accessible, although telephones and restrooms are in museum
Directions Subway: 1/9 to 79th St, then walk two blocks east; B or C to 81st St; Bus: M7, M10, M11, M79, M104 to 79th St; M79 to Central Park West
Parking On-site lot, enter from 81st St between Columbus Ave and Central Park West
Landmark Status National Register of Historic Places, New York City Landmark

City-owned, privately operated

Irving Dutcher, 1929

The American Numismatic Society

Broadway at 155th Street
New York, NY 10032
212-234-3130

Founded in 1858, the American Numismatic Society is the only American museum devoted exclusively to the preservation and study of coins, medals and paper money. Its museum houses nearly one million objects in addition to the world's most comprehensive library of numismatic literature.

Coins were first used about 2,600 years ago. The society's permanent exhibition, The World of Coins, tells the story of their evolution, focusing on the three main periods in the history of coinage: Ancient, Medieval and Modern. Highlights include an illustration of propagandistic coin use during Roman times; the innovation of international coinage after the campaigns of Alexander the Great; and the influence of Old World coins on the New World during exploration and settlement. The exhibit culminates with a complete set of United States coins to date. Also periodically on display is the famous Waterloo Medallion, which commemorates the defeat of Napoleon; commissioned in 1817, it took 30 years to produce. A second exhibition space features brief, periodic shows on various subjects.

The society is located on the former estate of American artist John James Audubon. Other buildings on the estate, now known as Audubon Terrace, house the Hispanic Society, the American Academy of Arts and Letters and Boricua College.

Round coin, China, ca. 1350; Oval coin, Japan, ca. 1850; Bottom, Pu-*shaped coin, China, 250 B.C.*

GENERAL INFORMATION

Hours Tues–Sat 9 am–4:30 pm; Sun 1–4 pm; closed Mon
Admission Free
Library Most comprehensive numismatic library in the world: 100,000 books, periodicals, manuscripts and catalogs
Disability Access None
Directions Subway: 1 to 157th St; A or B to 155th St; Bus: M4, M5 to 155th St; M100, M101 to 155th St; BX6 to Broadway
Landmark Status National Register of Historic Places, New York City Landmark

Americas Society

680 Park Avenue (at 68th Street)
New York, NY 10021
212-249-8950

The Americas Society was founded in 1965 to keep United States residents informed about its Western Hemisphere neighbors, particularly the Latin American, Caribbean and Canadian societies. To this end, it offers panel discussions relating to political, economic and social issues, as well as concerts, film screenings, art exhibitions and dramatic performances.

The society's Park Avenue gallery mounts four exhibits of contemporary art a year. Multinational in scope, roughly half of the shows focus on historic themes that demonstrate the rich heritage of North, Central and South American cultures. The gallery has introduced many artists from throughout the Western Hemisphere to U.S. audiences. A comprehensive program of lectures and gallery tours is offered in conjunction with each exhibition.

The literature department promotes Latin American literature in English translation through its journal. It also hosts lecture series, literary readings and writers' workshops. The programs featuring Latin American writers, scholars and translators are particularly popular.

The society is located in an historic neo-Federal mansion on Park Avenue, designed by McKim, Mead & White. Construction was completed on the building in 1911. From 1948 to 1963 it housed the Soviet Mission to the United Nations.

The Americas Society's 1911 neo-Federal mansion at 680 Park Avenue.

GENERAL INFORMATION

Hours Tues–Sun 12–6 pm; closed Mon
Admission Free
Library Art books, monographs and periodicals as well as an archive containing bibliographical documentation and slides of over 4,000 artists
Disability Access None
Directions Subway: 6 to 68th St; Bus: M1, M2, M3, M4 to 68th St; M66 to Park Ave
Landmark Status New York City Landmark

Anthology Film Archives

32 Second Avenue (at 2nd Street) 212-505-5181
New York, NY 10003

Anthology Film Archives (AFA) is a film and video exhibitor, reference center, archive, educational resource and publisher that originally opened in 1970 in spaces at the Public Theater. In 1988 it moved to permanent quarters in Lower Manhattan where it has two theaters, film vaults and offices.

AFA's activities embrace the entire range of film production, including documentary and narrative film. However, its special focus is experimental or breakthrough work best exemplified by film- and videomakers such as Jean Cocteau, Sergei Eisenstein and Nam June Paik.

Classic, independent and first-run motion pictures from all over the world are screened regularly. Each year AFA screens over 1,100 films and videos, stressing the individual contributions of the film- or videomaker. AFA is also active in film distribution and in the restoration and preservation of deteriorating motion pictures.

The institution is a popular venue for festivals showcasing films that are not exhibited by commercial houses or larger museums. Examples include the Algerian Film Festival, Cine de Reclama Film Festival, the Dance Film Association, the Irish Film Association, the New York Gay and Lesbian Experimental Film Festival and the Tibetan Film Festival.

GENERAL INFORMATION

Hours Screenings Fri–Sun evenings; office Mon–Fri 10 am–6 pm
Admission Adults $7, seniors and students $5, members $4, children under 14, $1.50
Giftshop AFA publications
Library World's largest collection of books, periodicals and primary-source material on independent and avant-garde film; call about access. Also a film/video archive of 1,900 avant-garde films, 3,000 documentaries and classic films, etc.
Disability Access First-floor spaces only
Directions Subway: 6 to Bleecker St; F to 2nd Ave; Bus: M21 to 2nd Ave; M15 to 2nd St

Aperture Foundation/ Burden Gallery

20 East 23rd Street 212-505-5555
(off Madison Avenue) Ext. 325
New York, NY 10010

The Burden Gallery is the exhibition arm of the Aperture Foundation, a leading nonprofit publisher of books and periodicals on photography. Housed in an historic brownstone (c. 1860), it acts as a laboratory for exhibitions of photography's classic and contemporary masters, as well as younger, emerging photographers. Five large exhibitions are mounted each year in the gracious 1,100-square-foot space. These shows often feature photographs published in Aperture publications. The gallery, which opened in 1984, also offers lectures, film screenings and other public programs. In addition, the gallery directs an extensive program of traveling exhibitions, collaborating with major museums around the world.

"Wall Street," by Paul Strand, New York, 1915, Aperture Foundation collection.

GENERAL INFORMATION

Hours Tues–Sat 11 am–6 pm; closed Sun, Mon
Admission Free
Giftshop Aperture Foundation publications, limited-edition prints, exhibition catalogs
Disability Access None
Directions Subway: N, R or 6 to 23rd St; Bus: M2, M3, M5 to 23rd St; M23 to 5th Ave

Archives of American Art–Smithsonian Institution

New York Regional Center
1285 Avenue of the Americas
(between 51st and 52nd Streets)
New York, NY 10019
212-399-5015

Founded in 1954, the Archives of American Art is the world's largest repository of primary source materials relating to the history of the arts in America. Its collections number over 12 million items, dating from 1620 to the present, including the letters, diaries and sketchbooks of artists; the papers of important galleries, collectors and critics; over half a million photographs of artists and their work; and more than 3,000 oral history interviews with art-world figures.

Of its five regional centers (Boston, Massachusetts; Washington DC; San Marino, California; Detroit, Michigan; New York City), only the New York facility offers regular exhibitions. These exhibits draw on the institution's own holdings and items borrowed from museums, collectors and dealers. Exhibitions have included "Roy Lichtenstein/Leo Castelli: Pop Artist/Pop Dealer," "Hiram Powers: An American Sculptor and His Private Patrons" and "Romare Bearden Draws, Too."

GENERAL INFORMATION

Hours Mon–Fri 9:30 am–4:45 pm; closed Sat, Sun
Admission Free
Library Ample work area in which to conduct research with above described materials
Disability Access Fully accessible; gallery at lobby level
Directions Subway: B, D or E to 7th Ave; 1/9 to 50th St; B, D, F or Q to 47th–50th St-Rockefeller Center; N or R to 49th St; Bus: M6, M7 to 52nd St; M27, M50 to 6th Aves

Art Students League of New York Gallery

215 West 57th Street
(between Broadway and
Seventh Avenue)
New York, NY 10019

212-247-4510

The Arts Students League of New York is an independent art school that was founded in 1875 by students from the National Academy of Design (see separate entry). Former students include Jackson Pollock and Norman Rockwell. Today the school offers classes taught by professional artists, many of international stature, and a popular exhibition series.

The gallery shows artwork by prominent living artists, current students and members. The permanent collection includes works by American artists who studied or taught at the Art Students League, in addition to works by other prominent American artists. The gallery was the first exhibition space in New York to show abstract art.

Built in 1892, the school's handsome French Renaissance home was designed by architect Henry J. Hardenbergh, who also designed the Plaza Hotel (59th Street and Fifth Avenue) and the Dakota (72nd Street and Central Park West). The gallery was modeled after the Georges Petit Gallery in Paris.

GENERAL INFORMATION

Hours Sun 1–4:30 pm; Mon–Fri 10 am–8:30 pm; Sat 9:30 am–4 pm; closed June–Aug
Admission Free
Disability Access No ramp, but call ahead for assistance; elevators available
Directions Subway: N or R to 57th St; B, D or E to 7th Ave; 1/9, A or C to Columbus Circle; Bus: M30, M57, M58 to 7th Ave; M5, M10, M104 to 57th St
Landmark Status National Register of Historic Places, New York City Landmark

Artists Space

38 Greene Street, Third Floor
(at Grand Street)
New York, NY 10013

212-226-39

Artists Space was founded in 1973 to exhibit the work of New York's expanding community of artists. In addition to providing exhibition opportunities, the organization supports artists with grants, materials and other services. Artists Space is renowned for embracing the full spectrum of cultures and esthetic sensibilities coexisting in New York, making for a diverse program of exhibitions.

The organization offers one-person and group exhibitions and installations, video programs, film screenings, readings and performances by local, national and international artists. Multimedia artworks employ everything from live performance to video images to John Cage–like found sound.

Exhibitions and installations have included the immensely popular "Putt Modernism," an 18-hole miniature golf course designed and built by artists; "HerStories in Color," a video program by women of

"Censorama," Pat Oleszko and Ward Shelly, inflated vinyl, 1989, from Putt Modernism.

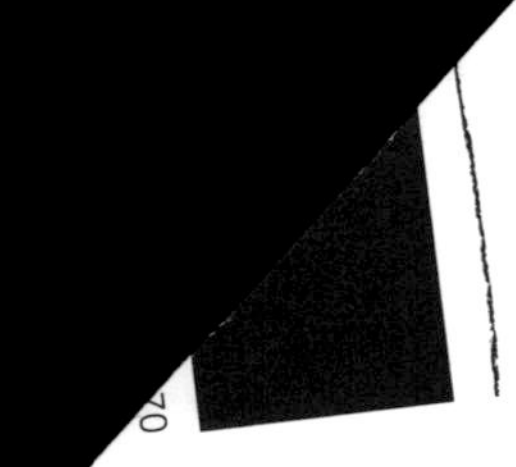

ɔr the Channeling
ˌ Elements"; "A New
ʼ the work of 48 artists
ʋn curio shop; and
ʼn," which presented
ɔn. Since 1983 the
e Mark Rothko
k of mid-career

INFORMATION

Hours Tues–Sat 12–6 pm; closed Sun, Mon
Admission Gallery free; performances: adults $5, seniors and students $3, members free
Library Computer registry tracks slides of work by 3,500 regional artists; open Wed–Sat 1–6 pm
Disability Access Fully accessible; ramp and elevator available
Direction Subway: 6, C or E, to Spring St; N or R to Prince Street; Bus: M1, M6 to Grand St

"Celestial Woman Undressed by a Monkey," probably Khajuraho, India, circa A.D. 975–1,000.

The Asia Society

725 Park Avenue (at 70th Street) 212-288-6400
New York, NY 10021

The Asia Society was created to build bridges of understanding between Americans and Asians. It achieves this through art exhibitions, workshops, international conferences, lectures, film series, performances and publications.

Masterworks of Asian art from the John D. Rockefeller III Collection, donated to the society in 1979, are at the heart of the Asia Society's permanent collection. These holdings include remarkable bronzes and celadons, Indian sculptures and miniatures, Japanese Buddhist paintings, Korean ceramics, Indonesian textiles, sumptuous silks and rugs, and rare photographs of an Asia long gone. There are also excellent examples of Cambodian and Thai sculpture.

Superb periodic exhibitions, lectures and performances address the complexity and richness of Asian civilizations. The society offers musical and theatrical events, including *Kathakali* (dance-drama of southern India), *Aak* (Korean court music and dance) and the films of many Asian nations.

Since 1981 the society has been housed in an attractive building designed especially for it by renowned architect Edward Larrabee Barnes. Constructed of red sandstone from Rajasthan, India, and polished red granite from Oklahoma, it physically symbolizes the benefits of harmonious cooperation between Asia and America.

GENERAL INFORMATION

Hours Sun 12–5 pm; Tues–Wed, Fri–Sat 11 am–6 pm; Thurs 11 am–8 pm; closed Mon
Admission Adults $3, students and seniors $1; Thurs 6–8 pm, free
Giftshop Large selection of books on Asia, also audio and videotapes, crafts and jewelry
Disability Access Fully accessible
Directions Subway: 6 to 68th St; Bus: M1, M2, M3, M4 to 70th St; M101, M102 to 70th St; M30, M66 to Park Ave
Landmark Status New York City Landmark

Asian American Arts Centre

26 Bowery, Third Floor 212-233-2154
(between Bayard and Pell Streets)
New York, NY 10013

Unbeknownst to many, Chinatown has developed a vibrant Asian-American artists' community in recent years as a result of the influx of new Asian immigrants. The Asian American Arts Centre exhibits and promotes the work of these artists and also hosts workshops and live performances.

Group exhibitions have included "A People's Folk Art Exhibition: From the Provinces of China to New York City," "And He Was Looking for Asia: Alternatives to the Story of Columbus Today" and "China: June 4, 1989," artists' responses to the Tiananmen Square Massacre. "White rice/mixed blood: stories from Amerasia" was a particularly well received multimedia performance.

The center, which was established in 1974 in a local library branch and later moved to the Bowery, also supports scholarly research into Chinese-American folk artists of the New York area, provides cross-cultural programs for New York schoolchildren and supports several artists-in-residence.

GENERAL INFORMATION

Hours Gallery open Mon–Fri 11 am–6 pm, Sat by appointment, closed Sun; call for performance schedule
Admission Gallery free; fee for performances
Library Slide archive of Asian-American artists' works; open by appointment
Disability Access None, third-floor walkup
Directions Subway: J, M, Z, N, R or 6 to Canal St; D to Grand St; Bus: M15, M102 to Chatham St

Austrian Cultural Institute

11 East 52nd Street
(between Fifth and Madison Avenues)
New York, NY 10022

212-759-5165

After 1945, Austria founded cultural centers in several world capitals to promote its contributions to world civilization. The Austrian Cultural Institute was established in New York in 1962 as the cultural branch of the Austrian Foreign Ministry. Since then it has sought to enhance cultural relations between the United States and Austria.

The institute has no permanent collection, but first-rate exhibitions throughout the year feature works by prominent Austrian artists. Concerts, film screenings, discussions, lectures and social gatherings are also offered. To house an expanding roster of activities, the institute will demolish its 1904 brownstone soon to construct a dramatic 20-story structure designed by Austrian architect Raimund Abraham. The new facility, based on the shape of a metronome, opens in 1995.

GENERAL INFORMATION

Hours Mon–Fri 9 am–5 pm; closed Sat, Sun
Admission Free
Library Reference library contains titles on Austrian history, music, literature, arts and folklore; music division equipped for listening to recordings; videotapes can be borrowed
Disability Access Fully accessible
Directions Subway: E or F to 5th Ave and 53rd St; Bus: M1, M2, M3, M4 to 53rd St

Model of the Austrian Cultural Institute's new home, a 20-story tower designed by Austrian architect Raimund Abraham.

Liselot van der Heijden

The Bard Graduate Center for Studies in the Decorative Arts.

Bard Graduate Center for Studies in the Decorative Arts

18 West 86th Street
(between Central Park West
and Columbus Avenue)
New York, NY 10024

212-721-4245

The Bard Graduate Center for Studies in the Decorative Arts, a new study and exhibition facility on Manhattan's Upper West Side, opened in 1993. The center's curriculum seeks to raise the decorative arts—furniture, jewelry, textiles, glass and so forth—to the level of the fine arts and expand the usual Western European and American decorative arts orientation to include Central and Eastern Europe, Scandinavia, Russia, Asia, Africa and Latin America.

The center's three to four annual exhibitions reflect this internationalist and non-hierarchical perspective. Exhibits have included "Along the Royal Road: Berlin and Potsdam in Porcelain and Painting, 1815–1848," focusing on the intimate relationship between the decorative and fine arts in the early 19th century, "Cast Iron from Central Europe: 1800–1850," "Baroque Goldsmiths' and Jewelers' Art from Hungary," "American Greek Revival Architecture" and "An Alliance of Art and Industry: The Brilliance of Swedish Glass, 1918–1939."

Founded in 1860, Bard College is located in Annandale-on-Hudson, 90 miles north of New York City. The Bard Graduate Center for Studies in the Decorative Arts, housed in a newly renovated 1906 Beaux Arts–style townhouse, contains three floors of exhibition space, classrooms, a research library and a roof garden.

GENERAL INFORMATION

Hours Tues, Wed, Fri–Sun 11 am–5 pm; Thurs 11 am–8:30 pm; closed Mon
Admission $2
Library 15,000 books, periodicals, slides and videos on decorative arts and related disciplines
Disability Access Fully accessible; elevators available
Directions Subway: 1/9, B or C to 86th St; Bus: M7, M10, M11 to 86th St; M86 to Central Park West

Symbol Key

 *Institutional Giftshop*

 *On-Site Food Services*

 *On-Site Library or Archive*

 *Full Accessibility*

 *On-Site Parking*

 *National Register of Historic Places and/or New York City Landmark*

Baruch College/ Sidney Mishkin Gallery

135 East 22nd Street
(between Park Avenue
and Irving Place)
New York, NY 10010

212-387-1006

Located in the historic Gramercy Park neighborhood, the Sidney Mishkin Gallery of Baruch College offers five exhibits a year ranging from scholarly and multicultural shows to one-person exhibitions of the work of mature artists. Exhibitions have included "Venezuela: The Next Generation," which introduced many contemporary Venezuelan artists to Americans for the first time; "Romare Bearden: Work with Paper," which comprised drawings, prints, watercolors and collages by the African-American artist; and "Marsden Hartley in Bavaria," focusing on a little-known but intensely productive period in the career of this American artist. Baruch College is one of the seven senior colleges of the City University of New York. The gallery is located in a restored 1940 building constructed during the Work Projects Administration.

GENERAL INFORMATION

Hours Mon–Fri 12–5 pm; Thurs 12–7 pm; closed Sat, Sun; closed Jan, June–Aug
Admission Free
Disability Access Fully accessible
Directions Subway: 6 to 23rd St; Bus: M23 to Park Ave; M1, M2, M3 to 23rd St

The Black Fashion Museum

155 West 126th Street
(between Adam Clayton Powell
and Malcolm X Boulevards)
New York, NY 10027

212-666-1320

The Black Fashion Museum, founded in 1979, chronicles the enormous contributions made by African-Americans to American fashion. In doing so, it documents their role in the larger realm of American culture. Dresses, costumes, photographs and memorabilia illustrate many little-known aspects of African-American heritage. Among the items on display is a yellow Sunday dress created by Rosa Parks, mother of the civil rights movement. Also featured is a copy of a dress made by former slave Elizabeth Keckley for Mary Todd Lincoln to wear to her husband's inaugural ball.

More recent examples of African-American fashion design include creations by some of today's most popular designers, including Jeffrey Banks and Geoffrey Holder. These works are complemented by original costumes designed and worn in the Broadway musicals "The Wiz," "Eubie" and "Grind." Two exhibitions are mounted yearly from items in the permanent exhibition. Exhibits have included "Costumes from Black Theater" and "Black Fashion: 1865–1965."

GENERAL INFORMATION

Hours Mon–Fri 12–8 pm, by appointment; closed Sat, Sun
Admission Suggested contribution: adults $1.50, students $1
Library Harlem Institute of Fashion Library, open to students, researchers and scholars
Disability Access None
Directions Subway: 2, 3, A, C, B or D to 125th St; Bus: M100, M101 to Lenox Ave; M2, M7, M102 to 125th St

Caribbean Cultural Center

408 West 58th Street 212-307-7420
(between Ninth and Tenth Avenues)
New York, NY 10019

The Caribbean Cultural Center focuses on the cultural activities of African descendants in the Americas, celebrating their rich traditions in music, dance, art, literature and belief systems. Exhibitions concentrate on painting, sculpture and hand-crafted items by African-American and Caribbean artists. Photographic exhibits document the history and contributions African descendants have made to cultures of the Western Hemisphere.

Concerts of contemporary and traditional music feature both African and American musicians. Gallery talks and conferences bring together artists, scholars, elected officials and community members to exchange information on the culture and societies of African descendants. The center also offers film screenings, an annual outdoor festival based on traditional African celebrations, and scholarly conferences on African belief systems in the Americas.

GENERAL INFORMATION

Hours Gallery: Tues–Fri 11 am–6 pm; closed Sat–Mon
Admission Adults $2, students and children $1
Giftshop Books, jewelry, T-shirts, musical instruments, films on videotape and other items
Library Reference collection, open by appointment
Disability Access None
Directions Subway: 1/9, A, C, B or D to 59th St–Columbus Circle; Bus: M11 to 58th St; M57 to 9th Ave

Leslie Jean-Bart

Puntilla Rios performing "Sacred Drums" at the Caribbean Cultural Center.

Carnegie Hall

Including Weill Recital Hall 212-247-7800
881 Seventh Avenue (at 57th Street) Box Office
New York, NY 10019

Carnegie Hall is the standard against which all other American concert halls are judged, in part because of its superb acoustics, in part because of its long history of attracting the world's most outstanding instrumentalists, conductors, orchestras and vocalists. It has also been a beacon to prominent dancers, politicians and crusaders. From Gustav Mahler to Kiri Te Kanawa, from John Philip Sousa to Frank Sinatra, from Booker T. Washington to Woodrow Wilson and from Ignace Jan Paderewski to Luciano Pavarotti, Carnegie Hall has hosted them all.

Here is just a partial list of some of the performers to appear on the Carnegie Hall stage throughout the decades: the Beatles, Maria Callas, Pablo Casals, Bob Dylan, Ella Fitzgerald, Judy Garland, Serge Koussevitzky, Yo-Yo Ma, Jessye Norman, Ivo Pogorelich, Leontyne Price, John Prine, Paul Robeson, Ravi Shankar, the Rolling Stones, Beverly Sills, Bessie Smith, the St. Paul Chamber Orchestra, the Tokyo String Quartet, Arturo Toscanini, Sarah Vaughan and virtually every major symphony orchestra in the world. The hall has also been the site for speakers like Ruth Draper, Ernest Hemingway, Mark Twain and others.

Steel magnate and philanthropist Andrew Carnegie provided $2 million toward the cost of the hall. The Italian Renaissance–style terra-cotta and brick building was designed by William Burnett Tuthill, in association with the firm of Adler and Sullivan, and consulting architect Richard Morris Hunt. The cornerstone was laid in 1890 and the hall opened in May of 1891 with a concert conducted by Peter Ilyich Tchaikovsky and Walter Damrosch.

Amazingly, in the late 1950s, Carnegie Hall was threatened with demolition to make way for a large, garish office building. Outraged citizens, including many musicians, led by violinist Isaac Stern, saved the building. In the mid-1980s Carnegie Hall underwent an extensive renovation which left it with a reconfigured lobby, restored auditorium and stage, and wing space in the new Carnegie Hall Tower next door. A smaller space was also refurbished and renamed the Weill Recital Hall. The renovation was planned by James Stewart Polshek Associates and the tower was designed by Cesar Pelli.

Steven J. Sherman

GENERAL INFORMATION

Hours Box office open Mon–Sat 11 am–6 pm, Sun and holidays 12–6 pm
Admission Tickets vary from $10 to $60; call for performance schedule and ticket availability
Giftshop Located at 154 West 57th St, 2nd floor, open 11 am–4:30 pm daily; merchandise also available prior to concerts on first-tier level
Food Service East Room (first-tier level) offers pre-concert buffet, for reservations call 212-903-9689; Cafe (parquet level) offers light dining; refreshment bars located throughout building during performances
Library Archives open Mon–Fri 9:30 am–5:30 pm by appointment; contains reference materials about the building's history and its tenants (many quite famous); 212-903-9629. The Rose Museum contains manuscripts, early construction plans and other objects; open 11 am–4:30 pm daily; closed Wed during Aug
Disability Access Wheelchair access arranged though House Manager, call 212-903-9605; earphones for hearing-impaired patrons and large-print programs for visually impaired patrons available
Directions Subway: 1/9, A, B, C or D to 59th St–Columbus Circle; N or R to 57th St; B, D or E to 7th Ave–53rd St; Bus: M5, M6, M7, M10, M104 to 57th St and Broadway; M30, M57, M58 to 57th St and 7th Ave
Landmark Status National Register of Historic Places, New York City Landmark

City-owned, privately operated

Castillo Cultural Center

500 Greenwich Street, Suite 201 212-941-5800
(between Spring and Canal Streets)
New York, NY 10013

The Castillo Cultural Center is a small community-supported organization containing a theater, a publishing house, an art gallery, a video studio and a darkroom. The center is particularly concerned with producing multicultural repertory theater works and to this end has encouraged some unusual cultural combinations, fusing the European avant-garde with African-American theater in one production, the Jewish vaudeville tradition with American country music in another. Productions have included "Emmy Gay & the Gayggles," a multicultural, improvisational comedy troupe; "The Task," by surrealist playwright Heiner Müller, about racial, economic and political disparities in the Third World; and "Explosions of a Memory," a multimedia event in which the audience interacts with the cast.

GENERAL INFORMATION

Hours Mon–Sat 10 am–10 pm; Sun 11 am–9 pm
Admission Gallery free; ticket prices for performances vary
Disability Access Fully accessible
Directions Subway: 1/9, A, C or E to Canal St; Bus: M10 to Hudson or Spring St

Castle Clinton National Monument

Battery Park 212-344-7220
New York, NY 10004

Castle Clinton was built as a fort just prior to the War of 1812 on a small island connected to Manhattan by a 300-foot causeway. It stood in defense of the city and the harbor from 1812 to 1823, but was never used in battle. From 1824 to 1855 it was known as Castle Garden, a concert hall with a promenade atop its eight-foot-thick sandstone walls. At this time the water between the island and Manhattan was displaced by a landfill creating Battery Park.

Lithograph of singer Jenny Lind's American debut at Castle Garden, 1850.

From 1855 to 1890, Castle Clinton was an immigrant processing depot where millions sought entry into the United States. Ellis Island ultimately assumed this function (see separate entry) in 1892. In 1896, McKim, Mead & White remodeled the castle, which then served as the New York Aquarium (see separate entry) until 1941, when the aquarium moved to Coney Island. Today Castle Clinton is both a monument and a museum containing exhibitions illustrating its role in historic events. It was restored by the firm of Beyer, Blinder, Belle in 1986.

GENERAL INFORMATION

Hours 8:30 am–5pm daily (except Christmas)
Admission Free
Giftshop Kiosk on parade grounds with books on immigration and New York history
Disability Access Limited access
Directions Subway: 1/9 to South Ferry; 4 or 5 to Bowling Green; Bus: M1, M6, M15 to South Ferry
Parking Garage at 70 Greenwich St
Landmark Status National Register of Historic Places, New York City Landmark
National Monument

The Cathedral of St. John the Divine

1047 Amsterdam Avenue 212-316-7540
(at 112th Street) Information
New York, NY 10025 212-662-2133
Box Office

The Cathedral of St. John the Divine is the largest Gothic cathedral in the world. Its floor space could accommodate two football fields, enough room for 6,000 people seated. At its highest point, the structure's vaulted ceiling is as tall as a 17-story building. On the West Front is the great Rose Window—40 feet wide and containing over 10,000 pieces of stained glass. The cathedral sits on a 13-acre site containing a green close and a biblical garden featuring papyrus, crocus, flax and four peacocks.

The cathedral's vigorous performing arts program features a number of dance, theater and music companies in residence. The Paul Winter Consort usually performs twice a year to sell-out crowds. And the annual free New Year's Eve Peace Concert—started by Leonard Bernstein—has become an extremely popular event. On display throughout the vast cathedral is a remarkable permanent collection of religious icons, tapestries and paintings from the 16th through the 20th centuries. There are also regular exhibits focusing on the work of New York City artists.

Art Garfunkel performing "The Animals' Christmas," written by Jimmy Webb, at the Cathedral of St. John the Divine.

Although the cornerstone was laid in 1892, the cathedral remains unfinished. Its style evolved from the Byzantine to the Romanesque to the French Gothic, which predominates. In 1982 construction resumed after a 41-year hiatus begun by the onset of World War II. It is estimated that the structure will be completed by the year 2000, relatively soon considering it took 840 years to finish Westminster Abbey. It is the seat of the Episcopal Bishop of New York.

GENERAL INFORMATION

Hours 7 am–5 pm daily
Admission Free except special concerts; call for ticket availability
Giftshop Broad selection of spiritual literature and gifts from around the world
Library 10,000 volumes in Cathedral House on religious matters; open by appointment
Disability Access Fully accessible, parking available, entrance ramp on 113th St. Special tours for hearing and visually impaired. First Sunday of every month religious services are signed
Directions Subway: 1/9 to 110th St–Cathedral Parkway; Bus: M4, M11, M104 to 112th St and Amsterdam Ave

Center for Book Arts

626 Broadway, Fifth Floor
(between Houston and
Bleecker Streets)
New York, NY 10012
212-460-9768

Exhibits and workshops at the Center for Book Arts explore the art and craft of bookmaking. Exhibits range from the traditional to the avant-garde. Some shows have celebrated various aspects of the typeface, while others have confronted the viewer with books made of unexpected materials like plexiglass, hairnets and, yes, concrete. One recent show challenged conventional notions of how a book functions: the text, stored on a floppy disk, self-destructed after a single reading.

The center's workshop provides members with a fully equipped professional studio with ample space to print and bind books. Instructors teach courses in traditional and contemporary bookmaking at every level of proficiency. Also offered are classes in letterpress and offset printing, papermaking and marbling, and small press management.

GENERAL INFORMATION

Hours Mon–Fri 10 am–6 pm; Sat 10 am–4 pm; closed Sun
Admission Free
Giftshop Exhibition catalogs
Library An archive traces the development of books through the ages; a slide library of book artists' work is also available
Disability Access Limited; call for information
Directions Subway: 6 to Bleecker St; B, D, F or Q to Broadway–Lafayette St; N or R to Prince St; Bus: M1, M5, M6 to Bleecker St

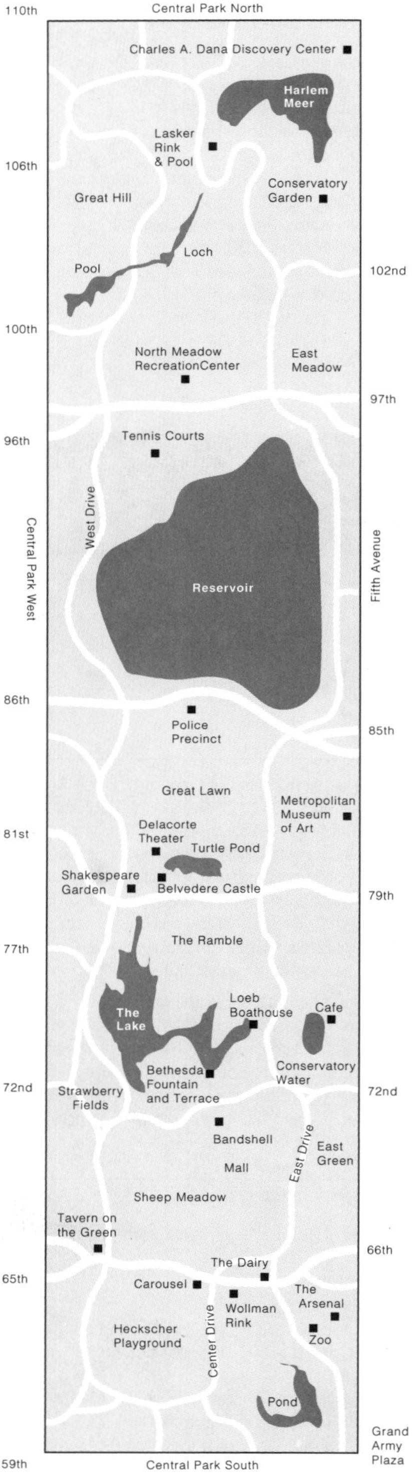

110th
Central Park North
Charles A. Dana Discovery Center
Harlem Meer
Lasker Rink & Pool
106th
Great Hill
Conservatory Garden
Loch
Pool
102nd
100th
North Meadow RecreationCenter
East Meadow
97th
96th
Tennis Courts
West Drive
Central Park West
Reservoir
Fifth Avenue
86th
Police Precinct
85th
Great Lawn
Metropolitan Museum of Art
Delacorte Theater
81st
Turtle Pond
Shakespeare Garden
Belvedere Castle
79th
The Ramble
77th
Loeb Boathouse
Cafe
The Lake
Conservatory Water
Bethesda Fountain and Terrace
72nd
Strawberry Fields
72nd
Bandshell
East Drive
East Green
Mall
Sheep Meadow
Tavern on the Green
66th
The Dairy
65th
Carousel
Wollman Rink
The Arsenal
Heckscher Playground
Center Drive
Zoo
Pond
Grand Army Plaza
59th
Central Park South

Central Park

Bordered by
Fifth Avenue,
Central Park South,
Central Park West
and Central Park North

212-315-0385
Central Park Conservancy
212-427-4040
Urban Park Rangers

Central Park was designed by Frederick Law Olmsted, America's greatest landscape architect, and Calvert Vaux in 1858. (Olmsted and Vaux also designed

Sheep Meadow, Central Park.

Morningside Park in Harlem; Riverside Park, flanking the Hudson River; and Brooklyn's Prospect Park, see separate entry.) Built between 1858 and 1873, the park comprises 6 percent of Manhattan's land area, 843 acres, and is 2.5 miles long and a half-mile wide. The most frequented urban park in the nation, it attracts over 14 million visitors yearly. It is the largest work of art in New York City.

Central Park's 26,000 trees and 132 acres of woodlands and meadows are both a haven for people and a natural habitat for wildlife. Water covers another 150 acres. There are 58 miles of pedestrian pathways that weave through an interlocking tapestry of meadows, lakes, forests and gardens. There are 4.7 miles of bridle trail, 22 playgrounds, 30 tennis courts, 26 baseball diamonds, two skating rinks, a swimming pool and a 1.6-mile running track around the reservoir.

Other park highlights include the Ramble, a wooded area of labyrinthine pathways, streams and concealed lawns; the Sheep Meadow, the great open lawn popular with sunbathers and picnickers; Bethesda Terrace, the only formal architectural element of Olmsted and Vaux's plan; and the Central Park Zoo (see separate entry). Adjacent to the Boathouse and its neo-Renaissance concrete basin is the oversize Alice in Wonderland sculpture, a favorite of children. Most of the 200 or so bridges throughout the park, many of them strikingly beautiful, were designed by Vaux.

Other attractions include ice skating in winter at Wollman Rink and, during summer, the largest free outdoor concerts in the U.S. by the New York Philharmonic and the Metropolitan Opera. The New York City Marathon, a major event each October, finishes in Central Park.

In 1980 the Central Park Conservancy was founded to work with the city's parks department to raise funds and set priorities for the maintenance and restoration of the park. Since the conservancy's establishment, over one -third of the park has been restored and the maintenance of 240 acres has been endowed in perpetuity.

The Arsenal

212-315-0385

The Arsenal, just off Fifth Avenue at East 64th Street, was originally built in 1848 to house the state's military explosives. When park construction began, it was purchased by the city. Shortly thereafter it became the first home of the American Museum of Natural History (see separate entry). The Arsenal Gallery offers changing exhibitions of contemporary art emphasizing urban park, recreational and historical themes.

GENERAL INFORMATION

Hours Mon–Fri 9 am–4:30 pm; closed Sat, Sun
Admission Free
Food Service Basement cafeteria
Disability Access Limited access
Directions Subway: N or R to 5th and 60th St; 4, 5 or 6 to 59th St; Bus: M1, M2, M3, M4 to 65th St; M66 to 5th Ave
Landmark Status National Register of Historic Places, New York City Landmark

Belvedere Castle

212-772-0210

Belvedere Castle has been the site of the city's weather station since 1919. Perched atop Vista Rock, the castle offers views of the park's Great Lawn and the city beyond. It was designed by Vaux in 1867. A scaled-down storybook castle, it possesses a particularly interesting combination of Norman, Gothic and Victorian architectural elements. Children, families and school groups visit the castle's Discovery Chamber, which contains exhibits on the park's natural history and an aquarium of species that inhabit nearby Belvedere Lake.

Belvedere Castle as seen from Turtle Pond.

GENERAL INFORMATION

Hours Spring–Summer: Tues–Sun 11 am–5pm, except Fri 1–5 pm; closed Mon; Fall–Winter: Tues–Sun 11 am–4 pm, except Fri 1–4 pm; closed Mon
Admission Free
Disability Access None
Directions Subway: 6 to 77th St; B or C to 81st St; Bus: M1, M2, M3, M4 to 79th St; M79 to Central Park West; M10 to 79th St
Landmark Status National Register of Historic Places, New York City Landmark

The Conservatory Garden

212-860-1382

The Conservatory Garden, facing Fifth Avenue at East 105th Street, consists of three interlocking horticultural planes. Nowhere else in Manhattan is there such a varied and wide collection of blooming plants—thousands of flowering trees and shrubs, annuals and perennials—from the rarest of old roses to common wildflowers. The geometric design of the six-acre public garden contrasts sharply with the soft, natural contours of the park. The garden was commissioned in 1934 by Parks Commissioner Robert Moses.

GENERAL INFORMATION

Hours 8 am–dusk daily; tours Sat 11 am
Admission Free
Disability Access Wheelchair access at 106th St gate
Directions Subway: 6 to 103rd St; Bus: M1, M2, M3, M4 to 105th St
Landmark Status National Register of Historic Places, New York City Landmark

The Dairy

212-794-6564

The Dairy is a Gothic Revival structure located between the zoo and the carousel. Built in 1870, it serves as the park's Information Center and houses exhibits about the design, architecture and history of the park. The Dairy offers educational events, tours for adults, concerts and exhibits.

GENERAL INFORMATION

Hours Spring–Summer: Tues–Sun 11 am–5pm, except Fri 1–5 pm; Fall–Winter: Tues–Sun 11 am–4 pm, except Fri 1–4 pm
Admission Free
Disability Access Fully accessible
Directions Subway: N or R to 5th Ave; B or Q to Lexington Ave; 6 to 68th St; Bus: M1, M2, M3, M4, M30 to 64th St
Landmark Status National Register of Historic Places, New York City Landmark

Central Park Zoo

off Fifth Avenue at 64th Street
New York, NY 10021

212-861-6030

Beautifully rebuilt during the late 1980s, the Central Park Zoo is home to 450 animals of over 130 species. A colonnade of tall brick-and-granite columns, topped by a pitched glass roof, surrounds the spacious central garden. Ranged around this axis are three major exhibits divided by climatic zone.

The Tropic Zone is a skylit structure containing a moist, dense jungle of towering tree trunks, waterfalls, tropical birds and primates. A school of red-bellied piranha from the Amazon Basin sit virtually motionless in their aquarium, invisible to land-roving prey. Black-and-white Colobus monkeys occupy a simulated forest canopy. Bats, golden-headed lion tamarins, flying geckos, Chinese water dragons, a green tree python, a red-throated parrot finch, a black-naped fruit dove and leaf-cutter ants are also on view.

In the Temperate Territory, Japanese macaques occupy an island in a lake. Unobtrusive vantage points allow visitors to get close to the animals. In their central pool, California sea lions sun themselves on rocks; they can also be watched underwater, through glass walls, swimming with remarkable speed and grace. Also on display are North American river otters, red pandas, Eastern painted turtles, mandarin ducks and black swans.

In the Polar Circle a multilevel polar bear habitat provides unobstructed above- and below-water views of the bears' enclosure. The Edge of the Icepack has above- and below-water views of chinstrap and gentoo penguins, as well as tufted puffins, in large breeding groups. Harbor seals and Arctic foxes occupy another habitat.

A small wildlife information center shows a video, narrated by John Chancellor, that explains the Wildlife

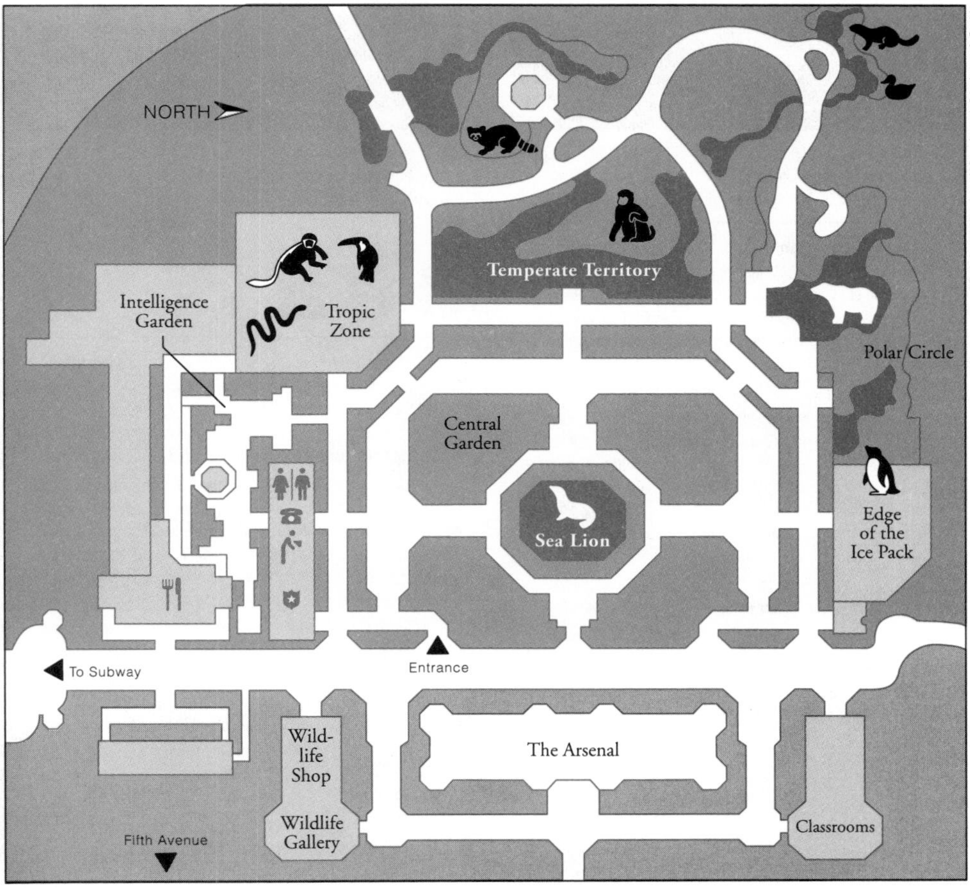

NORTH
Temperate Territory
Intelligence Garden
Tropic Zone
Polar Circle
Central Garden
Sea Lion
Edge of the Ice Pack
To Subway
Entrance
Wild-life Shop
Wildlife Gallery
The Arsenal
Classrooms
Fifth Avenue

Map design by Jean Wisenbough/Lindgren & Smith

Conservation Society's mission of animal exhibition, education and conservation. The nearby Zoo School has classrooms and auditoriums for large groups.

The city has operated a zoo in the park since 1864. Interestingly, park designers Olmsted and Vaux did not want one here. Park commissioners, however, were so overwhelmed with gifts of animals that they established a menagerie in the Arsenal (see Central Park entry), which remained until 1934, when the zoo was built next to it.

In 1980 the Wildlife Conservation Society agreed to renovate and operate the Central Park Zoo. During the late 1980s the zoo underwent a $40 million renovation. Old structures were torn down and replaced with attractive, naturalistic habitats. The restoration was designed by the architectural firm of Kevin Roche John Dinkeloo and Associates, which also designed the many new wings at the Metropolitan Museum (see separate entry).

The Central Park Zoo is managed by the New York Zoological Society/The Wildlife Conservation Society who also operates the Bronx Zoo, the Prospect Park Zoo, the Queens Zoo, the New York Aquarium (see separate entries) and the St. Catherines Wildlife Conservation Center in Georgia. It supervises some 150 wildlife conservation projects in 40 nations.

GENERAL INFORMATION

Hours April–Oct: Mon–Fri 10 am–5 pm; Sat and Sun 10:30 am–5:30 pm; Nov–March: 10 am–4:30 pm daily
Admission Adults $2.50, seniors $1.25, children 3–12, 50¢, children under 3 free
Giftshop Souvenirs, T-shirts, postcards, toys and books
Food Service Indoor/outdoor cafeteria near zoo's south gate
Disability Access Fully accessible; call 212-360-8134 for parking permit; restrooms available
Directions Subway: N or R to 5th Ave; Bus: M1, M2, M3, M4 to 64th St
Landmark Status National Register of Historic Places, New York City Landmark

City-owned, privately operated by New York Zoological Society/The Wildlife Conservation Society

Charas, Inc.

350–360 East 10th Street 212-982-0627
(between Avenues B and C)
New York, NY 10009

Charas, Inc. is a neighborhood cultural center on the Lower East Side. Well known for programs that address the cultural and ethnic diversity of the surrounding neighborhood, Charas presents plays, films, poetry readings, concerts, workshops, conferences and festivals.

The organization is located in former Public School 64 on East 9th Street, which has been partially renovated and renamed El Bohio, "the beach hut." This six-story structure now has three functioning floors, and efforts are under way to restore the others. Charas was founded in 1965 and in its early years worked with engineer Buckminster Fuller, adapting geodesic domes to the needs of poor communities.

GENERAL INFORMATION

Hours Mon–Fri 3–6 pm; Sat 12–4 pm; closed Sun
Admission Free
Disability Access None
Directions Subway: L to 1st Ave; 6 to Astor Place; F to 2nd Ave; Bus: M13, M14 to Aves A or D; M21 to 10th St

Children's Museum of Manhattan

212 West 83rd Street 212-721-1234
(between Broadway and
Amsterdam Avenue)
New York, NY 10024

The Children's Museum of Manhattan moved from Midtown to new and expanded spaces on the Upper West Side in the late 1980s. Youngsters of all ages and social backgrounds converge here to experience a rich assortment of exhibitions and public programs.

In the Media Center children take on the roles of engineers, camera operators, editors, sound technicians, writers and newscasters to produce their own newscasts and other programs. The performing arts space contains a theater with seating for 150 that on weekends features children's theater groups, dancers, musicians, puppeteers and storytellers.

Exhibits in the Scholastic Gallery give children an inside look at the art of children's book illustration. The gallery has original art from the finest children's books, of the past and present. Related art, bookmaking and writing workshops are conducted in nearby studios.

In the Family Learning Center preschoolers and their caregivers learn through interactive exhibits such as the Undersea Water World, the City Market and the Sandy Beach. Another gallery features children's art, and the Urban Tree House, a new outdoor exhibit made entirely from recycled materials, teaches environmental responsibility.

Youngsters at the Children's Museum of Manhattan produce their own television programming in the Media Center.

Courtesy of Time Warner Center for Media

GENERAL INFORMATION

Hours Mon, Wed, Thurs 1:30–5:30 pm; Fri–Sun 10 am–5 pm; closed Tues
Admission Children and adults $5, seniors $2.50, children under 2 free
Giftshop Educational toys, T-shirts, items related to exhibits
Library Children's and educational material; open by appointment only
Disability Access Fully accessible; restrooms, elevators, telephones, water fountains available
Directions Subway: 1/9 to 86th St; B to 81st St; Bus: M7, M10, M11, M104 to 83rd St; M79, M86 to Amsterdam Ave

Children's Museum of the Native American

Church of the Intercession 212-283-1122
550 West 155th Street
(at Broadway)
New York, NY 10032

At the Children's Museum of the Native American youngsters can play Indian games, go inside a tepee, sit in a dugout canoe and learn about the life and culture of America's indigenous peoples. The museum focuses on a different Native American culture each year. Past programs have been about Eskimos and Native Americans from the Eastern Woodlands, the Southwest, the Northwest Coast and the Plains.

Participatory demonstrations are an integral part of museum activities. In the Plains Indians program, for example, such hands-on activities were employed to teach children how these nomadic people traveled by horse and travois, hunted buffalo, designed and erected tepees, cared for their young and taught their children to respect the earth. A puppet show teaches the Cheyenne legend of "Jumping Mouse." Original puppets, music and songs are employed to tell this traditional tale.

Workshops emphasize the Native American love of nature. In these forums children sing chants, play games and learn sign language. The exhibition "The North American Indians" contains photographs that capture the dignity and spirit of the Indian way of life at the turn of the century. The museum is located in the Episcopal Church of the Intercession. Across the street is the Audubon Terrace Historic District, home to the American Academy of Arts and Letters, the Hispanic Society of America, the American Numismatic Society (see separate entries) and Boricua College.

Sioux Ghost Shirt

GENERAL INFORMATION

Hours By appointment only
Admission $3.50
Giftshop Books and items relating to Native American culture
Disability Access None
Directions Subway: 1/9 to 157th St; Bus: M4, M5 to 155th St; BX6 to Broadway
Landmark Status National Register of Historic Places, New York City Landmark

China Institute in America

125 East 65th Street 212-744-8181
(between Park and
Lexington Avenues)
New York, NY 10021

The China Institute in America is the only New York institution to focus solely on Chinese art, history and culture. It offers excellent exhibitions; lectures on art, culture and society; periodic firsthand reports from China; a speakers' forum; Chinese-language courses; studio classes in traditional Chinese arts; concerts; and children's workshops in conjunction with the public schools.

"Orchids and Flowers," Mao Yuyuan, ink and color on gold paper, 1651.

The China Institute Gallery features exhibitions ranging from the traditional to the contemporary. These have included "Views from Jade Terrace: Chinese Women Artists 1300–1912," "The Eccentric Painters of Yangzhou" and "Children in Chinese Art," as well as shows focusing on the techniques of ancient bronze casting, early photographs of borderland peoples and rare examples of Chinese glass.

The institute's close relationship with China's museums has enabled it to borrow outstanding works never before seen in the West. There are also guided tours to other museums and private collections containing important holdings. The institute's special access to Chinese film archives permits it to screen films of the '20s, '30s and '40s as well as works by contemporary filmmakers. And the annual Spring Concert introduces emerging Chinese composers and musicians to New York audiences.

When American philosopher John Dewey lectured at Peking University in 1919, he was impressed by his audience's understanding of the West. He wondered if a lecture in Chinese at Columbia University, where he was teaching, would be understood by more than a handful of people. To begin rectifying this imbalance of cultural understanding Dewey and colleagues in both America and China founded the institute in 1926.

GENERAL INFORMATION

Hours Mon, Wed–Fri 10 am–5 pm; Tues 10 am–8 pm; Sat 10 am–5 pm; closed Sun
Admission Suggested contribution: adults $3, seniors and students $1.50
Giftshop Books and items relating to Chinese culture, politics, society
Disability Access Limited access
Directions Subway: 6 to 68th St; B or Q to Lexington Ave; N or R to 59th St; Bus: M1, M2, M3, M4, M101, M102 to 65th St

Chinatown History Museum

70 Mulberry Street 212-619-4785
(at Bayard Street)
New York, NY 10013

The Chinatown History Museum seeks to rescue and reconstruct the history of Chinese-Americans and the community they built. One of the foremost facilities of its kind in the United States, the museum offers exhibitions, walking tours of Chinatown, an extensive physical archive and reference library, radio and video programs, and a slide show on Chinese-American history.

Through photographs, documents and ephemera the gallery tells the story of Chinese laundry workers, cooks, cigar makers, merchants and garment workers. Some past exhibits: "From Canton to New York: The Broken Tradition" and "Locke: A Chinese Community on the Sacramento Delta." There is also the permanent exhibition Remembering New York Chinatown.

The museum's growing archive includes family photographs of Chinese immigrants, the complete theatrical collection of a local Cantonese opera troupe, early Chinese-American newspapers, coaching books studied by immigrants in their efforts to circumvent exclusionary United States immigration laws, and over 300 hours of oral history tapes.

GENERAL INFORMATION

Hours Sun–Fri 12–5 pm; closed Sat
Admission Adults $1, children free
Giftshop Bookstore specializing in Chinese-American history and literature
Library Over 1,000 volumes relating to Chinese-American history; open by appointment only
Disability Access None
Directions Subway: 6, N, R, J, M or Z to Canal St; Bus: M101, M102 to Chatham Sq

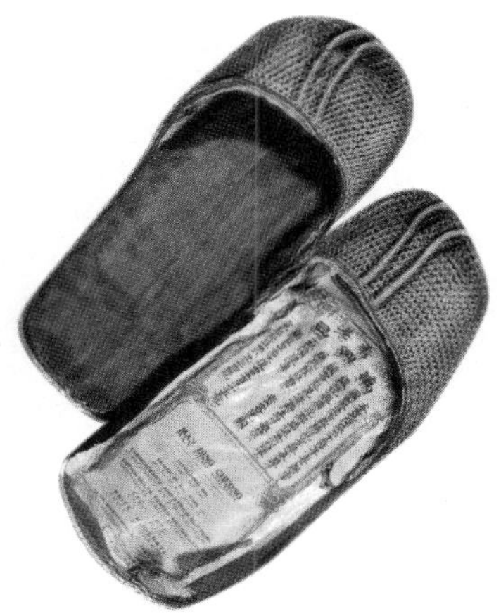

Slippers from the Chinatown History Museum, New York, circa 1890s.

Cinque Gallery

560 Broadway, Fifth Floor
(at Prince Street)
New York, NY 10012

212-966-3464

Joseph Cinque was an African who led a mutiny aboard the *Amistad*, a slave ship bound for America. He was so persistent in his cause that, eventually, the Supreme Court allowed the captives to return to their homeland. It is in this spirit of determination and pride that the Cinque Gallery was established.

Three African-American artists—Romare Bearden, Ernest Crichlow and Norman Lewis—founded the gallery in 1969 to foster the growth and development of young minority artists. Since that time it has sponsored over 300 exhibitions that have included work in a range of media. Originally opened in a donated space at the Public Theater, the gallery is now housed in its own SoHo exhibition space where it presents six to eight shows a year.

GENERAL INFORMATION

Hours Tues–Sat 1–6 pm; closed Sun, Mon
Admission Free
Disability Access Fully accessible
Directions Subway: N or R to Prince St; Bus: M5 to Broadway and Houston; M1, M6 to Prince St
Landmark Status National Register of Historic Places, New York City Landmark

City Center

Including Manhattan Theatre Club
131 West 55th Street (between Sixth and Seventh Avenues)
New York, NY 10019

212-581-1212 Box Office
212-645-5590 Manhattan Theatre Club

Constructed in 1924 as "Mecca Temple" by the fezzed Shriners, The City Center Theater acquired its name in 1943 when Mayor La Guardia saved the building from demolition and designated it a "cultural center for all New Yorkers." For the next 30 years, it served all the performing arts in New York City: dance, theater, musical theater, orchestral offerings and so on. The New York City Opera and George Balanchine's New York City Ballet had their beginnings at City Center.

In the early 1970s, when many resident artists moved to the new Lincoln Center for the Performing Arts (see separate entry), City Center was again threatened with demolition. This time it was saved to serve leading American dance companies, which today include Alvin Ailey American Dance Theater, Paul Taylor Dance Company, Martha Graham Dance Company, Merce Cunningham Dance Company, Joffrey Ballet, Lar Lubovitch Dance Company and Trisha Brown Company.

Visiting companies have included the Houston, San Francisco and Boston Ballets, Les Grands Ballets Canadiens and the Japanese Butoh troupe Sankai Juku.

The performance facilities include the 2,684-seat Main Stage and two smaller theaters, Stages I and II, home of the Manhattan Theatre Club. A full season of plays and the "Writers in Performance" series are presented on Stage I, and workshops and works-in-progress on Stage II.

Designed by Harry P. Knowles and the firm of Clinton & Russell, the structure has a mosquelike exterior dome. Equilateral arches on its 55th Street facade are clad in glazed tiles, and filigree throughout the interior suggests a Moorish influence. In the 1980s, the building was thoroughly restored and its sight lines improved.

GENERAL INFORMATION

Hours Box office 12–8 pm daily
Admission Ticket prices vary; subscription discounts; group, senior and student discounts
Disability Access Fully accessible; infrared sound system available
Directions Subway: 1, A or C to Columbus Circle; N or R to 57th St and 7th Ave; B to 57th St and 6th Ave; B, D or E to 53rd St and 7th Ave; Bus: M1, M2, M3, M4 to 55th St and 5th Ave; M5 to 59th St and 6th Ave; M7 to 56th St and 7th Ave; M10 to 55th St and Broadway; M104 to 57th St and Broadway
Landmark Status National Register of Historic Places, New York City Landmark
City-owned, privately operated

Jack Mitchell

Renee Robinson in "Cry," Alvin Ailey American Dance Theater, at City Center.

The Clocktower Gallery

108 Leonard Street (between Broadway and Lafayette Street)
New York, NY 10013
212-233-1096

The Clocktower Gallery was established in 1972 by the Institute for Contemporary Art, the same organization that operates P.S. 1 Museum in Long Island City, Queens (see separate entry). Its large main gallery and tower exhibition space are located on the top floors of an historic municipal office building in Lower Manhattan. Exhibitions have included "The Pop Project," a look at the history and future of Pop Art, and "Here and There: Travels," an exploration of travel in a variety of artistic disciplines.

Hundreds of single-artist and group shows have been mounted at the gallery, most recently a solo exhibition by Leningrad artist AfriKa and "Perspectives in Conceptualism," a group exhibition first shown and subsequently banned in the former Soviet Union. There are also occasional performances, such as those by Japanese Butoh artist Min Tanaka and the Polish performance ensemble Akadema Rucho.

GENERAL INFORMATION

Hours During exhibitions: Wed–Sat 12–6 pm
Admission Free
Disability Access None
Directions Subway: A, C or E to Canal St; 1/9 to Franklin St; Bus: M5, M6, M10 to Leonard St; M21 to Lafayette St
City-owned, privately operated

The Cloisters

Metropolitan Museum of Art
Fort Tryon Park (at 190th Street)
New York, NY 10040
212-923-3700

The Cloisters is a branch of the Metropolitan Museum of Art (see separate entry) devoted to the art and architecture of medieval Europe. Opened in 1938, the modern structure built in medieval style incorporates chapels, sections of monastic cloisters, a chapter house and fantastic examples of original Romanesque and Gothic architectural elements dating from the 12th through the 15th centuries.

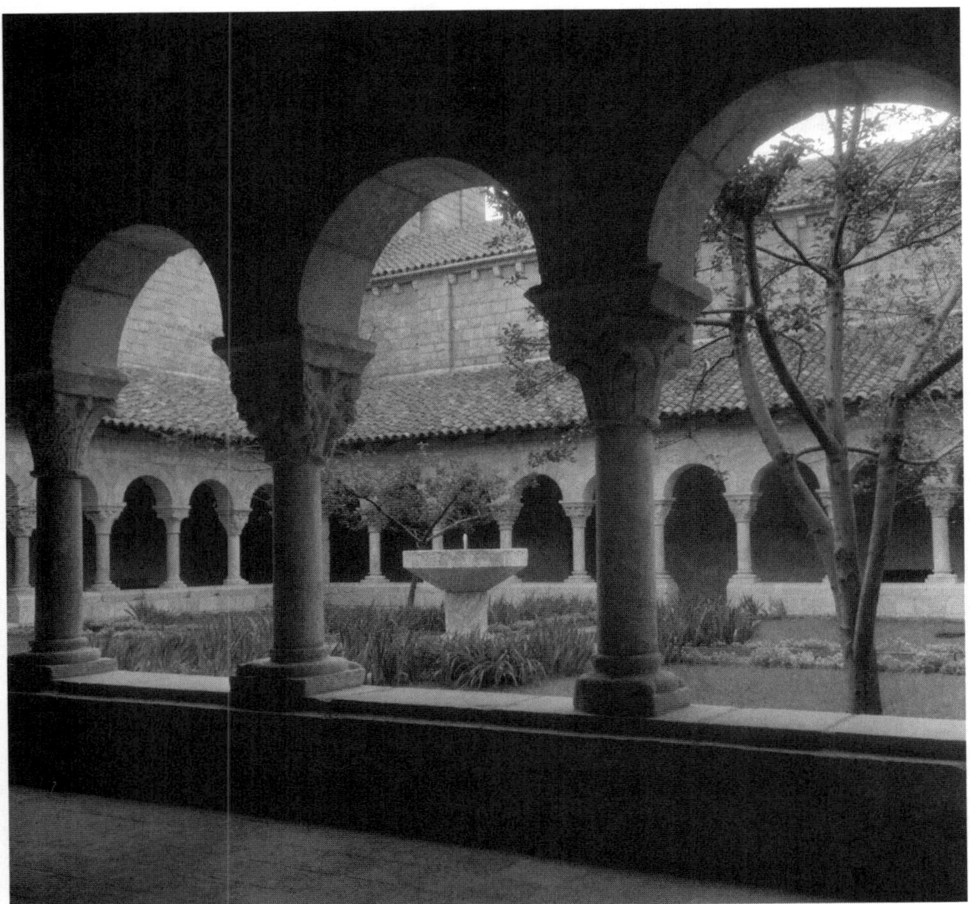

View of interior courtyard through the cloister from Saint-Michel-de-Cuxa.

At the Cloisters, one can view extraordinary medieval sculptures, the famed Unicorn Tapestries, the Annunciation Triptych by Robert Campin, finely illuminated manuscripts and paintings, intricate goldsmiths' work, brilliant jewel-like stained glass and one of the earliest known complete sets of playing cards. Among its other highlights are the beautiful flower and herb gardens containing more than 250 species of plants grown during the Middle Ages.

Early in the 20th century, American sculptor George Grey Barnard amassed the bulk of the collection seen at the Cloisters today. When the collection was put up for sale in the 1920s, John D. Rockefeller donated funds to the Metropolitan Museum for its purchase and exhibition, adding sculptures of his own. Later, Rockefeller gave land to New York City that would become Fort Tryon Park, reserving the high hilltop overlooking the Hudson River for a large medieval art museum. Charles Collens, architect of Riverside Church designed the building.

GENERAL INFORMATION

Hours March–Oct: Tues–Sun 9:30 am–5:15 pm, closed Mon; Nov–Feb: Tues–Sun 9:30 am–4:45 pm, closed Mon

Admission Suggested contribution: adults $6, seniors and students $3, children under 12 free (includes admission to The Metropolitan Museum of Art on the same day)

Giftshop Reproductions, postcards, guidebooks and exhibition catalogs

Library Titles, slides, photographs on medieval art and history; accessible to scholars and researchers by appointment

Disability Access Limited access; call ahead or check in with Security Office at entrance

Directions Subway: A to 190th St; Bus: M4 to Fort Tryon Park

Landmark Status New York City Landmark

Columbia University

Broadway and 116th Street
New York, NY 10027

212-854-1754
General Information

Columbia University, America's fifth-oldest institution of higher learning, was founded in 1754 as King's College. Every year 26,000 students attend this Ivy League instution's 15 schools, which offer 6,000 courses in virtually every field of professional endeavor—the liberal arts, education, engineering, journalism, law, medicine, the sciences, social work and so on. Columbia's 34 acres in Morningside Heights—actually its third Manhattan location—is the site of one of America's great urban campuses. Its spacious central plaza, dominated by the Roman Revival dome of Low Library, is surrounded and enclosed by numerous brick and limestone buildings designed by the firm of McKim, Mead & White in the Italian Renaissance style. There is much public sculpture too, including works by Rodin, Giacometti and Moore. Columbia offers many performing and visual arts activities open to the general public. Here is a selective survey of some of the most active programs.

GENERAL INFORMATION

Hours See descriptions below; several programs function intermittently, so call for schedule information
Admission Varies per venue: galleries usually free, sometimes a charge for live performances
Access See descriptions below
Directions Subway: 1/9 to 116th St; Bus: M4 to 116th St
Landmark Status New York City Landmark

Miriam & Ira D. Wallach Art Gallery

Schermerhorn Hall — 212-854-7288

Opened in 1986 by Columbia's Department of Art History and Archaeology, this space mounts exhibitions drawn from the university's permanent collection of European and American paintings, Oriental art, architectural drawings and work by contemporary artists. Shows have included "Actors, Courtesans and Famous Vistas: Japanese Art"; "Robert Smithson Unearthed: Works on Paper"; and "Notre-Dame, Cathedral of Amiens: An Orderly Vision." Lectures and symposia are offered in conjunction with the exhibitions.

GENERAL INFORMATION

Hours Sept–June: Wed–Sat 1–5 pm, closed Sun–Tues; closed July, Aug
Admission Free
Library None at gallery, but Columbia has numerous academic libraries for students only
Disability Access Call in advance for wheelchair access
Landmark Status New York City Landmark

Avery Hall

Graduate School of Architecture, Planning and Preservation
First Floor and Mezzanine

212-854-3414

Changing exhibitions of photographs, drawings and models of architectural projects reflect the wealth of one of the outstanding collections in the world. Shows have included "Hispanic Traditions in American Architecture and Urbanism."

GENERAL INFORMATION

Hours Vary, call for schedule
Admission Free
Disability Access Fully accessible
Landmark Status New York City Landmark

Low Memorial Library

The Rotunda — 212-854-2877

Formerly the university's library (that function is now served by Butler Library), Low Library's rotunda is the site of regular exhibitions and addresses. Exhibits have included "19th Century Photography at Columbia University" and "The Spanish Presence in American Architecture: Documents from Avery Library." A squarish, domed structure, Low Library is the pivotal structure of the highly symmetrical Columbia campus. In front of the building is Daniel Chester French's magisterial sculpture "Alma Mater," a campus icon.

GENERAL INFORMATION

Hours Mon–Fri 9 am–5:30 pm
Admission Free
Disability Access Fully accessible; take elevator adjacent to Dodge Hall to upper campus level
Landmark Status New York City Landmark

Morningside Heights Area

Grant's Tomb
Riverside Church
Riverside Park
Riverside Drive
Claremont Avenue
1/9 Subway
Broadway
W 122 nd St.
W 121 st St.
W 120 th St.
W 119 th St.
W 118 th St.
W 117 th St.
W 116 th St.
College Walk
W 115 th St.
W 114th St.
W 113 th St.
W 112 th St.
W 111 th St.
Amsterdam Avenue
Morningside Park
Morningside Avenue
Morningside Drive
Manhattan Avenue
Cathedral Church of St. John the Divine
1 2 3 4 5 6

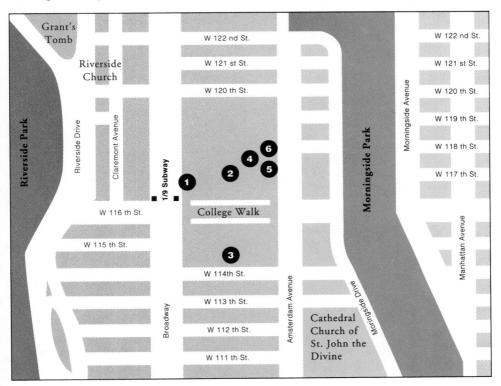

1 The Kathryn Bache Miller Theatre

2 Low Memorial Library

3 Rare Books & Manuscripts Library

4 Avery Hall

5 Postcrypt Arts Underground

6 Miriam & Ira D. Wallach Gallery

Joe Pineiro

Low Memorial Library & Plaza, Columbia University

Rare Books & Manuscripts Library

Butler Library, Sixth Floor 212-854-2231
114th Street between
Broadway and Amsterdam Avenue

This beautifully designed gallery, opened in the early 1980s, is a fine showcase for the astonishing rarities in Columbia's collection. Exhibitions have included "Jewish Literature through the Ages," a display of rare Judaica, and "The Fugitive Kind: The Theater of Tennessee Williams." Other shows have featured such items as a first edition of Walt Whitman's "Leaves of Grass" (1855), letters by Virginia Woolf and medieval illuminated manuscripts.

GENERAL INFORMATION

Hours Mon-Fri 9 am-4:45 pm
Admission Free upon request at Butler Library entrance; get security pass
Disability Access Fully accessible
Landmark Status New York City Landmark

Kathryn Bache Miller Theatre

Dodge Hall (116th Street and Broadway) — 212-854-7799 Box Office

The Miller Theatre offers performances of classical and contemporary music, jazz, literary readings and dance, as well as on-stage dialogues with artists, critics and cultural figures. "Profound Utterances: Composers and the Keyboard" is the theater's classical piano series. Other programs include "The Distinguished String Quartet: Exploring the Quintessential Quartet Repertoire"; "Symphonic Sundays"; "Echoes of Africa," examining the African-folk origins of popular music; and "Literary Evenings." The theater, whose season runs from September to April (concurrent with the academic year), underwent a thorough renovation in 1988.

GENERAL INFORMATION

Hours Box office open Mon–Fri 12–6 pm, closed Sat, Sun
Admission Varies, tickets generally $10-15; series subscriptions available; discounts for students, seniors, groups
Disability Access Fully accessible; call box office for more information
Landmark Status New York City Landmark

Postcrypt Arts Underground

St. Paul's Chapel, Lower Level (117th Street and Amsterdam Avenue) — 212-854-1953

Postcrypt Arts Underground consists of both a coffeehouse and an art gallery. The coffeehouse, established in 1964, features professional and amateur musical performers every Friday and Saturday night. Musical formats include (and transcend) blues, folk, jazz, rock, country and a cappella as well as performance art, poetry, comedy and storytelling. The intimate, stone-walled, candle-lit space seats 45. The art gallery, once a musty Sunday School classroom, mounts four shows a semester of works by artists of the university community, including students, faculty and administrators.

GENERAL INFORMATION

Hours Fri, Sat 9–12:30 pm, during academic year, Sept–April; closed Sun–Thurs
Admission Small cover charge
Food Service Coffeehouse has alcoholic and nonalcoholic beverages and pastry
Disability Access None
Landmark Status New York City Landmark

OTHER EXHIBITION SPACES

Arthur Ross Architecture Gallery
Buell Hall
212-854-6392

Butler Library Exhibition Space
Butler Library, Third Floor
212-854-8482

East Asian Library
300 Kent Hall
212-854-2578

Macy Gallery
444 Macy Hall, Teachers College
212-678-3419

Southern Asian Institute Reading Room
1134 School of International Affairs
212-854-5514

OTHER THEATER AND PERFORMANCE SPACES

Teatro Piccolo
Casa Italiana, Second Floor
212-854-2306

Horace Mann Theatre
525 West 120th Street, Teachers College
212-854-3408

Minor Latham Playhouse
Milbank Hall, Barnard College
212-854-2079

Schapiro Theatre
Schapiro Hall
212-854-3611

Sulzberger Parlor
Barnard Hall, Fourth floor
(chamber music)
212-854-5404

The Con Edison Energy Museum

145 East 14th Street (at Third Avenue) New York, NY 10003 212-460-6244

Inside Con Edison's Energy Museum one learns about the momentous day of September 4, 1882, when Thomas Edison's Pearl Street power plant began producing electricity for homes and businesses in the historic "First District," a square mile of Lower Manhattan. Starting with that seminal moment, the museum addresses the electrical age—past, present and future —through exhibits, artifacts and recorded narratives.

There are reconstructions of some of Edison's experiments and explanations of how electricity has changed our lives. Early examples of the "new" technology of electrical generation and underground distribution are on view, as well as antique kitchen appliances and an exhibit about factories and offices of the 1890s and 1920s.

One of the most popular displays lets visitors walk *beneath* a typical New York City street of today. Utility lines—electric, gas, steam, water, telephone and sewer—are colorfully illuminated, and a simulated passing subway adds an element of realism to the display. A question-and-answer display contains information on the use of electricity in New York City. For example, visitors discover when the first Major League night baseball game took place in the city (June 15, 1938). Energy conservation advice is also offered.

GENERAL INFORMATION

Hours Tues–Sat 9 am–5 pm; closed Sun, Mon
Admission Free
Disability Access Fully accessible; enter through Con Ed building at 4 Irving Place
Directions Subway: 4, 5, 6, N, R or L to 14th St–Union Sq; Bus: M14 to 3rd Ave; M101, M102 to 14th St

The Cooper Union for the Advancement of Science and Art

Third Avenue at Seventh Street New York, NY 10003 212-353-4195

Cooper Union offers public exhibitions, lectures, literary readings, film screenings and live performances related to its continuing education courses in art, architecture, graphic design, engineering, languages, writing and cultural studies.

The institution was established in 1859 by Peter Cooper (his granddaughters founded the Cooper-Hewitt Museum, see separate entry), an unschooled industrialist who, along with Samuel F.B. Morse, was responsible for laying the first trans-Atlantic cable.

Jose Pelaez

President Bill Clinton speaking in the Great Hall at Cooper Union, May 12, 1993.

He also designed America's first steam railroad engine and, with his wife, invented Jell-O. As a child Cooper wanted to study science, but he found no New York institution that would help him. He never forgot the futility of this search. Upon joining the ranks of America's richest men he created Cooper Union, one of the first colleges in the nation to offer an education free of charge, as it does today.

The institution's high-rise brownstone building, completed in 1859, is the oldest existing structure framed with steel beams in America. Italianate in style, it was designed by Frederick Peterson. The Great Hall has been the site of speeches by presidential candidates Lincoln, Roosevelt, Taft, Grant and Cleveland. Woodrow Wilson and Bill Clinton are the only incumbent presidents to have spoken there.

GENERAL INFORMATION

Hours Galleries open Mon–Fri 11 am–7 pm; Sat 12–5 pm; closed Sun
Admission Gallery is free; other programs $5–$10
Food Service First floor of Hewett Building, 3rd Ave, between 6th and 7th Sts, 10 am–3 pm weekdays only
Disability Access Great Hall and galleries fully accessible
Directions Subway: N or R to 8th St; 6 to Astor Place; Bus: M101, M102 to 8th St
Parking On-site lot
Landmark Status National Register of Historic Places, New York City Landmark

Cooper-Hewitt Museum

National Museum of Design/ Smithsonian Institution
2 East 91st Street (at Fifth Avenue)
New York, NY 10128
212-860-6868

The Cooper-Hewitt is the only museum in the United States devoted exclusively to historical and contemporary design. As such it is an important resource for architects, designers, studio artists, craftsmen and scholars. Four curatorial departments—Drawings and Prints, Decorative Arts, Textiles, Wallcoverings—maintain collections and mount exhibitions.

The museum has one of the largest design collections in the world—250,000 individual objects, collections and archives—including rare books, furniture, ceramics, glass, architectual drawings, metalwork and jewelry. The museum's collections are international, include both historic and contemporary design, and range from one-of-a-kind to mass-produced items. Emphasis is placed on the process of design from initial sketches, through working drawings, models and prototypes to finished products.

Exhibitions have included "Czech Cubism: Architecture and Design," "Tools for the Table: Designs for Dining," "Design and Fabric Technology: Pushing the Limits" and "Revolution, Life, and Labor: Soviet Porcelains 1918–1985." The Cooper-Hewitt Collections: A Design Resource chronicles the formation of the museum's collections from 1897 to the present.

The museum provides educational programs for children and adults, including lectures, seminars, workshops, tours of regional sites, gallery talks and family events. It also prepares interpretive materials for schools and teachers.

The museum was opened in 1897 by Sarah, Eleanor and Amy Hewitt. It was then located at Cooper Union in Lower Manhattan, which was founded by their grandfather, Peter Cooper. The sisters based their new museum on the Musée des Arts Décoratifs in Paris and what is now London's Victoria and Albert Museum. When Cooper Union could no longer afford to maintain the collection, it was adopted by the Smithsonian Institution, which created a new

Courtesy of the Decorative Arts Department at the Cooper-Hewitt Museum, Photo: John Parnell

Seven teapots, designed by Gerald Gulotta, produced by the Violet Sand Factory, Yixing, China, 1989.

museum for it in the former mansion of philanthropist and steel magnate Andrew Carnegie. Built in 1902, the 64-room house was donated to the Smithsonian by the Carnegie Corporation in 1972. It was designed by the architectural firm of Babb, Cook & Willard.

GENERAL INFORMATION

Hours Sun 12–5 pm; Tues 10 am–9 pm; Wed–Sat 10 am–5 pm; closed Mon
Admission Adults $3, seniors and students $1.50, children under 12 free; free admission to all Tues 5–9 pm
Giftshop Glassware, pottery, jewelry, furnishings, decorative objects related to collections; bookstore has titles on all aspects of design
Library 50,000-volume reference library; picture library of over one million images; and archive containing working papers, drawings and correspondence of important 20th-century designers
Disability Access Building fully accessible; limited access to grounds; ramps at entrance, restrooms available; lectures are frequently signed for the hearing-impaired
Directions Subway: 4, 5 or 6 to 86th St; Bus: M1, M2, M3, M4 to 91st St
Landmark Status National Register of Historic Places, New York City Landmark

Dance Theater Workshop

219 West 19th Street
(between Seventh and Eighth Avenues)
New York, NY 10011

212-924-0077
Box Office

Dance Theater Workshop provides promotional, administrative and technical services to artists work-ing in contemporary dance, theater, performance, music and the visual arts. Its Bessie Schönberg Theater, on 19th Street, is the site of nearly 200 performances a year. DTW's several performance series include "The Events," devoted to contemporary dance and performance, which focuses on five to nine dance artists in one or two-week presentations; "The 11 O'Clock New(s)," showcasing innovative dance, theater and performance artists exploring unusual performance concepts and material; "Fresh Tracks," concentrating on the work of emerging choreographers; and "Economy Tires Music Hall," offering concerts by independent composers whose work has had an impact on both the music and performance communities. The "Eyes Wide Open" series highlights original works by video artists working with the latest advancements in technology; and "Economy Tires Theater" presents independent theater, mime and performance artists working with unusual theatrical forms. DTW also presents rotating exhibits in its lobby gallery showcasing visual artists working in a variety of media.

DTW was founded in 1965 as a choreographers' cooperative with assistance from choreographer Jerome Robbins. It now serves a membership of more than 500 performing artists and companies.

Lois Greenfield

Choreographer Mark Morris performing his work "One Charming Night" at DTW.

GENERAL INFORMATION

Hours Mon–Fri 10 am–8 pm; Sat 1–8 pm; Sun 11 am–6 pm
Admission Tickets $12 or TDF voucher (Fri–Sun $5+TDF voucher), seniors $8, children under 12 half price
Giftshop Books and T-shirts
Disability Access None; many stairs, but management will carry patrons in wheelchairs if prior arrangements are made. TDD box office 212-691-6500; large-print performance programs available
Directions Subway: 1/9 to 18th St; 2 or 3 to 14th St; F to 14th St; A, C or E to 14th St; Bus: M10 to 18th St

Aaron Davis Hall for the Performing Arts

City College of New York
West 135th Street and
Convent Avenue
New York, NY 10031

212-650-7100
Box Office

Aaron Davis Hall is Harlem's principal performing arts center. Its three-theater complex serves ethnically diverse audiences with performances reflecting the broad spectrum of world cultures. Over 35 companies—including Dance Theatre of Harlem, Bill T. Jones/ Arnie Zane Dance Company, Opera Ebony and Boys Choir of Harlem—make Aaron Davis Hall their home.

Performance series include New Faces, New Voices, New Visions, presenting multicultural performers in the vanguard of new trends and innovations in the performing arts; the Jazz Institute of Harlem, curated by jazz legend Max Roach, which is regularly aired live on National Public Radio; and the annual Harlem Film Festival, screening the work of filmmakers of African descent from around the world.

Jazz musician Max Roach performing at Aaron Davis Hall.

Aaron Davis Hall was designed and constructed by Abraham W. Geller & Associates in 1979. A recent renovation has made it among the most technically advanced performance facilities in the city. The adjacent City College campus, with its towering Gothic cathedral and neo-Renaissance courtyard, is also of architectural interest.

GENERAL INFORMATION

Hours Box office open day of performance 12–8 pm
Admission Ticket prices vary; range from free to $25
Giftshop Items related to performances and Aaron Davis Hall
Food Service During performances
Disability Access Fully accessible; infrared listening system available
Directions Subway: 1 to 137th St; Bus: M11, M100, M101 to 135th St
Parking On-site lot
Landmark Status National Register of Historic Places, New York City Landmark

Dia Center for the Arts

212-431-9232

The Dia Center for the Arts, founded in 1974 as Dia Art Foundation, supports challenging visual art, especially large or unusual works that might not find acceptance elsewhere. Two examples of the realization of this mandate are Walter De Maria's "New York Earth Room," at 141 Wooster Street (second floor), a permanent exhibit consisting of a 3,500-square-foot room filled with soil to a depth of 22 inches; and the same artist's "Broken Kilometer," at 393 West Broadway, another permanent installation.

Exhibition Space

548 West 22nd Street
(off Eleventh Avenue)
New York, NY 10011

212-989-5912

Dia opened its West 22nd Street exhibition space in 1987 to show commissioned work from individual artists or collaborative teams of artists. Exhibitions, which frequently run for nine months or longer, have included Francesco Clemente's "Funerary Paintings"; "Laments," a sculptural work in stone and electric light by Jenny Holzer; and Joseph Beuys' "Fond" sculptures and "Codices Madrid" drawings. The permanent collection contains works by Beuys, Dan Flavin, Donald Judd, Barnett Newman, Cy Twombly and Andy Warhol, among others. Many of the Warhol holdings are now on view at the Andy Warhol Museum in Pittsburgh, which Dia was instrumental in creating.

A new facility, located across the street from the Dia Exhibition space on West 22nd Street, will permit the exhibition of Dia's extensive permanent collection of American and German art of the 1960s and '70s. This 50,000-square-foot museum facility is set to open in 1995.

"Rat King," a sculpture by the German artist Katharina Fritsch, exhibited at Dia in 1993.
Courtesy of Dia Center for the Arts, Photo: Bill Jacobson

GENERAL INFORMATION

Hours Thurs–Sun 12–6 pm; closed Mon–Wed; closed Jun–Aug
Admission Suggested contribution: $3
Giftshop Artists' books and publications; also see Printed Matter Bookstore at Dia, at 77 Wooster St
Food Service Rooftop coffee shop
Disability Access Fully accessible
Directions Subway: A, C or E to 23rd St; Bus: M23 to 11th Ave; M11 to 23rd St

Performance Space

155 Mercer Street (between Houston and Prince Streets)
New York, NY 10012
212-431-9232

A rehearsal and performance space is located at 155 Mercer Street, which Dia provides to dance companies either free or at minimal cost. Dozens of artists and companies appear in the space every year. Mercer Street also hosts seven or eight contemporary poetry readings every year. Featured poets have included James Merrill, Richard Wilbur, Lucille Clifton and Mark Strand. Panel discussions, lectures and symposia on issues in contemporary culture are also held here.

GENERAL INFORMATION

Hours Variable; call for performance schedule
Admission Generally $8–$12; various discounts available
Disability Access Limited access; steps to performance space
Directions Subway: B, D, F or Q to Broadway–Lafayette St; 6 to Bleecker St; N or R to Prince St; Bus: M5, M6 to Broadway and Houston St
Landmark Status National Register of Historic Places

Dixon Place

258 Bowery (between Houston and Prince Streets)
New York, NY 10012
212-219-3088

Dixon Place is a performance art space on Manhattan's Lower East Side that presents a varied palette of entertainments for those with decidedly nonmainstream tastes. An overview of activities during a single month provides the prospective visitor with a sense of the eclectic mix of offerings Dixon Place prides itself on. Such offerings have included "101 Humiliating Stories," a performance by Lisa Kron, member of Five Lesbian Brothers; the cathartic rampages of New York's only stand-up "tragic" (as opposed to comic), Heather Woodbury; "Bred by Exhibitor Dogs," by Kindness, Inc., a New York–based performance group; and "Eat My Shorts," a choreographic work-in-progress. At the annual "Cowboy Girl Show & Swap Meet" visitors can hear X-rated songs, enjoy theatrical skits and participate in the swap meet where, as Dixon Place literature states, one can "swap...old disco eight-tracks for a hardly used thighmaster." Other offerings include poetry and fiction readings, performance works in progress and open talent night.

GENERAL INFORMATION

Hours Box office opens 30 minutes before performances; call for schedule of events
Admission Tickets $5–8; discounts for seniors, students, groups; TDF vouchers accepted
Disability Access Limited; call ahead for assistance
Directions Subway: B, D, F or Q to Broadway–Lafayette St; 6 to Bleecker St; Bus: M101, M102 to Houston St; M21 to Bowery

Symbol Key

 *Institutional Giftshop*

 *On-Site Food Services*

 *On-Site Library or Archive*

 *Full Accessibility*

 *On-Site Parking*

 *National Register of Historic Places and/or New York City Landmark*

Downtown Art Co.

64 East 4th Street (between Bowery and Second Avenue)
New York, NY 10003

212-979-7362

Founded in 1987, Downtown Art Co. develops and presents contemporary performance work, ranging from traditional theater to more experimental multimedia art. Programmers seem particularly interested in nonmainstream perspectives on American culture.

Offerings have included "Our Mother and Other Visions," exploring religious issues, particularly the "miracle" phenomenon; "Washboard Jungle," a jug band performance art group; "Women in Black," a Hitchcockian murder mystery set in a convent and employing elements of "The Wizard of Oz"; "Walk of Fame," a theatrical collage addressing success and failure in Hollywood; and "Quintland," based on the commercial exploitation of the famous Dionne Quintuplets.

Downtown Art Co. also presents a guest artist series, offers residencies to assist those creating new works and provides a broad range of services to theater artists.

GENERAL INFORMATION

Hours Box office opens 30 minutes before performances; call for schedule of events
Admission Tickets $10; discounts for large groups; TDF vouchers accepted; pay what you can on Wed nights
Disability Access None
Directions Subway: N or R to 8th St; 6 to Astor Place; Bus: M15 to 8th St

The Drawing Center

35 Wooster Street
(between Grand and Broome Streets)
New York, NY 10013

212-219-2166

The Drawing Center is the only institution in the United States dedicated exclusively to the exhibition and study of drawing. As a showcase for unique works on paper, the center's gallery presents four or five group exhibitions each year focusing on the work of emerging artists. The gallery also mounts at least one historical exhibition a year highlighting the work of acknowledged masters and less celebrated artists whose work merits greater attention.

Exhibitions have included "Guercino: Drawings from Windsor Castle," "Inigo Jones: Complete Architectural Drawings" and "Picasso's 'Parade'." The center also presents related readings, lectures, symposia, performances and paper-conservation programs. The gallery is located on the ground floor of a five-story building with a faux cast-iron façade.

"Two Helmeted Soldiers on Horseback with Archers" by Guercino, ca. 1620, from the Drawing Center exhibition "Guercino: Drawings from Windsor Castle."

GENERAL INFORMATION

Hours Tues, Thur, Fri 10 am–6 pm; Wed 10 am–8 pm; Sat 11 am–6 pm; closed Sun, Mon
Admission Free
Giftshop Exhibition catalogs available
Library Artists' slide registry contains over 5,000 slides and resumés; access by appointment
Disability Access Fully accessible; wheelchair lift available
Directions Subway: 1/9, 6, A, C, E, N or R to Canal St; Bus: M21 to Greene St
Landmark Status National Register of Historic Places, New York City Landmark

Dyckman House Museum

4881 Broadway (at 204th Street) 212-304-9422
New York, NY 10034

Originally built of brick, fieldstone and wood in 1784, Dyckman House is Manhattan's last surviving Colonial farmhouse. The house contains English and early American Colonial furnishings, including a Bible and a cradle that were Dyckman family heirlooms. Relics from the Revolutionary War include pottery fragments, flint-tips, kitchen utensils and a replica of a military hut that has been reconstructed near its original site in the garden.

In 1661 Jan Dyckman arrived in New York from Westphalia and purchased several acres of remote land in northern Manhattan. He and his descendants expanded their landholdings until the house was the center of one of the largest estates in Manhattan's history—some 450 acres at its peak.

During the Revolutionary War, Dyckman House became the northernmost defense in New York City for the British, who ultimately burned it to the ground. Dyckman's grandson, William, constructed the present house on the old foundation in 1784. It is Dutch-American in style with a gambrel roof and double doors. The house remained in the family until the late 1800s. In 1916 it was reclaimed by several Dyckman descendants and donated to the city.

Annual events at Dyckman House Museum include the spring chamber music concert, the Inwood Arts Festival and the Folk Arts Festival.

Dorothy Zeidman

GENERAL INFORMATION

Hours Tues–Sat 11am–4 pm; closed Sun, Mon
Admission Free
Disability Access None
Directions Subway: 1/9 to 207th St; A to 207th St; Bus: M100, BX7 to 204th St and Broadway
Landmark Status National Register of Historic Places, New York City Landmark
City-owned and operated

Educational Alliance

Lee Kohns Cultural Arts Center 212-475-6200
197 East Broadway (between Jefferson and Clinton Streets)
New York, NY 10002

The Educational Alliance is a settlement house, community center and social service agency that serves a diverse city population. It addresses a range of problems and needs—aging, AIDS, early childhood education, homelessness, parenting and substance abuse, to mention a few. The group also provides numerous cultural enrichment programs.

The Alliance Art School was founded in 1917. Among the artists studying there have been Adolph Gottlieb, Louise Nevelson, Zero Mostel, Mark Rothko and Ben Shahn. The school's New Gallery offers shows by community artists or arts groups; these generally run for three weeks.

The Lee Kohns Cultural Arts Center presents cultural activities throughout the year. Concerts, dance recitals, theatrical presentations, art lectures, children's programs, holiday celebrations, films and poetry readings are held in the Mazer Theater.

The Educational Alliance was established over a century ago as a settlement house for Eastern European Jews settling on the Lower East Side. Today it serves everyone, regardless of race or religion, at sites in Manhattan, Brooklyn, Staten Island and upstate New York.

GENERAL INFORMATION

Hours Gallery: Mon–Thurs 8 am–10 pm, Fri 8 am–6 pm; closed Sat, Sun; various performance times
Admission Gallery free; ticket prices for performances vary
Disability Access Limited access; ramp available
Directions Subway: F to East Broadway; Bus: M9 to East Broadway and Clinton St; M14 to Clinton and Grand Sts; M22 to Madison Ave and Jefferson St

Ellis Island Immigration Museum

Ellis Island
New York, NY 10004

212-363-8340
Information
212-269-5755
Ferry Service

A symbol of America's immigrant heritage, Ellis Island functioned from 1892 to 1924 as the gateway for the greatest tide of migrating humanity in United States history. Some 16 million people landed at Ellis Island. Today their descendants account for almost 40 percent of the country's population.

Originally a three-acre island, the land expanded over the years to almost 28 acres supporting 36 buildings. Despite expansion, facilities were always inadequate. In 1924 immigration quotas stemmed the tide. No longer needed for mass processing, the station became a detention and deportation center for undesirable aliens. In 1954 it was permanently closed as an immigration station. President Johnson declared it a national monument in 1965.

In 1987 the Main Building was refurbished and transformed into the Ellis Island Immigration Museum, in time for the depot's 1992 centennial. Covering 200,000 square feet, the museum features exhibits, restored areas and an interactive learning center for children.

Highlights include more than 30 separate galleries filled with artifacts, historic photographs, posters, maps, oral histories and ethnic music; two theaters featuring Island of Hope, Island of Tears, a film-documentary; the exhibition Treasures from Home, displaying priceless family heirlooms brought to America by immigrants; an innovative learning center with computer technology that teaches schoolchildren about their cultural heritage; and The Peopling of America, a series of eleven graphic arrays chronicling four centuries of immigration history.

The massive brick-and-limestone Main Hall, which once housed dormitories, examination rooms and offices, was constructed in 1898 after a design by Boring & Tilton. The $160 million Ellis Island renovation was designed by the New York firm of Beyer, Blinder, Belle. The museum is operated by the National Park Service.

New Americans, shortly after arriving at Ellis Island for processing, ca. 1920.

GENERAL INFORMATION

Hours 9:30 am–5 pm daily; last ferry at 3:30 pm
Admission Ferry ticket includes admission to both Statue of Liberty and Ellis Island: adults $6, seniors $5, children under 17, $3; $5 per person for groups of 20 or more.
Giftshop T-shirts, mugs, postcards and other items
Food Service Fast food available
Library Oral history collection containing hundreds of taped interviews with immigrants; open by appointment
Disability Access Fully accessible
Directions Subway: N or R to Whitehall St; 1/9 to South Ferry; 4 or 5 to Bowling Green; Bus: M6 to Bowling Green; then take ferry
Landmark Status National Register of Historic Places
National Monument

The Equitable Center and Gallery

787 Seventh Avenue 212-554-4818
(between 51st and 52nd Streets)
New York, NY 10019

The Equitable Center houses a small gallery and some of the largest public art works in Manhattan. The 3,000-square-foot Equitable Gallery presents works in all media, including shows originating outside New York that would not otherwise have a presence in the city, as well as shows culled from important New York private collections. The gallery mounts four exhibitions a year, each on view for about ten weeks. Exhibits have included "Telling Tales: 19th Century Narrative Painting from the Pennsylvania Academy of Fine Arts," "Alone in a Crowd: Prints of the 1930s and 1940s by African-American Artists" and "Thomas Jefferson and the Design of Monticello."

Installations of public art throughout the Equitable Center include Roy Lichtenstein's "Mural with Blue Brushstroke," an immense work that is a compendium of the Pop artist's signature images; Thomas Hart Benton's ten-panel mural "America Today," originally commissioned by the New School for Social Research in 1930; and Sol LeWitt's "Wall Drawing..," which is mounted in the exterior courtyard passageway linking 51st and 52nd streets. Also located here are two bronze works by British sculptor Barry Flanagan, "Young Elephant" and "Hare on Bell." Sandro Chia's immense four-panel mural "Palio," celebrating the fabled Siena horse race, is located in the bar of the Italian restaurant of the same name.

Dorothy Zeidman

The Equitable Gallery

Equitable Center occupies the entire block between Avenue of the Americas and Seventh Avenue, and comprises two office buildings: Equitable Tower, sheathed in polished rose-granite, was constructed in 1985 and designed by Edward Larrabee Barnes Associates; the PaineWebber Building, including the PaineWebber Art Gallery (see separate entry), was designed by Skidmore, Owings & Merrill.

GENERAL INFORMATION

Hours Mon–Fri 11 am–6 pm; Sat 12–5 pm; closed Sun
Admission Free
Giftshop Next door to gallery; operated by the Brooklyn Museum
Disability Access Fully accessible
Directions Subway: B, D or E to 7th Ave; N or R to 49th St; 1/9 to 50th St; B, D, F or Q to 47th–50th St; Bus: M5, M7 to 52nd St; M27, M50 to 7th Ave

Exit Art/The First World

548 Broadway, Second Floor 212-966-7745
(between Prince and Spring Streets)
New York, NY 10012

Exit Art/The First World is a multidisciplinary cultural center with an atmosphere that is decidedly eclectic and experimental. It is located in a former SoHo warehouse that has been transformed into a 17,000-square-foot space with two galleries, a 100-seat theater-performance space, a store and a cafe.

The galleries present thematic exhibits, installations and special projects featuring younger and mid-career artists, and historical exhibitions. Exhibitions have included "Fever," which consisted of 200 works by 50 young artists focusing on contemporary issues; "1920: The Subtlety of Subversion, the Continuity of Intervention," a showcase for women's art of the last 25 years that takes its name from the year women got the vote; and "Poverty Pop," a show of emerging artists using recycled materials in their sculptures. A second gallery called Foreign Affairs showcases international artists.

The First World Theater stages experimental performances, dramas, music programs, and film and video screenings.

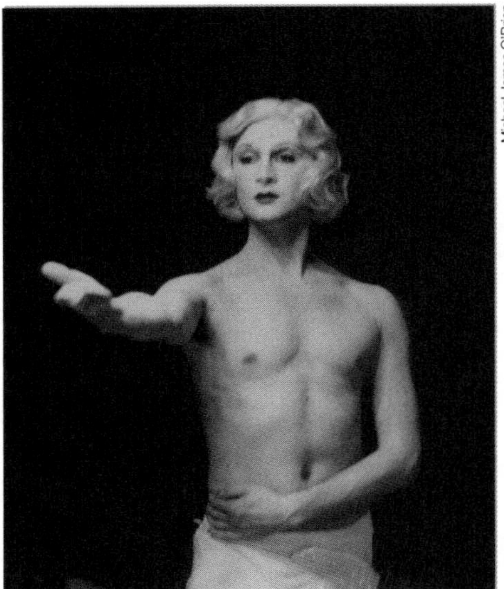

Michael James O'Brien

Performance artist John Kelly, photographed by Michael James O'Brien, from the Exit Art exhibit "Assembling Gender."

GENERAL INFORMATION

Hours Tues–Fri 10 am–6 pm; Sat 11 am–6 pm; closed Sun, Mon
Admission Suggested contribution: $2
Giftshop The Apartment Store, a retail shop of artist-made functional objects, furnishings and gifts
Food Service Cafe Cultura, with baked items, coffees, etc.
Disability Access Fully accessible; elevator to gallery and restrooms available
Directions Subway: N or R to Prince St; B, D, F or Q to Broadway–Lafayette St; 6 to Spring St ; Bus: M1 to Prince St; M21 to Broadway
Landmark Status National Register of Historic Places, New York City Landmark

Fashion Institute of Technology

The Museum at F.I.T. 212-760-7760
State University of New York
Shirley Goodman Resource Center
27th Street at Seventh Avenue
New York, NY 10001

The Fashion Institute of Technology is a professional school for those seeking careers in the apparel industry. Its galleries, located in the Shirley Goodman Resource Center, offer regular shows on all aspects of fashion and its satellite industries, from design and illustration to textiles and photography. Shows have included "The Undercover Story," a history of lingerie, 1780–present; "All American: A Sportswear Tradition"; "Fashion and Surrealism"; "Halston: Absolute Modernism"; and "Extravagant Lengths: Velvet, Plush and Velveteen." The work of design-related artists has also been showcased, including Andy Warhol, who started his career as an illustrator of stylish footwear, and Tiffany's jewelry master Elsa Peretti. Highlights each season are shows of work by students and faculty.

GENERAL INFORMATION

Hours Tues–Fri 12–8 pm; Sat 10 am–5 pm; closed Sun, Mon
Admission Free
Library Fashion-related rare books, manuscripts, drawings, illustrations and periodicals
Disability Access Fully accessible; elevators and restrooms available
Directions Subway: 1/9 to 27th St; A, E or F to 23rd St; Bus: M10 to 27th St; M23 to 7th Ave

Federal Hall National Memorial

26 Wall Street (at Nassau Street) 212-264-8711
New York, NY 10005

Federal Hall has been the site of government activity for almost 300 years. Three successive buildings have stood at the corner of Wall and Nassau streets, each playing a role in momentous national historic events.

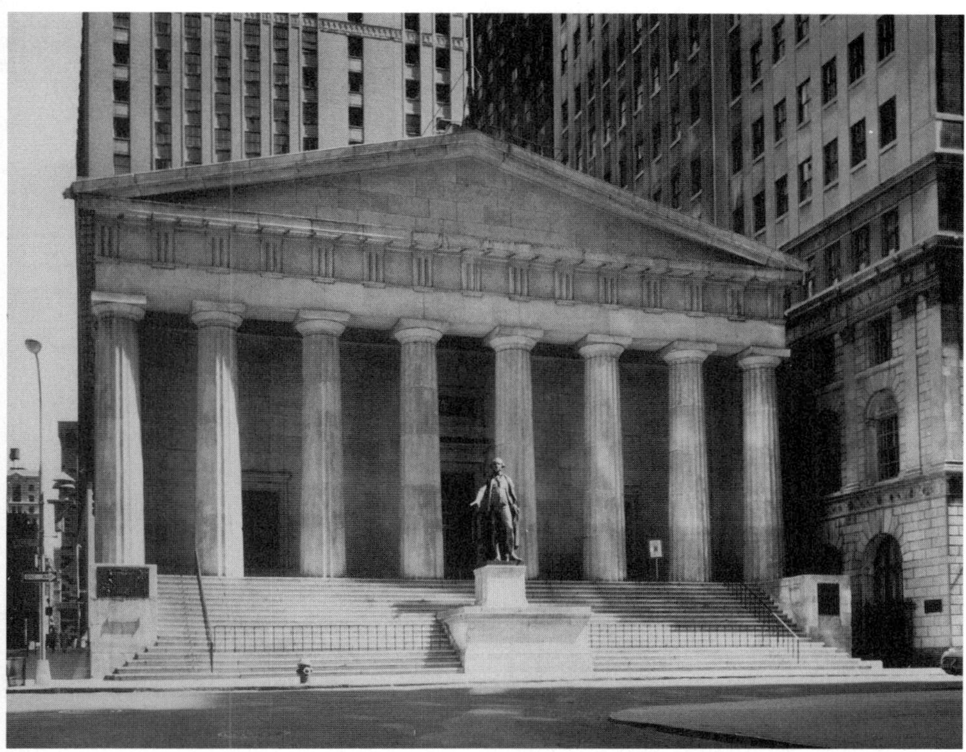

Federal Hall National Memorial, the site of George Washington's inauguration.

The earliest, built in 1702, was New York's first City Hall. This is where John Peter Zenger was tried and acquitted of seditious libel in 1735, marking the country's first great freedom of the press trial. In 1765, the Stamp Act Congress met to protest English taxation, and resistance to "taxation without representation" spread across America.

Six years after the Revolutionary War, New York City became the first capital city of the United States. In 1789 old City Hall was renovated and renamed Federal Hall, becoming the young nation's first capitol building. On March 4 of that year the government of the United States of America began to function there under the present constitution. Eight weeks later George Washington, standing on an open-air balcony on the second floor, took the oath of office to become the nation's first president. Today's Supreme Court and the Departments of State, Defense and the Treasury can trace their beginnings to Federal Hall. In 1812, after the seat of government moved south, this second structure was razed and sold for scrap, fetching $425.

The present building, an excellent example of Greek Revival architecture, was constructed in 1842 as a custom house. The Independent Treasury System was established here in 1862 and the Federal Reserve System in 1913. In 1939 the Secretary of the Interior declared the structure a National Historic Shrine. In 1955 Congress renamed it Federal Hall National Memorial in honor of the earlier edifice.

There are guided tours, and the second-floor galleries mount temporary exhibitions for all ages. These shows, which are organized by other galleries and museums, have included a New York City/Tokyo exchange show of children's art, a pictorial display of the city boroughs and a Smithsonian exhibit about everyday life in Colonial America.

GENERAL INFORMATION

Hours Mon–Fri 9 am–5 pm; closed Sat, Sun
Admission Free
Giftshop Books and documents; open 9:30 am–4:30 pm
Library Archive and curatorial collection accessible by appointment only; call curator
Disability Access Fully accessible; back entrance on Pine St has bell, ramp and elevators
Directions Subway: N or R to Rector St; 4 or 5 to Wall St; M or J to Broad St; 2 or 3 to Wall St; Bus: M1, M6 to Broadway and Wall St; M15 to Wall St
Landmark Status National Register of Historic Places, New York City Landmark

National Memorial

Forbes Magazine Galleries

Forbes Building
62 Fifth Avenue (between
12th and 13th Streets)
New York, NY 10011
212-206-5549

During his life Malcolm Forbes cultivated a range of exotic tastes and interests. The seven galleries within the Forbes Building, which opened in 1985, are filled with the late publisher's personal collections and attest to the scope of his esthetic sensibilities.

Permanent exhibits include a display of over 500 toy boats, the largest flotilla of its kind in the country, in the Toy and Trophy Room, along with 12,000 miniature soldiers and a wide assortment of antique trophies. Twelve of the fabled Imperial Easter Eggs made by the House of Fabergé for the last two Russian czars are among over 300 jeweled items and objets d'art on display.

Otto E. Nelson

Malcolm S. Forbes—publisher, financier, collector, adventurer—from the Forbes Magazine Collection, New York. Portrait by Claudio Bravo, 1978.

In the Picture and Autograph Galleries, rare manuscripts, including Abraham Lincoln's Emancipation Proclamation, are on view. There are also periodic short-term exhibits of paintings, photographs and manuscripts from the permanent collection.

The Forbes Building was designed by Carrère and Hastings, architects of the New York Public Library and the Frick Collection (see separate entries), in collaboration with Shreve and Lamb, the firm that would later design the Empire State Building. It was constructed in 1925.

GENERAL INFORMATION

Hours Tues–Sat 10 am–4 pm; closed Sun, Mon (guided group tours on Thurs, must be arranged months in advance)
Admission Free
Disability Access Limited access; ramps available
Directions Subway: N, R, 4, 5 or 6 to 14th St–Union Square; 1, 2 or 3 to 14th St; Bus: M1, M2, M3, M5 to 12th St

14 Sculptors Gallery

164 Mercer Street (between
Prince and Houston Streets)
New York, NY 10012
212-966-5790

In 1973 fourteen sculptors founded this gallery exclusively for the exhibition of contemporary sculpture. Shows change about every three weeks and emphasize both figurative and abstract work. Exhibits have included "Sculptors' Proposals for Large-Scale Works," architectural models and drawings; "Industrialization: Before and After," featuring the work of Central and South American artists; and "Columns," a group show focusing on the city's architecture. The gallery presents works by members and invited sculptors.

GENERAL INFORMATION

Hours Sept–July: Tues–Sun 11 am–6 pm, closed Mon; June–Aug closed
Admission Free
Disability Access None
Directions Subway: N or R to Prince St; B, D, F or Q to Broadway–Lafayette St; C or E to Spring St; 6 to Bleecker St; Bus: M1 to Broadway and Houston St; M5 to Houston and Greene Sts; M21 to Houston and Mercer Sts
Landmark Status National Register of Historic Places, New York City Landmark

Franklin Furnace Archive

112 Franklin Street
(between Church Street
and West Broadway)
New York, NY 10013

212-925-4671

Franklin Furnace Archive emphasizes avant-garde art of the past and present through historical and thematic exhibitions, performance art, readings and educational programs.

Exhibitions, installations and performance art pieces at Franklin Furnace range from the ethereal to the shocking. Exhibitions have included "The Avant-Garde Book: 1900-45," "Picasso's Sketchbooks" and "The King Is Gone but Not Forgotten," an homage to Elvis Presley. Installations have included "I Refused the Hysterectomy of My Desire," exploring the female experience of pornography, and "Sleep of Reason," in which ecological issues were examined through animatronic sculpture. The institution's performance art offerings represent the cutting edge of creativity in the field.

For many years Franklin Furnace maintained a collection of book and book-like objects made by artists. In 1993, it sold this collection to the Museum of Modern Art, because of MoMa's superior conservation and long-term storage facilities, while retaining the right of access for future exhibitions. Artists represented in the 18,000–object trove include Sol Lewitt, Claes Oldenburg, Joseph Beuys and Jenny Holzer.

Cubist Books

Franklin Furnace has expanded educational outreach in recent years, bringing artists, many internationally renowned (Eric Bogosian, Laurie Anderson), into the public schools to work with students in the areas of storytelling, bookmaking and performance art.

GENERAL INFORMATION

Hours Tues–Sat 12–6 pm; closed Sun, Mon
Admission Gallery free; fee for performances
Giftshop Publications and posters
Library Archive accessible with staff assistance
Disability Access Access arranged with advance notice
Directions Subway: 1/9 to Franklin St; A, C or E to Canal St; N, R, 5, 6, M or Z to Canal St; Bus: M6, M10 to Franklin St

Symbol Key

 *Institutional Giftshop*

 *On-Site Food Services*

 *On-Site Library or Archive*

 *Full Accessibility*

 *On-Site Parking*

 *National Register of Historic Places and/or New York City Landmark*

Fraunces Tavern Museum

54 Pearl Street
(at Broad Street)
New York, NY 10004

212-425-1778

The Fraunces Tavern Museum, which opened in 1907, is located in a reconstructed 18th-century building that was the frequent gathering spot of American Revolutionary leaders. Its permanent collection contains important early American prints, paintings, decorative arts and artifacts dating from the Colonial period to the mid-19th century.

The Visitor Orientation Exhibit provides an illustrated history of Fraunces Tavern within the context of early New York City and the Revolutionary War. Temporary exhibits examine different aspects of American history and culture, such as Jewish life in early New York,

Fraunces Tavern Museum

medicine and the healing arts in early America, drinking traditions and temperance movements in early America, the changing image of George Washington and the Revolutionary War. Related lectures are also offered.

The museum houses two fully reconstructed period rooms: the Long Room, site of George Washington's emotional farewell to his officers at the end of the Revolutionary War; and the Clinton Dining Room, where Dewitt Clinton, the first American-born governor of New York, commemorated the British evacuation of North America.

The museum building was constructed in 1719 by Etienne DeLancey as a residence. Samuel Fraunces purchased it in 1762 and made it a popular tavern.

GENERAL INFORMATION

Hours Mon–Fri 10 am–4:45 pm; Sat 12–4 pm; closed Sun
Admission Adults $2.50, students and seniors $1
Disability Access None
Directions Subway: 4 or 5 to Bowling Green; 1/9 to South Ferry; 2 or 3 to Wall St; N or R to Whitehall St; E to World Trade Center; Bus: M1, M6, M15 to South Ferry
Landmark Status National Register of Historic Places, New York City Landmark

French Institute/ Alliance Française

22 East 60th Street (between Madison and Park Avenues)
New York, NY 10022
212-355-6100

Best known for its language courses, the French Institute/Alliance Française offers a rich *potpourri* of French culture designed especially for Americans. Located in a beautiful Beaux-Arts building, circa 1925, the institute contains a lending library, a bookstore, two theaters and classrooms for teaching French.

Performing arts facilities include the 125-seat Tinker Auditorium, host to slide lectures, poetry readings, film and video screenings, and symposiums on subjects ranging from art history and literature to dance and politics. Lectures have included "A Survey of French Design Today," "Literature and the Arts" and "Society and Politics."

The new 400-seat Florence Gould Hall is a multi-purpose theater equipped for concerts, dance, dramatic theater and operatic performances. Events in this state-of-the-art facility have included a lecture by Dominique Perrault, architect of France's controversial new national library, a production of Emmanuel Chabrier's opéra bouffe "L'Étoile" and the "Lolli-Pops Concerts" for children 3–5. Florence Gould Hall is also home to Ciné-Club, which presents classic French films weekly and regular premieres of new French films, all with English subtitles.

The institute also holds book signings and receptions honoring writers, artists, speakers, film directors and performers. The French Institute/Alliance Française was founded at the beginning of the 20th century by American Francophiles for the purpose of encouraging the appreciation of French language and culture and fostering friendly exchange between the two countries. It is an independent institution, unaffiliated with the French government.

GENERAL INFORMATION

Hours Mon–Thurs 10 am–8 pm; Fri 10 am–6 pm; Sat 10 am–1:30 pm; closed Sun
Admission Free; various membership benefits available
Giftshop "Les Belles Lettres" bookstore has titles on French art, literature, history and culture
Food Service Cafe, hours vary
Library Lending library has holdings on all periods of French literature, art, history and every aspect of French civilization; large selection of current

newspapers and magazines, reference books, dictionaries; tours of library first Thurs of each month; call for reservations
Disability Access Fully accessible
Directions Subway: 4, 5 or 6 to 59th St; N or R to 5th Ave; E or F to 5th Ave and 53rd St; B or Q to Lexington Ave ; Bus: M1, M2, M3, M4, M30, M31 to 60th St; M32, M57, M58 to Madison Ave

The Frick Collection

1 East 70th Street
(at Fifth Avenue)
New York, NY 10021

212-288-0700

The Frick Collection exhibits one of the world's most important private collections of paintings, sculptures and decorative arts. The artworks, dating from the 14th through the 19th centuries, are housed in a neoclassical mansion designed by Thomas Hastings and constructed in 1913–14.

Visitors can stroll about the interior of the house, originally the residence of steel magnate Henry Clay Frick, and enjoy the sculpture of the Renaissance and later periods, French and Italian furniture, oriental and French porcelains, Limoges enamels, oriental rugs, silver, prints and drawings. An interior courtyard with fountain offers a quiet respite from the hectic pace of the city. Outside, formal gardens enhance the structure's beauty.

Perhaps the Frick Collection's most conspicuous strength is in Old Master paintings. Among its more famous holdings are Bellini's "St. Francis in the Desert," El Greco's "St. Jerome," Vermeer's "Officer and Laughing Girl," Van Gogh's "Flowering Garden" and Rembrandt's "The Polish Rider." Also on permanent display are works by Boucher, Constable, Duccio, Fragonard, Goya, Hals, Hogarth, Holbein, Renoir, Reynolds, Titian, Turner, Van Dyck, Van Eyck and others. Most of these priceless artworks were collected by Frick during his lifelong pursuit of fine art, although acquisitions have been made since his death.

The Frick lecture series features prominent scholars and art historians. The Frick Art Reference Library, housed in an adjacent 13-story building, is a major scholarly resource containing almost 800,000 photographic images of artworks and nearly 250,000 publications. Free concerts of classical music are presented throughout the year.

GENERAL INFORMATION

Hours Tues–Sat 10 am–6 pm; Sun 1–6 pm; closed Mon
Admission Adults $3, students and seniors $1.50, children under 10 not admitted
Giftshop Reproductions, books, postcards related to collection
Library Frick Art Reference Library is a leading center for research in the history of art; open to scholars, students, artists; call: 212-288-8700
Disability Access Limited access; wheelchairs provided
Directions Subway: 6 to 68th St; Bus: M1, M2, M3, M4 to 70th St
Landmark Status National Register of Historic Places, New York City Landmark

Interior courtyard of The Frick Collection.

Gallery 62

National Urban League
Equal Opportunity Building
500 East 62nd Street
(between First and York Avenues)
New York, NY 10021
212-310-9045

Gallery 62's art exhibitions, sponsored by the National Urban League, have the singular goal of stimulating creative self-expression among African-American artists. Since its founding in 1978, the gallery has mounted individual and group exhibits two to three times a year, presenting work in virtually all media. The National Urban League was founded in 1910. It is committed to eliminating poverty and racism and sponsors a variety of programs through its 113 affiliates nationwide.

GENERAL INFORMATION

Hours Mon–Fri 10 am–4 pm; closed Sat, Sun
Admission Free
Giftshop Exhibition catalogs, reproductions of work by minority artists, original works
Disability Access Fully accessible
Directions Subway: 4, 5 or 6 to 59th St; Bus: M58 to York Ave; M1, M2, M3, M4, M15, M31, M101, M102 to 62nd St

Gallery 1199

Martin Luther King Jr. Labor Center
310 West 43rd Street
(between Eighth and Ninth Avenues)
New York, NY 10036
212-582-1890 Ext. 3027

At Gallery 1199, short-term thematic exhibitions of painting, drawing and photography focus on labor and social issues throughout American history. The gallery mounts six exhibits a year, including offerings such as "Angola," an exhibition curated by the Angolan Mission to the United Nations, and "Plant Closings in Ohio." Established in 1972, the gallery is named after Local 1199, the Drug, Hospital, and Health Care Employees Union, headquartered in the same building.

GENERAL INFORMATION

Hours Mon–Fri 10 am–8 pm; closed Sat, Sun
Admission Free
Disability Access Fully accessible
Directions Subway: A, C or E to 42nd St; 1/9, 2, 3, 7, S, N or R to 42nd St–Times Square; Bus: M10, M16, M27, M42 to 42nd St and 8th Ave

General Grant National Memorial

Riverside Drive at 122nd Street
New York, NY 10027
212-666-1640

Dedicated in 1897, the General Grant National Memorial is the largest mausoleum in America. Its sheer size reflects the immense reverence Americans felt for this former general and president, who was considered the savior of the Union. Through major battlefield victories—including those at Fort Donelson, Shiloh, Vicksburg and Chattanooga—he changed the tide of the Civil War in the Union's favor. After the war he was elected president, advocating amnesty for Confederate leaders and protection for freed African-Americans. At his death, Grant was almost universally respected by both Northerners and Southerners.

Architect John Duncan based his design on Mausoleus' Tomb at Halicarnassus of 350 B.C. The structure rises 150 feet from a bluff overlooking the Hudson River. It was built between 1891 and 1897, utilizing the labor of hundreds of men and over 8,000 tons of granite. Two exterior figures, probably personifying Victory and Peace, support a plaque reading "Let Us Have Peace." The interior is of Carrara and Lee marbles. Allegorical reliefs on the vaulting represent Grant's birth, military life, civilian career and death. The bronze busts in the crypt, sculpted under the Work Projects Administration in 1938, portray some of Grant's best generals—Sherman, Sheridan and MacPherson among them.

The colorful tile-mosaic seating that encircles the tomb is the result of a 1970s community beautification project. The site is administered by the National Park Service.

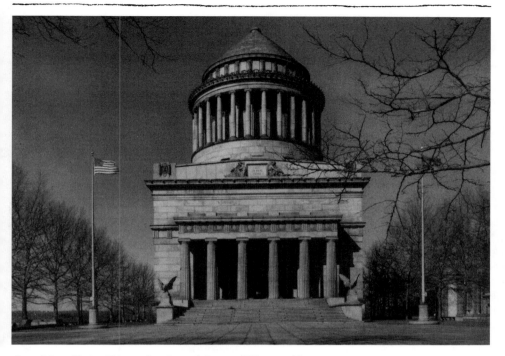

General Grant National Memorial, on Riverside Drive and West 122nd Street.

GENERAL INFORMATION

Hours Wed–Sun 9 am–5 pm; closed Mon, Tues
Admission Free
Giftshop Postcards, books and memorabilia relating to Grant, his presidency and the Civil War
Disability Access Limited access; parking available
Directions Subway: 1/9 to 125th St; Bus: M4, M5, M104 to 122nd St; M100, M101 to Riverside Dr
Landmark Status National Register of Historic Places, New York City Landmark

National Memorial

Goethe House New York—German Cultural Center

1014 Fifth Avenue (at 82nd Street)
New York, NY 10028
212-439-8700

Johann Wolfgang von Goethe, a polymath known primarily for his writings, is one of the greatest artists Germany has ever produced. The facility named after him on upper Fifth Avenue is part of an international network of German cultural centers sponsored by that nation's Foreign Office. Goethe House provides a varied schedule of exhibitions, film screenings, performances, classes and symposiums focusing on German language and culture.

Contemporary German artists are the primary focus of the exhibition program here. The exhibit "Parallax View: New York–Köln," for example, focused on the developing dialogue between artists in two of the art world's epicenters. One of Goethe House's best-known projects is "Berlin Now," a collaborative undertaking of 140 exhibits, theatrical productions, concerts and lectures, and a retrospective of 40 German films dating from 1919 to 1945, that was featured at venues throughout the city.

Goethe House's film series is one of its greatest strengths. A recent sequence of films examined the life and work of German Expressionist artist Max Ernst; another series explored aspects of society and the arts during the period of Nazi rule. Goethe House conferences have included "The Legacy of the STASI Archives in Unified Germany" and "Women and German Unification." Short-term, intensive German-language courses are also offered.

Goethe House was founded in 1957 and became a branch of the multinational Goethe-Institut in 1963. It also hosts the German-American Partnership Program, a student exchange initiative that pairs American and German secondary schools.

GENERAL INFORMATION

Hours Mon–Thurs 9 am–5 pm; Fri 9 am–4 pm; closed Sat, Sun; starting times for films, concerts and conferences vary; call for calendar of events
Admission Free
Library 11,000 volumes; strengths are in classic and contemporary German literature, arts, social sciences, history and geography; open to the public Tues and Thurs 12–7 pm; Wed, Fri, Sat 12–5 pm
Disability Access None
Directions Subway: 4, 5 or 6 to 86th St; Bus: M1, M2, M3, M4 to 82nd St; M79, M86 to 5th Ave
Landmark Status New York City Landmark

The Governor's Room at City Hall

City Hall Park, Second Floor
(between Broadway
and Park Row)
New York, NY 10007

212-788-3081
(Art Commision of the
City of New York)

Once a private office for the governor of New York State during his visits to the city, the Governor's Room at City Hall now serves as a civic museum and stylish reminder of early 19th century elegance.

The Governor's Room was designed by the original architects of City Hall, Joseph F. Mangin and John McComb, and completed in 1816. Today the space contains a permanent exhibition of early American furniture, art and artifacts, including a series of 12 commissioned portraits by John Trumbull, whose subjects included Alexander Hamilton and George Washington.

To reach the Governor's Room—actually a three-room suite—visitors may cross City Hall's rotunda and climb a double-curved stairway, two of the building's outstanding features. Most of the furniture in the Governor's Room was commissioned by the City in 1812. There are also a pair of high-backed settees and a writing table used by George Washington.

Courtesy of the Art Commision of the City of New York

Governor's Room, New York City Hall

GENERAL INFORMATION

Hours Mon–Fri 10 am–12 pm, 1–4 pm; closed Sat, Sun
Admission Free
Giftshop Related titles at City Books, 61 Chambers St; call 212-669-8245 for hours and information
Library Photograph and document archive, open by appointment; call 212-788-3071 (Art Commission of the City of New York)
Disability Access Fully accessible; restrooms available
Directions Subway: 2 or 3 to Park Place; 4, 5 or 6 to Brooklyn Bridge; A, C, E, J, M or Z to Chambers St; N or R to City Hall; Bus: M1, M6, M9, M10, M15, M22, M101, M102, B51 to City Hall
Landmark Status National Register of Historic Places, New York City Landmark

Gracie Mansion

East 88th Street and
East End Avenue
New York, NY 10128

212-570-4751

Before Archibald Gracie built his famous mansion on the tract of land overlooking Hell's Gate (where the East River, Harlem River and Long Island Sound converge), George Washington recognized the site for its strategic military value. Washington had a fort built on the site with a battery of cannon facing the East River. The fort and an adjacent residence were eventually destroyed by British bombardment.

Gracie, who emigrated from Scotland in 1784, established a trading company and became one of the city's richest men, built a handsome frame house on his newly acquired East River property in 1799. The two-story mansion featured wooden trellis roof rails and a porch on three sides. This was the Gracie family's

Holland Wemple

Gracie Mansion, home of the Mayor of New York City, viewed from the East River.

country home; at that time the city was several miles south. He staged elegant parties at the mansion, attended by Alexander Hamilton and James Fenimore Cooper, among others.

Gracie sold the mansion in 1823. In 1896 the city appropriated the property, its 11 acres becoming the nucleus of the new East End Park. In 1920 civic groups, recognizing the site's historic importance, lobbied to have it restored. From 1923 to 1932 it was the home of the Museum of the City of New York (see separate entry). In 1942 Parks Commissioner Robert Moses convinced city authorities to make it the mayor's official residence. Fiorello H. La Guardia became the first mayoral resident.

As the need for space grew, architect Mott B. Schmidt was retained to design an addition, which he created to reflect the character of the original Federal-period mansion. The Gracie Mansion Conservancy was established in 1981. Under its direction, a team of architects, engineers, curators and designers planned and carried out a thorough restoration.

GENERAL INFORMATION

Hours Open by appointment only; 50-minute guided tours on Wed at 10 am, 11 am, 1 pm, 2 pm; school tours given on Thurs
Admission Adults $3, seniors $2, children free
Giftshop Gracie Mansion mugs, bags, address books, etc.
Disability Access Fully accessible
Directions Subway: 4, 5 or 6 to 86th St; Bus: M1, M2, M3, M4, M15, M31 to 86th St; M86 to York Ave
Landmark Status National Register of Historic Places, New York City Landmark

Grand Central Art Galleries

24 West 57th Street, Seventh Floor
(between Fifth and Sixth Avenues)
New York, NY 10019
212-867-3344

The Grand Central Art Galleries were founded as a means of changing the perception, prevalent during the early 20th century, that American artists were lesser talents than their European counterparts. In 1923 the galleries opened on the top floor of the Grand Central Station to exhibit and promote the work of American artists. John Singer Sargent, one of the earliest artists involved, donated three paintings to raise "seed money" for the fledgling outfit. Works by many well-known figures in American art and design have been featured, such as John Sloan; Louis Comfort Tiffany; Gutzon Borglum, sculptor of Mount Rushmore; and Daniel Chester French, creator of the Lincoln Memorial.

Today the galleries still present an ambitious exhibition program, mounting 16 shows a year. Group shows and exhibits of the work of solo artists are regularly held. In 1959 Grand Central Art Galleries moved to the Biltmore Hotel. Upon the hotel's demolition in 1981, they moved to the 57th street location.

GENERAL INFORMATION

Hours Wed–Fri 10 am–5:30 pm; Sat 10 am–4 pm; July and Aug, closed Sat
Admission Free
Giftshop Books on art education and exhibiting artists
Library Archives and literary collection available to art students and scholars
Disability Access Fully accessible; elevator available
Directions Subway: E or F to 5th Ave and 53rd St; N or R to 57th St and 7th Ave; Bus: M1, M2, M3, M4, M5 to 57th St; M57, M58 to 5th Ave

Greenwich House Pottery

16 Jones Street (between West 4th and Bleecker Streets)
New York, NY 10014
212-242-4106

Greenwich House Pottery is one of the city's leading ceramic arts center. In addition to exhibitions it offers ceramic instruction for all ages as well as workshops and lectures.

The Jane Hartsook Gallery mounts a different show each month featuring work by established ceramic artists as well as students. Exhibitions have included "The Illusion of Space–Tableware," "Artists On Their Own–2nd Annual Juried Exhibition" and "Majolica–An Invitational." A second space, the Office Gallery, features student work in monthly shows.

Greenwich House Pottery offers classes for beginners and advanced students in studios that are equipped for all aspects of pottery making. Greenwich House Pottery was established in 1909 as a part of Greenwich House , a human services agency founded in 1902 to serve Lower Manhattan residents.

GENERAL INFORMATION

Hours Tues–Sat 1–5 pm; closed Sun, Mon
Admission Free
Library Book and slide library, and permanent collection of historic ceramic art, open to members
Disability Access None
Directions Subway: A, B, C, D, E, F or Q to West 4th St; 1/9 to Christopher St; Bus: M10 to West 4th St
Landmark Status National Register of Historic Places

The Grolier Club

47 East 60th Street (between Madison and Park Avenues)
New York, NY 10022
212-838-6690

Named after leading Renaissance bibliophile Jean Grolier, the Grolier Club is an organization for book collectors. Although the club is private, the public is invited to regular exhibitions of rare books, manuscripts, prints and memorabilia. Subjects explored in these exhibits have included the Gothic novel, natural history, the art of illustration, murder mysteries, Japanese prints and famous authors, such as John Donne and Edith Wharton, on their significant anniversaries.

Since it was founded in 1884, the club has published over 145 volumes on the arts of papermaking, design, illustration, printing and bookbinding. The club's Georgian-style building, erected in 1917, was renovated in 1984, enlarging the main exhibition hall and adding an environmentally controlled storage facility for books.

GENERAL INFORMATION

Hours Mon–Sat 10 am–5 pm; closed Sun; closed Aug
Admission Free
Library 90,000 volumes on the history and art of books, open to scholars and bibliophiles by appointment
Disability Access Fully accessible; restrooms available
Directions Subway: N or R to 5th Ave; 4, 5, 6 to 59th St; Bus: M1, M2, M3, M4 to 60th St

Solomon R. Guggenheim Museum

1071 Fifth Avenue (at 88th Street)
New York, NY 10128
212-423-3500

The Solomon R. Guggenheim Museum acquires and exhibits modern and contemporary painting and sculpture in one of the most famous museum buildings in the world. It reopened in 1992 after a two-year

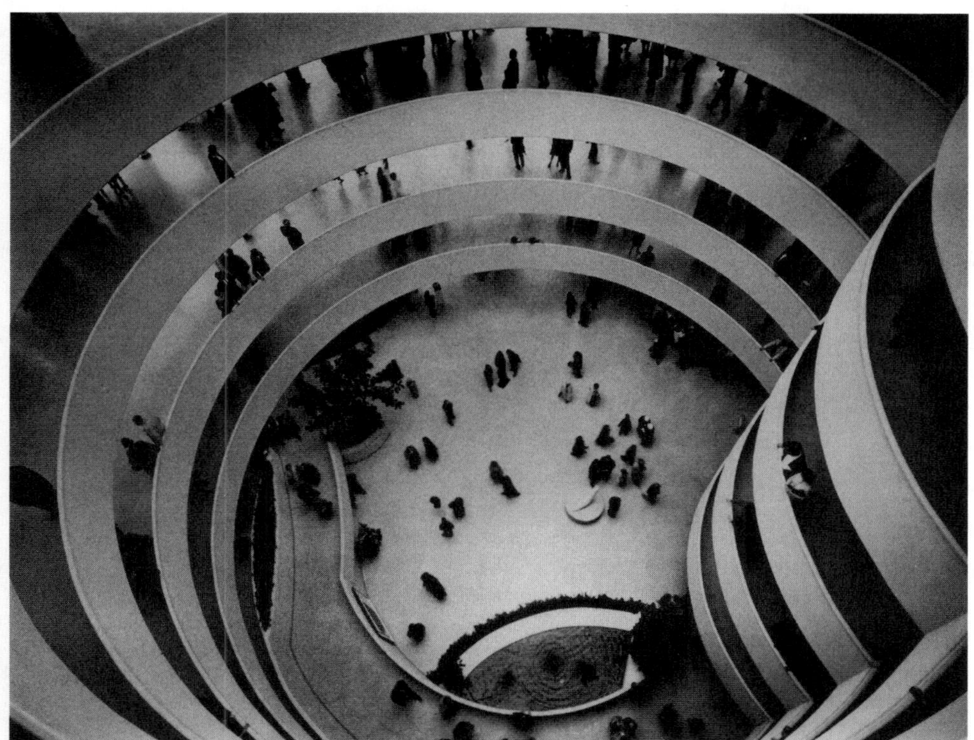

Spiral rotunda of Frank Lloyd Wright's Guggenheim Museum.

expansion and renovation. In addition to a thorough refurbishment of Frank Lloyd Wright's masterpiece—inspired by the spiral structure of the chambered nautilus—the museum added a 10-story tower, designed by Gwathmey Siegel & Associates. Offices have been moved to a newly constructed subterranean "vault," so the entire Wright building is fully accessible to the public for the first time.

The new tower provides 31,000 square feet of exhibition, public and administrative space. It contains four floors of galleries, most with double-height ceilings for showing large works. A fifth-floor sculpture terrace offers dazzling views of Central Park and the city. The expanded Wright building, the tower galleries and the new Guggenheim Museum SoHo branch (see separate entry) allow more works to be shown from the museum's extensive permanent collection than ever before.

The Guggenheim has one of the largest collections of Wassily Kandinsky's paintings in the world. Paul Klee, Franz Marc, Robert Delaunay, Marc Chagall and Fernand Léger are among the other modern masters featured in its collection. The Justin K. Thannhauser Foundation Collection of Modern Art is particularly strong in Impressionist and Post-Impressionist works. An ongoing series of exhibitions draws on the permanent collection of over 6,000 works and loans from other institutions. Lectures, concerts, dance performances and poetry readings are also offered.

Solomon R. Guggenheim, the fourth of seven brothers, was from an old New York family with a financial empire based in mining. In the 1920s he began collecting the work of avant-garde artists. As the fame of his collection grew, he opened his apartment to the art world and began to lend works for exhibition. In 1937 the Guggenheim Foundation was created, opening two years later as the Guggenheim Collection of Non-Objective Paintings. In 1943 Wright was commissioned as the architect for a new museum. However, due to the museum's controversial design—and New York's conservative building codes—it would be 16 years before it would open.

GENERAL INFORMATION

Hours Fri–Wed 10 am–8 pm; closed Thurs
Admission Adults $7, students and seniors $4, children under 12 free; Tues 5–8 pm voluntary contribution; dual-admission pass to both Solomon R. Guggenheim Museum and Guggenheim Museum SoHo, adults $10, students and seniors $6

Robert E. Mates

"The Zouave," a drawing by Vincent van Gogh, 1888, from the collection of the Guggenheim Museum.

Giftshop Exhibition catalogs, art books, prints, posters and cards; open Fri–Wed 10 am–8 pm, Thurs 11 am–6 pm
Food Service Cafe open Fri–Wed 8 am–9 pm, Thurs 8 am–3 pm
Library Open by appointment
Disability Access Fully accessible; TDD 212-423-3607
Directions Subway: 4, 5 or 6 to 86th St; Bus: M1, M2, M3, M4 to 88th St
Landmark Status New York City Landmark

Guggenheim Museum SoHo

575 Broadway (at Prince Street) 212-423-3500
New York, NY 10012

The Solomon R. Guggenheim Museum (see previous entry) opened this branch in 1992 as part of a strategy to make more of its extraordinary permanent collection accessible to the public. Like its Upper East Side parent, it is dedicated to the presentation of contemporary and modern painting and sculpture. The new branch adds 30,000 square feet of exhibition space to the museum. Thus far exhibitions have included "Robert Rauschenberg: The Early 1950s," "Photography in Contemporary German Art" and "Chagall's Jewish Theater Murals."

The Guggenheim Museum SoHo is located in a former commercial-loft building in SoHo's landmark Cast-Iron Historic District. Construction on the building was begun in 1881, for John Jacob Astor III, on the site of his family's original estate office. Interiors of the new branch were designed by Pritzker Prize–winning architect Arata Isozaki. The Guggenheim Museum SoHo is located on the same block as the New Museum of Contemporary Art and the Museum for African Art (see separate entries).

GENERAL INFORMATION

Hours Sun, Mon, Wed 11 am–6 pm; Thurs–Sat 11 am–8 pm; closed Tues
Admission Adults $5, seniors and students $3, children under 12 free; dual-admission pass to both Solomon R. Guggenheim Museum and Guggenheim Museum SoHo, adults $10, students and seniors $6
Giftshop Exhibition catalogs, art books, jewelry, gifts, posters; open Sun–Wed 11 am–6pm, Thurs–Sat 11 am–10 pm
Disability Access Fully accessible; TDD 212-423-3607
Directions Subway: 6 to Spring St; N or R to Prince St; Bus: M1, M5, M6 to Prince St
Landmark Status National Register of Historic Places, New York City Landmark

Guinness World of Records Exhibition

Empire State Building 212-947-2335
Concourse Level
350 Fifth Avenue (at 34th Street)
New York, NY 10118

You've read the book—now see the exhibition. Housed in the Empire State Building, this exhibition complements the bestselling "Guiness Book of World Records," which catalogs numerous record-breaking achievements. With its giant video screens, realistic replicas and collection of original record-breaking objects, the exhibition is a fascinating compilation of bizarre but true facts and events that must be seen to be believed. Visitors can compare their height to a life-size statue of 8'11" Robert Wadlow, the world's tallest man. Other displays reveal the world's most expensive shoes, the biggest Raggedy Ann doll, the smallest insect, the smallest bicycle and other interesting arcana.

GENERAL INFORMATION

Hours 9 am–8 pm daily; spring and summer open until 10 pm
Admission Adults $7, students and seniors $6, children under 12, $3.50
Giftshop Guinness books and coins, other items with logo
Disability Access Fully accessible; elevator available
Directions Subway: A, C, E, 1, 9, 2 or 3 to 34th St–Penn Station; Bus: M1, M2, M3, M4, M5 to 34th St; M16, M34 to 5th Ave
Landmark Status National Register of Historic Places, New York City Landmark

Henry Street Settlement

Louis Abrons Arts Center 212-598-0400
466 Grand Street (between
Pitt Street and Bialystoker Place)
New York, NY 10002

Henry Street Settlement was founded in 1893 to provide health and human services to immigrant populations on Manhattan's Lower East Side. Similarly, its arts program was started to cultivate the esthetic sensibilities of disadvantaged persons and thereby improve their lives. Today, in addition to individual and family counseling services, Henry Street Settlement offers performances, exhibitions and arts classes to a diverse, underprivileged community.

The Louis Abrons Arts Center, which opened in 1975 at 466 Grand Street, was designed to serve a diverse lower-income population. It presents exhibitions in all media by artists-in-residence, faculty and local artists. Shows have included photographs of the Lower East Side from the 1940s and '50s; "On the Way Home," works by homeless women in collaboration with their artist instructors; and "Voices of Henry Street," photographic portraits of people helped by the organization over the past 75 years. Theater performances have included a selection of new works by young playwrights and readings of stories set on the Lower East Side.

Professional artists, students, children and adults converge at the center for instruction in the arts. Current instructional offerings include instrumental music, modern dance, creative writing and cartooning. Henry Street Settlement also offers the Arts for Family Series and the Family Literacy Program and sponsors various ethnic arts festivals.

GENERAL INFORMATION

Hours 12–6 pm daily
Admission Gallery free; performances $3.50–$10
Disability Access Fully accessible
Directions Subway: F to East Broadway or Delancey St; B, D or Q to Grand St; J or M to Essex St; Bus: M9, M14, M15 to Grand St; M22 to Montgomery St
Landmark Status National Register of Historic Places

The Hispanic Society of America

Audubon Terrace 212-926-2234
613 West 155 Street (at Broadway)
New York, NY 10032

The Hispanic Society of America was founded in 1904 to establish a free museum and research library representing the culture of Spain and the peoples it has influenced.

The society's holdings range from prehistoric art to 19th- and 20th-century paintings. Exhibitions have concentrated on the work of individual artists, illustrated manuscripts, Spanish interiors and laces, and other subjects. The two-story terra cotta main court is lined with paintings by Goya, Velázquez, Morales and others, and archways frame 15th- and 16th-century tomb

Courtesy of the Hispanic Society of America

Upper and lower galleries of the Main Court at the Hispanic Society of America.

sculpture and Roman mosaics. There are also wood carvings, ivories, examples of hand-crafted gold and silver, as well as contemporary works.

The library contains over 200,000 books relating to the art, history and society of Spain, Portugal and colonial Hispanic America including more than 16,000 books that were printed before 1701. The library also holds valuable rare maps, globes, prints, Bibles, historical chronicles, and books on chivalry and incunabula.

The Hispanic Society's collections were started in 1892, when the institution's founder, Archer Milton Huntington, made his first trip to the Iberian Peninsula. It is located in an attractive neoclassical building on Audubon Terrace, the former estate of American artist John James Audubon. Audubon Terrace is also the site of the American Academy of Arts and Letters, the American Numismatic Society (see separate entries) and Boricua College.

GENERAL INFORMATION

Hours Tues–Sat 10 am–4:30 pm; Sun 1–4 pm; closed Mon
Admission Free
Giftshop Publications relating to the collections and prints, slides, posters, etc.
Library See description above; open Tues–Fri 1–4:15 pm, Sat 10 am–4:15 pm, closed Aug
Disability Access None
Directions Subway: 1 to 157th St; Bus: M4, M5 to 155th St
Landmark Status National Register of Historic Places, New York City Landmark

The Horticultural Society of New York

128 West 58th Street 212-757-0915
(between Sixth and
Seventh Avenues)
New York, NY 10019

Since 1900 the Horticultural Society of New York has been furthering knowledge about the world of plants. Its best-known event is the New York Flower Show, mounted each spring at Pier 92 on the Hudson River, featuring the work of hundreds of landscape and horticultural artists. Regular art exhibits at the society's gallery focus on botanical subjects. Shows have emphasized Japanese embroidery, botanical illustration, and watercolors from the society's workshops. The Horticultural Society is an important informational resource as well, with a large library (see below). It also offers courses and tours of local gardens.

GENERAL INFORMATION

Hours Mon–Fri 10 am–6 pm; closed Sat, Sun
Admission Free, except for select events
Giftshop Retail greenhouse shop
Library 15,000 volumes, extensive clipping file, slides, photographs, seed and nursery catalogs, etc.; open to the public
Disability Access Broad access, except for 2nd-floor classrooms; Pier 92 Flower Show fully accessible
Directions Subway: 1/9, A, B, C or D to 59th St–Columbus Circle N, R to 57th St; B, Q to 57th St Bus: M57, M58 to 6th Ave; M5, M6 to 57th St

IBM Gallery of Science and Art

590 Madison Avenue (at 57th Street) New York, NY 10022 — 212-745-6100

The IBM Gallery fills a gap by presenting engaging science and art exhibitions that do not find a slot in the schedules of the city's museums. Its installation quality is equal to that of the best museums.

Art exhibitions have showcased works of the Northwest Coast tribes, prints of Japanese woodblock master Ando Hiroshige, examples of contemporary Swedish design, and Impressionist and Post-Impressionist paintings. Other exhibits include "Post-Modern Visions: Contemporary Architecture 1960–1985," "Corot to Monet: The Rise of Landscape Painting in France" and "Picturing History: American Painting, 1770–1930."

Scientific exhibitions have explored the nature of light and vision, space photography, microscopy, the contributions to physics by Sir Isaac Newton, artists' use of computers and the history of information technology.

The gallery opened in 1983 at the same time as the structure in which it is housed—the 42-story polished granite and glass IBM building. Designed by American architect Edward Larrabee Barnes, the structure has one corner that is cantilevered over the sidewalk at 57th and Madison, seeming to defy natural forces. The glass atrium on the ground floor provides an ideal spot for a brief respite.

GENERAL INFORMATION

Hours Tues–Sat 11 am–6 pm; closed Sun, Mon
Admission Free
Disability Access Fully accessible
Directions Subway: 4, 5 or 6 to 59th St, then walk west to Madison Ave; 1/9, 2 or 3 to 59th St, then walk east to Madison Ave; Bus: M1, M2, M3, M4 to 57th St; M57, M58 to Madison Ave

INTAR Hispanic American Arts Center

420 West 42nd Street (between Ninth and Tenth Avenues) New York, NY 10036 — 212-695-6551

INTAR (International Arts Relations) Hispanic American Arts Center was founded in 1966 in response to the dearth of opportunities for Hispanic-American theater and visual artists. Today it is an arts center providing residencies to playwrights, staging theatrical productions and mounting exhibits in its Latin American Gallery. In 1977 INTAR became the only Latino company to join the newly developed Theatre Row complex, where it has shifted to a program of both Spanish and English-language productions.

The theater program supports the creation and development of plays, musicals and opera, children's theater and performance art pieces. Productions have included "Daedalus in the Belly of the Beast," by Chilean play-

Actors performing 'Divinas Palabras,' by Ramon del Valle-Inclan, at INTAR.

wright Marco Antonio de la Parra; "Culture Clash Unplugged," by a Chicano-Latino comedy troupe from Los Angeles; "El Greco: the Opera"; and "The Popol Vuh Project," a multimedia operatic work based on the Mayan creation myth.

The Latin American Gallery features exhibitions by emerging and established Hispanic, Asian-American, African-American and Native American artists. Exhibitions have included "Self-Portraits: Twelve Puerto Rican Visual Artists"; Josely Carvalho's "Diary of Images: Cirandas," a multimedia installation of silkscreens, photographs and texts about children and violence; and "Martí-Martyr: A Discovery of José Martí," a multimedia show by Arturo Cuenca. The gallery also installs site-specific works and provides various artist services and youth education programs.

GENERAL INFORMATION

Hours Mon–Fri 12–6 pm; closed Sat, Sun
Admission Gallery, readings, workshops free; performances \$5–\$30
Disability Access Theater has limited access; gallery has none
Directions Subway: A, C, E, N, R, 1/9, 2, 3, 7 or S to 42nd St–Times Sq; Bus: M10, M11 to 42nd St; M16, M42 to 9th Ave

International Center of Photography

1130 Fifth Avenue (at 94th Street) New York, NY 10128 — 212-860-1777

Midtown Gallery
1133 Avenue of the Americas (Sixth Avenue at 43rd Street) New York, NY 10036 — 212-768-4682

The International Center of Photography is New York's predominant exhibiting and educational institution in the photographic arts. It operates uptown and midtown exhibition spaces. Each venue has large galleries for temporary exhibitions, smaller galleries for displaying works from the permanent collection and a screening room for video and exhibition-related films.

The International Center of Photography mounts 15 to 20 exhibits a year, each on view for about two months, which reflect the history of the medium and the broad spectrum of photography's expressive style. Exhibits examine photography of every kind, ranging from documentary and photojournalism to fine art, video and digital imaging. Exhibitions have included "A Moment

Robert Capa

"Barcelona, 1936" by Robert Capa, from the permanent collection of the International Center of Photography.

Before: Jews in the Soviet Union," by Frederick Brenner; "Karsh: American Legends," a selection of the photographer's portraits; and "Motion and Document—Sequence and Time: Eadweard Muybridge and Contemporary American Photography."

The permanent collection contains over 12,000 original photographic prints representing some 600 photographers. Major permanent holdings include the Robert Capa Archive and the Roman Vishniac Archive, and large holdings by Wegee (Arthur Fellig), Diane Arbus, Lewis Hine, Berenice Abbott and Henri Cartier-Bresson.

The main Fifth Avenue location houses darkroom facilities and offers an impressive educational program addressing every aspect of photography. ICP evolved out of the International Fund for Concerned Photography, founded in 1966 by Life magazine photographer Cornell Capa. Its Fifth Avenue headquarters, an elegant neo-Georgian house that was the former home of the National Audubon Society, was built in 1915 by Delano & Aldrich for the founder of The New Republic, Willard Straight.

GENERAL INFORMATION

Hours Tues 11 am–8 pm; Wed–Sun 11 am–6 pm; closed Mon
Admission Adults $4, seniors and students $2.50; Tues 5–8 pm voluntary contribution
Giftshops More than 1,000 titles on photojournalism, photo theory, practice and esthetics; also exhibition catalogs, prints, T-shirts, postcards, etc.
Library ICP Resource Library has books and periodicals on photography and related fields; biographical files on over 8,000 photographers and 3,000 slides; open Tues–Fri 11 am–5 pm (5th Ave only)
Disability Access ***Uptown-*** limited, call to arrange access; ***Midtown-*** fully accessible
Directions ***Uptown-*** Subway: 4, 5 or 6 to 96th St; Bus: M1, M2, M3, M4 to 94th St; M19 to 5th Ave
Midtown- Subway: B, D, F or Q to 42nd St; 1/9, 2, 3, N, R or 7 to 42nd St–Times Sq; Bus: M1, M2, M3, M4, M5, M6, M7 to 42nd St; M42, M104 to 6th Ave
Landmark Status ***Uptown-*** National Register of Historic Places, New York City Landmark

Intrepid Sea Air Space Museum

Hudson River at
46th Street and Twelfth Avenue
New York, NY 10036

212-245-0072

The aircraft carrier USS *Intrepid* is an historic, battle-scarred veteran of 37 years of naval service. During World War II, the *Intrepid* and her air wing fought many campaigns in the Pacific Ocean, sinking 200 enemy ships and destroying over 600 planes. During these engagements the ship suffered seven bomb hits, five *kamikaze* attacks and one torpedo strike. In 1960 the ship was twice the primary recovery vessel for manned space flights. The *Intrepid* also served during the Vietnam conflict.

Shipboard exhibition spaces include Navy Hall, simulating the sights and sounds of today's navy, and the Carrier Operations Theater, which visually recounts the ship's World War II service. Visitors can tour vital operational spaces, including the Combat Information Center and Traffic Control. The *Intrepid* also presents short-term exhibits on undersea exploration, satellite communication, ship and aircraft design, and other landmarks of American military and technological achievement.

An F-6 Hellcat on the USS Intrepid's hangar deck.

On the flightdeck are 40 aircraft, including a Lockheed A-12 Blackbird. Built for CIA surveillance missions, this jet is capable of speeds up to Mach 3.6 and altitudes of 90,000 feet. The *Intrepid* is today the center of a virtual flotilla. Docked nearby and open for public inspection are the missle submarine USS *Growler* and a destroyer, the USS *Edson*.

Construction of the *Intrepid* began six days before the Japanese attacked Pearl Harbor and was completed in 18 months. The carrier opened to the public at its current location in 1982.

GENERAL INFORMATION

Hours Summer (Memorial Day–Labor Day): 10 am–5 pm daily; Winter: Wed–Sun 10 am–5 pm, closed Mon, Tues; last admission at all times: 4 pm
Admission Adults $7; seniors and veterans $6, children under 12, $4, under 6 free; active Armed Forces free; ticket booth closes 4 pm
Giftshop Books on navy, maritime, aviation and armed forces; ship models and souvenirs
Food Service Portside Grill Cafe during summer
Library Research library and photo archive, open by appointment
Disability Access Limited access; parking available
Directions Subway: A, C, E, 1, 2, 3, N, R, S or 7 to 42nd St–Times Sq; Bus: M42, M50 to West Side Highway
Landmark Status National Register of Historic Places

Irish Arts Center

553 West 51st Street
(at Eleventh Avenue)
New York, NY 10019
212-757-3318

For over 20 years, the Irish Arts Center has been the home of Irish culture in the New York region. Its gallery mounts periodic exhibitions of painting and photography by contemporary Irish and Irish-American artists. The education program offers, on a trimester basis, classes in acting, dancing, filmmaking, music, creative writing, Gaelic language and Celtic history. The 73-seat theater features three dramatic productions a year, as well as film screenings, lectures and poetry readings. The center also sponsors a traditional Irish music festival every year at an outdoor site. Members keep apprised of the center's diverse activities, and other events in the region related to Irish culture, through its quarterly publication, Irish Arts.

GENERAL INFORMATION

Hours Mon–Fri 12–6 pm; closed Sat, Sun
Admission Free
Disability Access Limited access
Directions Subway: 1/9, C or E to 50th St; Bus: M50 to 11th Ave; M11 to 50th St

Elsa Mott Ives Gallery

YWCA
610 Lexington Avenue
(at 53rd Street)
New York, NY 10022
212-755-4500

The Elsa Mott Ives Gallery shows the work of emerging and nationally known artists working in a variety of media. Exhibitions are usually in the form of group shows, some focusing on social themes. Such exhibits have included "Transcending Boundaries," an investigation of the divisions between craft and art; "Contemporary Woodturning," which explored the physical and esthetic aspects of the turned object; and "Sculpture in the Sky," for which six urban sculptors, granted the freedom of ample space on the Y's midtown rooftop, created works in steel, aluminum, wood and ceramic. There are also periodic faculty and student shows highlighting work of the Y's Craft Students League. A series of panels and workshops coincide with the exhibitions and further explore subjects, ideas and media presented in the gallery. One unexpected treat is the gallery's original Tiffany window.

GENERAL INFORMATION

Hours Mon–Fri 11 am–7 pm; Sat 11 am–3 pm; closed Sun
Admission Free
Disability Access Fully accessible
Directions Subway: E or F to Lexington Ave; 6 to 51st St; Bus: M101, M102 to 53rd St and Lexington Ave

Japan Society

Japan House 212-832-1155
333 East 47th Street
(between First and Second Avenues)
New York, NY 10017

The Japan Society is dedicated to fostering cross-cultural understanding between Japan and the United States through exhibitions, dance performances, theater and music recitals, film series and educational programs.

The society's gallery is a showcase for traditional and contemporary Japanese arts: painting, sculpture, architecture, photography, calligraphy, ceramics, printmaking and lacquerware. Exhibits have focused on Shinto art, 16th- to 19th-century textiles, *ukiyo-e* prints and paintings, objects from *Horyu-ji* (one of Japan's most important temples) and the work of well-known and rising contemporary artists.

Traditional and modern Japanese performing arts, from the ancient arts of *Noh* and *Kabuki* to the most contemporary dance groups, are presented in the Lila Acheson Wallace Auditorium. The C.V. Starr Library includes a fine collection of English-language books on Japanese history and culture. The langua
tion in both Japanese and Engl
presents Japanese film in all its
classic work of such masters a
the experimental work of a new

Designed by Tokyo architects
and George Shimamoto, Japan
American materials and Japane

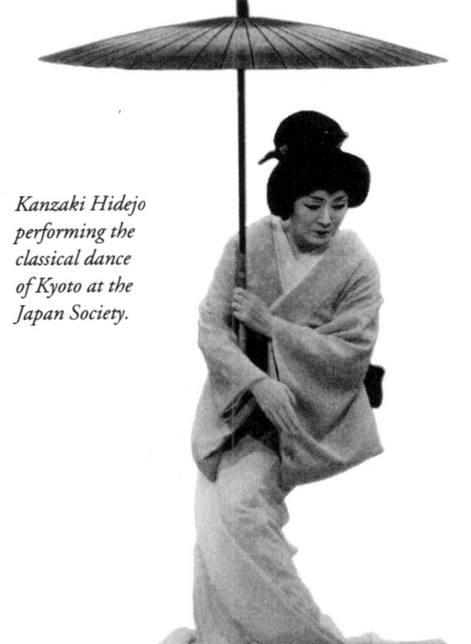

Kanzaki Hidejo performing the classical dance of Kyoto at the Japan Society.

GENERAL INFORMATION

Hours Gallery: Tues–Sun 11 am–5 pm; closed Mon
Admission Suggested contribution: $2.50
Giftshop Catalogs and books on Japan
Library C.V. Starr Library: large number of English-language titles on Japanese history, culture, politics, arts, economics and religion
Disability Access Fully accessible
Directions Subway: 6 to 51st St; E or F to Lexington Ave and 53rd St; Bus: M15 to 47th St; M101, M102 to 47th St; M27, M50 to 1st Ave

The Jewish Museum

1109 Fifth Avenue at 92nd Street 212-423-3200
New York, NY 10128

The Jewish Museum is one of the world's largest and most important institutions devoted solely to exploring the scope and diversity of Jewish culture. It was founded in 1904 in the library of the Jewish Theological Seminary, where it was housed for decades. In 1944 Frieda Schiff Warburg donated her family's Fifth Avenue mansion to the seminary. This elegant structure has been the home of the Jewish Museum since 1947.

Early exhibitions at the Fifth Avenue location featured avant-garde art, but in the 1970s the museum broadened its focus to encompass all of Jewish culture, including the development of an ancient Israelite archaeology collection and exhibition, and an education department. Exhibitions have included "Gardens and Ghettos: The Art of Jewish Life in Italy," "Painting a Place in America: Jewish Artists in New York, 1900–1945," "A Tribute to the Educational Alliance Art School" (see separate entry) and "Bridges and Boundaries: African-Americans and American Jews."

In 1993 the museum completed a $36 million renovation and expansion. The centerpiece of the expansion is a two-floor permanent exhibition exploring Jewish identity over 4,000 years. The show—Culture and Continuity: The Jewish Journey—showcases a significant portion of the museum's permanent collection of 27,000 objects. This collection, considered among the

...nt in the world, includes fine art, ethno... ...aterial, archaeological artifacts and ...onial objects. Because of its encyclopedic ...adth, the permanent exhibit provides a frame of ...eference for subjects explored in the temporary shows.

In addition to doubling the museum's exhibition space, the expansion features a 232-seat auditorium, a conservation laboratory, a cafe, two museum shops and an education center with classrooms, a children's gallery and a conference room. The education department presents a diverse array of programs for individuals, groups, families and schools.

The original Warburg mansion was designed by architect Charles Gilbert and completed in 1908. The renovation and expansion, designed by Kevin Roche John Dinkeloo and Associates, is unusual in that it extends the original limestone facade of the mansion to the entire building, giving the appearance of a late French Gothic chateau. The structure is one of Fifth Avenue's architectural high points.

"The Dancer," a sculpture in cherry wood by Elie Nadelman, 1918-19, from the Jewish Museum's permanent collection.

The Jewish Museum, New York
under the auspices of The Jewish Theological Seminary of America

GENERAL INFORMATION

Hours Sun, Mon, Wed, Thurs 11 am–5:45 pm; Tues 11 am–8 pm; closed Fri, Sat
Admission Adults $6, seniors and students $4, children under 12 free; Tues 5–8 pm, free
Giftshop Books, catalogs, audio and video tapes, children's items; open museum hours plus Fri 11 am–3 pm; design shop at 1 East 92nd Street
Food Service Cafe Weissman serves cafeteria fare
Disability Access Fully accessible; ramp at main entrance
Directions Subway: 4, 5 or 6 to 86th St; Bus: M1, M2, M3, M4 to 92nd St; M86 to 5th Ave
Landmark Status National Register of Historic Places, New York City Landmark

The Joseph Gallery

Hebrew Union College–
Jewish Institute of Religion
Brookdale Center
One West 4th Street (between
Broadway and Mercer Street)
New York, NY 10012

212-674-5300
Ext. 205

The five or six exhibitions mounted at the Joseph Gallery every year explore Jewish history and culture. Exhibits have included the work of painters addressing themes of the Holocaust and the Spanish Inquisition, photographic documentaries on the Jews of Greece and Ethiopia as well as African-American and Jewish relations today, ancient maps of Jerusalem and contemporary ritual objects. There have also been exhibits about the preservation of Jewish monuments around the world, the Moroccan Jewish community and the celebration of Passover through contemporary crafts.

Hebrew Union College, founded in 1875 in Cincinnati, Ohio, was the first Jewish institution of higher learning in America. Its Jewish Institute of Religion was established in New York in 1922. It also operates campuses in Cincinnati, Los Angeles and Jerusalem.

GENERAL INFORMATION

Hours Mon–Thurs 9 am–5 pm; closed Fri–Sun
Admission Free
Disability Access Fully accessible
Directions Subway: 6 to Astor Place; N or R to 8th St; A, B, C, D, E, F or Q to West 4th St; Bus: M1, M2, M3, M4, M5 to 8th St; M10 to 4th St
Landmark Status New York City Landmark

Michael O'Neill

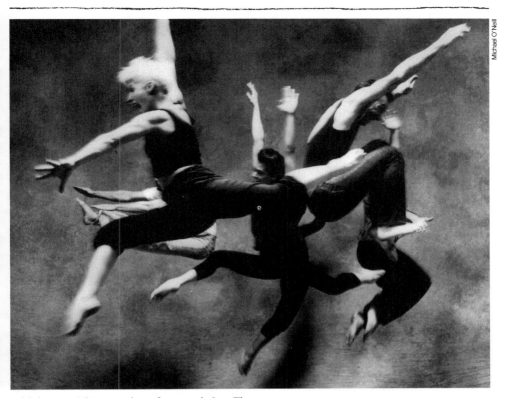

Pilobolus Dance Theatre, regular performers at the Joyce Theater.

The Joyce Theater

175 Eighth Avenue
(at 19th Street)
New York, NY 10011

212-242-0800
JoyceCharge

Eliot Feld, director of the Feld Ballet, conceived of the Joyce Theater in the late 1970s. At that time, the only workable New York venues for dance were either high-rent, full-size theatrical venues or awkwardly configured downtown lofts. The old Elgin Theater, a former Eighth Avenue art-film house, offered a unique compromise between these two extremes. The facility was purchased, given a $3.5 million renovation and opened as the Joyce Theater in 1982. Since then it has emerged as one of the nation's foremost venues for dance.

One typical Joyce season might feature 25 modern, ballet and ethnic dance troupes presenting dozens of premieres in addition to repertory works. Companies appearing since the theater's opening include the Erick Hawkins Dance Company; Japan's Takarazuka Dance Company; the Florence Dance Theatre, a contemporary Italian ballet company; Montreal's Desrosiers Dance Theatre; Minneapolis' Zorongo Flamenco Dance Theatre; the American Indian Dance Theater; Ballet Hispanico; Lucinda Childs Dance Company; Classical Dance Company of Cambodia; and the companies of Merce Cunningham and Laura Dean.

The Joyce also presents some of the country's top theater companies. Productions have included the Mark Taper Forum's "In the Belly of the Beast," based on the book by convicted murderer Jack Henry Abbott; the State Theater of Lithuania's production of "Uncle Vanya," by Anton Chekhov; and the legendary Living Theater production of "Antigone" by Samuel Beckett.

The Art Moderne building was originally constructed in 1942 after a design by Simon Zelnik. The early 1980s renovation was designed by Hardy Holzman Pfeiffer Associates. Audiences have widely praised the new 472-seat theater for its intimate and comfortable spaces. The Joyce education program serves some 5,000 city school children a year with free performances by some of the nation's finest dance companies.

Molissa Fenley in "State of Darkness" at the Joyce Theater.

GENERAL INFORMATION

Hours Box office open 2–6 pm daily
Admission Ticket prices vary; members get 40 percent discount; groups of 20 or more, 20 percent discount; students and seniors get disounts within one hour of curtain time
Food Service Bar in lobby, lower level
Disability Access Fully accessible, but seating arrangements should be made in advance
Directions Subway: A, C or E to 14th St; 1/9 to 18th St; Bus: M10, M11 to 18th St; M14 to 8th Ave

Kampo Cultural and Multi-Media Center

31 Bond Street (between Lafayette Street and Bowery)
New York, NY 10012
212-228-3063

Plays, exhibitions, and classes in dance, shamanism, Japanese language and calligraphy: the Kampo Cultural and Multi-Media Center is involved in all of these activities as a means of promoting cross-cultural awareness. Exhibitions of sculpture, painting and other media are mounted for periods of one to several weeks. Classes are offered in aikido, a martial art; Hatha Yoga; *Sumi-e* brush painting; Haitian dance and song; and Ayurvedic healing (traditional Indian medicine). In addition, Kampo leases a small, top-quality video sound stage and control room to professionals in the film and music business as well as independent creative artists. Kampo Harada—master Japanese calligrapher, collector and promoter of cultural exchange—established Kampo in New York City in the 1970s. Renovated in 1986, the center is located in Manhattan's NoHo (north of Houston Street) neighborhood.

GENERAL INFORMATION

Hours Office: Mon–Fri 10 am–6pm; closed Sat, Sun
Admission Gallery is free; performances and workshops $10–$15
Disability Access Fully accessible; elevator available
Directions Subway: B, D, F or Q to Broadway–Lafayette St; 6 to Bleecker St; Bus: M1, M5, M6 to Bleecker St

Sylvia and Danny Kaye Playhouse

Hunter College of the City University of New York
695 Park Avenue (at 68th Street)
New York, NY 10021
212-772-4448 Box Office

Thanks to funds from the Sylvia and Danny Kaye Foundation, the former Hunter College Playhouse underwent an extensive $5.2 million renovation in the early 1990s. This revitalization and the diverse new performance schedule have reestablished the theater as one of the city's premier performing arts venues.

The 664-seat auditorium features top artists in international dance, music, theater and opera. The Manhattan Theatre Club also stages various dramatic works. Emerging performers are featured in two free programs: the "New Soloists Six O'Clock Series" and the "Young Performers Series," co-produced with the Chamber Music Society of Lincoln Center.

The newly renovated Sylvia and Danny Kaye Playhouse marks the revitalization of a long history of performing arts events at Hunter College. Hunter is where Martha Graham presented new works, Jonathan Miller directed his celebrated "Hamlet" and Daniel Barenboim and Pinchas Zukerman made their New York recital debuts.

GENERAL INFORMATION

Hours Box office open Mon–Sat 12–6 pm
Admission Price varies, generally $15–$35
Food Service Concessions at performances
Disability Access Fully accessible; restrooms available
Directions Subway: 6 to 68th St–Hunter College; Bus: M101, M102 to 68th St; M1, M2, M3, M4 to 68th St, then walk east
Landmark Status New York City Landmark

Kenkeleba House New York

214 East 2nd Street (between Avenues B and C)
New York, NY 10009
212-674-3939

Named for a West African plant believed to possess spiritual powers, Kenkeleba House is dedicated to the exhibition of artworks by African-American, Latino, Asian-American and Native American artists.

Kenkeleba House sponsors eight to ten exhibitions a year of four to five weeks duration, often exploring historical or thematic issues. Exhibits have included "Unbroken Circle," a show of works by African-American artists produced during the Work Projects Administration; and "In the Spirit of Wood," a multi-ethnic exhibit of artists who use that medium. Kenkeleba has a substantial collection of contemporary American paintings, especially works by established and emerging African-America artists.

The main Kenkeleba House facility has a 6,000-square-foot gallery and 14 studios for visual artists. A second facility, at 219 East Second Street, has a smaller exhibition space and housing for 26 artists. Founded in 1973, the organization also hosts literary events, concerts, lectures and gallery tours.

GENERAL INFORMATION

Hours Wed–Sat 11 am–6 pm; call ahead to confirm
Admission Suggested contribution $2
Giftshop Kenkeleba House publications, small crafts, one-of-a-kind gifts made by artists
Library Books and records on African and African-American history, art and culture; partially open to general public; uncataloged holdings available only to scholars and researchers
Disability Access Assisted access over two steps at 214 (call ahead); ramp access at 219
Directions Subway: F to 2nd Ave; Bus: M9 to East 2nd St and Ave B; M14 to East 3rd St and Ave A; M15 to East 3rd St and 1st Ave; M21 to East Houston St and Ave B

The Kitchen Center for Video, Music, Dance, Performance, Film and Literature

512 West 19th Street (between Tenth and Eleventh Avenues)
New York, NY 10011
212-255-5793

The Kitchen is home to some of the nation's finest experimental work in the performing and visual arts. As its name indicates, the focus is decidedly multidisciplinary. The Kitchen presents independent artists, companies and festivals, providing them with a venue and support services.

The Annual "Bang on a Can" festival, for example, uses the Kitchen as the location for its week-long melange of minimalist theater, computer-generated music, shadow theater and rap soliloquies. Another independent festival was "SPEW/New York," described in Kitchen literature as "an unofficial gathering, linking 'zine culture, alternative music, video productions, unorthodox feminisms and queer sex practices." In addition, The Kitchen mounts exhibitions of painting, sculpture, photographs and the like.

The Kitchen, founded in 1971, was originally located in what had been the kitchen of the Broadway Central Hotel. After relocating on Broome Street in SoHo, it moved to larger quarters on 19th Street in 1985. Once an icehouse, the complex has two floors of theater space and a third floor containing video-editing facilities.

Symbol Key

 *Institutional Giftshop*

 *On-Site Food Services*

 *On-Site Library or Archive*

 *Full Accessibility*

On-Site Parking

 *National Register of Historic Places and/or New York City Landmark*

Rehearsal and performance space, the Kitchen.

GENERAL INFORMATION

Hours Hours vary; call for information
Admission Price varies; call for information; various discounts available
Library Video archive; call for details
Disability Access Fully accessible
Directions Subway: A to 14th St; C or E to 23rd St; Bus: M11 to 20th St; M14 to 11th Ave; M23 to 11th Ave

Korean Cultural Service

460 Park Avenue, Sixth Floor
(between 57th and 58th Streets)
New York, NY 10022

212-759-9550

Korea's rich cultural heritage is celebrated through performance and exhibition programs presented by the Korean Cultural Service. A service of the Consulate General of South Korea, the organization exhibits the work of contemporary South Korean artists, hosts lectures by noted experts on the country, screens Korean feature films and presents performances of traditional and modern Korean dance, theater and music. Large-scale performances are staged in well-known halls throughout the city, while solo artists perform at the Park Avenue location.

Drawing on collections of Korean art and artifacts from museums around the world, exhibits in Gallery Korea have included "Modern [Korean] Embroidery," "Color and Shape: East and West," "5000 Years of Korean Art" and an exhibit of traditional musical instruments. Lectures on topics such as "An Introduction to Korean Culture" and "Korean-U.S. Relations" are open to the public.

GENERAL INFORMATION

Hours Mon–Fri 9 am–5 pm; closed Sat, Sun
Admission Free
Library Large bilingual library offers books on Korean history, culture and society as well as a film and video lending service and a slide archive
Disability Access Limited access
Directions Subway: 4, 5 or 6 to 59th St; N or R to Lexington Ave; Bus: M1, M2, M3, M4, M15, M101, M102 to 57th St; M57, M58 to Park Ave

The Kosciuszko Foundation

15 East 65th Street
(between Madison
and Fifth Avenues)
New York, NY 10021

212-734-2130

In 1925, on the 150th anniversary of Tadeusz Kosciuszko's enlistment in the American Revolutionary cause, the Kosciuszko Foundation was established with the aim of promoting cross-cultural understanding between Poland and the United States. Today the foundation is the largest public institution in North America devoted solely to Polish art.

The sculpture, oils, watercolors, lithographs, woodcuts, drawings, ceramics, tapestries, masks and photographs that make up its permanent collection are displayed in the gallery on a rotating basis. The permanent collection, started in 1945 with a famous portrait of Kosciuszko, now contains works by more than 50 Polish artists—the largest collection of 19th century Polish painting in America.

The gallery is located on the second floor of the foundation's spectacular, four-story Renaissance-style townhouse. The structure's ample public rooms serve as the site not only for exhibitions but also for the popular chamber music series, the annual Chopin Piano Competition (once won by Van Cliburn), film screenings, a lecture series and literary readings in English and Polish.

GENERAL INFORMATION

Hours Mon–Fri 9 am–5 pm, appointment recommended. Concerts, exhibits, lectures evenings and weekends; call for schedule of events
Admission Free
Giftshop Books on Polish history and culture
Disability Access None
Directions Subway: 6 to 68th St; B or Q to Lexington Ave; Bus: M1, M2, M3, M4 to 65th St; M30, M72 to 5th Ave
Landmark Status New York City Landmark

La Mama E.T.C.

74A East 4th Street
(between Second
and Third Avenues)
New York, NY 10003

212-475-7710

La Mama is perhaps the greatest crucible for experimental theater that America has ever produced. La Mama presents the works of new playwrights; engages new directors, designers and performers to execute that work; showcases the international avant-garde; and is a major performance venue for composers and choreographers. The organization mounts 60 to 70 productions a year reflecting the ethnic diversity not just of New York but of the world.

Founded by Ellen Stewart in 1961, La Mama was the first home to many of today's most popular playwrights, including Harvey Fierstein, Lanford Wilson and Sam Shepard. Over the years La Mama works have been honored with over 60 OBIE Awards and dozens of Drama Desk Awards.

Since its inception, La Mama has grown from a simple basement theater to a complex of four buildings housing two theaters, a cabaret, seven floors of rehearsal space, an educational and performance workshop space, and an archive. Educational programs are geared for high school and college students. La Mama also hosts young playwrights' workshops and plays-in-progress series.

GENERAL INFORMATION

Hours Box office open 10 am–10 pm daily
Admission Price varies; member, student and group discounts available; ask about ticket subsidies that allow students, seniors and handicapped to attend free
Library Archive documents Off Off Broadway theater; call about access
Disability Access Limited
Directions Subway: 6 to Astor Place; N or R to West 4th St; B, D, F or Q to Broadway–Lafayette St; Bus: M15 to 2nd Ave and 4th St; M101 to 3rd Ave and 4th St

Peter Moore

The Ridge Theater performing "Everyday Newt Burman" at La Mama E.T.C.

Lincoln Center

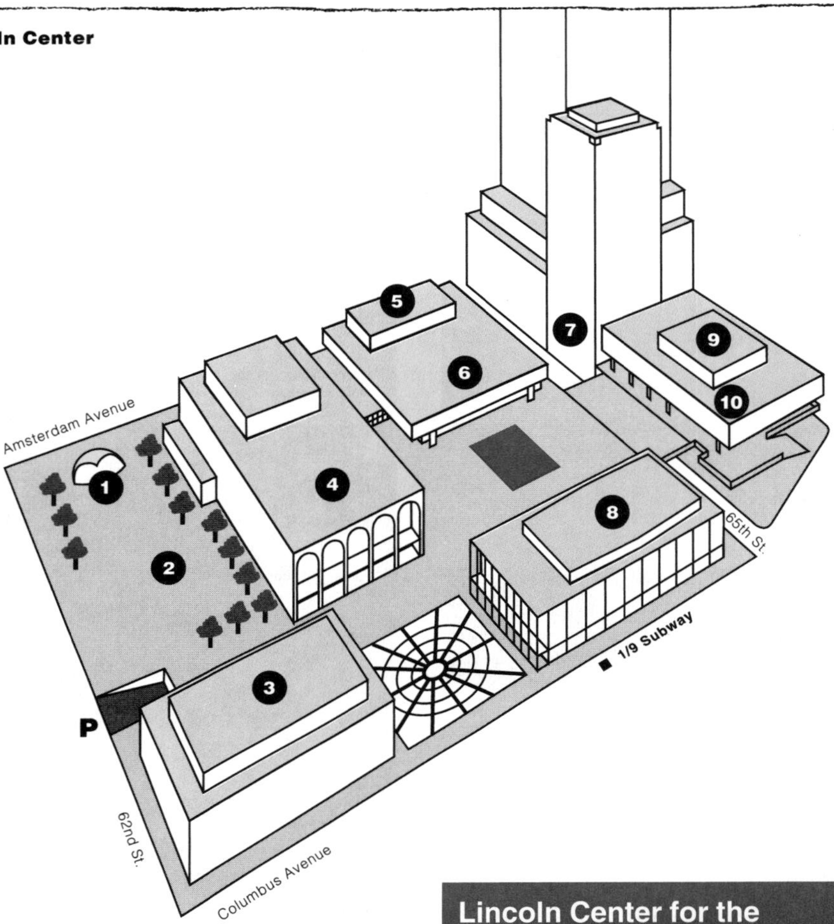

Amsterdam Avenue
65th St.
1/9 Subway
62nd St.
Columbus Avenue
P

1 Guggenheim Bandshell

2 Damrosch Park

3 New York State Theater
New York City Ballet
New York City Opera

4 Metropolitan Opera House

5 New York Public Library for the Performing Arts

6 Vivan Beaumont & Mitzi E. Newhouse Theaters
Lincoln Center Theater Company

7 Walter Reade Theater
Film Society of Lincoln Center

8 Avery Fisher Hall
New York Philharmonic

9 The Juilliard School

10 Alice Tully Hall
Chamber Music Society of Lincoln Center

Lincoln Center for the Performing Arts

Columbus Avenue between
62nd and 66th Streets
New York, NY 10023

212-875-5000
General Number
212-721-6500
CenterCharge
212-875-5350
Tour Information

Lincoln Center is the preeminent performing arts complex in the United States. The companies residing within its six marble-clad structures offer works primarily in traditional formats—opera, ballet, theater, orchestral and chamber music—although more experimental fare is occasionally featured. New York public works baron Robert Moses is credited with conceiving of Lincoln Center during the 1950s. Built from 1962 to 1968, the complex transformed an area of urban blight into one of esthetic pleasures.

Lincoln Center for the Performing Arts, Inc., as distinct from the resident companies described in separate sections below, manages the complex and also presents five series annually: **Mostly Mozart**, a popular and popularly-priced concert series each summer; **Jazz at Lincoln Center**, presenting classic and new music in several halls; **Serious Fun!**—a festival of artists and companies working in nontraditional, frequently multidisciplinary formats; the **Great Performers** series, featuring the best in chamber music, virtuoso recitals, symphonic offerings and visiting companies; **Lincoln Center Out-of-Doors**, showcasing dance companies from around the world, jazz, chamber music and family events ("Just for Kids," "Clown Theater Day") on the center's spacious plaza; and occasional performances in the Guggenheim Bandshell, located in Damrosch Park between the New York State Theater and the Metropolitan Opera House. Between Thanksgiving and New Year's the **Big Apple Circus** performs in an intimate, one-ring tent in the park.

Lincoln Center has three notable constituents which are primarily educational: the Juilliard School, the School of American Ballet and the Lincoln Center Institute. The Juilliard School and the School of American Ballet, each preeminent in its field, offer occasional public performances.

Note: The New York Public Library for the Performing Arts, located at Lincoln Center, is listed separately.

GENERAL INFORMATION

Hours Hours vary; see venue-related information sections below; facility tours daily 10 am–5 pm
Admission Price varies; see venue-related information sections below; tours: adults $7.50, seniors and students $6.50, children $4.25
Giftshop Performing Arts Shop on concourse level under main plaza; open Mon–Sat 10 am until second performance intermission; Sun 12–6 pm; 212-580-4356
Food Service Fountain Cafe on plaza serves cold entrees, desserts and beverages; open daily mid-May through Sept, 11:30 am until performance starts, weather permitting; see venue-related information sections below for other food service options
Library See separate entry for New York Public Library for the Performing Arts
Disability Access See venue-related information sections below; to request the Lincoln Center Accessibility Guide, call 212-875-5357; wheelchair tours available
Directions Subway: 1/9 to 66th St; Bus: M5, M7, M11, M66, M104 to Lincoln Center
Parking On-site lot, enter on 62nd or 65th Sts between Columbus and Amsterdam Aves

Vivian Beaumont Theater/ Mitzi E. Newhouse Theater

Lincoln Center Theater Company 212-362-7600 General Number

The Vivian Beaumont Theater and the Mitzi E. Newhouse Theater are the home of the Lincoln Center Theater Company. The 1,050-seat Beaumont is the larger venue, adjacent to the sculpture-bedecked reflecting pool on the main plaza. The more intimate, 280-seat Newhouse space is frequently the site of one-person shows. Eero Saarinen & Associates, collaborating with Jo Mielziner, designed the structure. One interesting note: the thick travertine slab that sits atop the Beaumont is not part of the theater, but houses reading rooms of the New York Public Library for the Performing Arts (see separate entry).

Since its reorganization in 1985, the Lincoln Center Theater Company has presented dozens of productions in its two performance spaces, as well as on and Off Broadway. Dramatic offerings have included Mustapha Matura's "Playboy of the West Indies," John Guare's "Six Degrees of Separation," Spalding Gray's "Gray's Anatomy" and Samuel Beckett's "Waiting for Godot."

GENERAL INFORMATION

Hours Box office open Mon–Sat 10 am–8 pm, Sun 12–7:30 pm
Admission Price varies
Giftshop See Lincoln Center general information section above
Food Service Lobby bar, light refreshments during performances
Disability Access Limited access, wheelchair seating upon request; enter at concourse level and take elevator to 2 for Newhouse theater or 5 for Beaumont; restrooms accessible; infrared listening systems available
Directions and Parking See Lincoln Center general information section above

Avery Fisher Hall

New York Philharmonic 212-875-5030 Box Office

Avery Fisher Hall is home to the New York Philharmonic, the Mostly Mozart Festival and many visiting performers.

The New York Philharmonic, founded in 1842, is the oldest orchestra in the United States. It plays about 200 concerts every year and is seen regularly on PBS's "Live from Lincoln Center" telecasts. Its conductors and music directors have included founder Ureli Corelli Hill, Gustav Mahler, Arturo Toscanini, Dimitri Mitropoulos, Leonard Bernstein, Pierre Boulez, Zubin Mehta and Kurt Masur, the present music director.

Mostly Mozart is a multiweek series that each summer presents some of the best orchestras and instrumentalists in the world. The festival has lately offered an informal comparison between the works of Mozart and other Classical and Romantic masters, such as Mendelssohn, Strauss, Brahms and others. Many concerts in the Great Performers series take place in Avery Fisher Hall, as do the opening and closing nights of the New York Film Festival.

Chris Lee

Kurt Masur, Music Director, New York Philharmonic.

Cork Gallery is a lower lobby of Avery Fisher Hall which opened in 1971. It has about 90 feet of wall space and two bay windows for sculpture and presents more than 25 shows a year. Exhibitors include art schools, such as the Art Students League and the National Academy of Design (see separate entries), and artists' organizations, among others.

Within an arcade of slim travertine columns, Avery Fisher Hall's multilevel lobby can be viewed through clear glass walls. The hall was an acoustical failure upon opening in 1962. In 1976, with funds from stereo-equipment magnate Avery Fisher, its auditorium was demolished and rebuilt. The original architect was Max Abramovitz; the firm of Johnson/Burgee designed the renovation. The suspended sculpture in the lobby is by Richard Lippold. The hall seats 2,738.

GENERAL INFORMATION

Hours Box office open Mon–Sat 10 am until performance time; Sun 12 noon until performance time; Cork Gallery open 10 am until closing of hall
Admission Price varies; student discounts available
Giftshop Shop in the hall open during performances; also see Lincoln Center general information section above
Food Service Panevino Ristorante, moderate prices, located in east lobby, plaza level, open Mon–Sat for dinner and lunch on matinee days, reservations 212-874-7000; Cafe Vienna Kaffeehaus and Dinner Buffet, located in west lobby, plaza level, open Tues–Sat 5–8 pm, reservations 212-874-7000
Disability Access Fully accessible, wheelchair seating upon request, call 212-875-5005. Infrared listening devices available; braille and large-type programs available for selected performances
Directions and Parking See Lincoln Center general information section above

Metropolitan Opera House

212-362-6000 Box Office

The Metropolitan Opera House offers lyric theater on a grand scale and of the highest standard. The entire stage is on an elevator and it is breathtaking to see this immense, opulently designed stage ascend into the air, another rising beneath it to take its place. In the lobby are two huge murals by Marc Chagall. The white, red and gold house, designed by Wallace Harrison and completed in 1966, seats 3,788.

Winnie Klotz

Kathleen Battle and Tatiana Troyanos in Act II of the Metropolitan Opera's production of "Der Rosenkavalier" by Richard Strauss.

Founded in 1883, the Metropolitan Opera is one of the world's great opera companies. A repertory company in the truest sense, it stages more than 200 performances during a 30-week season, as well as free performances in city parks during summer. In early summer the house usually presents visiting ballet companies, such as the Paris Opera Ballet and American Ballet Theatre.

GENERAL INFORMATION

Hours Box office open Mon–Sat 10 am–8 pm, Sun 12–6 pm
Admission Price varies per performance. Opera House tours, rates stated above
Giftshop Opera Shop in lobby has audio and video recordings, opera-related memorabilia; open Mon–Sat 10 am until second intermission of performance, Sun 12–6 pm, 212-580-4090. Also see Lincoln Center general information section above
Food Service The Grand Tier Restaurant open Mon–Sat for dinner and intermission; also serves lunch for Wed and Sat matinees; open two hours before performance for ticketholders; 212-799-3400. Revlon Bar, Champagne Bar, Family Circle Bar and Founder Hall are open during intermission
Disability Access Fully accessible, wheelchair seating upon request; infrared listening systems available at south checkroom, concourse level; large print programs available
Directions and Parking See Lincoln Center general information section above

New York State Theater

New York City Ballet 212-870-5570
New York City Opera Box Office

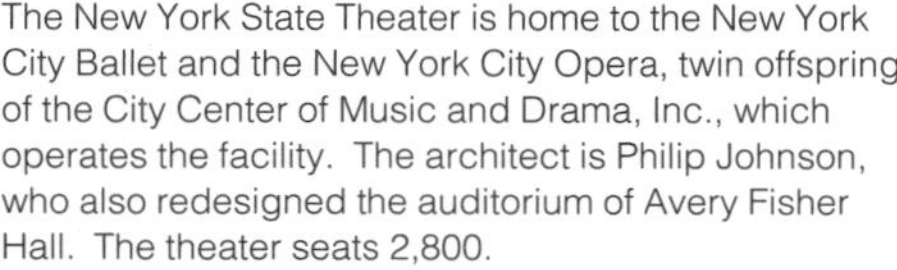

The New York State Theater is home to the New York City Ballet and the New York City Opera, twin offspring of the City Center of Music and Drama, Inc., which operates the facility. The architect is Philip Johnson, who also redesigned the auditorium of Avery Fisher Hall. The theater seats 2,800.

The New York City Ballet was founded in 1948 by George Balanchine and Lincoln Kirstein. Today it is one of the world's greatest ballet companies, maintaining a repertory of more than 100 works by Balanchine, Jerome Robbins, Peter Martins and others. Currently under Martins' direction, the company was run by Balanchine until his death in 1983. The company's education department introduces public school students to the art of classical ballet.

The New York City Opera was founded in 1944 to offer an alternative style and repertory to the Metropolitan

Opera. It showcases first-rate performers in a repertory of both opera and the classics of American musical theater. City Opera has persevered in offering the controversial supertitles—English translations of the libretto projected above the stage—loved by those new to opera, disdained by the purists. City Opera normally offers about 100 performances of 14 productions during its 16-week season. Every season dozens of young American artists debut with the company, which, since its establishment, has presented more than 2,200 singers, 99 percent of them American.

GENERAL INFORMATION

Hours Box office open Mon 10 am–7:30 pm, Tues–Sat 10 am–8:30 pm, Sun 11:30 am–7:30 pm
Admission Price varies; student and group discounts available. Opera ticketst range from $10 to $70
Giftshop Books, photos and compact discs on sale to ticketholders
Food Service Promenade bar offers coffee and light refreshments
Disability Access Fully accessible, wheelchair seating upon request; NYC Opera provides infrared listening systems
Directions and Parking See Lincoln Center general information section above
City-owned, privately operated

Walter Reade Theater

Film Society of Lincoln Center 212-875-5600 Box Office

The Walter Reade Theater is home to the Film Society of Lincoln Center. Designed by Davis, Brody and Associates, the 268-seat cinema was completed in 1991 and is considered one of the best in the country.

The Film Society's programs range from national film series to retrospectives that highlight the accomplishments of outstanding directors, performers, cinematographers, screenwriters and other film artists. Thematic programs look at film genres and periods as well as timely issues and ideas. Recent series have focused on the work of actress Judy Davis, the early films of Alfred Hitchcock, Martin Scorsese's entire body of work and new films from Taiwan.

The Film Society sponsors the New York Film Festival and the New Directors/New Films series. New Directors/

Wendy Whelan and Albert Evans in George Balanchine's "Stravinsky Violin Concerto."

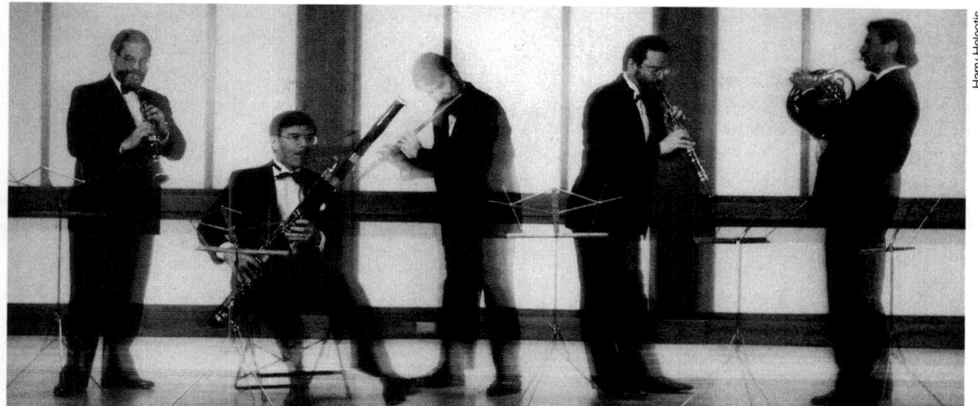

Harry Heleotis

Musicians David Shifrin, left, Milan Turkovic, Ransom Wilson, Stephen Taylor and Robert Routch—regular performers in concerts presented by the Chamber Music Society of Lincoln Center.

New Films takes place each winter at the Museum of Modern Art, its co-sponsor. Additional programs include summer retrospective screenings; Film-in-Education, which allows filmmakers to introduce public school students to the art of film; and special events, such as the premiere of the restored D. W. Griffith masterpiece "Intolerance."

GENERAL INFORMATION

Hours Box office open daily 1:30 pm until 15 minutes after the start of the last screening
Admission Adults $7, members $5, seniors $4 (weekday matinees only), children under 12, $4 ("Movies for Kids" only)
Giftshop See Lincoln Center general information section above
Disability Access Fully accessible, wheelchair seating upon request, call 212-875-5601; receivers available for hearing-impaired
Directions and Parking See Lincoln Center general information section above

Alice Tully Hall

Chamber Music Society of Lincoln Center

212-875-5050 Box Office

Alice Tully Hall is home to the Chamber Music Society of Lincoln Center and three special series: the New York Film Festival, Serious Fun! and Jazz at Lincoln Center. Many other concerts and recitals are also presented. Designed by Pietro Belluschi, Alice Tully Hall contains a 1,096-seat theater yet is an intimate room for chamber music.

The Chamber Music Society maintains a permanent roster of nine noted virtuosi, who work together in various combinations and collaborate with distinguished guest artists. It has given more than 1,000 performances since it was founded in 1969 by pianist Charles Wadsworth.

GENERAL INFORMATION

Hours Box office open Mon–Sat 10 am–6 pm, Sun 12–6 pm; performance times vary
Admission Price varies; student discounts available
Giftshop See Lincoln Center general information section above
Food Service Lobby bar, light refreshments during performances
Disability Access Fully accessible, wheelchair seating available in the loge upon request; Infrared listening devices available in the east lobby; large-print and braille programs for selected performances
Directions and Parking See Lincoln Center general information section above

Symbol Key

 *Institutional Giftshop*

 *On-Site Food Services*

 *On-Site Library or Archive*

 *Full Accessibility*

 *On-Site Parking*

 *National Register of Historic Places and/or New York City Landmark*

Lower East Side Tenement Museum

97 Orchard Street
(between Broome and
Delancey Streets)
New York, NY 10002

212-431-0233

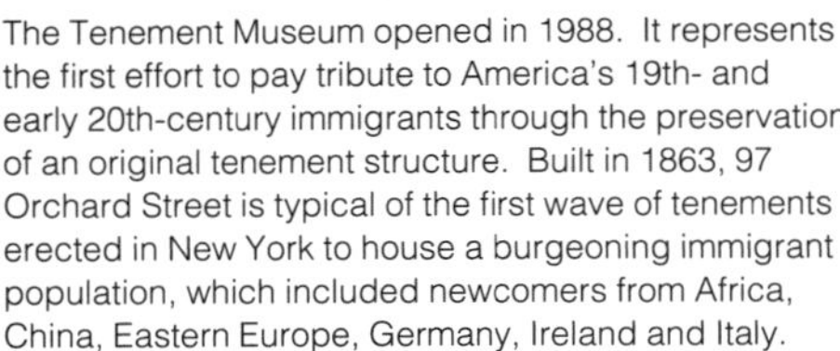

The Tenement Museum opened in 1988. It represents the first effort to pay tribute to America's 19th- and early 20th-century immigrants through the preservation of an original tenement structure. Built in 1863, 97 Orchard Street is typical of the first wave of tenements erected in New York to house a burgeoning immigrant population, which included newcomers from Africa, China, Eastern Europe, Germany, Ireland and Italy.

The permanent exhibition consists of photographs and domestic tableaux in period rooms. Regular exhibits, displaying authentic costumes and artifacts, explore every aspect of the immigrant experience. Curators have even been able to determine the names and reconstruct the histories of many families that lived in the tenement during its 72 years of residential service. It is estimated that as many as 100 people lived in the five-story building at a time, with seven to 20 people sharing a three-room flat.

The museum also offers programs that embrace the surrounding neighborhood. The "Peddler's Pack" walking tour, for instance, features a costumed guide who leads visitors to Lower East Side sites that were an integral part of the community in the 19th and early 20th centuries, such as teahouses, synagogues, sweatshops, public baths and union halls. The play "Family Matters" makes use of archival materials and the memoirs of an immigrant family to dramatize day-to-day life during the period.

GENERAL INFORMATION

Hours Sun 10 am–5 pm; Tues–Fri 11 am–5 pm; closed Sat, Mon
Admission Free Tues–Fri; Sun, adults $3, children 17 and under $1
Giftshop Books, postcards and posters relating to immigration history
Library Not open to public, but staff will answer research questions
Disability Access None
Directions Subway: F to Delancey St; B, D or Q to Grand St; J, M or Z to Essex St; Bus: M15 to Allen and Delancey Sts
Landmark Status National Register of Historic Places, New York City Landmark

Merkin Concert Hall

at Elaine Kaufman Cultural Center
Abraham Goodman House
129 West 67th Street (between
Broadway and Amsterdam Avenue)
New York, NY 10023

212-362-8719

The Elaine Kaufman Cultural Center celebrates Jewish culture through music, dance, art and theater, and uses the arts to unite people of different cultural backgrounds. It includes a school of music and dance, concert and recital halls, an art gallery, a music library and a state-of-the-art digital recording studio.

Merkin Concert Hall is the center's primary performance space. It seats 457 and offers events 270 nights a year. Merkin Concert Hall has been acclaimed by critics for its excellent acoustics. The smaller, 100-seat Ann Goodman Recital Hall is used for lectures, community concerts, and recitals by students and faculty of the center's Lucy Moses School of Music and Dance. The art gallery shows work by contemporary Jewish artists from many countries and documentary exhibitions complementing Merkin Concert Hall presentations.

Founded as the Hebrew Arts School in 1952 when it opened in two borrowed classrooms, the organization today occupies a handsome modern facility, the Abraham Goodman House, on West 67th Street.

GENERAL INFORMATION

Hours Mon–Thurs 10 am–6 pm; Fri 10 am–4 pm; Sat, one hour before performance time; Sun 12–4 pm; on performance evenings box office is open through intermission
Admission Price varies; student and senior discounts on day of performance
Giftshop Open before performances and during intermission
Library Birnbaum Music Library contains books, manuscripts, scores and standard reference texts on Jewish and Israeli music
Disability Access Fully accessible; infrared listening devices available
Directions Subway: 1/9 to 66th St; 2, 3 to 72nd St; Bus: M5, M7, M11, M104 to 68th St; M66 to Broadway

The Metropolitan Museum of Art

Fifth Avenue and 82nd Street
New York, NY 10028
212-879-5500

The Metropolitan Museum of Art is one of the greatest museums in the world in terms of its size and the quality and encyclopedic scope of its collections. The Met's vast holdings include more than three million works of art—several hundred thousand of which are on view—spanning more than 5,000 years of world culture from prehistory to the present. The collections are divided into 18 departments and fill more than 220 galleries.

The Met is the most popular tourist attraction in New York and has an annual attendance of 4.4 million.

One of the Met's newest attractions is the 19th Century European Paintings and Sculpture Galleries—exhibition spaces containing America's finest collection of Romantic, Barbizon, Impressionist and Post-Impressionist masterpieces. Like several other Met departments, these galleries constitute a museum-within-a-museum.

Included among the Met's 3,000 European paintings are Italian masterpieces by Mantegna, Botticelli and Bronzino; Dutch and Flemish works by Rubens, Rembrandt and Vermeer; and Spanish works by El Greco, Velázquez and Goya. The collection also includes important early French paintings by de la Tour, Poussin and Watteau.

The American Wing houses one of the nation's largest collections of American paintings, sculptures and decorative arts. Exhibited are masterpieces by Cole, Sargent, Eakins and Homer. Decorative arts date from early Colonial times to the 20th century, and 25 period rooms offer an unparalleled view of American art history and domestic life. Various neoclassical and Beaux-Arts sculptures stand in the Engelhard Court.

Works of ancient and Near Eastern art range from sixth millennium B.C. to the Arab conquest of A.D. 626, and come from Mesopotamia, Iran, Syria, Anatolia and other lands. Holdings of Islamic art span the 7th through the 19th centuries and consist of objects from Morocco in the west to Indonesia in the east.

The institution's nearly 4,000 drawings are particularly rich in Italian and French works from the 15th through the 19th centuries. The print collection includes works by virtually every master printmaker and is augmented by more than 12,000 books containing prints. The bulk of the photography collection came from Alfred Stieglitz between 1928 and 1949, augmented by numerous more recent acquisitions as well.

The 20th-century art department maintains 8,000-plus works, the emphasis being primarily on American artists. Holdings include paintings by the Eight, modernist works of the Stieglitz circle, Abstract Expressionist and Color Field paintings as well as Art Nouveau and Art Deco furniture and metalwork.

Temple of Dendur, Nubia, Egypt. Early Roman Period, circa 15 B.C. Given to the United States by Egypt, 1965, awarded to The Met, 1967.

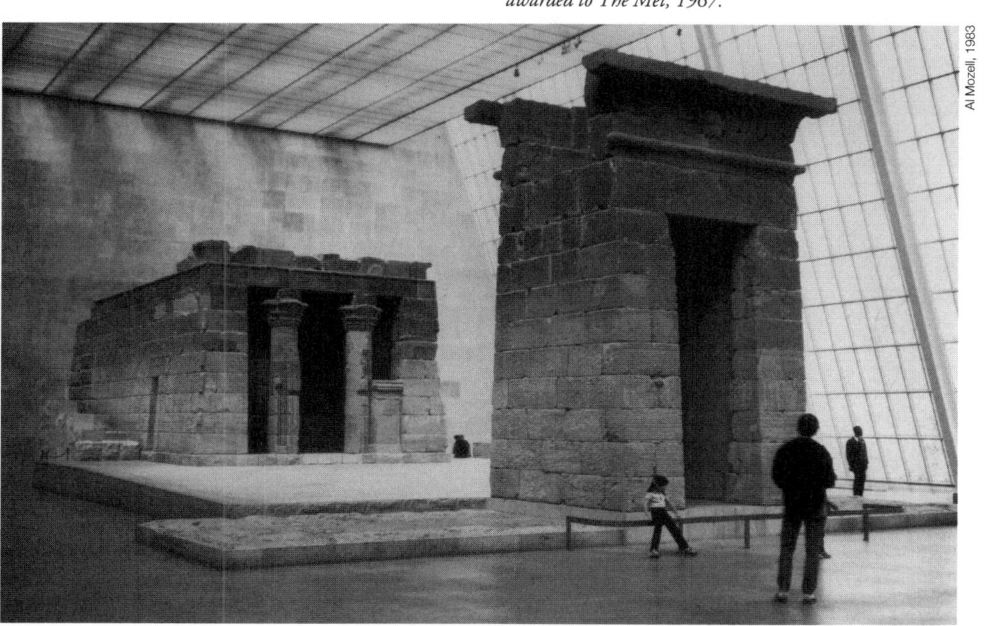

Al Mozell, 1983

The Greek and Roman art collection covers several cultures. In addition to works from the Classical period, it contains pre-Greek artworks of the eastern Mediterranean (Cypriot, Minoan and Mycenaean) and the pre-Roman art of Italy (Etruscan and Italic).

About 2,000 objects from Africa, the Pacific Islands and the Americas are exhibited. The African collection has superb examples of bronze sculpture from Benin (Nigeria) and wooden sculpture from West and Central Africa. Works from the Pacific area include sculpture from the Asmat people of New Guinea and from the island groups of Melanesia and Polynesia. Pre-Columbian cultures of Mexico and Central and South America are represented by important holdings in gold, ceramics and stone. Native arts of North America are represented by groups of Inuit and Indian artifacts.

The medieval art collection, one of the richest in the world, encompasses the 4th through the 16th centuries. Strengths include early Christian and Byzantine silver, jewelry of the barbarian tribes, liturgical vessels, stained glass and tapestries. Many of this department's greatest works are exhibited at the Cloisters (see separate entry).

Other museum highlights include art from China, Japan, Korea, India and Southeast Asia, dating from the third millennium B.C. to the present; the Egyptian art department, with works dating from 3100 B.C. to the eighth century A.D.; the arms and armor collection of more than 14,000 weapons from Europe, the Near East, Asia and the Americas; the Costume Institute, containing 45,000 pieces dating from the 17th century to the present; and the nearly 4,000 objects from six continents that make up the holdings of the department of musical instruments.

"Portrait of the Princess de Broglie" by Jean August Dominique Ingres, French, ca. 1850, Robert Lehman Wing, Metropolitan Museum of Art.

Gallery talks and recorded tours are offered in several languages. Subscription lectures, films and concerts, and symposiums are offered regularly.

The creation of the Met was first proposed in 1866 by John Jay, grandson of the eminent jurist, when he and other Americans gathered in Paris to celebrate the Fourth of July. Later, back in New York, he rallied civic leaders, art collectors and philanthropists to the cause. The Metropolitan Museum of Art was incorporated in 1870 and moved to its present location in Central Park in 1880.

Many architects have had a role in creating the Met. The original musuem was designed by Calvert Vaux and J. Wrey Mould. Expansion since then has left only the exterior of this modest structure visible inside the Lehman Wing. The neo-Renaissance, Fifth Avenue facade was designed and built in two stages: the central section by Richard Morris Hunt (1902) and the side wings by McKim, Mead & White (1906). Physical growth in the second half of the 20th century has been monumental. In the late 1970s the Met began an expansion program that has more than doubled its gallery space. The many new wings and galleries called for by the plan were designed by the firm Kevin Roche, John Dinkeloo and Associates.

GENERAL INFORMATION

Hours Sun, Tues–Thurs 9:30 am–5:15 pm; Fri, Sat 9:30 am–8:45 pm; closed Mon
Admission Suggested contribution: adults $6, students and seniors $3, members and children under 12 with an adult free (includes admission to the Cloisters on the same day)
Giftshop Bookstore has broad selection of art history books, postcards, prints, exhibition catalogs and other Met publications; shops also feature reproductions produced by the museum
Food Service Cafeteria, cafe and restaurant; hours vary with each facility. Great Hall Balcony Bar open Friday and Saturday evenings only
Libraries Watson Library, Media Center Library, Uris Library and Resource Center, Goldwater Library of Primitive Art, Lewisohn Costume Reference Library, Print and Study Room Library, Photography Library and Reference Collection, and Slide Library; hours vary, inquire about access
Disability Access Fully accessible; wheelchairs available; parking available; various special programs; TDD 212-879-0421
Directions Subway: 4, 5 or 6 to 86th St; Bus: M1, M2, M3, M4 to 82nd St
Parking On-site lot, entrance at 80th St and 5th Ave
Landmark Status National Register of Historic Places, New York City Landmark

City-owned, privately operated

Morris-Jumel Mansion, built in 1765 for British Colonel Roger Morris.

Midtown Y Photography Gallery

Educational Alliance 212-475-6200
197 East Broadway Ext. 376
(between Jefferson and Clinton Streets)
New York, NY 10002

Opened in 1971 at the YWHA on 14th Street, the Midtown Y Photography Gallery moved to spaces at the Educational Alliance in the early 1990's. It presents the work of 18 to 20 photographers a year. Exhibits change every four to six weeks and feature the work of two or three artists. The gallery has a permanent collection containing the work of photographers who have exhibited in the gallery over the years, and it frequently offers lectures related to the exhibitions.

GENERAL INFORMATION

Hours Mon–Thurs 10 am–10 pm; Fri and Sun 10 am–6 pm; closed Sat
Admission Free
Giftshop Photographic works for sale
Disability Access Fully accessible
Directions Subway: F to East Broadway; Bus: M9 to East Broadway and Clinton St (or Rutgers St); M22 to Madison and Jefferson Sts

Morris–Jumel Mansion

65 Jumel Terrace at 160th Street 212-923-8008
New York, NY 10032

The Morris-Jumel Mansion is one of the city's few remaining pre–Revolutionary War buildings and a Harlem landmark. The house was originally constructed by British Colonel Roger Morris in 1765 as a summer villa for his family. At that time it was 12 miles from New York City, and the estate, first named Mount Morris, stretched over 130 acres from the Harlem to the Hudson Rivers.

Facing south, the mansion has been erected in a Georgian-Federal style with Tuscan columns. Inside, the drawing room features Chinese wallpaper and American and English Chippendale furniture. Upstairs, in Madame Jumel's boudoir, are the original bed and two chairs covered in gold damask which are believed to have been owned by Napoleon.

George Washington used the mansion during the war as headquarters of the Continental Army. Its commanding views and large size made it ideal for military use. In the rear rooms, over the drawing room, visitors can see the private quarters where Washington slept, planned maneuvers and wrote reports to Congress.

In 1810 Stephen Jumel purchased and restored the mansion. It has been a museum since 1904. Exhibitions focus on historical events that occurred during the structure's heyday. There are also periodic lectures and concerts.

GENERAL INFORMATION

Hours Wed–Sun 10 am–4 pm; closed Mon, Tues
Admission Adults $3, seniors and students $2, children under 10 free
Giftshop Books and souvenirs
Library Archival collection on the history of the mansion and museum; open by appointment only
Disability Access None
Directions Subway: A (Sat, Sun) or B (Mon–Fri) to 163rd St; Bus: M3 to 160th St
Landmark Status National Register of Historic Places, New York City Landmark
City-owned, privately operated

Mulberry Street Theater

70 Mulberry Street, Second Floor 212-349-0126
(corner of Bayard Street)
New York, NY 10013

The only performance space in Chinatown, Mulberry Street Theater is a home base for touring and local dance artists. Visitors will not find household names performing here; instead, emerging modern dance choreographers present a diversity of dance expression of the highest quality. The 70-seat "black box" theater has been used by dance artists from around the world, including Japan, Taiwan, China and Hong Kong, and elsewhere in the United States.

Carol Rosegg/Martha Swope Associates

Chen & Dancers, resident company of Mulberry Street Theater, performing "Opening the Gate."

The Children's Matinee Series (kindergarten through sixth grade) includes the programs "Modern Dance from the Asian Heritage" and "Traditional Chinese Dance." These lecture/demonstrations explain the basics of choreography and teach lessons in Chinese history and culture. Mulberry Street Theater also provides the surrounding Asian-American community with space for lectures, film screenings and concerts.

GENERAL INFORMATION

Hours Hours vary; call for schedule of events
Admission Price varies; TDF vouchers accepted
Disability Access None
Directions Subway: N, R, 4, 5 or 6 to Canal St; Bus: M1 to Center and White Sts; M9 to Mott and Worth Sts; M15 to Center and Worth Sts; M102, B51 to Bowery and Bayard Sts

Municipal Archives of New York City

Department of Records 212-788-8580
and Information Services
31 Chambers Street, Room 103
(between Centre Street and
City Hall Park)
New York, NY 10007

The Municipal Archives maintain the administrative remnants of New York's 300-year history. The scope of the collections is immense—80,000 cubic feet—and these materials are used by researchers of all kinds: architectural historians and preservationists, genealogists, urban archaeologists, journalists and writers.

A brief sampling of the holdings includes original Brooklyn Bridge construction plans, genealogical records (1795–1956), court records (1808–1935), photographs of New York public works projects (1936–43), manuscripts related to the Work Projects Administration Federal Writers' Project (1936–43), Department of Parks' records (1850–1960) and mayoral papers (1849–present).

The permanent Windows on the Archives exhibit illustrates the breadth of the collections. Periodic rotating shows are drawn from the archives and other Department of Records documents. The 31 Chambers Street facility has a well-lit, comfortable reading room that is open to the public.

Surrogates Court/Hall of Records, where the Department of Records is housed, is a seven-story Beaux-Arts structure topped with a mansard roof, that recalls the days when grandeur was a requirement in municipal architecture. The building, completed in 1911, was designed by John Thomas and the firm of Horgan and Slattery. Its elaborate lobby features a mosaic-tableau ceiling depicting deities and zodiac symbols.

GENERAL INFORMATION

Hours Mon–Fri 9 am–4:30 pm; closed Sat, Sun
Admission Free
Library See description above
Disability Access Limited access; elevators available
Directions Subway: 4, 5 or 6 to Brooklyn Bridge; Bus: M1, M6 to Reade St and Broadway; M9 to Park Row and Spruce St; M15 to City Hall; M22 to Chambers and Centre Sts
Landmark Status National Register of Historic Places, New York City Landmark

El Museo del Barrio

1230 Fifth Avenue
(at 104th Street)
New York, NY 10029

212-831-7952

El Museo del Barrio is one of the foremost Latin American cultural institutions in the United States. Its permanent collection—10,000 paintings, sculptures, photographs, works on paper, films, pre-Columbian objects, and farm and household implements—illustrates for the visitor a Latin American culture of astounding depth and richness.

Regular exhibitions in the museum's first-floor galleries display these holdings in a variety of contemporary and historical contexts. Exhibits have included "Voyages to Freedom: 500 Years of Jewish History in Latin America and the Caribbean" and "Another Face: Mexican Masks in the Permanent Collection."

The museum also offers bilingual screenings of classic and contemporary Latin American films; a variety of live musical, dramatic and dance performances; workshops; lectures; scholarly symposiums; festivals; special educational programs for children; an artists' register and a residency program for artists and writers.

El Museo del Barrio was founded in 1969 in a public school classroom in Spanish Harlem. In 1977 it moved to its present location along the city's celebrated Museum Mile in the city-owned Heckscher Pavillion. The institution recently reopened after an extensive expansion and renovation.

Museum Mile

105th St.
• Museo del Bario
• Museum of the City of New York
Conservarory Garden •
96th St.
Fifth Avenue
Central Park
• International Center of Photography
• Jewish Museum
• Cooper Hewitt Museum
• National Academy of Design
• Guggenheim Museum
86th St.
• YIVO Inststitute for Jewish Research
• Goethe House
• Metropolitan Museum of Art
79th St.

GENERAL INFORMATION

Hours Wed–Sun 11 am–5 pm; closed Mon, Tues
Admission Adults $2, students and seniors $1, children under 12 free
Giftshop Exhibition catalogs and museum souvenirs
Library Artist file open by appointment
Disability Access Fully accessible; restrooms, telephones available
Directions Subway: 6 to 103rd St; Bus: M1, M3, M4 to 104th St

City-owned, privately operated

The Museum for African Art

593 Broadway
(at Houston Street)
New York, NY 10012

212-966-1313

The Center for African Art was founded in 1984 on Manhattan's Upper East Side. In 1993 the organization changed its name to the Museum for African Art and moved to larger quarters in SoHo. The museum works to increase public appreciation of African art through high-quality exhibitions, many of which have received strong critical praise; a publications program (the museum is one of the world's foremost publishers on African art); educational programs; and excursions to Africa.

Carved pedestal, Yoruba, Nigeria, from the exhibition "Faces of the Gods: Art and Altar of the Black Atlantic World," Museum for African Art.

One recent exhibit examined how secrecy functions in African societies to create both cohesion and boundaries and to define and express power and authority. Another show featured two contemporary African sculptors whose work, a concatenation of imaginary buildings, comments on the evolving contours of African identity. Documentary and feature films focus on various aspects of African culture or the work of a single African filmmaker. Saturday afternoon family workshops include interactive storytelling, video, dance and music programs.

The interior of the Museum for African Art was designed by architect Maya Lin, who is responsible for the Vietnam Veterans Memorial in Washington, DC. The museum is located in SoHo's landmark cast-iron district on the same block as the Guggenheim Museum SoHo and the New Museum of Contemporary Art (see separate entries).

GENERAL INFORMATION

Hours Sun 12–6 pm; Tues–Fri 10:30 am–5:30 pm; Sat 12 am–8 pm; closed Mon
Admission Adults $4, students and seniors $2
Giftshop Various creations by African potters, weavers, dyers, jewelers and basket makers; also numerous books on African art
Disability Access Fully accessible
Directions Subway: 6 to Spring St; N or R to Prince St; Bus: M1, M6 to Houston St; M21 to Broadway
Landmark Status National Register of Historic Places, New York City Landmark

Museum of American Financial History

26 Broadway (opposite Bowling Green Park)
New York, NY 10004

212-908-4110

The Museum of American Financial History, founded in 1988, collects and exhibits historical financial artifacts. Exhibits at its gallery in New York's financial district examine episodes in the history of America's capital markets. Its premier exhibition was "U.S. Capital Markets: A Retrospective." Subsequent exhibits have included "Alexander Hamilton: First Secretary of the Treasury," "The Art of Engraving on Stocks and Bonds," "Politicians and the Financial Markets" and "The Financing of the Civil War," which explored financial policies of the Union and the Confederacy and the role they played in determining the outcome of the war. The museum has also exhibited artifacts from the New York Stock Exchange in commemoration of its 200th anniversary. The museum is in the old Standard Oil Building, which was designed by the firm of Carrère and Hastings and completed in 1922. Its unusual curving facade works to integrate the structure with neighboring buildings.

GENERAL INFORMATION

Hours Mon–Fri 11:30 am–2:30 pm and by appointment; closed weekends
Admission Free
Giftshop Gifts and publications relating to the development of America's capital markets and New York Stock Exchange
Disability Access None
Directions Subway: 4 or 5 to Bowling Green; 1/9 to Rector St; N or R to Whitehall St–South Ferry; Bus: M1, 6, x25 to Battery Pl

Museum of American Folk Art

Two Lincoln Square
(66th Street and
Columbus Avenue)
New York, NY 10023

212-595-9533

The Museum of American Folk Art is the only institution in the United States devoted exclusively to the exhibition of American folk art. The museum's outstanding collection of 2,500 objects, many of them masterpieces, offers a telling glimpse into the social and historical settings in which they were created.

A large gallery displays works from the permanent collection. This exhibit, America's Heritage, contains fine examples of portraits, landscapes, seascapes, trade signs, weathervanes, whirligigs, decorated tin, carousel horses, hand-crafted furniture, pottery, decoys, quilts and other objects from the mid-1700s to the present day. Other galleries contain temporary shows, several of which are mounted annually. These exhibits have included "Young America: A Folk Art History," "Muffled Voices: Folk Artists in Contemporary America" and "The Jewish Heritage in American Folk Art."

The museum opened in 1963. In 1989 it reopened in a modern structure opposite Lincoln Center (see separate entry) on Manhattan's Upper West Side. It eventually plans to construct a new building on 53rd Street near the Museum of Modern Art. Exhibition-related lectures, gallery tours and workshops give visitors a full understanding of the cultural, social and historical context of the artworks.

Weathervane, East Branch, New York, ca. 1850. Figure represents semi-mythical Indian Chief Tammany.

GENERAL INFORMATION

Hours Tues–Sun 11:30 am–7:30 pm; closed Mon
Admission Free
Giftshop Hand-made and one-of-a-kind objects crafted in the folk tradition, also books on folk and decorative arts; call 212-496-2966. Additional shop at 62 West 50th St; call 212-247-5611
Library 8,000 volumes on American folk art, photo archive of 5,000 slides; access by appointment
Disability Access Fully accessible
Directions Subway: 1/9 to 66th St; Bus: M5, M7, M10, M104 to 66th St; M66 to Columbus Ave

Museum of American Illustration

Society of Illustrators
128 East 63rd Street
(between Park and Lexington
Avenues)
New York, NY 10021

212-838-2560

The Society of Illustrators' collection of 1,500 works by many of America's most famous illustrators is on rotating, permanent display in its Museum of American Illustration. The museum sponsors about 14 exhibitions a year on contemporary and historical themes as well as the work of individuals and groups. Exhibits have highlighted the best in children's book art, Edward Sorel's illustrations and the work of member illustrators. The "Illustrator's Annual" exhibition features the best in editorial, advertising and book art.

For a small fee, students can hone their skills in the society's sketch class under the tutelage of experienced illustrators. An ongoing program of lectures, films, slide shows and workshops is also offered.

The Society of Illustrators was founded in 1901. Early members included American artists William Glackens and Charles Dana Gibson. During the World Wars members were engaged in poster campaigns to boost morale and conscription. One of their most famous works is the Uncle Sam "I Want You" poster, created by James Montgomery Flagg.

GENERAL INFORMATION

Hours Tues 10 am–8 pm; Wed–Fri 10 am–5 pm; Sat 12–4 pm; closed Sun, Mon
Admission Free
Giftshop Books, catalogs, souvenirs
Library Titles on illustration, including biographical and historical materials; open by appointment
Disability Access Limited; call for information
Directions Subway: 4, 5 or 6 to 59th St; R or N to Lexington Ave; Bus: M101, M102 to 63rd St

Museum of the American Piano

211 West 58th Street (at Seventh Avenue)
New York, NY 10019
212-246-4646

Before the electronic age, the piano was the center of home entertainment. During the 19th century, hundreds of American companies manufactured pianos, employing thousands of workers. Today there are only eight such concerns. The Museum of the American Piano is the only museum devoted to preserving the record of how these keyboard instruments were made and used in the United States.

The museum's exhibit of restored instruments and memorabilia illustrates the evolution of the piano, which has been adopted by Western musicians of every stripe: rock, jazz, classical and so on. The permanent collection features over 40 pianos—including a small square piano built in 1825; a Chickering Cocked Hat grand piano, made in 1857; and a Weber upright from the 1870s with lion-head carvings. One popular highlight: the concrete grand. Important piano-making tools and machinery are also displayed.

A course in piano tuning and technology is offered, as well as classes in the restoration and maintenance of antique keyboard instruments. Music recitals on contemporary and period pianos are frequently held. This is a hands-on museum that encourages visitors to sit down and play. Nearby are the piano showrooms of the Steinway (109 West 57th Street) and Baldwin (205 West 58th Street) companies.

GENERAL INFORMATION

Hours At publication time, the museum was temporarily open only to researchers; call to see if it has reopened to the general public
Admission Free
Library Piano-related titles open to scholars and technicians by appointment
Disability Access Call ahead to arrange access
Directions Subway: 2, 3, A, B, C or D to 59th St–Columbus Circle; N or R to 57th St; Bus: M11 to 58th St; M7, M10, M103, M104 to Columbus Circle; M28 to Broadway

The Museum of Modern Art

11 West 53rd Street (between Fifth and Sixth Avenues)
New York, NY 10019
212-708-9480

"A torpedo moving through time" is how Alfred H. Barr Jr., the Museum of Modern Art's charismatic first director, described the institution's permanent collection. Since its 1929 opening exhibition—"Cézanne, Gaugin, Seurat, Van Gogh"—held with borrowed works in rented rooms on Fifth Avenue, MoMA has become one of the most significant critical forces in modern art. Its collection, rivaled by few other museums, spans the major

"Hirondelle–Amour" by Joan Miró, 1933-34, permanent collection of the Museum of Modern Art, gift of Nelson A. Rockefeller.

MoMA's Abby Aldrich Rockefeller Sculpture Garden designed by Philip Johnson. The work in the foreground is "Woman Standing" by Gaston Lachaise, 1932.

movements in European and American art since 1880. In addition, MoMA was the first museum in the United States to recognize film, photography, architecture and design as legitimate art forms worthy of collection and study.

MoMA's painting and sculpture collection contains many of the world's best-known modern works, such as Picasso's "Les Demoiselles d'Avignon," Pollock's "One" and Van Gogh's "The Starry Night." Brancusi, De Chirico, Malevich, Matisse, Miró, Mondrian and O'Keeffe are well represented. Landmark exhibitions have included "Cubism and Abstract Art" (1936), "The New American Painting and Sculpture: The First Generation" (1969), "Pablo Picasso: A Retrospective" (1980) and the Matisse retrospective (1992–93).

The drawings department features works of Dubuffet, Ernst, Klee, Rauschenberg, Schwitters and others. The department's holdings, many of which are studies for particular paintings or sculptures, are often displayed to complement such works during exhibitions. Particularly strong are drawings of the School of Paris, the Dada and Surrealist schools, and those relating to the theater arts.

The film department has one of the most complete international film collections in the country. Programming includes retrospectives of prominent directors and actors, national film cycles and series devoted to new filmmakers. The earliest works in the Department of Photography date to the 1840s, about when the medium was born. The collection here is diverse, including work not only by artists, but also by journalists, scientists and amateurs. Photographers represented include Steichen, Atget, Cartier-Bresson, Weston, Arbus and Mapplethorpe.

Cheese slicers, watches, a sports car and typewriters are just some of the items collected by the Department of Architecture and Design. With its rich collection of objects, graphic works, architectural models and drawings, the department has organized shows such as "Machine Art" and "Bauhaus: 1919–1928." The prints and illustrated books department is an important repository of art edition texts, with original Toulouse-Lautrec prints, graphic works by Munch, Redon, Klee and Johns, and first editions of significant art books.

The original MoMA building was designed by Edward Durell Stone and Philip L. Goodwin. Built in 1939, it was a fine example of the International Style. The sculpture garden on 54th Street, pictured above, was constructed in 1964 and designed by Philip Johnson. The West Wing and residential tower above it were designed by Cesar Pelli and Associates and constructed in 1984 when the museum underwent an extensive expansion and renovation.

The education department offers lectures and symposia by prominent artists and scholars, as well as regular gallery talks, films and live performances.

GENERAL INFORMATION

Hours Sun–Tues, Sat 11 am–6 pm; Thurs, Fri 12–8:30 pm; closed Wed
Admission Adults $7.50, students and seniors $4.50, children under 16 free; Thurs, Fri 5:30–8:30 pm voluntary contribution
Giftshop Store adjacent to museum: large selection of art books, posters, exhibition catalogs and cards; MoMA Design Store at 44 West 53rd St (across the street), open Fri–Wed 11am–5:45 pm, Thurs 11 am–8:45 pm
Food Service Garden Cafe open Sat–Tues, 11–5 pm; Thurs–Fri, 12–7:45 pm; Sette MoMA, open 12–3 pm, 5–11:30 pm, reservations required; both closed Wed
Library Main library with 80,000 volumes, plus separate study centers in photography, architecture and design, drawings, prints and illustrated books, film; all open by appointment
Disability Access Fully accessible; wheelchairs available at checkroom. Theaters have infrared system for hearing-impaired; inquire at information desk 212-708-9500; TDD 212-247-1230
Directions Subway: E, F, to 5th Ave and 53rd St; Bus: M1, M2, M3, M4, M5 to 53rd St; M27, M50 to 5th Ave

The Museum of Television and Radio

25 West 52nd Street (between Fifth and Sixth Avenues) New York, NY 10019 — 212-621-6600

The Museum of Television and Radio (formerly the Museum of Broadcasting) is the first institution in the United States dedicated solely to the collection, preservation and exhibition of television and radio programs. It was founded in 1975 by William S. Paley, also founder of the CBS television network. Its collection contains more than 60,000 programs—from news, public affairs programs and documentaries to the performing arts, children's shows, sports, comedy and advertising—covering over 70 years of television and radio history. Virtually all of these recordings are quickly accessible to the public through a new computerized catalog and playback system.

The museum's striking new facility, designed by Philip Johnson and John Burgee, opened in 1991. It houses a 200-seat theater, a 90-seat theater, two 45-seat screening rooms, 96 radio and television consoles for individual screening or listening and a listening room for radio programming. Major exhibitions and screening–listening series focus on topics of social, historical, popular or artistic interest.

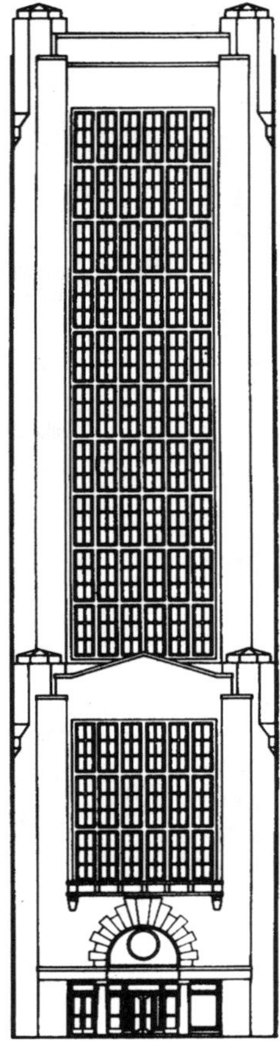

Architectual drawing of the Museum of Television and Radio's new West 52nd Street facility.

Recent exhibitions have included "The New York Philharmonic: A Radio and Television Tradition," in commemoration of the orchestra's 150th anniversary; "Madison Avenue Meets Gasoline Alley: Automobile Advertising on Radio and Television"; and, during the 1992 campaign, a reexamination of past presidential debates. In addition, a retrospective of PBS's acclaimed series "American Playhouse," seven previously unseen sketches of Jackie Gleason's "The Honeymooners" and memorable episodes of "Star Trek: The Next Generation" have been offered.

Three galleries house exhibits of television and radio artifacts. These have included original costumes worn by Elizabeth Taylor and others on television; apparel, masks and photographs used in the "Star Trek" series; and innovative poster art created to promote the PBS series "Masterpiece Theatre" and "Mystery!" Seminars feature discussions with writers, producers, directors, actors and others who have created landmark programming. The education department engages students with special programs at all grade levels.

GENERAL INFORMATION

Hours Tues, Wed, Sat, Sun 12–6 pm; Thurs 12–8 pm; Fri 12–9 pm; closed Mon
Admission Suggested contribution: adults $5, students $4, children under 13 and seniors $3
Giftshop Books on radio and television, tapes of classic programs, memorabilia, museum publications
Library See description above
Disability Access Fully accessible; elevators available
Directions Subway: E or F to 5th Ave and 53rd St; 6 to 51st St; N or R to 49th St; Bus: M1, M2, M3, M4, M5 to 52nd St; M27, M50 to 5th Ave

Museum of the City of New York

Fifth Avenue at 103rd Street
New York, NY 10029
212-534-1672

The complex narrative of New York City—from its start as a small Dutch trading post to its status today as one of the world's largest and most important cities—unfolds through the diverse collections of the Museum of the City of New York.

The museum's permanent collection contains over three million items, which are maintained by six curatorial departments—costumes, decorative arts, paintings and sculpture, prints and photographs, theater, and toys. Highlights include apparel worn at George Washington's inaugural ball, silver objects from the studios of Louis Comfort Tiffany, paintings by members of the Hudson River School, Currier & Ives prints, artifacts from New York theatrical productions and several original handwritten scripts by Eugene O'Neill.

In addition to period rooms and permanent exhibits, short-term displays explore the city's cultural diversity, architecture and economic significance. Shows have included "Is It Phyfe?," a display of the cabinetmaker's Federal-style furniture; "Songs of My People: The New York Melody," photographs by youngsters reflecting the pride of New York's African-Americans; "Building Bridges: Japanese Artists in New York City"; and "Family Treasures: Toys and Their Tales."

Founded in 1923, the museum first opened in Gracie Mansion (see separate entry). In 1932 it moved to its permanent home, a five-story neo-Georgian building designed by Joseph Freedlander. To display more of its holdings, the museum plans a seven-story addition to be completed in 1998, on its 75th anniversary. The education department offers concerts, walking tours, lectures, family programs and special children's events.

GENERAL INFORMATION

Hours Wed–Sat 10 am–5 pm; Tues 10 am–2 pm for preregistered groups; Sun 1–5 pm; closed Mon, Tues
Admission Suggested contribution: adults $5, families $8, seniors, students and children $3
Giftshop Books, toy reproductions, greeting cards, posters, gifts, collectibles relating to the art, culture and history of New York City
Library Photographs and archival materials on New York; open Mon–Fri 9 am–5 pm and by appointment
Disability Access Fully accessible; ramp at 104th St, restroom available. Services for the blind and hearing-impaired with advance notice
Directions Subway: 6 to 103rd St; Bus: M1, M3, M4 to 104th St
Landmark Status New York City Landmark
City-owned, privately operated

Courtesy of the Museum of the City of New York

Dressing room of the residence of John D. Rockefeller Sr., period room at the Museum of the City of New York.

National Academy of Design

1083 Fifth Avenue (at 89th Street) 212-369-4880
New York, NY 10128

In 1825 Samuel F.B. Morse, artist and inventor of the telegraph, working with the artists Rembrandt Peale, Thomas Cole and others, founded the National Academy of Design for the advancement and exhibition of American art. Peripatetic during its early years, today this organization operates out of a striking Beaux-Arts townhouse on Fifth Avenue, just north of the Guggenheim Museum (see separate entry).

The academy's permanent collection of over 4,000 works from the 19th and 20th centuries draws primarily on the realist tradition, with examples by American masters (and former academy members) such as Church, Cole, Eakins, Homer, Saint-Gaudens and Sargent. Exhibitions reveal the breadth of the academy's holdings and document its considerable artistic activity in the United States throughout its history. Exhibits have included the annual juried exhibitions, "Dreams and Shadows: Thomas Hotchkiss in 19th-Century Italy" and "Model to Mold: 19th and 20th Century Sculpture." In addition, the academy mounts traveling exhibits on loan from other museums.

The academy's School of Fine Arts offers multi-year programs in painting, sculpture and other disciplines taught by an outstanding faculty. Seminars, lectures, gallery talks, performances and concerts complete the academy's year-round slate of activities.

GENERAL INFORMATION

Hours Wed–Sun 12–5 pm; Fri 12–8 pm; closed Mon, Tues
Admission Adults $3.50, seniors, students and children under 16, $2; free on Wed for art students with ID; free for everyone Fri 5–8 pm
Giftshop Exhibition catalogs, design-related books, posters, cards, etc.
Library Contains titles on the decorative arts, prints, antiques, costumes, museum collections, artistic technique, art history, architecture and other subjects; access by appointment
Disability Access Fully accessible
Directions Subway: 4, 5 or 6 to 86th St; Bus: M1, M2, M3, M4 to 90th St

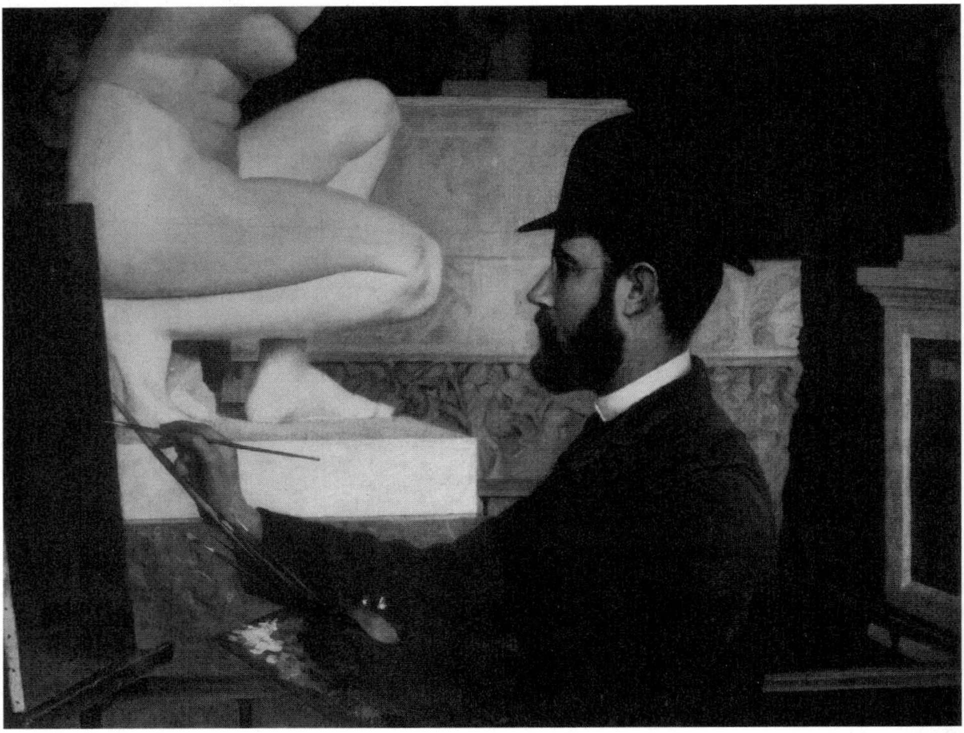

"Portrait of Charles C. Curran," by William J. Whittemore, 1988, from the permanent collection, National Academy of Design.

The National Museum of the American Indian

The George Gustav Heye Center
Smithsonian Institution
Alexander Hamilton
United States Custom House
One Bowling Green
(at State Street)
New York, NY 10004

212-283-2420

For over 60 years the Museum of the American Indian was an independent institution operating out of Audubon Terrace in Upper Manhattan. In 1989—in recognition of its outstanding collections and tenuous financial condition—an act of the United States Congress made it part of the Smithsonian Institution. This new affiliation has engendered enormous changes that should bring the museum international recognition.

In October 1994 the new National Museum of the American Indian will open an exhibition facility in the refurbished Alexander Hamilton United States Custom House in Lower Manhattan. By the end of the decade, the museum will open its flagship, $106 million facility, next to the National Air and Space Museum in Washington, DC; this new building will permit the museum to exhibit more of its vast collection, most of which has been in storage over the years. A third facility, the Museum Support Center, will open in Suitland, Maryland, in 1997.

The National Museum of the American Indian possesses one of the world's finest and most comprehensive assemblages of Indian artifacts, spanning 10,000 years of Native American heritage. Assembled by George Gustav Heye (1874–1957), an engineer and scion of a wealthy New York family, the holdings are distinguished by wood, horn and stone carvings from the northwest coast of North America; painted hides and garments from the North American plains; kachina dolls and basketry from the southwestern United States; archaeological objects from the Caribbean; textiles from Peru and Mexico; goldwork from Colombia, Peru and Mexico; jade from the Olmec and Mayan peoples; and Aztec mosaics.

Located in New York's financial district, the Custom House is an architectural jewel. Designed by Cass Gilbert and completed in 1907, the structure originally functioned as a site for the collection of customs duties. Today it is regarded as one of the most splendid Beaux-Arts buildings in New York. Ironically, it sits on what was once the southern end of the *wiechquaekeck* trail, an old Algonquin trade route.

Shirt produced by the Chilkate Indians of Alaska, from the collection of the National Museum of the American Indian.

GENERAL INFORMATION

Hours 10 am–5 pm daily (upon opening, Oct '94)
Admission Free
Giftshop Native American jewelry, pottery, beadwork, basketry, weavings, plus postcards and related books
Library Huntington Free Library, with 40,000 titles on Native Americans, is at 9 Westchester Sq, Bronx; open by appointment, Mon–Fri
Disability Access Fully accessible
Directions Subway: 1/9 to South Ferry; 4 or 5 to Bowling Green; N or R to Whitehall St–South Ferry; M, J or Z to Broad St; Bus: M1, M6, M15 to Bowling Green

SoHo Area Map

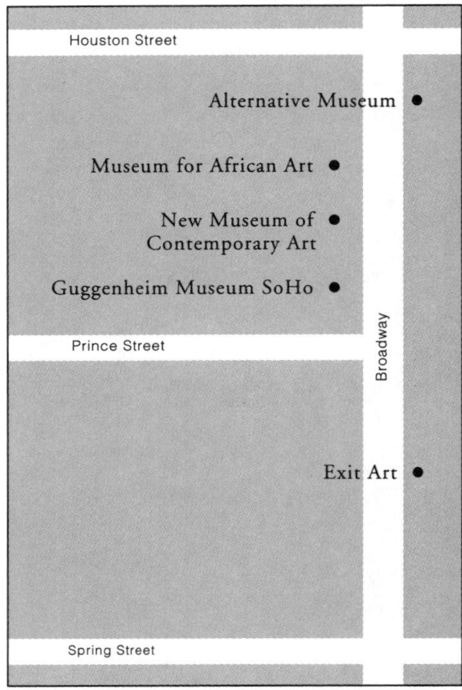

The New Museum of Contemporary Art

583 Broadway (between Prince and Houston Streets)
New York, NY 10012
212-219-1355

The New Museum of Contemporary Art is a haven for nontraditional and experimental art that other museums will not or cannot show. You will find art here that challenges and perhaps provokes you, but it is a virtual certainty you will never be bored. The museum's curators are interested in what art is and how it relates to individuals and society, and this is the thematic thread that pulls together an institution which prides itself on giving voice to a diversity of world views and esthetic sensibilities.

The New Museum presents three or four major exhibitions each year and up to 12 smaller shows. A range of curatorial approaches is employed: thematic shows, solo exhibits for artists in mid-career, guest-curated exhibitions, installations, commissioned works and exhibits organized elsewhere, such as "The 1970s: New American Painting," which toured Europe. The On View series presents smaller shows emphasizing the recent work of emerging artists.

The museum maintains a unique semipermanent collection, acquiring art for a ten-year period and then disposing of the collection after mounting a large, fully documented exhibition. Then the cycle begins again. The museum also offers symposiums, lectures and educational programs for everyone from elementary school children to adults.

The New Museum was founded in 1977 by Marcia Tucker, formerly a curator at the Whitney Museum of American Art. Since 1983 it has operated from the landmark Beaux-Arts Astor Building, originally constructed for John Jacob Astor. The museum is located in SoHo's landmark cast-iron district on the same block as the Guggenheim Museum SoHo and the Museum for African Art (see separate entries).

GENERAL INFORMATION

Hours Sun, Wed–Fri 12–6 pm; Sat 12–8 pm; closed Mon, Tues
Admission Adults $3.50, students and seniors $2.50, children under 12 free; free, Sat 6–8 pm
Giftshop Books, catalogs, maps, guides and limited-edition artworks
Library SoHo Center Library, a world-class resource on contemporary art, criticism and theory containing over 48,000 volumes; temporarily closed at publication time
Disability Access Limited access; wheelchairs on ground floor only
Directions Subway: 6 to Spring St or Bleecker St; N or R to Prince St; A, C or E to Spring St; B, D or F to Broadway–Lafayette St; Bus: M1, M5, M6, M21 to Houston St or Broadway
Landmark Status National Register of Historic Places, New York City Landmark

The New York Academy of Sciences

2 East 63rd Street
(at Fifth Avenue)
New York, NY 10021
212-838-0230

Originally the Lyceum of Natural History when it was established in 1817, the New York Academy of Sciences is one of the oldest scientific societies in America. Its "Art at the Academy" exhibitions focus on science-related art. Exhibits have included "Kenneth Snelson: the Nature of Structure," an exploration of the artist's career and his distinctive tube-and-cable sculptures;

and "Recent Photographs: Hans Danuser," images of technical and scientific activity.

The academy hosts some 20 international conferences annually, bringing together thousands of distinguished scientists for face-to-face intellectual exchange. Smaller workshops focus on single scientific issues. Early academy members included Charles Darwin, Thomas Huxley, Louis Pasteur and Thomas Edison. Science education is a big part of the academy's mission and it sponsors many programs for school students at all grade levels.

GENERAL INFORMATION

Hours Sept–June: gallery open Mon–Fri 10 am–4 pm; call for hours during July and Aug
Admission Free
Disability Access Call in advance for assistance
Directions Subway: N or R to 5th Ave; Bus: M1, M2, M3, M4 to 63rd St; M66 to 5th Ave
Landmark Status National Register of Historic Places

New York City Fire Museum

278 Spring Street
(between Hudson
and Varick Streets)
New York, NY 10013

212-691-1303

The New York City Fire Museum displays the richest collection of fire memorabilia in the United States, dating from the mid-18th century to the present. Beautifully preserved horse- and hand-drawn rigs, helmets, hoses and interactive videos show visitors how firefighting technology has changed as knowl-

Fireman's Helmet, ca. 1890, at the New York City Fire Museum.

edge about the behavior [illegible] museum is located in a [illegible] firehouse in SoHo.

Working Firehouse, th[illegible] is organized around [illegible] Colonial times to the [illegible] leather fire buckets [illegible] and The Hope, a r[illegible] the dedication of the [illegible]

The second floor exhibit celebrat[illegible] city's volunteer firefighters. (New York firefi[illegible] now highly trained, full-time professionals.) Visitors can step into the boots of firefighters, don helmets and sit atop rigs. Exhibits have explored the causes and aftermath of New York's most famous fires as well as 19th- and 20th-century firefighting toys. The small reference library and study area are open by appointment. A fire-safety awareness program consists of lectures and museum tours.

GENERAL INFORMATION

Hours Tues–Sat 10 am–4 pm; closed Sun, Mon
Admission Suggested contribution: adults $3, children 50¢
Giftshop Fire-related items: official Fire Department of New York and museum T-shirts, toy fire engines, badges, books, puzzles and mugs
Library Open by appointment
Disability Access Fully accessible; elevator available. Call about arrangements for blind and hearing-impaired
Directions Subway: 1/9 to Houston St, then walk three blocks south on Varick to Spring St; C or E to Spring St, then walk west past Varick; Bus: M21 to Spring St

City-owned, operated by New York City Fire Department

New York Public Library

Central Research Library
Fifth Avenue and 42nd Street
New York, NY 10018

212-870-1630

The New York Public Library's research collections contain over 39 million items making it one of the world's greatest libraries. About 11.5 million of these items are books. The balance is in the form of periodicals, manuscripts, photographs, maps, newspapers, microfilms, prints, paintings, ephemera, CD-ROM and on-line resources.

1990 Casey Cronin

Collection highlights include a Gutenberg Bible, the first five folios of Shakespeare's plays, ancient Torah scrolls, a handwritten copy of George Washington's Farewell Address to his troops, paintings by Rembrandt Peale and the Hudson River School, rare cylindrical recordings, prints by the Japanese master Hokusai, illustrations by British satirist Hogarth and Alexander Hamilton's handwritten draft of the United States Constitution.

Over one million visitors use the library's four Manhattan research facilities every year. They are the Central Research Library at 42nd Street, the focus of this entry; the Schomburg Center for Research in Black Culture (see separate entry); the New York Public Library for the Performing Arts at Lincoln Center (see next entry); and the new Science, Industry and Business Library, now in the planning stages. The library also operates 82 branch libraries in the Bronx, Manhattan and Staten Island. (Brooklyn and Queens each has its own library system.)

The Central Research Library's holdings focus on the humanities, social sciences and special collections. In addition, the library mounts exhibitions in four galleries. Exhibits in Gottesman Hall, the main gallery, have included "Flora Photographica: The Flower in Photography, 1835–Present"; "King Arthur: Looking at the Legend," tracing the Arthurian legend from its 12th century origins to today through rare books, musical scores and photographs; and "On the Edge: Photographs from 100 Years of Vogue," which included works by Cecil Beaton, Edward Steichen, Richard Avedon and others.

Salomon Room exhibits have featured the working papers of Truman Capote; "Documents of Dissent," recent political dissent around the world as chronicled through posters, underground newspapers and the like; and "Shelley: Unacknowledged Legislator," an examination of the poet's role as political activist. "Edna St. Vincent Millay, 1892–1950" and "Walt Whitman: In Life and Death Forever" were mounted in the Berg Exhibition Room, and the Third Floor Gallery has offered "Revelations and Revolution: German Expressionist Prints and Books" and "Recent Acquisitions: Photography."

The library was founded in 1895 when the private libraries of John Jacob Astor and James Lenox were merged with monies from the Samuel Tilden Trust. The Beaux-Arts building is perhaps the crowning achievement of the architectural firm of Carrère & Hastings, possessing one of the most opulent interiors in New York. The structure, completed in 1911, took ten years to build at a cost of $9 million. During the 1980s the New York Public Library undertook a successful $307 million fundraising campaign. A portion of these funds were used to thoroughly restore the deteriorating Central Research Library to its former neo-classical glory.

The Central Research Library also offers a fine public education program that features top writers, critics and historians discussing their work, as well as political figures, fashion designers, filmmakers and others.

GENERAL INFORMATION

Hours Mon, Thurs–Sat 10 am–6 pm; Tues, Wed 11 am–7:30 pm; closed Sun; call for schedule of exhibitions, lectures, etc.
Admission Free
Giftshop Books, art reproductions, postcards, gift items, toys, posters, jewelry, desk accessories
Library See description above
Disability Access Fully accessible; ramp at 42nd St entrance
Directions Subway: 1/9, 2 or 3 to 42nd St–Times Square, then walk east to 5th Ave; 4, 5 or 6 to Grand Central–42nd St, then walk west to 5th Ave; 7 to 5th Avenue; B, D, F or Q to 42nd St; Bus: M1, M2, M3, M4, M5, M6, M7, M104, Q32 to 42nd St
Landmark Status National Register of Historic Places, New York City Landmark
City-owned, privately operated

Above: Fortitude, one of the two concrete lions (the other one's name is Patience) guarding the hallowed portals of the New York Public Library.

Opposite page: One of Alexander Calder's famous stabiles outside the Lincoln Center Plaza entrance of the New York Public Library for the Performing Arts; to the left is the Metropolitan Opera House; to the right is the Vivian Beaumont Theater.

New York Public Library for the Performing Arts

40 Lincoln Center Plaza 212-870-1600
(enter Lincoln Center Plaza
or Amsterdam Avenue
and 65th Street)
New York, NY 10023

The heavy slab of travertine marble above Lincoln Center's Vivian Beaumont Theater and the glass wall behind the theater facing Amsterdam Avenue are, respectively, the reading rooms and exhibition spaces of the New York Public Library for the Performing Arts. Conveniently located at Lincoln Center (see separate entry), the nation's premier performing arts complex, this is one of the four Manhattan research facilities of the New York Public Library (see previous entry).

The research collections here focus on dance, theater, music and recorded sound. Collection highlights include Oscar Wilde's original typescript of "The Importance of Being Earnest"; the Jerome Robbins Dance Archive, containing films and videos of hundreds of choreographed dances by masters of the art; a similar theater archive that records comedies, dramas, musicals and cutting-edge performance art for future reference that would otherwise not be preserved on permanent media; a vast collection of popular and classical recordings accessible through listening carrels; and original scores in the hand of Mozart, Haydn, Mahler and others.

Exhibitions are a prominent feature of the New York Public Library for the Performing Arts. Exhibits regularly feature costumes and set designs, posters, playbills, autographed scores, original letters, prints and photographs. Shows have included "Zurich: The Fugitive's Haven," surveying the history of the Zurich theater, formed when artists fled Nazi Germany; "Body and Soul: The Alvin Ailey American Dance Theater," tracing the history of the company from its 1958 founding to the present; and "The Theater Magic of Jusaburo Tsujimura," the Japanese puppet master.

Concerts and lectures are offered in the Bruno Walter auditorium, and occasionally plays, theatrical readings and special events are presented.

GENERAL INFORMATION

Hours Mon, Thurs 12–8 pm; Wed, Fri, Sat 12–6 pm; closed Tues, Sun
Admission Free
Library See description above
Disability Access Fully accessible
Directions Subway: 1/9 to 66th St; A, B, C or D to 59th St–Columbus Circle; Bus: M5, M7, M10, M11, M66, M104 to 66th St
Parking On-site lot, beneath Lincoln Center
City-owned, privately operated

Susan Oristaglio

New York School of Interior Design Gallery

170 East 70th Street
(between Lexington
and Third Avenues)
New York, NY 10022

212-472-1500
Ext. 36

The forte of this small gallery is design and architecture. The space—an exhibition area of ten by twenty feet leading into extended hallways—features two shows during the school year (September–May) and student work during the summer. Exhibitions have included "Paris in the Belle Époque," rare photographs of the French capital in the years 1880–1914; "Vanishing Irish Country Houses," a look at the preservation crisis facing these magnificent structures; "The Painted Surface," exploring techniques of *faux bois* and *faux marbre*; "The New Classicism," showcasing trends in current furniture design; "Perspective on Perspective," about the subtle art of rendering interiors and exteriors; and "The Artist as Decorator," bridging the gap between the fine and decorative arts with displays of fabrics and pottery by major American and European artists. The gallery's Thursday evening lectures have included an examination of lessons learned from French architecture and a survey of Paris' *Grands Projets* undertaken during the Mitterrand era.

GENERAL INFORMATION

Hours Mon–Thurs 12–6 pm; Fri 12–5 pm; closed weekends
Admission Free
Disability Access Fully accessible; elevator available
Directions Subway: E or F to Lexington Ave–53rd St; 4, 5, 6, N or R to Lexington Ave–59th St; Bus: M98, M101, M102 to 56th St; M31, M57, M58 to 3rd Ave

New York Shakespeare Festival

212-598-7100

The New York Shakespeare Festival was founded by Joseph Papp in 1954 in a church basement on Manhattan's Lower East Side. Today the New York Shakespeare Festival encompasses the Public, with five stages and a cinema under one roof; free Shakespeare at the Delacorte Theater; and Broadway productions, national and international tours, television and motion pictures. Shakespeare Festival productions have won 28 Tony Awards, 96 Obies, 29 Drama Desk Awards and three Pulitzer Prizes. Seventeen productions have gone to Broadway, including "A Chorus Line," "The Pirates of Penzance" and "The Secret Rapture."

Joseph Papp Public Theater

425 Lafayette Street (between
East Fourth Street and Astor Place)
New York, NY 10003

212-598-7150
Box Office

For the year-round production of new American plays, Joseph Papp saved the old Astor Library from demolition and renamed it the Public Theater. The city now owns and supports the building, which has been meticulously renovated with public and private funds. "The Public," as it is known to New Yorkers, opened in 1967 with the original production of "Hair."

The Public also offers poetry readings; informal encounters with actors, directors and playwrights; and a series with cabaret acts, performance artists, comedians and music.

The Public was built in three phases between 1853 and 1881. It is considered a fine example of *Rundbogenstil*, a German variation of Romanesque Revival. John Jacob Astor had the red brick and brownstone structure built as New York's first public library. Its collections later became part of the New York Public Library (see separate entry).

GENERAL INFORMATION

Hours Box office open 1–8 pm daily, except Mon 1–6 pm
Admission Price varies; single tickets usually $15–$37.50; some discount tickets available day of performance

Giftshop Lobby theater giftshop; open Tues–Fri 4 pm through performance; Sat, Sun 1 pm through performance
Food Service Light refreshments available during performances
Library Archival materals at the New York Public Library for the Performing Arts (see separate entry)
Disability Access Fully accessible
Directions Subway: N or R to 8th St; 6 to Astor Place; F to Broadway–Lafayette; Bus: M1 to 8th St
Landmark Status National Register of Historic Places, New York City Landmark

City-owned, privately operated

Delacorte Theater

Central Park
(enter at 81st Street from Central Park West or at 79th Street from Fifth Avenue)
212-861-7277

In 1962 the Delacorte Theater, funded by New York philanthropist and publisher George Delacorte, was built near Central Park's Belvedere Lake for free performances of Shakespeare's plays during the summer. The New York Shakespeare Festival is now in the midst of a multi-year effort to produce all 38 of the bard's plays, some staged at the Public, others at the Delacorte. Recent productions have included "Much Ado About Nothing," with Kevin Kline and "Twelfth Night," with F. Murray Abraham. During some summers, productions of the Festival Latino are also staged at the Delacorte.

The Delacorte Theater in Central Park, Manhattan's Upper West Side in background.

GENERAL INFORMATION

Hours Box office open 1–8 pm daily
Admission Free, tickets are distributed first come, first serve; no advance distribution of tickets, day of performance only; get there early to avoid the lines.
Disability Access Fully accessible, but call in advance
Directions Subway: 6 to 77th St, walk west, enter park at 79th St; A, B, C, D, 2 or 3 to 72nd St, walk east, enter park at 81st St; 1/9 to 79th St, walk east, enter park at 81st St; Bus: M1, M2, M3, M4 to 79th St; M90 to 5th Ave; M10, M79 to 81st St
Landmark Status National Register of Historic Places, New York City Landmark

City-owned, privately operated

New York Studio School Gallery

8 West 8th Street
New York, NY 10011
212-673-6466

During the 1920s, Gertrude Vanderbilt Whitney, sculptor and arts patron, kept a small studio on MacDougal Alley, directly across from the graceful mews and carriage houses of Washington Square. These small dwellings were converted into more studio space over the years as Mrs. Whitney began acquiring buildings and opening spaces for artists to exhibit and work. Thus began the Whitney Studio Club, which later became part of the Whitney Museum of American Art. When the museum moved to the Upper East Side in the mid-1960s, the New York Studio School of Drawing, Painting and Sculpture was founded.

The gallery at the New York Studio School mounts five or six shows from October through June, drawing largely from the works of its faculty and students. The school offers classes, workshops and lectures, maintaining an atelier atmosphere where artists can learn and teach.

GENERAL INFORMATION

Hours Sept–July: Mon–Fri 10 am–6 pm; Sat, Sun 10 am–4 pm; closed Aug
Admission Free
Disability Access None
Directions Subway: N, R, 4, 5 or 6 to 8th St; A, C, E, B, D or F to West 4th St; Bus: M13 to Ave of the Americas (6th Ave); M2, M3, M5, M6 to 8th St
Landmark Status National Register of Historic Places, New York City Landmark

New York University Area Map

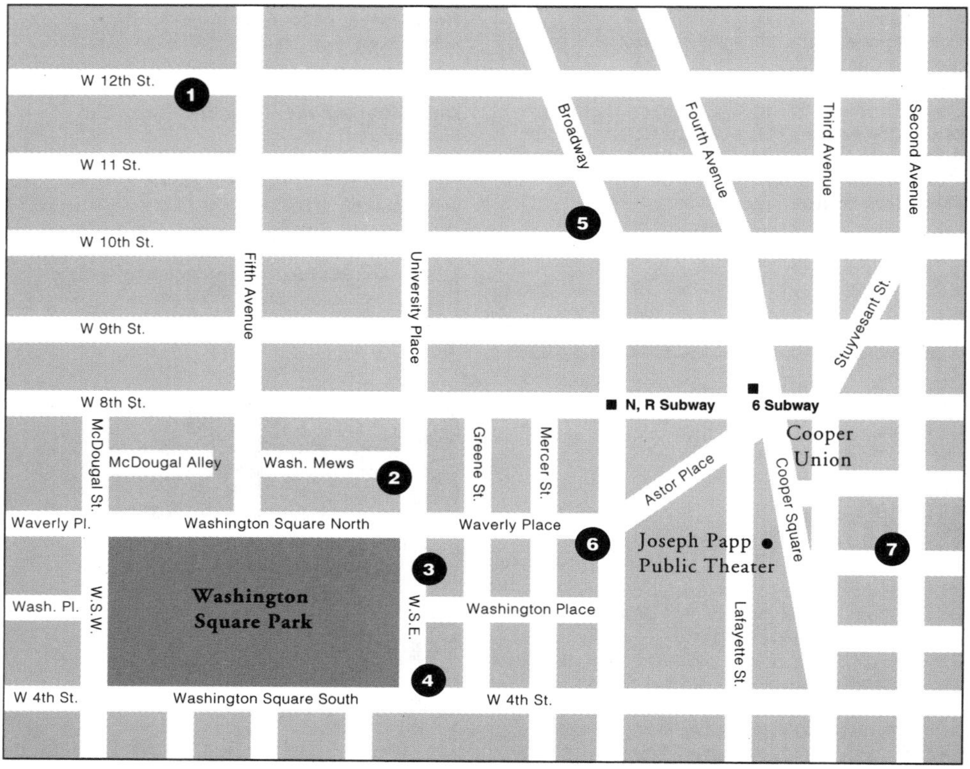

1 Casa Italiania Zerilli-Marimo

2 La Maison Française

3 Grey Art Gallery and Study Center

4 80 Washington Square East Galleries

5 Broadway Windows

6 Tisch School/Photography Galleries

7 Tisch School/Graduate Acting Program

New York University

50 West Fourth Street
New York, NY
(See entries below for addresses/telephone numbers)

212-998-1212
General Information

Founded in 1831, New York University is today the largest private university in the United States. Its 13 schools, colleges and divisions serve some 49,000 students annually. Unlike Columbia University—with its distinctive plaza—NYU has no central campus. Its classrooms, libraries and residence halls are scattered throughout Greenwich Village and other New York neighborhoods. This gives NYU a decentralized character unusual in American universities as well as a sense of integration with the workaday life of the city.

What follows are capsule descriptions of some of the most active visual arts and performing arts activities at NYU open to the public.

GENERAL INFORMATION

Hours See descriptions below; several programs function intermittently, so call for schedule information
Admission Varies per venue: galleries usually free, sometimes a charge for live performances
Disability Access See descriptions below
General directions to Greenwich Village
Subway A, B, C, D, E, F or Q to West 4th St; N or R to 8th St; 6 to Astor Place; Bus M1, M2, M3, M5, M6 to University Place
Landmark Status
National Register of Historic Places

80 Washington Sq. East Galleries

at West 4th Street 212-998-5747

Established in 1975 as the exhibition facility of the NYU Department of Art and Art Education, 80 Washington Square East Galleries exhibits work by students seeking their master's degrees within the studio art program. Special events, such as the "Annual Small Works Competition," occupy all the galleries. Occasionally non-student shows are mounted. The galleries are located next to Goddard Hall.

GENERAL INFORMATION

Hours Tues 11 am–7 pm; Wed, Thurs 11 am–6 pm; Fri, Sat 11 am–5 pm; closed Sun, Mon
Admission Free
Disability Access Fully accessible via 79 Washington Square East

The Washington Arch in Washington Square Park, designed by Stanford White of McKim, Mead & White, 1895.

Casa Italiana Zerilli-Marimo

24 West 12th Street (off Fifth Avenue) 212-998-8728

Exhibitions, usually by Italian artists or on Italian subjects, have included "American Sketchbook: 1957-90," oils, watercolors and drawings by Luciano Guarnieri; and photographic shows exploring ancient Etruscan tumulus architecture and Italian-American culture.

GENERAL INFORMATION

Hours Mon–Fri 10 am–5 pm; closed weekends
Admission Free
Disability Access Fully accessible

Grey Art Gallery and Study Center

33 Washington Place (at Washington Square East) 212-998-6780

Two exhibition spaces feature shows in virtually all aspects of the fine and applied arts: painting, sculpture, decorative arts, architecture, film, video and performance art. Exhibits have included "Camera as Weapon: Worker Photography Between the Wars," "Against Nature: Japanese Art in the Eighties" and "Sonia Delaunay: A Retrospective." Exhibition-related gallery talks, lectures and symposiums are also offered.

GENERAL INFORMATION

Hours Tues, Thurs, Fri 11 am–6 pm; Wed 11 am–8:30 pm, Sat 11 am–5 pm
Admission Suggested contribution: $2.50
Disability Access Fully accessible

La Maison Française

16 Washington Mews (between University Place and Fifth Avenue) 212-998-8750

The emphasis here, not surprisingly, is on French artists. Exhibitions have included "Haiti: Flesh and Spirit," a sequence of black-and-white photographs;

"Artists at the Court of Burgundy" and "Photographs of France and Beyond."

GENERAL INFORMATION

Hours Mon–Fri 10 am–6 pm; reopens at 7:45 for evening engagements; closed weekends
Admission Free
Disability Access Fully accessible

Photography Galleries

Tisch School of the Arts 212-998-1930
721 Broadway, Eighth Floor
(at Waverly Place)

Throughout the year the Tisch School of the Arts offers photo exhibitions which include work by faculty, students and other visitors. Shows have focused on new directions in fine art, documentary and electronic genres including Peter Smith's large murals of contemporary dancers on stage.

GENERAL INFORMATION

Hours Mon–Fri 10–5 pm; Sat 12–5 pm; closed Sun
Admission Free
Disability Access Fully accessible

Graduate Acting Program

111 Second Avenue 212-998-1921
(between 6th and 7th Streets)

Productions within the Tisch School of the Arts Graduate Acting Program have included Joe Orton's "What the Butler Saw" and Ivan Turgenev's "A Month in the Country." The program also uses two small theaters at the Tisch School, 721 Broadway (at Waverly Place).

GENERAL INFORMATION

Hours Varies with performance
Admission Free, but reservations are required
Disability Access Fully accessible

OTHER CULTURAL ACTIVITIES AT NYU

Broadway Windows
Five streetside display windows serve as a gallery for exhibitions of contemporary art
Broadway and East 10th Street
212-998-5751

Center for Music Performance
Classical and jazz concerts throughout the year
Loeb Student Center, 566 LaGuardia Place
212-998-5252

Gallatin at La Mama Project
Original short plays presented at La Mama E.T.C. (see separate entry) by the NYU Gallatin Division
212-998-7370

NYU Creative Writing Program
Prose and poetry readings by some of the foremost writers and poets working today
Locations vary.
212-998-8816

School of Education, Dance and Dance Education Program
Performances by students and faculty
35 West 4th Street
212-998-5400

School of Education Program in Educational Theater
Locations vary.
212-998-5868

Tisch School of the Arts Dance Program
Performances by students and faculty
111 Second Avenue space (between 6th and 7th Streets)
212-998-1980

Tisch School of the Arts Undergraduate Drama Program
721 Broadway (at Waverly Place)
212-998-1850

New-York Historical Society

170 Central Park West
(at 77th Street)
New York, NY 10024

212-873-3400

Founded in 1804, when a group of New York merchants, politicians and professionals set out to "discover, procure and preserve the...history of the United States... and of this State in particular," the New-York Historical Society operates New York's oldest museum. Its collection of 1.6 million objects includes fine examples of painting, furniture, prints, maps, books and manuscripts that preserve the American past.

At the time of this guide's publication only the library and print room were open to the public. The galleries were closed as the institution was being reorganized, a regrettable situation because the society's fine and decorative art collections contain an interesting mix of items. Examples include an assortment of late 19th-century carriages, numerous paintings by artists of the Hudson River School, works by early New York silversmiths, lamps from the studios of Louis Comfort Tiffany and all but one of the original watercolors used by John James Audubon for his great book "The Birds of America."

Anthony Holmes

"Snowy Egret" from John James Audubon's "The Birds of America," Watercolor, 1832.

The library holds some of the landmark documents in American history, including one of 23 surviving copies of the Declaration of Independence (1776), George Washington's proposed plan for retaking British-occupied New York City (1781) and a copy of "Freedom's Journal" (1827), the first paper published by African-Americans for their fellow citizens.

In 1904 the society built its current home, a neo-classical building on Central Park West. The granite facade was designed by the firm of York and Sawyer. The north and south wings, designed by Walker and Gillette, were added 30 years later.

GENERAL INFORMATION

Hours Library open Mon–Fri 10 am–5 pm (subject to change; call to confirm). Call for gallery reopening date
Admission Free
Library A major source of primary and secondary materials on New York history: 650,000 volumes; 2 million manuscripts, documents and letters; 30,000 maps, atlases, etc.
Disability Access Limited access; call for information
Directions Subway: A, B, C or D to 77th St; Bus: M10 to 76th St
Landmark Status National Register of Historic Places, New York City Landmark

Nikon House

620 Fifth Avenue at
(between 49th and 50th Streets)
Rockefeller Center
New York, NY 10020

212-586-3907

The first floor of Nikon House is an information center and product showroom for Nikon camera equipment. On the second and third floors, 12 to 15 exhibits by both established and emerging professional photographers are mounted each year. Nikon House has exhibited works by such well-known photographers as Pulitzer Prize winners John White and David Turnley. Annually the gallery hosts the "Ford Modeling: New Photo Faces" exhibit and the "Small World" show of microscopic photography. In addition, educational and instructional workshops, led by Nikon's technical staff, are offered free of charge.

GENERAL INFORMATION

Hours Tues–Sat 9:30 am–5:30 pm; closed Sun, Mon
Admission Free
Disability Access Limited access
Directions Subway: B, D, F or Q to 47th–50th Sts; N or R to 49th St; Bus: M27, M50 to 5th Ave; M1, M2, M3, M4, M5 to 49th St
Landmark Status National Register of Historic Places, New York City Landmark

92nd Street Y

1395 Lexington Avenue (at 92nd Street) New York, NY 10128 — 212-996-1100

The 92nd Street Y—a hybrid institution that has attributes of both a performing arts center and a college—operates out of a complex of buildings on Manhattan's Upper East Side. Particularly impressive is the range of notable figures the Y is able to engage year after year to perform, lecture, give interviews and participate in panel discussions.

During just one fall season such luminaries included journalist and former hostage Terry Anderson, former Secretary of State Henry Kissinger, choreographer Merce Cunningham, restaurant critic Gael Greene, actors Dustin Hoffman and Michael Douglas, artist David Salle, novelist/filmmaker Nora Ephron, New York Governor Mario Cuomo, playwrights Wendy Wasserstein and Tony Kushner, diplomat Jeane Kirkpatrick, attorney Alan Dershowitz and many more.

Subjects addressed in Y courses and public lectures include New York architecture and archaeology, personal investment strategies, the earth's threatened biodiversity, U.S. foreign policy, advancing media technology, dining out, personal growth, smoking cessation and language instruction. There are also many activities and courses in Jewish culture and religious life, and Jewish holiday celebrations.

In addition, the Poetry Center, without parallel in the United States, organizes readings by some of the world's greatest poets and writers. Readings have been given by Nobel Prize winners Nadine Gordimer, Czeslaw Milosz, Toni Morrison and Derek Walcott, as well as Margaret Atwood, Salman Rushdie, Joyce Carol Oates, Norman Mailer, Mavis Gallant, Anthony Hecht, James Merrill, Mario Vargas Llosa, Tracy Kidder, Galway Kinnell and Terrence McNally. Readings also feature emerging novelists and poets. The Poetry Center conducts writing workshops as well.

The 92nd Street Y concert series includes performances highlighting orchestral and chamber music, jazz piano, string quartets and young concert artists. The Y also offers a range of courses in the arts through its School of Music, Dance Center and Arts Center.

The Young Men's Hebrew Association was founded in 1874 and opened a downtown branch eight years later to assist new immigrants. In 1900 the 92nd Street Y opened on Lexington Avenue. It was replaced with a larger structure 30 years later.

GENERAL INFORMATION

Hours Box office: open Mon–Thurs 1–9 pm; Fri 11 am–4 pm; Sat 6–9 pm; Sun 12–8 pm
Admission Price varies; 50 percent discounts for seniors and students on day of performance; Late Rate Card may be purchased for discounts to ticketed events. Course tuition varies; call for catalog
Library Buttenwieser Library focuses on Jewish history and culture; open to members and, for a $45 annual fee, to nonmembers
Disability Access Fully accessible; elevators, ramp, restrooms, public phones available; infrared listening system for hearing-impaired; guide dogs admitted with visually impaired
Directions Subway: 4, 5 or 6 to 86th St; Bus: M1, M2, M3, M4, M101, M102 to 92nd St

Symbol Key

 *Institutional Giftshop*

 *On-Site Food Services*

 *On-Site Library or Archive*

 *Full Accessibility*

 *On-Site Parking*

 *National Register of Historic Places and/or New York City Landmark*

Old Merchant's House

29 East 4th Street
(between Lafayette
Street and Bowery)
New York, NY 10003

212-777-1089

Standing amid Greenwich Village's garages, lofts and factories is the Old Merchant's House—a five-story row house that is among the finest surviving examples of late-Federal and Greek Revival architecture in New York. Built in 1832, the house is the only 19th-century home in Manhattan with all of its original furnishings intact.

Milliner Joseph Brewster built the house in 1832. It was purchased by hardware merchant Seabury Tredwell in 1835. Tredwell's descendants lived there until 1933, when his last surviving daughter died. The house was then purchased by a cousin and established as a museum in 1936. It was restored during the 1970s and again in the 1980s, reopening in 1991.

The house's rich red brick and white marble exterior recalls the beauty and order of entire city blocks now razed. The front door opens onto a handsome *faux marbre* vestibule. Beyond, the parlor contains ornate gasoliers, mahogany furniture, crimson draperies and carpets. Upstairs the four-poster double bed is hung with a red wool damask canopy and gilded wood ornaments.

Exhibitions have included "Once in a Lifetime," displaying the Tredwells' 19th century apparel. The museum has also hosted New York University symposiums, including one on "Authenticity in American Antique Furniture." Special group tours can be arranged. The Old Merchant's House is the only historic house museum in Greenwich Village.

GENERAL INFORMATION

Hours Sun–Thurs 1–4 pm; closed Fri, Sat; closed Aug
Admission Adults $3, seniors and students $2
Giftshop 19th-century reproduction toys, vintage textiles and books
Disability Access None
Directions Subway: 6 to Astor Place; N or R to 8th St; A, B, C, D, E, F or Q to West 4th St; Bus: M1, M2, M3, M101, M102 to 4th St
Landmark Status National Register of Historic Places, New York City Landmark

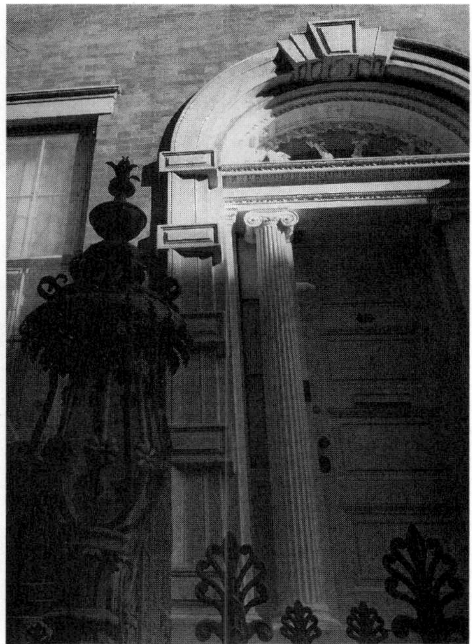

Old Merchant's House, 29 East 4th Street.

P.S. 122 (Performance Space 122)

150 First Avenue (at 9th Street)
New York, NY 10009

212-477-5288
Box Office

Started in 1980 in a disused public school building on Manhattan's Lower East Side, P.S. 122 is an arts center specializing in experimental multimedia performance. It presents 300 to 400 events a year in two small theaters. Artists and companies working here are largely concerned with exploring the contextual interrelationships of movement/dance, text, media, visual art and sound.

P.S. 122 series include "Avant-Garde-Arama," two-day mini-festivals of new performance, dance, music and film; "The Hearings," a music concert program; "Reel Time," featuring work by independent and experimental filmmakers; and "La Misma Onda," a Latino film series. "Spacecase: Art in the Lobby" mounts small exhibitions of photography, painting and other visual media.

The organization also offers numerous support services for artists. P.S. 122 is in many ways a product of the long tradition of radical thought that has flourished for generations among the immigrant and artistic communities of the Lower East Side.

GENERAL INFORMATION

Hours Box office open half hour before curtain
Admission Price varies; usually $6–$8; discounts for students and other groups; TDF voucher accepted
Disability Access Limited access: first floor accessible; second floor by prior arrangement only, call for information
Directions Subway: L to 1st Ave; N or R to 8th St; 6 to Astor Place; Bus: M8 to East 9th St and 1st Ave; M14 to Ave A and East 9th St; M15 to 1st Ave and St. Mark's Place

City-owned, privately operated

© Dona Ann McAdams

Dancer Ron Brown performing at P.S. 122.

Pace Downtown Theater

Schimmel Center for the Arts
One Pace Plaza (Spruce Street between Park Row and Gold Street)
New York, NY 10038

212-346-1715 Box Office

Pace Downtown Theater is on the New York City campus of Pace University. Just five minutes from Chinatown, across the street from City Hall, the 659-seat theater offers a range of events embracing everything from jazz to Chinese drama, from baroque dance to chamber music. It is well known for modern dance offerings and its Highlights in Jazz series.

GENERAL INFORMATION

Hours Box office open Mon–Fri 1–5 pm or until curtain time on performance nights
Admission Price varies, usually $5–$20 per ticket; discounts available
Disability Access Limited access
Directions Subway: 4, 5 or 6 to City Hall; A to Fulton St; N or R to City Hall; 1/9 to Park Place; Bus: M101, M102 to Park Row; M1, M6 to City Hall

PaineWebber Art Gallery

1285 Avenue of the Americas
(between 51st and 52nd Streets)
New York, NY 10019

212-713-2885

PaineWebber Art Gallery opened in 1985 in the lobby of PaineWebber's corporate headquarters. Located next to Equitable Center (see separate entry), it features short-term exhibitions from New York cultural institutions. For example, exhibits exploring children's art, Mayan weavings, landscape design, contemporary folk art and sports photography have come to the gallery from organizations such as the Americas Society, the Studio Museum in Harlem, the Queens Museum of Art, and Studio in a School. About four or five shows are mounted yearly.

Star Black

An artist at Studio in a School exhibit at PaineWebber Art Gallery.

GENERAL INFORMATION

Hours Mon–Fri 8 am–6 pm; closed Sat, Sun
Admission Free
Disability Access Fully accessible
Directions Subway: 1/9 to 50th St; B, D or E to 7th Ave; B, D, F or Q to 47th-50th St; N or R to 49th St; Bus: M27, M50 to 6th Ave; M5, M6, M7 to 51st St

Park Avenue Atrium

237 Park Avenue
(between 45th and 46th Streets; enter on Lexington Avenue)
New York, NY 10017

212-850-9786

Within the tree-lined, glass-enclosed inner court of the Park Avenue Atrium is 300 linear feet of wall space reserved for exhibitions. This large, sprawling gallery offers four to six exhibits annually, each containing up to 100 works. Exhibits are eclectic in nature and have included "Originals: The Cartoonist's Art"; "Testing: Behind the Scenes at Consumer Reports," an off-beat photography show; and a show on the history of pinball machine design. Park Avenue Atrium sits over part of the original Grand Central Terminal. It was thoroughly redesigned in the 1980s by Edward Durell Stone Associates.

GENERAL INFORMATION

Hours Mon–Fri 8 am–6 pm; closed Sat, Sun
Admission Free
Disability Access Fully accessible
Directions Subway: 6 or 7 to 42nd St–Grand Central; Bus: M1, M2, M3, M4, M32, M101, M102 to 49th St; M27, M42, M104 to Lexington Ave; M1, M2, M3, M5, M6, to 10th St

Pen and Brush

16 East Tenth Street
(between Fifth Avenue and University Place)
New York, NY 10003

212-475-3669

Founded in 1893, Pen and Brush is the oldest professional organization for women writers and artists in the United States. It presents the work of members in about ten exhibitions a year. These include two oil and two watercolor shows, a graphics show, a crafts show, an invitational pastel exhibition and a juried sculpture show. The gallery space is used by other arts organizations for their own exhibits.

The institute also offers lectures, numerous concerts, art and craft demonstrations and slide presentations related to the arts; all are open to the public. Illustrious Pen and Brush members have included Anne Morrow Lindbergh, Marianne Moore and Eleanor Roosevelt. Pen and Brush is housed in a landmark 1843 brownstone in Greenwich Village. Its spacious, high-ceilinged parlors, arched doorways, marble fireplaces and inlaid wood floors represent the very finest in early American craftsmanship.

GENERAL INFORMATION

Hours Vary, call for information
Admission Free
Giftshop Holiday craft sale in Dec
Disability Access None
Directions Subway: N or R to 8th St; Bus: M9, M102 to 15th St and Irving Place
Landmark Status National Register of Historic Places, New York City Landmark

The Pierpont Morgan Library

29 East 36th Street (at Madison Avenue)
New York, NY 10016
212-685-0610

The Pierpont Morgan Library is a fine museum as well as a repository for books and manuscripts. Its holdings rank among the world's greatest and include rare treasures such as one of 23 copies of the first printing of the Declaration of Independence; an edition of the collected works of Phillis Wheatley, one of the first known African-American poets; Mozart's handwritten score of the "Haffner" symphony; the only known partial manuscript of "Paradise Lost," dictated by John Milton to his daughter; one of the most important collections of Mesopotamian seals; and a manuscript article by Einstein describing how he developed his General Theory of Relativity. The library has a fine collection of medieval and Renaissance illuminated manuscripts and many Old Master drawings and prints.

"Adam and Eve" by Albrecht Dürer, pen and ink, 1504, from the permanent collection, The Pierpont Morgan Library.

The Morgan, in addition to maintaining a great collection of primary source materials for scholars, mounts four major exhibits and eight smaller exhibits a year. Drawing on its own holdings and the collections of other institutions, these shows present some of the greatest works ever rendered on paper—ranging from Edward Curtis' photographs of Native Americans, taken early in the 20th century with J.P. Morgan's sponsorship, to drawings from some of the most important European collections.

The library is yet another architectural wonder by the firm of McKim, Mead & White, which also designed much of the campus of Columbia University, the Brooklyn Museum (see separate entries) and dozens of other structures throughout the United States. In 1906 J.P. Morgan, a financier of immense wealth and avid collector, had the library built adjacent to his 36th Street home. Constructed of pinkish-white Tennessee marble, the library combines features of Italian Renaissance garden casinos and urban palazzi. The richly colored and ornamented interior is breathtaking. In 1988 the library expanded to an adjacent 45-room brownstone that had once been the residence of J.P. Morgan Jr.

GENERAL INFORMATION

Hours Sun 1–5 pm; Tues–Sat 10:30 am–5 pm; closed Mon
Admission Suggested contribution: adults $5, seniors and students $3
Giftshop Exhibition catalogs, books, pamphlets and cards relating to the collections
Library See description above; collections are open to scholars, graduate students, dealers and collectors by appointment only
Disability Access Fully accessible; restrooms and telephones available
Directions Subway: 6 to 33rd St; Bus: M2, M5 to 34th St; M16, M34 to Madison Ave
Landmark Status National Register of Historic Places, New York City Landmark

Police Academy Museum

235 East 20th Street (between Second and Third Avenues)
New York, NY 10003
212-477-9753

The Police Academy Museum possesses the country's largest collection of police equipment and memorabilia. Housed in a large, one-room gallery are over 50 exhibits displaying truncheons, handcuffs, badges, counterfeit money, even a Prohibition-era tommy gun.

Established in 1929, the museum functions as an important part of police recruit training, introducing cadets to the rich history of the New York City Police Department.

Photo courtesy of the New York City Police Department

GENERAL INFORMATION

Hours Mon–Fri 9 am–3 pm; closed weekends; call to confirm hours
Admission Free
Disability Access Limited access
Directions Subway: 6 to 23rd St; Bus: M15, M101, M102 to 23rd St; M23 to 7th Ave

City-owned, operated by the New York City Police Department

Pratt Manhattan Gallery

Puck Building
295 Lafayette Street, Second Floor
(at Houston Street)
New York, NY 10012

212-925-8481

The Pratt Institute began as a trade school in 1887. Today it is one of New York City's foremost academies, offering programs in the humanities, architecture, design and engineering. Its main campus is in Brooklyn, but courses are also offered in Manhattan at the Puck Building.

In 1975 the institute opened the Pratt Manhattan Gallery in the Puck Building. The gallery mounts about eight exhibits a year. Shows encompass the pure arts of painting and sculpture, but also embrace the applied arts of graphic and interior design as well as architecture. Some exhibits originate at Schafler Gallery on the Brooklyn campus (see separate entry).

The gallery is located on the second floor of the nine-story Romanesque Revival structure called the Puck Building. From 1887 to 1918 it housed the editorial offices and printing plant of the satirical weekly magazine Puck.

GENERAL INFORMATION

Hours During academic year, Sept–May: Mon–Sat 10 am–6 pm; closed Sun
Admission Free
Disability Access Limited access
Directions Subway: 6 to Bleecker St; B, D, F or Q to Broadway–Lafayette St; Bus: M5, M6 to Houston St; M21 to Lafayette St
Landmark Status National Register of Historic Places, New York City Landmark

Nicholas Roerich Museum

319 West 107th Street
(at Riverside Drive)
New York, NY 10025

212-864-7752

Nicholas Roerich—artist, philosopher, archaeologist and author—led a life rich in artistic and humanitarian achievement. Born in St. Petersburg in 1874, he was a highly disciplined man who seemed to live several lives at once. He created over 6,000 paintings, wrote numerous books, and undertook extensive archaeological expeditions in Russia and Central Asia. One of his greatest achievements, the Roerich Pact, sought to protect, in war and peace, world cultural treasures. This project led to his nomination for the Nobel Peace Prize in 1929.

The Nicholas Roerich Museum houses works and memorabilia from all periods of the great man's life, including his set designs for operas by Rimsky-Korsakov, his collaborations with Stravinsky, and the paintings he made from expeditions to India and Tibet. The work of established and emerging artists is also featured. Lectures on art, music and science are offered, as are recitals by concert artists and chamber music ensembles, exhibits of handicrafts by Native American and foreign artisans, and poetry readings.

GENERAL INFORMATION

Hours Tues–Sun 2–5 pm; closed Mon
Admission Free
Giftshop Reproductions of Roerich paintings, books on his work, postcards, etc., at main desk
Disability Access None
Directions Subway: 1/9 to 110th St; Bus: M4 to Broadway and 110th St; M5 to Riverside Dr and 108th St; M104 to Broadway and 106th St

Theodore Roosevelt Birthplace

28 East 20th Street (between Broadway and Park Avenues)
New York, NY 10003
212-260-1616

When "Teddie" Roosevelt was growing up on the site of this four-story brownstone, he was a frail child prone to asthma. At age 12 his father built a backyard gymnasium for him to further his improving health. It worked. In time he became a robust man with an active life: a cowboy in the Dakotas, a colonel of the Rough Riders regiment during the Spanish-American War and a hunter-naturalist on three continents. At 23 he was elected to the New York State legislature. In 1901, on the death of President McKinley, he became President, the only native New Yorker to hold that office.

The 26th President of the United States, age 8.

The Theodore Roosevelt Birthplace is a reconstruction of his opulent childhood home and a fine example of a fashionable Victorian residence. Rooms of the period 1865 to 1872 contain many original family furnishings. Color schemes and layouts were provided during the reconstruction by Roosevelt's sisters and wife. The parlor—the most elegant room—is furnished in the Rococo Revival style popular at the time. The master bedroom has its original rosewood and stainwood veneered furniture, and the crib and rush-seated chair in the nursery are said to have been the future president's. An exhibit traces Roosevelt's life from childhood through his presidency, highlighting his political career and naturalist concerns.

Theodore Roosevelt Sr. and his wife Martha Bulloch resided in the house from 1854 until 1872, when Theodore Jr. was 14. After a year in Europe, the family moved to 57th Street because 20th Street had become increasingly commercial. In 1916 the Roosevelt home was completely demolished and replaced with a two-story commercial building. At Roosevelt's death in 1919, prominent citizens purchased the site, razed the shop and reconstructed the former president's boyhood home as a memorial. It was opened to the public in 1923. In 1963 the Theodore Roosevelt Association donated it to the National Park Service.

GENERAL INFORMATION

Hours Wed–Sun 9 am–5 pm; guided tours until 3:30 pm; closed Mon, Tues
Admission $2
Giftshop Books, pamphlets, postcards, etc.
Disability Access None
Directions Subway: 6, F, N or R to 23rd St; Bus: M2, M3, M5 to 20th St; M23 to 5th Ave
Landmark Status National Register of Historic Places, New York City Landmark
National Historic Site

Roulette

228 West Broadway
(at White Street)
New York, NY 10013
212-219-8242

Roulette is a laboratory for experimentation by established and developing musical artists. It presents 50 to 90 concerts a year in a specially equipped 1,000-square-foot loft. Performances showcase the work of innovative composers, musicians and interdisciplinary collaborators, and nearly all feature premieres of new compositions.

A range of genres is presented, including contemporary music, new jazz, electronic and computer-generated music, world music, experimental rock, audio art and performances on homemade instruments. "Piano Festivals" celebrate the diversity of new music for that instrument, and the annual "Mixology Festival" focuses on new uses of technology in music. "Le Salon de Roulette" provides a time for artists and audience members to meet informally.

The organization's own descriptions perhaps best convey the kind of musical works it presents: "an electro-acoustic reconstruction of Debussy's 'La Mer'," "an evening of audio installations and interactive hi-tech innovations," "the voices of anxious objects as empowered by a multi-media artist in an audio-visual expedition," "humor, collisions, thoughtful spontaneity."

Roulette was founded in 1978 by its current directors, Jim Staley and David Weinstein.

GENERAL INFORMATION

Hours Most performances Thurs–Sun, beginning at 9 pm
Admission $7 per ticket; TDF vouchers accepted
Giftshop CDs from Roulette's "Einstein" label available at performances
Library Archive of recordings not open to the general public; however, scholars might gain access
Disability Access None
Directions Subway: 1 to Franklin St; A, C or E to Canal St; Bus: M10 to White St
Landmark Status New York City Landmark

Salmagundi Club

47 Fifth Avenue (between 11th and 12th Streets)
New York, NY 10003

212-255-7740

"Salmagundi" comes from the papers of Washington Irving, where the word was used to refer to a stew of many ingredients. In 1880 a group of young artists borrowed it to describe their nascent club, being, as it was, a loose alliance of artists with diverse views and ideals. Today the club offers exhibitions, open to the public, as well as lectures and demonstrations by artist members, and sketch classes. Past Salmagundians have included Childe Hassam, William Merritt Chase, Augustus Saint-Gaudens, John Philip Souza and Stanford White. The club is in a landmark building that was constructed in 1853. The interior is beautifully restored.

Library and reading room, Salmagundi Club.

GENERAL INFORMATION

Hours 1–5 pm daily
Admission Gallery is free
Library Art Reference Library open to researchers Tues 10:30 am–5 pm, Wed 6–8:30 pm
Disability Access None
Directions Subway: 1/9, 2, 3, B, D, F or Q to 14th St; L to 6th Ave; Bus: M5 to 8th St; M14 to 5th Ave
Landmark Status National Register of Historic Places, New York City Landmark

The Schomburg Center for Research in Black Culture

The New York Public Library
515 Malcolm X Boulevard
(at 135th Street)
New York, NY 10037
212-491-2200

The Schomburg Center is one of the world's most important centers for the study of the history and culture of peoples of African descent. A research facility of the New York Public Library (see separate entry), it possesses over five million books and other items. Rarities include a handwritten prayer by Phillis Wheatley, one of the first known African-American poets; a 19th-century reprint of Jupiter Hammon's 1781 "Address to the Negroes of the State of New York"; the original typescript of Richard Wright's masterpiece "Native Son"; and the scrapbook of Ira Aldridge, a black Shakespearean actor of the 19th century.

Arthur Alfonso Schomburg, (1874–1938), drawing by Albert Smith.

The Schomburg Center also collects rare African art—bronzes, wood carvings, weaponry, religious artifacts, musical instruments and other items—as well as works by contemporary artists. In the main gallery, four to five exhibits drawn from the collections are mounted each year. Exhibitions have included "Mandela in New York," photographs documenting Nelson Mandela's 1991 visit to the city; "JazzArts," paintings and photographs showing the influence of jazz on the visual arts; and "New World Africans: 19th-Century Images of Blacks in South America and the Caribbean." In addition, there are displays of sculpture and painting throughout the center by Romare Bearden, Augusta Savage and others.

The center was named after Arthur Alfonso Schomburg. Born in Puerto Rico in 1874, Schomburg spent much of his life recovering the history of people of African descent. He was spurred on to this work by an early teacher who said that black people had no history. During the Harlem Renaissance of the 1920s and '30s, he was an active figure, hosting scholars, playwrights and philosophers. In 1925 the Division of Negro History was opened in the New York Public Library with Schomburg's private collection at its core. In 1932 he was appointed its curator.

The center began in the 135th Street branch, which was built with funds from philanthropist Andrew Carnegie in the early 1900s. In 1980 it moved to a new, larger building next door designed by Bond Ryder Associates. Growth of the center's collections and usership continued unabated, however, and the center underwent another burst of institutional expansion in the late 1980s. The idle Carnegie branch was renovated and enlarged to include galleries, reading rooms and collection-support facilities. A 350-seat auditorium was constructed on the lot between it and the modern structure. Theatrical and dance works, literary readings, scholarly symposia and community events are held in the auditorium, named after the preeminent African-American writer Langston Hughes.

GENERAL INFORMATION

Hours Mon–Wed 12–8 pm; Thurs–Sat 10 am–6 pm; closed Sun.
Admission General library use and galleries free. Ticket charge for some auditorium events such as concerts and plays
Giftshop Books, posters, postcards, gift items, etc.
Library See description above
Disability Access Fully accessible
Directions Subway: 2 or 3 to 135th St; Bus: M7, M102 to 135th St
Landmark Status National Register of Historic Places, New York City Landmark

City-owned, privately operated

The Sculpture Center Gallery

167 East 69th Street
(between Lexington
and Third Avenues)
New York, NY 10021

212-879-3500

The Sculpture Center Gallery mounts experimental, occasionally controversial exhibits by outstanding young and mid-career artists. The ground-floor exhibition space features monthly shows concentrating on the work of individual artists or specific themes. Exhibits have included "Narrative Sculpture," with works by Red Grooms among others; "New Orleans Sculptors in New York"; and "Showdown: A Regional Exhibition by Artists of the Southwest." Gallery talks and tours are an important part of the center's activities. The Sculpture Center is housed in an old coach house in a landmark Upper East Side neighborhood. Above the gallery are studios where artists teach all phases of sculpture making.

GENERAL INFORMATION

Hours Tues–Sat 11 am–5 pm; closed Sun, Mon
Admission Free
Giftshop No formal shop, but most work displayed is for sale
Library Extensive slide collection; access by appointment
Disability Access Fully accessible
Directions Subway: 6 to 68th St; Bus: M1, M2, M3, M4 to 68th St
Landmark Status National Register of Historic Places, New York City Landmark

Seagram Gallery

375 Park Avenue, Fourth Floor
(between 52nd and 53rd Streets)
New York, NY 10152

212-572-7000

On the fourth floor of the famous Seagram Building is a small gallery where shows drawn from the Seagram collection and traveling exhibits from other galleries are presented three or four times a year.

Richard Pare

Pablo Picasso's painted stage curtain for the ballet "Le Tricorne," 1919, from the Joseph E. Seagram & Sons, Inc. Collection.

The Seagram collection features photographs of American urban life, antique glass, American and European paintings, tapestries and prints. Exhibits, often with an emphasis on urban topics, have included "Summer Pastimes: Photographs from the Seagram Collection," featuring works by Walker Evans, Weegee (Arthur Fellig), Garry Winograd and others; "California Photography from a Seventies Perspective"; and "Other Places: America Beyond New York City," concentrating on man's impact on the landscape.

Ludwig Mies van der Rohe designed the Seagram Building, which was constructed in 1958. Because of its classic proportions, masterful use of materials (bronze and bronze-colored glass) and innovative use of the streetside plaza, it is considered one of his masterpieces and one of the greatest buildings in New York. The building's influence on post-modern architecture has been enormous. The lobby features the largest Picasso in New York—a painted theater curtain designed in 1919 for Diaghilev's ballet "Le Tricorne." The interiors were designed by Philip Johnson.

GENERAL INFORMATION

Hours Mon–Fri 9 am–5 pm; closed Sat, Sun
Admission Free
Food Service Cafeteria on premises; also in Seagram building are the Four Seasons restaurant and the Brasserie
Disability Access Limited access
Directions Subway: 6 to 51st St; E or F to Lexington Ave; Bus: M1, M2, M3, M4, M5, M101, M102 to 52nd St
Parking On-site lot
Landmark Status New York City Landmark

South Street Seaport Museum

207 Front Street (off Fulton Street)
New York, NY 10038
212-669-9400

South Street Seaport preserves vestiges of that time when Lower Manhattan was a thriving seaport ringed with ships, when its narrow cobbled streets were lined with counting houses, ship chandleries, tobacconists, tanners, sailors' bars, flophouses and fish merchants.

This 12-square-block landmark district consists of a tract of historic buildings, various shops, the Fulton Fish Market, historic ships moored at Piers 15 and 16, and the South Street Seaport Museum. The museum mounts exhibitions in six restored buildings, drawing on a collection of paintings, photographs, models and tools relating to shipbuilding, maritime history and the surrounding historic district.

Exhibitions have included "The Whaleman's Art of Scrimshaw"; "Model-Making in New York City," focusing on the work of 12 contemporary modelers; and "Of Sailing Ships and Sealing Wax: 25 Years of Collecting," a retrospective commemorating the museum's 25th anniversary and featuring paintings, decorative arts, artifacts, drawings, maps and nautical decor.

Historic ships berthed nearby include the *Peking* (1911), a steel four-masted bark; the *Wavertree* (1855), an iron full-rigged ship; the *Pioneer* (1885), a cargo schooner; and the *Lettie G. Howard* (1893), a wooden fishing schooner and others. Several have on-board exhibitions.

There are crafts workshops at the Children's Center and storytelling for children and adults at Pier 16. A working 19th-century print shop demonstrates printing techniques and displays antique typefaces and presses. For architecture enthusiasts, there are tours of adjacent buildings which feature an eclectic mix of architecture—from the 19th century Federal rowhouses of Schermerhorn Row to neoclassical and Greek Revival buildings.

In 1967 the South Street Seaport Museum was chartered to reclaim an area of neglected buildings, many of which were slated for demolition. The Rouse Company, developers of Baltimore's Inner Harbor and Boston's Faneuil Hall Marketplace, is responsible for the overall design of the seaport. The City of New York has played an important role in the development of South Street.

GENERAL INFORMATION

Hours 10 am–5 pm daily; during summer until 6 pm on Sat and Sun
Admission Adults $6, seniors $5, students $4, children $3; tickets at Museum Visitors Center, 12 Fulton St, or Pier 16 ticket booth
Giftshop The Chandlery, 209 Water St, has books, charts, nautical gifts; 14 Fulton St shop has South Street Seaport and New York City gifts and souvenirs
Food Service Numerous restaurants throughout seaport
Disability Access Fully accessible
Directions Subway: 2, 3, 4, 5, J, M or Z to Fulton St; A or C to Broadway–Nassau St; E to World Trade Center; Bus: M15 to Fulton St
Parking 5 lots throughout district
Landmark Status National Register of Historic Places, New York City Landmark

1 Circle Line
2 *Lettie G. Howard* (1893)
3 *W.O. Decker* (1930)
4 *Ambrose* (1908)
5 *Pioneer* (1885)
6 *Peking* (1911)
7 Pilot House
8 Ticketbooth
9 Container Store
10 *Wavertree* (1855)
11 Maritime Crafts Center
12 Boat Building Shop
13 A.A. Low Building
14 Childrens Center
15 Visitors Center
16 Museum Shop
17 Museum Gallery
18 Herman Melville Library
19 Bowne & Company Stationers
20 The Chandlery
21 Titanic Memorial Lighthouse

Design: Two Twelve Associates, Inc., Map drawing: Lieu & Silks

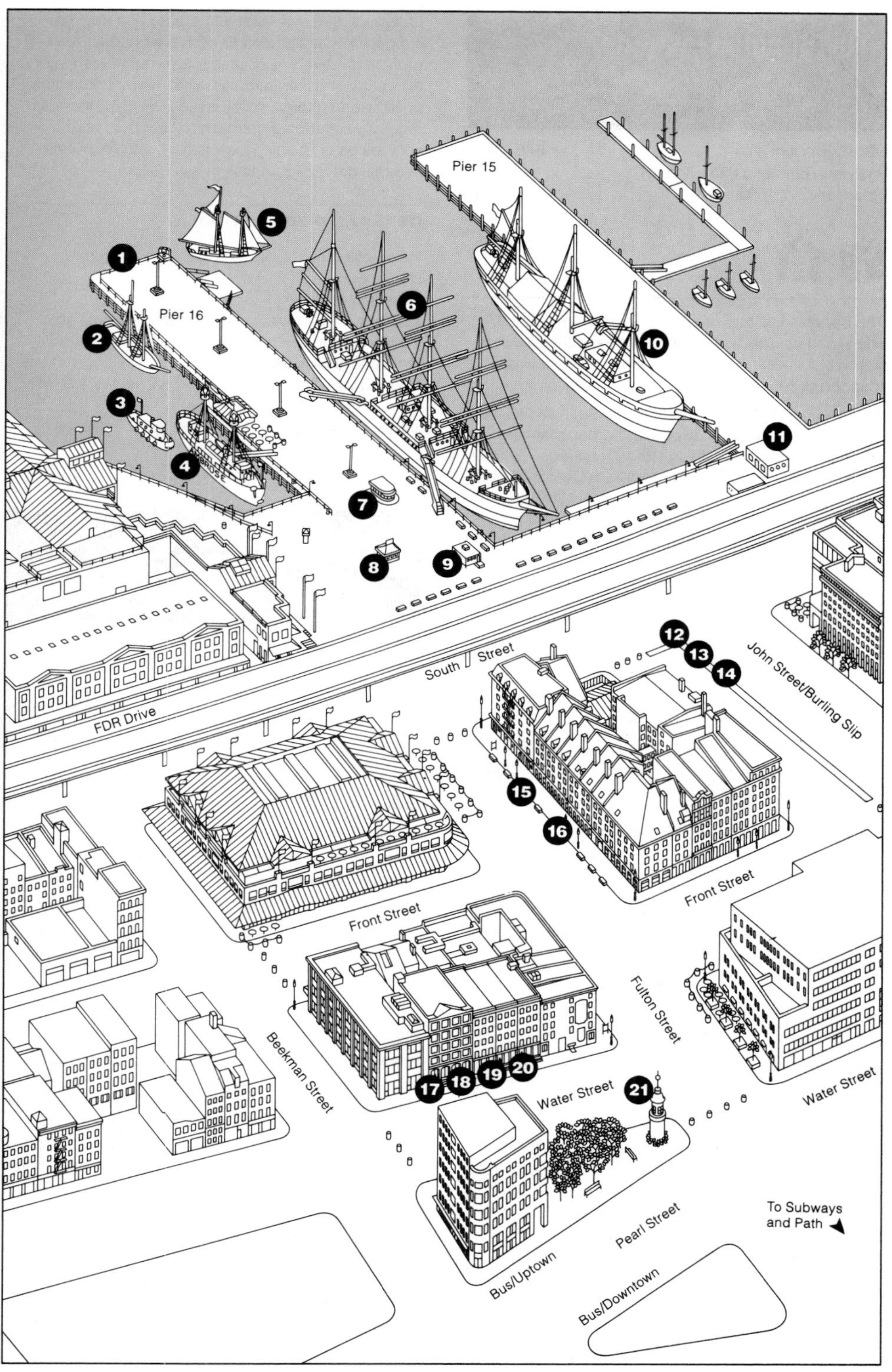
Pier 15
Pier 16
1
2
3
4
5
6
7
8
9
10
11
12
13
14
15
16
17
18
19
20
21
South Street
FDR Drive
John Street/Burling Slip
Front Street
Front Street
Fulton Street
Beekman Street
Water Street
Water Street
Pearl Street
Bus/Uptown
Bus/Downtown
To Subways
and Path

The Spanish Institute

684 Park Avenue
(between 68th and 69th Streets)
New York, NY 10021

212-628-0420

The Spanish Institute promotes Spain's rich cultural, social and political history and, more specifically, that nation's historic influence on the Americas. It was founded in 1954.

About four exhibitions a year focus on Spanish painting, sculpture, architectural design and urban planning, photography and graphic arts from all periods. Exhibits have included "From the Volcano: 20th Century Artists from the Canaries," "Valencian Painters: 1860–1936," "The Spanish Vision: Contemporary Photography, 1970–1990" and "The Gold and Silver Coins of Mexico."

Language classes—both structured and informal—in Spanish, Catalan and English are conducted at all proficiency levels. Lectures address political history, art history and literature as well as current economic, political and foreign policy issues. Further, there are regularly scheduled dramatic readings, concerts, screenings of Spanish feature films and *tertulias*, informal gatherings with Spanish visitors.

GENERAL INFORMATION

Hours Mon–Fri 10 am–6 pm; Sat 11 am–5 pm; closed Sun
Admission Free
Library Tinker Library contains small collection of literary and historical titles
Disability Access None
Directions Subway: 6 to 68th St; Bus: M1, M2, M3, M4 to 68th St; M66 to Park Ave
Landmark Status National Register of Historic Places, New York City Landmark

St. Mark's Church in-the-Bowery

131 East 10th Street
(at Second Avenue)
New York, NY 10003

212-674-8194
Danspace Project
212-420-1916
Ontological at St. Mark's
212-674-0910
Poetry Project

St. Mark's Church is an unofficial cultural center for the East Village, an important venue that for decades has offered the finest in contemporary poetry, dance and theater. It also functions as a lively church providing a variety of social services for Lower East Side residents. Its Ontological at St. Mark's Theater, an Off Off Broadway venue, specializes in experimental fare.

The Danspace Project stages performances in the renovated 300-seat sanctuary of the church. Dance is programmed for about 20 weeks every year. Works have been presented here by Bill T. Jones and Meredith Monk. Although Danspace was founded in 1974, dance performances at St. Mark's go back to the 1920s and '30s, when Isadora Duncan, Martha Graham and Ruth St. Denis performed here.

The Poetry Project offers Monday, Wednesday and Friday night readings, weekly writing workshops and monthly lectures. Poets appearing over the years have included Robert Lowell, Allen Ginsberg, Frank O'Hara, John Ashbery, Amiri Baraka, Adrienne Rich and Galway Kinnell.

St. Mark's Church in-the-Bowery was completed in 1799 on the site of a chapel originally built by Peter Stuyvesant, Governor of New Amsterdam—New York City's Dutch predecessor. Alexander Hamilton provided legal help to incorporate the church as the first Episcopal parish in America. It was built in roughly three stages: the original Federal structure (1799), the Greek Revival steeple (1828) and the cast-iron portico (circa 1858).

GENERAL INFORMATION

Hours Hours vary; call for schedule of events
Admission Price varies
Disability Access Limited; call about access 212-674-6377
Directions Subway: 6 to Astor Place; Bus: M15 to 2nd Ave and East 9th St
Landmark Status National Register of Historic Places, New York City Landmark

Statue of Liberty National Monument

Liberty Island, NY 10004

212-363-3200 Information
212-269-5755 Ferry Servce

The Statue of Liberty is one of the most enduring of American images. So strong is the statue's message of freedom, hope and prosperity that many émigrés have told the story of entering New York harbor and finding themselves and their fellow travelers in tears at the mere sight of "her."

The monument was first discussed in 1865 at the Paris home of Edouard René Lefebvre de Laboulaye, legal scholar and authority on America, who saw it as an opportunity to further republican ideals in France. Laboulaye discussed the idea with his dinner guest, the sculptor Auguste Bartholdi, who was later commissioned to make the statue. It was formally presented to the United States on July 4, 1884, and dedicated in 1886.

The statue's iron skeleton was engineered by Alexandre Gustave Eiffel and mounted on a base designed by American architect Richard Morris Hunt. Clad in beautifully oxydized copper skin, the statue towers over 151 feet and weighs 225 tons. The index finger is eight feet long; the mouth, three feet wide; 12 people can fit within the torch. Inside, visitors take an elevator, then climb 168 steps to the crown, which offers a breathtaking view of the harbor.

The Statue of Liberty Exhibit on the second level depicts the history and evolving national and international symbolism of the monument through models and replicas. On the third level, the Immigration Exhibit uses text, artifacts and photographs to depict the arrival of millions of new Americans to the United States and their contributions to the country.

"Liberty Enlightening the World," by Auguste Bartholdi, 1884, a gift to Americans from the people of France.

The statue was completely refurbished for its 1986 centennial. For two years French and American craftsmen worked on it, replacing corroded iron ribs with stainless steel. They strengthened the uplifted arm, which had been incorrectly installed in 1886. In keeping with the statue's original design, French metal crafters replaced the old glass flame, lit from inside, with a gold-plated copper flame lit with reflected light. The $140 million restoration was carried out simultaneously with the Ellis Island renovation (see separate entry).

GENERAL INFORMATION

Hours 9:30 am–5 pm daily; last ferry at 3:30 pm
Admission Ferry ticket includes admission to both Statue of Liberty and Ellis Island: adults $6; seniors $5; children under 17, $3; groups of 20 or more $5 per person
Giftshop T-shirts, mugs, postcards and other items
Food Service Concession stand open seven days a week
Library Call for information; access by appointment only
Disability Access Fully accessible, except crown
Directions Subway: N or R to Whitehall St–South Ferry; 1/9 to South Ferry; 4 or 5 to Bowling Green; then take ferry to Liberty Island; Bus: M6 to Bowling Green
Landmark Status National Register of Historic Places, New York City Landmark
National Monument

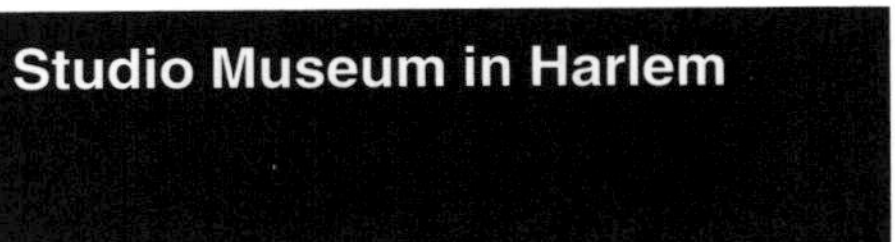

Studio Museum in Harlem

144 West 125th Street
(between Lenox and
Seventh Avenues)
New York, NY 10027

212-864-4500

The Studio Museum in Harlem is the foremost presenter of African-American artists in the country. The museum mounts about a dozen exhibitions a year examining themes such as "Ritual and Myth: A Survey of African-American Art"; "Artists Respond: The 'New World' Question," in which artists explored divergent cultural and historical viewpoints; and "Home: Contemporary Urban Images by Black Photographers."

The permanent collection contains the works of James Van Der Zee, who photographed Harlem scenes during the 1920s, '30s and '40s; important African and Caribbean artifacts; and paintings by post–World War II artists. These works are shown on a rotating basis. A new outdoor sculpture garden displays large-scale pieces.

Also offered are professional conferences ("Contemporary Issues in the Visual Arts"), panel discussions ("The New World Question"), literary readings (Toni Morrison, Amiri Baraka), jazz concerts (Fred Ho and the Afro-Asian Music Ensemble), dance performances (Bill T. Jones/Arnie Zane and Co.) and film programs.

The museum is housed in the former Kenwood Building, a 60,000-square-foot turn-of-the-century office structure. It was restored by Bond Ryder James Associates in 1982, the same concern responsible for the

"Conjur Woman" Romare Bearden, photo projection on paper, 1964, collection from the Studio Museum in Harlem.

Schomburg Center for Research in Black Culture (see separate entry). The Studio Museum in Harlem was founded in 1968.

GENERAL INFORMATION

Hours Wed–Fri 10 am–5 pm; Sat, Sun 1–6 pm; closed Mon, Tues
Admission Adults $5; seniors and students $3; children under 12, $1; members free
Giftshop Exhibition catalogs, art books, jewelry, T-shirts, etc.
Disability Access Fully accessible; ramps and elevators available
Directions Subway: A, B, C, D, 2, 3, 4, 5 or 6 to 125th St; Bus: M2, M7, M10, M100, M101, M102, BX15 to 125th St

Swiss Institute

35 West 67th Street
(between Columbus Avenue
and Central Park West)
New York, NY 10023

212-496-1759

Traditional and contemporary works by Swiss artists are featured in several exhibits each year at the Swiss Institute. The visitor will find a broad range of artistic styles and techniques on display, from representational paintings of Switzerland's farmers to abstract/nonobjective and experimental work in a variety of disciplines: painting, sculpture, photography, drawing, lithography, filmmaking, etc. The institute also offers screenings of recent Swiss films and videos, as well as dance performances and concerts. Related lectures and symposia are also presented. The Swiss Institute opened in 1986.

GENERAL INFORMATION

Hours Tues–Sat 2–7 pm; closed Sun, Mon
Admission Free
Disability Access None
Directions Subway: 1/9 to 66th St; Bus: M5, M7, M104 to 66th St; M66 to Columbus Ave
Landmark Status National Register of Historic Places

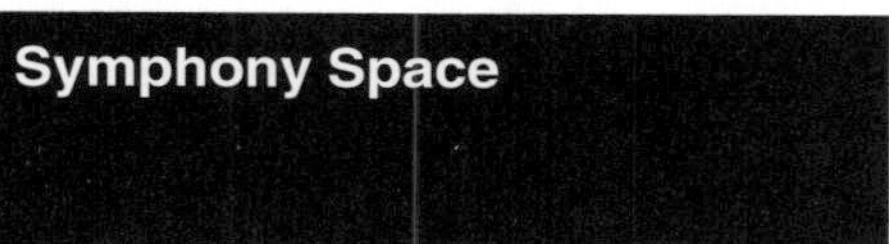

Symphony Space

2537 Broadway (at 95th Street)
New York, NY 10025

212-864-5400
Box Office

Located halfway between midtown Manhattan and Harlem, Symphony Space is a meeting place for New York City's diverse citizenry, drawing audiences from the metropolitan area and beyond for 200 music, dance, drama, literature, film and children's programs every year. Founded in 1978 in an abandoned movie house on Manhattan's Upper West Side, Symphony Space presents a full calendar of inexpensive, often free programs.

Its signature presentations include the annual free "Wall to Wall" music marathons, each celebrating a different composer; the popular literary series "Selected Shorts: A Celebration of the Short Story"; the provocative composers' forum "Face the Music"; the annual James Joyce tribute "Bloomsday on Broadway"; and the "Curriculum Arts Project," which combines arts programs with the curriculum for seventh-to ninth-grade students in city schools.

Symphony Space events in literature, music and film have included "Russian Weekend," featuring prominent American and Russian actresses reading the works of Chekhov, Tolstoy and Akhmatova; "Coyote Walks Around," focusing on stories, dance, music and song of Native Americans; "Carnaval!," consisting of an Afro-Caribbean Mardi Gras celebration in concert and film; and "Intolerance: Film and Censorship," featuring some of the most controversial motion pictures ever made.

Symphony Space is also a major presenter of independent performing groups—many of them black and Latino, but also many others (Chinese, Czech, Gay/Lesbian, Irish, Israeli, Italian, Russian) which together make up the city's proverbial "gorgeous mosaic."

Members of the performing groups Spirit Ensemble and Women of the Calabash on stage at Symphony Space.

GENERAL INFORMATION

Hours Box office open Tues–Sun 12–7 pm
Admission Price varies, generally $10–$25; discounts for groups, members
Giftshop Performance-related gift items; refreshments available
Disability Access Fully accessible
Directions Subway: 1/9, 2 or 3 to 96th St; Bus: M104 to 96th St; M19 to Broadway

Synchronicity Space

55 Mercer Street (between Broome and Grand Streets)
New York, NY 10013
212-925-8645

The term "synchronicity," defined as the simultaneous occurrence of events, was adopted by this small SoHo theater and gallery space because of the multitude of activities taking place here at any given time. Eight resident theater companies—including the Eleventh Hour Collective, the Red Earth Ensemble and the No Pants Theater Company—use Synchronicity Space as a base of operations and produce staged works in a variety of styles. A larger auditorium in the basement is used for dramatic readings.

GENERAL INFORMATION

Hours Box office open 7–8 pm on performance nights; gallery open Tues–Sat 12–6 pm
Admission Price varies, generally $8–$12; student, member and group discounts; TDF vouchers accepted. (Reservations and general information 12–6 pm daily)
Disability Access Limited seating; one step up to theater; restrooms accessible by elevator
Directions Subway: 6, C or E to Spring St; N or R to Prince St; 1/9, J, M or Z to Canal St; Bus: M1 to Broadway and Grand St; M6 to Broadway and Broome St; B51 to Broadway and Canal St
Landmark Status National Register of Historic Places, New York City Landmark

Taller Boricua Gallery

1685 Lexington Avenue
(at 106th Street)
New York, NY 10029
212-831-4333

Taller Boricua Gallery is a Latino creative arts organization located in East Harlem. The organization's programming is designed to strengthen appreciation of arts and culture among residents of this largely Puerto Rican and African-American community. Activities include six to eight exhibitions of contemporary art a year by established and emerging artists, an artist-in-residence program for minority artists and a filmmaking and video program that focuses on pressing community issues. The Mural Project, a public art program, trains youngsters as commercial painters, and the Hidden Treasures/ Seniors Project provides cultural enrichment for older residents.

GENERAL INFORMATION

Hours Tues–Sat 1–6 pm; closed Sun, Mon
Admission Free
Disability Access Limited, gallery only
Directions Subway: 6 to 103rd St; Bus: M19, M98, M101, M102 to 103rd St

Town Hall

123 West 43rd Street
(between Sixth Avenue and Broadway)
New York, NY 10036
212-840-2824
Box Office

Town Hall was founded in 1921 by a women's group seeking a public forum for the political enlightenment of women.

Among the thinkers, cultural leaders and artists who have spoken at Town Hall are W.H. Auden, Winston Churchill, Buckminster Fuller, Thomas Mann, Anaïs Nin, Eleanor Roosevelt, Carl Sandburg, Kurt Vonnegut, Booker T. Washington and William Butler Yeats. The famous "America's Town Meetings of the Air" were broadcast weekly from the Town Hall stage from 1935 to 1956, bringing world leaders debating global issues into the homes of millions.

Town Hall

The hall's fine acoustics make it an excellent venue for concerts. Marian Anderson, Joan Baez, Béla Bartók, Leonard Bernstein, David Byrne, Cab Calloway, Miles Davis, Duke Ellington, Billie Holiday, Marilyn Horne, Meredith Monk, Steve Reich, Max Roach, Pete Seeger, Andres Segovia and Igor Stravinsky, among others, have appeared on the Town Hall stage over the years.

In the 1980s the hall launched its "New Traditions" performance series, which includes classical music, drama, film screenings, jazz, and ethnic and contemporary music. This multicultural and multidisciplinary series features both emerging and established artists in a virtually unlimited range of styles.

Town Hall, a Georgian Revival-style building, was designed by McKim, Mead & White.

GENERAL INFORMATION

Hours Box office located at 113 West 43rd St, open Mon–Sat 12–6 pm; closed Sun
Admission Price varies; group discounts available
Disability Access Fully accessible
Directions Subway: B, D, F or Q to 42nd St; N, R, 1/9, 2 or 3 to 42nd St–Times Sq; Bus: M6, M7 to 42nd St; M42, M104 to 6th Ave
Landmark Status National Register of Historic Places, New York City Landmark

Tribeca Performing Arts Center

Borough of Manhattan Community College
199 Chambers Street
(off Greenwich Street)
New York, NY 10007

212-346-8510
Box Office

The Tribeca Performing Arts Center is the largest presenter of performing arts events in Lower Manhattan. The name Tribeca is a contraction of "Triangle Below Canal," referring to the district just south of Canal Street and SoHo where many artists live and galleries have flourished since the 1970s. Home to the popular family weekend series "Kids Arts Tribeca," the center is also a popular venue for international theater, dance and music performances. Companies using the center have included the San Francisco Mime Troupe, Circle Rep, Dublin's Abbey Theater, Mabou Mines, the Acting Company, China's Ningxia Yinchuan Beijing Opera Troupe, Izulu Dance Theater and Music, and Maria Benitez Estampa Flamenco. Built in the early 1980s, the attractive theater has excellent sight lines and acoustics.

GENERAL INFORMATION

Hours Box office open Mon–Fri 10 am–5 pm; closed Sat, Sun
Admission Price varies, $5–$10; discounts for groups, students, seniors
Disability Access Fully accessible
Directions Subway: A, C, E, J, M, 1/9, 2 or 3 to Chambers St; 4, 5 or 6 to Brooklyn Bridge; N or R to City Hall; Bus: M6, M22 to Chambers St

Trinity Museum at Trinity Church

Broadway at Wall Street
New York, NY 10006

212-602-0872

Trinity Church, an Episcopal parish that once owned a large part of Manhattan, is one of New York City's oldest institutions. The wealth of the parish, which derives from a land grant bestowed by Queen Anne in 1705, is reflected in the architecture and decoration of both Trinity Church and nearby St. Paul's Chapel (Broadway at Fulton Street), which is part of Trinity Parish.

A permanent exhibit in the Trinity Museum traces church history from the 1600s to the present. Sections of the exhibition include A Colonial Church in a Colonial Society, The American Revolution: Trinity in an Occupied City, and A New Church in a New Nation. Most exhibits are permanent, while changing exhibits draw on historical documents, maps, prints and drawings that relate to the social and religious life of the parish. "It Is Done" commemorated the 200th anniversary of George Washington's inauguration. (Washington worshiped at nearby St. Paul's Chapel, the oldest church in New York City.) Both Trinity Church and St. Paul's Chapel have ongoing free music programs.

The tomb of American patriot Alexander Hamilton, Trinity Church cemetery.

In the adjacent cemetery are the Greco-Egyptian tomb of Alexander Hamilton and the first memorial to unknown servicemen of the Revolutionary War. The building was designed by Richard Upjohn and completed in 1846. It is a classic example of Gothic Revival architecture. The bas-relief doors, illustrating scenes from the Bible, were designed by Richard Morris Hunt. This is actually the third Trinity Church. The first, built in 1696, was destroyed in the Great Fire of 1776, which consumed much of the city. The second, a rectangular building with a 200-foot steeple, was razed because of structural problems.

GENERAL INFORMATION

Hours Museum: Mon–Fri 9–11:45 am and 1–3:45 pm; Sat 10 am–3:45 pm; Sun 1–3:45 pm
Admission Free
Giftshop Religious items: icons, stained glass, ceramics and brochures about the church; Tues–Fri 11:30 am–5:30 pm, Sun 12:30–4 pm, closed Sat, Mon
Library Large archive on New York City and Trinity Church Parish history since 1600s; access by appointment, call 212-602-0847
Disability Access Limited access
Directions Subway: 1, N or R to Rector St; 2, 3, 4 or 5 to Wall St; J or M to Broad St; A or C to Broadway–Nassau St; A or E to Chambers St; Bus: M1, M6 to Broadway and Thames St
Landmark Status National Register of Historic Places, New York City Landmark

Symbol Key

 *Institutional Giftshop*

 *On-Site Food Services*

 *On-Site Library or Archive*

 *Full Accessibility*

 *On-Site Parking*

 *National Register of Historic Places and/or New York City Landmark*

Ukrainian Museum

203 Second Avenue
(between 12th and 13th Streets)
New York, NY 10003
212-228-0110

The Ukrainian Museum was established in 1976 by Ukrainian immigrants who wished to preserve and promote their cultural heritage. The museum's permanent collection includes folk art, handwoven rugs, textiles, wood carvings, metalwork and costumes, virtually all produced in the 19th and 20th centuries. Exhibitions draw on these holdings and loans from other institutions.

"The Lost Architecture of Kiev" was a photographic exhibit about the churches and other architectural landmarks demolished by the Soviet regime during the 1930s. "To Preserve a Heritage: The Story of Ukrainian Immigration to the United States" explored the life of these new Americans during the past century. There have also been exhibits of *pysanky*, (handpainted Easter eggs); *rushnyky* (Ukrainian ritual cloths); and various other artifacts.

The education program offers courses for children and adults in embroidery and wood carving. The workshops in traditional handcrafted Christmas ornaments and Easter egg decoration are popular, as are gallery tours and courses in Ukrainian crafts and culture. Lectures and film screenings augment these activities.

Ceramic tile, villiage of Kosiv, Ivano-Frankivs'ka Oblast, 1930s. From the collection of the Ukrainian Museum.

GENERAL INFORMATION

Hours Sun, Wed–Sat 1–5 pm; closed Mon, Tues
Admission Adults $1, seniors and students 50¢, children under 6 free
Giftshop Ukrainian crafts, artworks, embroidery, books, exhibition catalogs
Library Large photographic archive focusing on Ukrainian immigration; open by appointment
Disability Access Fully accessible
Directions Subway: 6 to Astor Place; N or R to 8th St; L to 1st Ave; Bus: M15 to 12th St

Urban Center Galleries

457 Madison Avenue
(between 50th and 51st Streets)
New York, NY 10022
212-935-3960

Located in the landmark Villard Houses, the Urban Center Galleries explore aspects of architecture, city planning, land use and historic preservation. "Steel, Stone and Backbone: New York Builds in Hard Times," "Stanford White's New York," "Perspectives on the New York Waterfront: Planning the City's Edge" and "The New New Yorkers: The Changing Face of the City" are some of the exhibitions that have been featured in the first-floor galleries. Exhibits have also explored a major development proposed for Columbus Circle and the redevelopment of 42nd Street.

Both the Municipal Art Society and the Architectural League, which are quartered in the Villard Houses, present lectures and forums on architecture, planning and design. One series, for instance, features writers discussing their newly published books on contemporary public sculpture, the history of Central Park, urban redevelopment and other subjects.

The Villard Houses, sitting at the base of the Helmsley Palace Hotel, are five neo-Renaissance brownstones built in 1886 by McKim, Mead & White for Austrian railroad baron Henry Villard. They were used as residences until 1945, when they were converted to office space, first for Random House and then for the Roman Catholic Archdiocese of New York (St. Patrick's Cathedral is across the street). In 1980, when the houses were renovated and converted to form part of the hotel, the northern wing was dedicated to public use as the Urban Center.

Municipal Art Society's Urban Center

GENERAL INFORMATION

Hours Mon–Wed, Fri, Sat 11 am–5 pm; closed Thurs, Sun
Admission Free
Giftshop Urban Center Bookstore, the most comprehensive of its kind in New York City, sells titles on architecture, design, landscape design, historic preservation, graphic design, urban planning and New York City history; 212-935-3595
Library Information Exchange/Greenacre Reference Resource has books and periodicals on preservation, urban planning, etc.; open Mon–Fri 10 am–1 pm
Disability Access Fully accessible; entrance on 51st St
Directions Subway: 6 to 51st St; Bus: M1, M2, M3, M4, M18 to 51st St; M27, M50 to Madison Ave
Landmark Status National Register of Historic Places, New York City Landmark

Visual Arts Museum

School of Visual Arts 212-592-2144
209 East 23rd Street (between Second and Third Avenues)
New York, NY 10010

The Visual Arts Museum, established in the mid-1960s at the School of Visual Arts (SVA), presents the work of noted professionals working in the fine and applied arts. Guest curators mount four exhibitions a year. Theme, style and theory vary widely from show to show in accordance with curatorial vision.

Every fall the museum sponsors a retrospective exhibition honoring a significant 20th century visual communicator. Known as the Masters Series Laureates, this distinguished group has so far included Paul Rand, Milton Glaser, Massimo Vignelli and Lou Dorfsman.

In addition, the museum offers symposiums and discussions on issues in the fine and applied arts. Each exhibiting artist is invited to present a slide lecture free to the public.

Founded in 1947, SVA today offers undergraduate and graduate degrees as well as continuing education courses. The school also operates several small galleries throughout the city which feature work of SVA students and alumni.

GENERAL INFORMATION

Hours Mon–Thurs 9 am–8 pm; Fri 9 am–5 pm; closed Sat, Sun
Admission Free
Giftshop Student and alumni artwork for sale at smaller SVA galleries throughout the city
Library Accessible to SVA students only
Disability Access Fully accessible
Directions Subway: 6, N or R to 23rd St; Bus: M26 to 2nd Ave; M15 to 23rd St

White Columns

154 Christopher Street, 212-924-4212
Second Floor (between Washington and Greenwich Streets)
New York, NY 10014

White Columns is New York City's oldest alternative exhibition space. The gallery, founded in 1969, exhibits the work of over 200 visual artists each year. Every year the "White Room" program offers new work by 18 emerging artists. White Columns also organizes ten thematic exhibitions each season and commissions new installations.

Programming spans a variety of disciplines and media. "Speed Trials" was a celebration of so-called art rock music. "Science and Prophecy" showcased emerging artists who incorporate technology and fine art materials into their work. White Columns' new West Village facility opened in 1991.

GENERAL INFORMATION

Hours Sun, Wed–Sat 12–6 pm; closed Mon, Tues
Admission Free
Library Files of artists' slides open to curators, art writers and dealers by appointment
Disability Access Fully accessible
Directions Subway: 1/9 to Christopher St–Sheridan Sq; Bus: M10, M13 to Christopher St
Landmark Status National Register of Historic Places

Whitney Museum of American Art

945 Madison Avenue 212-570-3600
(at 75th Street)
New York, NY 10021

The Whitney Museum has the world's most comprehensive permanent collection of 20th-century American art—over 10,000 works. Virtually every artist of any significance is represented: Arbus, Bearden, Calder, Close, de Kooning, Diebenkorn, Dove, Flavin, Grooms, Hartley, Johns, Kelly, O'Keeffe, Lichtenstein, Nevelson, Serra, Stella, Pollock, Rothko, Warhol, Wyeth, Oldenburg and many others.

The museum mounts about 15 exhibitions a year, encompassing individual and group shows, historical surveys and retrospectives. These have included "Hand-Painted Pop: American Art in Transition, 1955–62"; "Edward Hopper: Selections from the Permanent Collection"; "Image World: Art and Media Culture," exploring artists' responses to the influence of mass media on American culture; "Thomas Hart Benton" and "Maurice Prendergast," two retrospectives; and "The New Sculpture 1965–75: Between Geometry and Gesture." The Whitney Biennial is a series of invitational exhibitions of work by living American artists. Started in 1932, its often controversial surveys highlight recent American art.

The New American Film and Video Series exhibits independently produced films, videos, and film and video installations. Lectures, seminars and symposiums are offered several times a year. Occasionally the museum hosts programs of dance, music and poetry.

The Whitney also operates a satellite gallery and sculpture court in the Philip Morris building at Park Avenue and 42nd Street. "The Call of the Street," photographs by Sylvia Plachy; "Isamu Noguchi: Portrait Sculpture"; and the sculpture shows "Out of Wood" and "Miniature Environments" are just some of the exhibits mounted there since it opened in 1986. Call 212-878-2550 for current exhibits and hours.

Gertrude Vanderbilt Whitney established the museum in 1930. It initially opened in 1931 in four remodeled brownstones on West 8th Street, using Whitney's 700 American works as the nucleus of its permanent collection. The museum moved to its second home in

"Second Story Sunlight" by Edward Hopper, 1960, from the collection of the Whitney Museum of American Art, New York.

1954, a new building on West 54th Street near the Museum of Modern Art. In 1966 its current facility opened on Madison Avenue. The structure—resembling an inverted staircase fronted by a moat-like well—was designed by Marcel Breuer and Hamilton Smith. It is sheathed in unpolished granite.

GENERAL INFORMATION

Hours Sun, Wed 11 am–6 pm; Thurs 1–8 pm; Fri–Sat 11 am–6 pm; closed Mon, Tues
Admission Adults $6, students and seniors $5
Giftshop Store Next Door at 943 Madison Ave: furniture, jewelry, household objects, etc., by leading American artists, architects, craftsmen and designers; also art books, exhibition catalogs and posters; open 10 am–6 pm daily, Thurs until 8 pm
Food Service Sarabeth's at the Whitney, various hours; call 212-570-3670
Library Works on and by American artists; open by appointment only, call 212-570-3628
Disability Access Fully accessible; sign language tours first Thurs evening of each month
Directions Subway: 6 to 77th St; Bus: M1, M2, M3, M4, M30 to 77th St; M79 to Madison Ave
Landmark Status National Register of Historic Places

Winter Garden

Arts and Events Program 212-945-0505
The World Financial Center
West Street (between Liberty and Vesey Streets)
New York, NY 10281

Launched in 1988, the World Financial Center's Arts and Events Program has featured over 300 events by artists and cultural organizations. Events have included the unveiling of commissioned works created especially for the World Financial Center, previews of works scheduled to appear at other cultural venues, exhibitions from major museums and small-scale traveling exhibits.

Dance performances have been given at the Winter Garden by the Trisha Brown Company, Pilobolus Dance Theater, Les Grands Ballets Canadiens and many others. Among musicians appearing have been the McCoy Tyner Trio, the Shostakovich String Quartet, the Artie Shaw Orchestra, Buster Poindexter and His Banshees of Blue, the Brooklyn Philharmonic, John Cale, and the Abyssinian Baptist Church Sanctuary Choir.

Exhibitions have included "Underwater Cities: the World of the Coral Reef," "Art from the Exploratorium" and "Homefront: New Yorkers During World War II."

A concert at the Winter Garden, Battery Park City.

Robin Holland

There have also been installations of the AIDS Memorial Quilt and the Tropical Rain Forest Sound Installation by Brian Eno.

Most programs are staged or mounted within the Winter Garden's vaulted glass-and-steel dome enclosing a grove of palm trees almost five stories tall. Designed by architect Cesar Pelli, the dome is about the size of Grand Central Terminal's main waiting room. Just outside is a 3.5-acre park on the Hudson River where special summer events are held.

About 75 performances and four exhibits are presented every year. Performances are scheduled at lunchtime, in the evening and on weekends.

GENERAL INFORMATION

Hours 7 am–11 pm daily; call for performance times
Admission Free; no tickets needed, seating on a first-come first-served basis
Giftshop Numerous retail shops in complex; open Mon–Fri 11am–7 pm, Sat 12–6 pm, Sun 12–5 pm
Food Service Numerous restaurants in complex
Disability Access Fully accessible
Directions Subway: 1/9, N or R to Cortlandt St; A, C, E or Path Train to Chambers St–World Trade Center; Bus: M9, M10, M22 to Battery Park City

Yeshiva University Museum

2520 Amsterdam Avenue (at 185th Street) New York, NY 10033 — 212-960-5390

Exhibitions at Yeshiva University Museum explore virtually all aspects of Jewish life and tradition. Numerous disciplines are examined—including art, architecture, history, literature and the sciences—through fine and decorative art works, ceremonial objects, textiles, rare books and photographs.

Exhibitions have included "Synagogue Life in Odessa," photos by Alexander Royzman; "Solomon Nunes Carvalho: Painter, Photographer and Prophet in 19th Century America"; "Jewish Ceremonial Objects"; "Dreams of the Bible," paintings by Uri Shaked; and "Aishet Hayil: Woman of Valor," illuminating a famous biblical acrostic, which inaugurated the museum's newly renovated gallery.

Since its establishment in 1973, the permanent collection has grown significantly. It includes a live biblical garden, scale models of ten historic synagogues, a Sephardic costume collection and paintings and graphics by Israel's early artists. One recent acquisition of particular interest: a rare, 512-year-old transcript of a famous trial that resulted in the destruction of a Jewish community in northern Italy. The museum building, designed by Armand Bartos, is meant to resemble stacks of books.

GENERAL INFORMATION

Hours Sun 12–6 pm; Tues–Thurs 10:30 am–5 pm; closed Mon, Fri and Sat
Admission Adults $3, seniors and children 4–16 $1.50, children under 3 free
Giftshop Books and gift items relating to Jewish heritage; open Sun, Tues–Thurs 11 am–3 pm; closed Fri, Sat
Library University library open to guests with visitor's pass; inquire at Security Office
Disability Access Access to some galleries
Directions Subway: 1/9 to 181st St; Bus: M3, M4, M5, M101 to 185th St

YIVO Institute for Jewish Research

1048 Fifth Avenue (at 80th Street) New York, NY 10028 — 212-535-6700

Although primarily a scholarly institute dedicated to the study of Eastern European Jewry, the YIVO Institute also presents cultural programs. Two large exhibitions are mounted each year drawing on YIVO's vast collection of books, photographs and manuscripts. These shows are historical in nature and have included "Revolutions in Print: Jewish Publishing Under the Tsars and the Soviets," "From the Archives of the Jewish Labor Bund" and "Monument of Memory: Photographs of Ira Nowinski," commemorating the 50th anniversary of the Warsaw Ghetto uprising. Lectures, conferences and concerts are also offered.

Founded in Poland in 1925, YIVO opened a New York branch during World War II to ensure that Jewish culture and tradition would be preserved. YIVO conducts graduate and post-doctoral training in Jewish studies. It is located in the Louis XIII-style mansion once owned by Mrs. Cornelius Vanderbilt.

GENERAL INFORMATION

Hours Mon 9:30 am–8:30 pm; Tues–Thurs 9:30 am–5:30 pm; close Fri–Sun
Admission Free
Library 300,000 volumes on Jewish culture
Disability Access Limited access
Directions Subway: 4, 5 or 6 to 86th St; Bus: M1, M2, M3, M4 to 86th St; M19 to 5th Ave
Landmark Status New York City Landmark

In 1635 the Dutch became the first Europeans to settle in what is today the county of Queens. When the British subsequently occupied the area they named it Queens County in honor of Catherine of Braganza, wife of Charles II. In 1683 it became one of ten counties chartered to form the "colony" of New York. George Washington lost Queens to British troops during the Battle of Long Island (1776), the first of several engagements leading to the British occupation of New York City for the duration of the American Revolution.

The western portions of Queens voted to join the City of New York in 1898, splitting with the eastern section which became Nassau County. Early 20th-century growth in Queens was driven by construction of the Queensborough Bridge (1904) and a railroad tunnel under the East River (1910). The great influx of people into Queens since the second World War—from almost every nation on earth—has made it the most ethnically diverse county in the United States.

Queens possesses the largest land area of all five boroughs—109 square miles. It is divided into distinct neighborhoods—such as Jackson Heights, Corona and Elmhurst—many of them old farm towns which still retain their small-scale ambiance even as they have grown into metropolitan communities.

The history of Queens is recalled not only through the many historic houses in the borough—Bowne House and Kingsland Homestead among them—but also by the cultural institutions located in buildings originally constructed for the 1939 and 1964 World's Fair—such as the New York Hall of Science and the Queens Museum of Art—both of which were held in Flushing Meadow Park. In addition, the Museum of the Moving Image reflects the early history of American filmmaking, which was active in Queens before the rise of Hollywood. The more recent phenomenon of artists living in Queens has produced the Isamu Noguchi Garden Museum, Socrates Sculpture Park and P.S. 1.

Queens

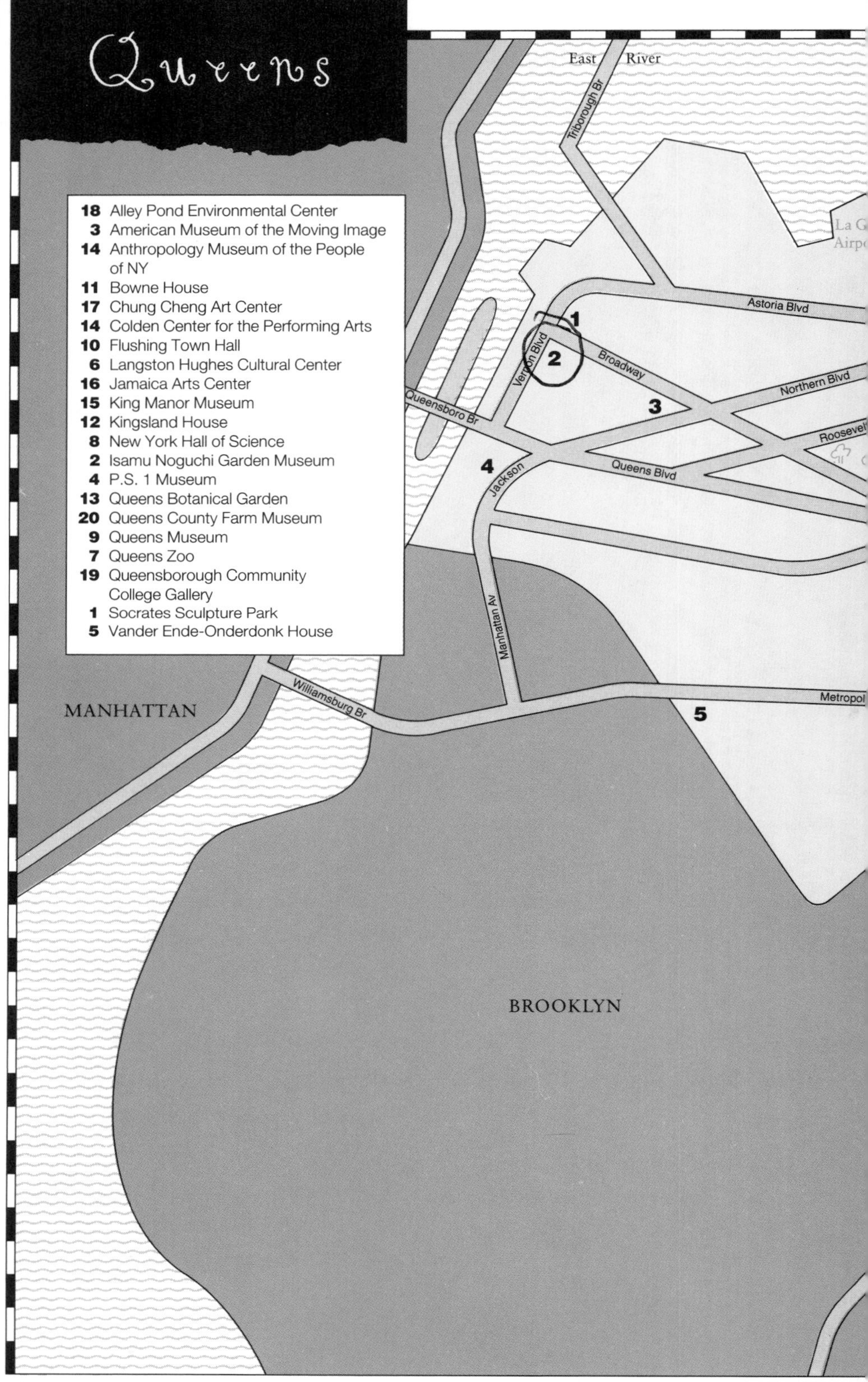
18 Alley Pond Environmental Center
3 American Museum of the Moving Image
14 Anthropology Museum of the People of NY
11 Bowne House
17 Chung Cheng Art Center
14 Colden Center for the Performing Arts
10 Flushing Town Hall
6 Langston Hughes Cultural Center
16 Jamaica Arts Center
15 King Manor Museum
12 Kingsland House
8 New York Hall of Science
2 Isamu Noguchi Garden Museum
4 P.S. 1 Museum
13 Queens Botanical Garden
20 Queens County Farm Museum
9 Queens Museum
7 Queens Zoo
19 Queensborough Community College Gallery
1 Socrates Sculpture Park
5 Vander Ende-Onderdonk House
East River
Triborough Br
Astoria Blvd
Vernon Blvd
Broadway
Northern Blvd
Queensboro Br
Queens Blvd
Jackson
Manhattan Av
Williamsburg Br
MANHATTAN
BROOKLYN

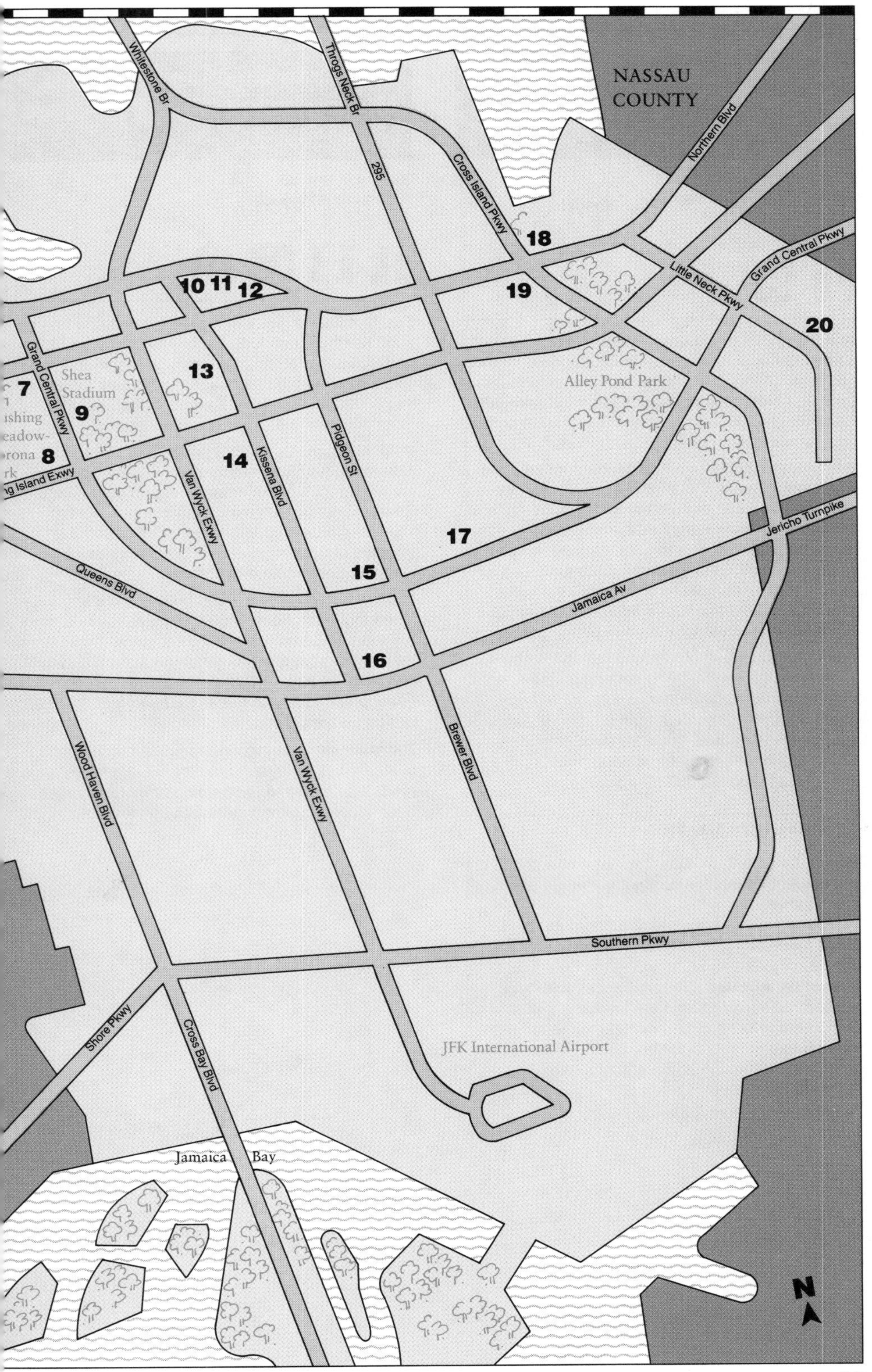
NASSAU
COUNTY
Whitestone Br
Throgs Neck Br
295
Cross Island Pkwy
Northern Blvd
18
Grand Central Pkwy
Little Neck Pkwy
10 11 12
19
20
Grand Central Pkwy
Shea
Stadium
13
7
9
ushing
eadow-
orona
rk
8
Alley Pond Park
Pidgeon St
14
Kissena Blvd
Van Wyck Exwy
ng Island Exwy
17
Jericho Turnpike
Queens Blvd
15
Jamaica Av
16
Wood Haven Blvd
Van Wyck Exwy
Brewer Blvd
Southern Pkwy
Shore Pkwy
Cross Bay Blvd
JFK International Airport
Jamaica Bay
N

Alley Pond Environmental Center

228-06 Northern Boulevard (off the Cross Island Parkway)
Douglaston, NY 11363
718-229-4000

Alley Pond Park is an undeveloped, 700-acre area of eastern Queens that attracts over 300 species of birds and other wildlife. Bird-watchers and nature enthusiasts can follow trails here that lead to fresh and saltwater marshes; glacial moraine expanses with kettle ponds; flood plains; upland forests; and beaches.

The Alley Pond Environmental Center is an educational organization founded in 1976 to encourage understanding and preservation of the environment. Located in a newly renovated structure at the northern end of the park, the center offers lessons in the diverse ecosystems of the park to thousands of schoolchildren every year. Exhibits, discussions and hands-on discovery of rabbits, snakes and turtles in the center's mini-zoo contribute to the learning experience.

Other permanent exhibits include salt and freshwater aquariums and several demonstration projects, including an organic garden and an apiary. Workshops address environmental issues ranging from endangered species to toxic waste. The Alley Pond Environmental Center has been designated a National Environmental Study Area by the National Park Service.

GENERAL INFORMATION

Hours Tues–Fri 9 am–4 pm; Sat, Sun 9:30 am–3:30 pm; closed Mon; closed Sun during summer
Admission Free
Giftshop Nature-related items for children
Food Service No concessions; picnic area behind building
Disability Access Building is accessible, trails are not; parking, restrooms and fountains available. Opportunities for hearing-impaired volunteers
Directions Subway: 7 to Main Street–Flushing, then take Q12 bus to 228th St; Bus: Q12 to 228th St
Parking On-site lot
City-owned, privately operated

American Museum of the Moving Image

35th Avenue at 36th Street
Astoria, NY 11106
718-784-4520

The American Museum of the Moving Image is the first institution in the United States devoted to the art, history and technology of motion pictures, television and video. The museum is directly across the street from the famous Astoria Studios, originally Paramount Pictures' East Coast facility.

A 7,200-square-foot permanent exhibit, Behind the Screen, traces the evolution of film and television productions from creative inception to public screening. Through participatory exhibits visitors can explore various acting styles, learn about the transforming wonders of makeup, mix soundtracks and view antique fan magazines and movie posters.

The museum's 200-seat Riklis Theater and 60-seat screening room offer over 500 programs yearly, among them rarely seen film and video treasures. Other viewing theaters include a 1960s-style living room complete with shag rug and vinyl furniture that seats six, and Tut's Fever, an amusing homage to the neo-Egyptian–style picture palaces of the 1920s.

The museum's collection includes 70,000 objects related to the history and practice of film and television production, marketing and distribution. The museum does not collect films, videotapes or kinescopes.

A landmarked three-story building was renovated for the museum by Gwathmey Siegel & Associates. The building is part of the 1920s Astoria Studios complex. Renamed Kaufman Astoria Studios, the complex has been revitalized as a multimedia center for the production of film, television, commercials and rock videos. It has been used by such filmmakers as Woody Allen, Martin Scorsese and Sidney Lumet.

David Allison

RCA Victor portable television set, 1959.

Collection of Museum of the Moving Image

GENERAL INFORMATION

Hours Tues–Fri 12–4 pm; Sat, Sun 12–6 pm; closed Mon
Admission Adults $5, seniors $4, children and students free
Giftshop Books, posters, cards and toys related to collection
Food Service Cafe serves beverages and pastries
Disability Access Fully accessible
Directions Subway: R or G to Steinway St; E or F to Queens Plaza or Roosevelt Ave, transfer to R or G, exit at Steinway St; Bus: Q101 to Steinway St and 35th Ave; Q66 to 35th Ave
Parking On public streets
Landmark Status New York City Landmark

City-owned, privately operated

The Anthropology Museum of the People of New York

Queens College of the
City University of New York
65-30 Kissena Boulevard
Flushing, NY 11367

718-428-5650

In 1977 Margaret Mead and other anthropologists founded the Anthropology Museum of the People of New York to promote cross-cultural understanding among the city's many cultural groups, while encouraging ethnic pride. The museum offers panel discussions, traveling photography exhibits, demonstrations, field trips, art shows and socials.

With the underlying goal of promoting goodwill toward different ethnic cultures, museum exhibitions display artifacts to emphasize and illustrate similarities among various ethnic groups. Past student-produced exhibitions have included "Quest for Cures," which explored connections among folk, scientific and holistic medicine. The permanent collection contains artifacts relating to ancient Greek culture, and there are fossils demonstrating human evolutionary development.

Since it has no permanent facility of its own, the museum presents events on the Queens College campus and at various off-campus sites. Call for information about off-campus shows.

GENERAL INFORMATION

Hours Various; call for hours and program schedule
Admission Free
Library Field research papers, slides and cultural artifacts of contemporary ethnic groups; open to scholars by appointment
Handicapped Access All Queens College facilities are fully accessible; inquire about off-campus events
Directions Subway: 7 to Main St–Flushing, transfer to Q17 or Q25-34 bus to Queens College; R, E or F to Continental Ave, transfer to Q65-A bus to Jewel Ave and Kissena Blvd; Bus: Q17, Q25-34 to Queens College; Q65-A to Jewel Ave and Kissena Blvd
Parking On public streets, on site by permission only

Bowne House

37-01 Bowne Street
(at Congressman
Rosenthal Avenue)
Flushing, NY 11354
718-359-0528

Built in 1661 by John Bowne, this is one of the oldest surviving buildings in New York City. Considered a fine example of vernacular Dutch-English architecture, it was named one of the 20 most important structures in the nation by the American Institute of Architects. It differs little today from the house that Bowne built.

The original sections of the house consist of the kitchen, two small adjoining rooms and sleeping quarters upstairs. In 1680 Bowne added the dining room with its pegged floors, hand-hewn beams and handsome fireplace. The dining room gives the impression that the Bowne family had prospered since construction of the earlier wing and that their lives had taken on an air of greater leisure and elegance.

In 1945, after occupancy by nine generations of Bownes, the house was purchased by the Bowne House Historical Society. Today it contains a magnificent collection of 17th-, 18th- and 19th-century furniture, paintings, artifacts and documents belonging to the Bowne family. There are four special exhibits each year, an antiques auction in the spring and a winter quilt raffle.

In this house, John Bowne took his stand against the outlawing of the Quaker sect by Peter Stuyvesant, governor of New Netherland, the Dutch colony's name at the time. Bowne's advocacy of freedom of conscience, which caused him to be banished to Holland (he was later vindicated), contributed to the adoption more than a century later of the First Amendment to the Constitution. The Bowne House is located next to the 18th-century Kingsland Homestead (see separate entry).

GENERAL INFORMATION

Hours Tues, Sat, Sun 2:30–4:30 pm; school groups, weekday mornings by appointment
Admission Adults $2, seniors and children under 12, $1
Giftshop Postcards, stationery, quills and memorabilia
Library Archives open by appointment only
Disability Access Limited wheelchair access
Directions Subway: 7 to Main St–Flushing;
Bus: Q12, Q13, Q14, Q15, Q16 to Bowne St
Parking On public streets
Landmark Status National Register of Historic Places, New York City Landmark

Chung-Cheng Art Gallery Center of Asian Studies

Sun Yat-Sen Hall
St. John's University
8000 Utopia Parkway
Jamaica, NY 11439

718-990-1525

The Chung-Cheng Art Gallery was named to honor Chiang Kai-shek (1887–1975), founder of the Republic of China, whose formal name was Chiang Chung-Cheng. The gallery contains objects dating from the seventh century to the present and is located at St. John's University in the golden pagoda, a yellow-brick structure with a red and gold roof decorated with carved demon figures.

There are 1,000 items on display, including a samurai sword and a number of scabbards of gold, bronze and cloisonné depicting fish, generals, sages and landscapes; delicate blue and white porcelain and cloisonné plates; brush pots of iron, bamboo, jade and porcelain; a lacquerware writing box with gold-inlay cover and gold powder sprinkled on the instruments; beautifully glazed vases and ivory carvings; and an ink set made as a tribute to Emperor K'ang-hsi (1662–1722). The pure white porcelain figure is Kuanwin, the Buddhist goddess of mercy. About half the items are Chinese, the other half Japanese. Changing exhibitions usually center on the work of contemporary Asian artists, many of them exhibiting in the United States for the first time.

GENERAL INFORMATION

Hours Mon–Fri 10 am–8 pm; Sat, Sun 10 am–4 pm
Admission Free
Library Gallery has collection of books on Chinese and Japanese art, literature and history
Disability Access Fully accessible
Directions Subway: E or F to Kew Gardens, then transfer to bus; Bus: From Kew Gardens, Q46 to 173rd St and Union Turnpike
Parking On-site lot

Colden Center for the Performing Arts

Queens College of the
City University of New York
65-30 Kissena Boulevard
Flushing, NY 11367

718-793-8080
Box Office

Known affectionately to loyal patrons as the "Lincoln Center of Queens," Colden Center for the Performing Arts has offered New Yorkers a sophisticated range of classical music, dance, jazz and children's theater programs at moderate prices for over 30 years.

The center maintains three performance spaces: Colden Auditorium, 2,100 seats; Queens College Theatre, 450 seats; and Queens College Concert Hall, 489 seats. This last space, built in the early 1990s, is renowned

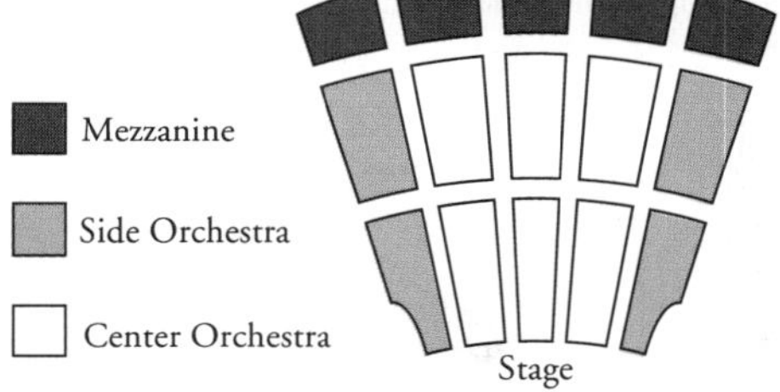

for its superior acoustics. The center has offered performances in the past by Luciano Pavarotti, Itzak Perlman, Tony Bennett, Joan Sutherland, Mel Torme and Ella Fitzgerald, among others.

The "Revelations" series is geared to schoolchildren, with special daytime performances of native African and Chinese dance, Western music and ballet, and contemporary music of Puerto Rico. There is also a pop and jazz series.

GENERAL INFORMATION

Hours Box Office: Mon, Thurs, Fri 10 am–4 pm; Wed 2–8 pm; closed Tues, Sat, Sun
Summer hours: Mon–Thurs 10 am–4 pm; closed Fri–Sun
Admission Tickets generally $18 to $20
Food Service Concessions during performances
Disability Access Orchestra level fully accessible; restrooms available
Directions Subway: E, F, R, G or 7 to Union Turnpike–Kew Gardens or Main St –Flushing;
Bus: Q17, Q25-34, Q88, Q74 to Kissena Blvd and Horace Harding Expressway
Parking On-site lot, between exits 23 and 24 of Long Island Expressway

Flushing Town Hall

137-35 Northern Boulevard 718-463-7700
(at Linden Place)
Flushing, NY 11354

Flushing Town Hall, home of the Flushing Council on Culture and the Arts, has just completed an extensive $6 million restoration. Thanks to much-needed structural improvements, the hall now accommodates a variety of cultural events, including art exhibitions, concerts, educational programs, cultural festivals and plays.

The Town Hall Gallery is a lively venue for contemporary art, emphasizing artists who live or work in Queens. Exhibits change about five times a year. The council is also responsible for outdoor sculpture installations in nearby Flushing Meadow Park. A permanent exhibit in the Visitors' Center depicts the hall's role in the social, political and cultural life of the late 19th century, as well as the story of the building's reclamation. The intimate, wood-paneled Jazz Cafe is used for a Thursday-night series featuring jazz legends as well as mid-career and emerging musicians.

Built in 1862 in the Romanesque Revival style, Town Hall has served Flushing over the years in a variety of ways. During the Civil War, it was an assembly point for Union recruits. P. T. Barnum, the sideshow impresario, used the structure as a showcase for the likes of Tom Thumb and singer Jenny Lind. It has also been used as a bank, police station, jail, grand ballroom and courthouse.

GENERAL INFORMATION

Hours Wed–Fri 10 am–5 pm; Thurs, live jazz at 8 and 10 pm; Sat, Sun 12–5 pm; closed Mon, Tues
Admission Adults $2, seniors and students $1, children under 12 free
Giftshop Books and souvenirs
Disability Access Fully accessible; restrooms available
Directions Subway: 7 to Main St–Flushing; Bus: Q12, Q17, Q26, Q44 to 41st Ave
Parking On public streets
Landmark Status National Register of Historic Places, New York City Landmark
City-owned, privately operated

Langston Hughes Community Library and Cultural Center

102-09 Northern Boulevard 718-651-1100
(at 103rd Street)
Corona, NY 11368

The Langston Hughes Community Library and Cultural Center was founded in 1969 to serve the Corona/East Elmhurst area's predominantly African-American population. The center's cultural programs range from theatrical presentations to music concerts, from literary readings to exhibitions.

The exhibition program presents both established and emerging artists, working in all media, with an emphasis on Third World and women artists. The center also offers at least two film festivals a year emphasizing the work of independent filmmakers from around the globe. Workshops in drama, textiles, crafts, photography, writing, dance and ceramics are regularly offered. Events such as the Caribbean Festival and Kwanza Celebration are a significant part of the center's ongoing commitment to focus on African and African-American artists.

Langston Hughes (1902–1967).

GENERAL INFORMATION

Hours Mon, Fri 10 am–6 pm; Tues 1–6 pm; Wed, Thurs 1–8 pm; Sat 10 am–5 pm; closed Sun
Admission Free
Library Black Heritage Reference Center contains over 20,000 volumes on African-American culture; circulating collection is open to the public
Disability Access Library is accessible; gallery is not
Directions Subway: 7 to Corona Plaza; Bus: Q66 to 101st St; Q23 to 103rd St
Parking On public streets

Jamaica Arts Center

161-04 Jamaica Avenue (between 161st and 162nd Streets) Jamaica, NY 11432 — 718-658-7400

The Jamaica Arts Center presents exhibitions of local and nationally known artists in its three galleries. Workshops in ceramics, photography, dance, acting, printmaking, painting, drawing and other areas offer a high level of personalized attention and are open to all ages and skill levels.

The center was started in 1972 as part of the redevelopment of downtown Jamaica, and in 1974 it opened in the building that formerly housed the Register of Titles and Deeds for the County of Queens. The Italian Renaissance style building was designed in 1898 by the firm A.S. MacGregor.

GENERAL INFORMATION

Hours Gallery: Tues–Sat 10 am–5 pm; closed Sun, Mon
Admission Free
Disability Access Fully accessible; restrooms available
Directions Subway: E, Z or J to Jamaica Center; Bus:Q42, Q54, Q56, Q83, Q85 to Jamaica Ave
Parking Adjacent lot, across Jamaica Ave
Landmark Status National Register of Historic Places, New York City Landmark
City-owned, privately operated

King Manor Museum

King Park
Jamaica Avenue (between 150th and 153rd Streets)
Jamaica, NY 11432 — 718-523-0029

King Manor is the centerpiece of an 11-acre historic park in Jamaica. The 18th- and 19th-century house takes its name from Rufus King (1755–1827), one of the most distinguished figures in this nation's early political history. King was a member of the Continental Congress, a framer and signer of the Constitution, one of the first two senators from New York State and the first ambassador to Great Britain, under presidents Washington, Adams and Jefferson.

In 1805 King bought an existing farm that included an 18th-century Dutch-style house with an attached Long Island–style "half house." A year after moving in, he added a kitchen to the rear of the Dutch house. He further expanded the structure four years later to its stylish Georgian grandeur by adding a dining room and two bedrooms. After King's death, his son, John, lived in the house and added the Greek Revival exterior details, such as the classical portico and entranceway. The house remained with King's heirs until 1896, when it was purchased by the Village of Jamaica. Two years later it was transferred to the city.

The just-completed reconstruction of King Park has created a more appropriate setting for the manor, including period landscaping with native plants and wildflowers. The new history museum inside the house gives visitors of all ages an introduction to King's family, home, farm, village and nation. Several rooms have been furnished in period style.

King Manor Museum

GENERAL INFORMATION

Hours Open on a limited basis; call in advance for information on hours
Admission Fees per program: free–$2
Disability Access Limited access; ramp on first floor
Directions Subway: E, J or Z to Jamaica Center; F or R to Parsons Blvd; Bus: Q24, Q42, Q43, Q44, Q54, Q56, Q83 to Archer Ave and Parsons Blvd
Parking On public streets
Landmark Status National Register of Historic Places, New York City Landmark
City-owned, privately operated

Symbol Key

 *Institutional Giftshop*

 *On-Site Food Services*

 *On-Site Library or Archive*

 *Full Accessibility*

 *On-Site Parking*

 *National Register of Historic Places and/or New York City Landmark*

Kingsland Homestead

Queens Historical Society
(between Parsons Boulevard and Bowe Street)
143-35 37th Avenue
Flushing, NY 11354
718-939-0647

Located in Weeping Beech Park, the Kingsland Homestead is a graceful example of the unique Long Island–style "half houses" popular in the late 18th and early 19th centuries. The house is a blend of Dutch and English Colonial styles featuring a gambrel roof, a crescent-shaped window in a side gable and a Dutch-style front door. The house is fully restored. Its only furnished period room is a second-floor parlor decorated as if it belonged to a middle-class family.

The first floor is used for local history exhibitions that draw on the collections of the Queens Historical Society, which owns Kingsland, and local residents. Exhibits have included "The Civil War: A Queens Perspective" and "Work Projects Administration: Relief, Reform and Recovery," a survey of Depression-era Queens. Other shows have focused on the 1939 World's Fair, antique toys and costumes and the history of local communities.

In 1785 Charles Doughty built the house on land inherited from his father. During the Revolutionary War the estate was plundered by the British. Doughty, nevertheless, returned to prosperity after the war and restored the house. In 1799 he became the first local slave owner to free a slave. The house was designated a New York City Landmark in 1966. Kingsland Homestead is located next to 17th-century Bowne House (see separate entry).

GENERAL INFORMATION

Hours Tues, Sat, Sun 2:30–4:30 pm; closed Mon, Wed–Fri
Admission Adults $2, seniors and children $1
Giftshop Publications and items related to exhibits and Queens history
Library Primary and secondary source materials covering Queens 300-year history; open Mon–Sat 9:30 am–4:30 pm, by appointment only
Disability Access Upgrading amenities; call about status
Directions Subway: 7 to Main St–Flushing; Bus: Q12 to Parsons Blvd; Q13 to Parsons and Northern Blvds; Q16 to Union and Northern Blvds
Parking Adjacent lot, 38th and Roosevelt Ave
Landmark Status National Register of Historic Places, New York City Landmark

New York Hall of Science

47-01 111th Street
(at 46th Avenue)
Flushing Meadows Corona Park
Queens, NY 11368

718-699-0005

The New York Hall of Science works to improve public understanding of science and technology. The Hall's 25,000-square-foot facility contains some 150 hands-on, interactive exhibits divided into thematic sections.

Seeing the Light is a journey into the world of color, light and perception. Visitors cast colored shadows, blow giant soap bubbles and explore how humans perceive color in this exhibition, created by the Exploratorium in San Francisco.

The Realm of the Atom teaches participants about the invisible building blocks of matter. Viewers can examine and manipulate the world's first three-dimensional, dynamic model of an atom in this foray into quantum physics.

Hidden Kingdoms—The World of Microbes is the nation's largest interactive microbiology exhibition. Microscopes in this section allow visitors to see everything from yeast cells and penicillin microbes to amoebas; a working, scanning electron microscope magnifies objects 25,000 times.

The exhibits grouped under the heading Feedback allow museumgoers to interact with machines that sense and respond to environmental changes. A windmill's direction, for instance, is changed by switching on different fans, and the mechanism of an antique steam engine is explained.

Traveling and temporary exhibitions have included artist installations such as Ned Kahn's 20-foot tornado, "Temple of Whirlwinds," and larger programs like "Dawn of the Molecules," a multimedia presentation.

Live daily science demonstrations, as well as films and workshops for children and adults, are also offered. The hall's multimedia library provides reference services for the public and circulation services to school teachers and members.

Recognizing that a sophisticated understanding of science represents a survival skill for Americans in a technologically competitive world, the hall has instituted programs to inspire students to pursue careers in science teaching and research.

The tall concrete structure housing the New York Hall of Science is a futuristic piece of architecture in the form of undulating curves. It was designed by Wallace Harrison for the 1964 World's Fair. The hall has just begun a ten-year $80 million renovation and expansion project that will add laboratories, classrooms, an observatory, a planetarium and additional exhibition space to the building.

GENERAL INFORMATION

Hours Wed–Sun 10 am–5 pm; closed Mon, Tues
Admission Adults $3.50, seniors and children $2.50
Giftshop Variety of science-related items: books, experiments, etc.
Food Service Small seating area with vending machines
Library Science Access Center, lending library for members and staff only
Disability Access Fully accessible
Directions Subway: 7 to 111th St; Bus: Q23 to 108th St and 48th Ave; Q48 to Roosevelt Ave and 111th St; B58 to 111th St and Corona Ave
Parking On public streets

City-owned, privately operated

Noguchi n Museum

32-37 Vernon Boulevard
(corner of 33rd Road)
Long Island City, NY 11106

718-204-7088

This museum, situated in a quiet industrial neighborhood of Long Island City, is dedicated to the life and work of the internationally recognized Japanese-American sculptor Isamu Noguchi (1904–1988).

Three hundred works in stone, metal, wood and clay from all phases of Noguchi's career reflect the sculptor's esthetic sensibility and interest in the natural world. Twelve galleries and an outdoor sculpture garden house the pieces, which range from Noguchi's early portrait busts to his late basalt stone works. The collection also features the sculptor's *Akari* light sculptures, his stage designs for Martha Graham and George Balanchine, and documentation of his gardens and playgrounds. The museum itself, designed by Noguchi, may be one of his greatest creations.

Shigeo Anzai

"Core (Cored Sculpture)," by Isamu Noguchi, 1978.

The building, converted from a photo-engraving plant, was once used by Noguchi as a studio. When he transformed it into an exhibition space, he retained the character of the original studio: sculptures are displayed on the floor on rough-hewn wood bases, and simple lighting illuminates most of the space. The outdoor sculpture garden is planted with birches, juniper, weeping cherry and bamboo, and landscaped with gravel paths and streams. Across the street, two parks offer magnificent East River views of Manhattan: Rainey Park and Socrates Sculpture Park (see separate entry).

GENERAL INFORMATION

Hours April–Nov: Wed, Sat, Sun 11 am–6 pm; closed Mon, Tues, Thurs, Fri
Admission Suggested contribution: adults $4, seniors and students $2
Giftshop Books and lamps for sale
Library Artist file and library open to public by appointment only
Disability Access Main floor and parts of garden are accessible; second floor is not
Directions Subway: N to Broadway (Queens), then 15-minute walk west to Vernon Blvd; Bus: Sat and Sun shuttle service from Asia Society (70th St and Park Ave, Manhattan), call for information
Parking On public streets

P.S. 1 Museum

46-01 21st Street
(at 46th Avenue)
Long Island City, NY 11101

718-784-2084

In 1976 the Institute for Contemporary Art, an enterprise dedicated to securing studio space for artists whose work was overlooked by New York's museum establishment, took possession of a large 19th-century red-brick school building in Long Island City and refurbished it. Today, this 85,000-square-foot structure, known as P.S. 1, is one of the largest alternative art spaces in North America.

Three to five times a year, P.S. 1 mounts major exhibits in all media. Thematic exhibitions have included "New York/New Wave," which presented the early work of Jean-Michel Basquiat, Keith Haring and Kenny Scharf; "German New Expressionism"; and "Slow Art: Painting in New York Now."

P.S. 1 houses film and video screening rooms, a large auditorium for dance and performance presentations, ambitious sculptural installations and more than a dozen galleries. The Institute for Contemporary Art also supports over 20 artists-in-residence annually at P.S. 1, providing them with studio facilities and sponsoring group shows of their work. The Clocktower Gallery in Lower Manhattan (see separate entry) is also administered by the institute.

GENERAL INFORMATION

Hours During exhibitions: Wed–Sun 12–6 pm; closed Mon, Tues
Admission Suggested contribution $2
Giftshop Institute books for sale at main desk
Disability Access None
Directions Subway: E or F to 23rd St–Ely Ave; 7 to 45th Rd–Courthouse Sq; G to 21st St–Van Alst Rd; Bus: None
Parking On public streets
City-owned, privately operated

Queens Botanical Garden

43-50 Main Street 718-886-3800
Flushing, NY 11355

The Queens Botanical Garden was created to preserve a garden exhibit developed for the 1939 World's Fair in Flushing Meadows Corona Park. It was moved to its current 38-acre site in 1962. Considering the garden's modest size, it contains an impressive range of plantings. The Formal Display Gardens contain 80,000 tulips; after these bloom in early spring, the beds are replanted with annual flowers in the style of 17th- and 18th-century formal European gardens. The Wedding Garden is based on Victorian designs and has a stream, a large weeping willow, rose trees, flowering fruit trees and perennial and annual borders. The Bird Garden contains plantings that provide food, shelter and nesting materials for birds. The Bee Garden contains nine working hives stocked with honey-producing bees that promote propagation throughout the Queens Botanical Garden. There is also a six-acre rose garden, one of the largest in the Eastern United States; a collection of 93 conifer varieties; and an herb garden with aromatic, culinary and medicinal varieties. Educational programs are offered for all age groups and there is special instruction for schoolchildren, seniors and handicapped audiences.

GENERAL INFORMATION

Hours Mid–April to mid–Oct: Tues–Sun 10 am–6 pm; closed Mon
Mid–Oct to mid–April: Tues–Sun 10 am–4:30 pm; closed Mon
Admission Free, donations welcomed
Giftshop Gardening items; indoor/outdoor plants
Food Service Vending machines; concessions during summer
Disability Access Fully accessible
Directions Subway: 7 to Main St–Flushing; Bus: Q44 to the garden
Parking On-site lot
Landmark Status New York City Landmark
City-owned, privately operated

Queens County Farm Museum

73-50 Little Neck Parkway 718-347-3276
Floral Park, NY 11004

It's a little hard to believe, but amid the houses and apartment buildings of Floral Park, Queens, sits a 17th-century farm with ducks, geese, sheep and orchards of apple and pear trees. This is the Queens County Farm Museum, a 47-acre spread that has been the site of continuous farming for over 200 years and is now a museum chronicling the agricultural history of New York City.

The 18th-century farmhouse is in the Dutch-Flemish style featuring four-foot eaves, hand-split shingles and window sashes. Inside are plank floors, wainscoted walls and beamed ceilings. The outbuildings, which date from 1927, include greenhouses, a potting shed, wagon shed, cow barn and brooder house. These are probably the last farm buildings constructed in Queens.

The farm was started in 1772 by Jacob and Catherine Adriance. It was bought and sold thereafter by various families of Dutch descent. New York State purchased it in 1926 for use by adjoining Creedmoor Psychiatric Hospital. In 1975, after the state declared the farm to

Queens County Farm Museum Highlights

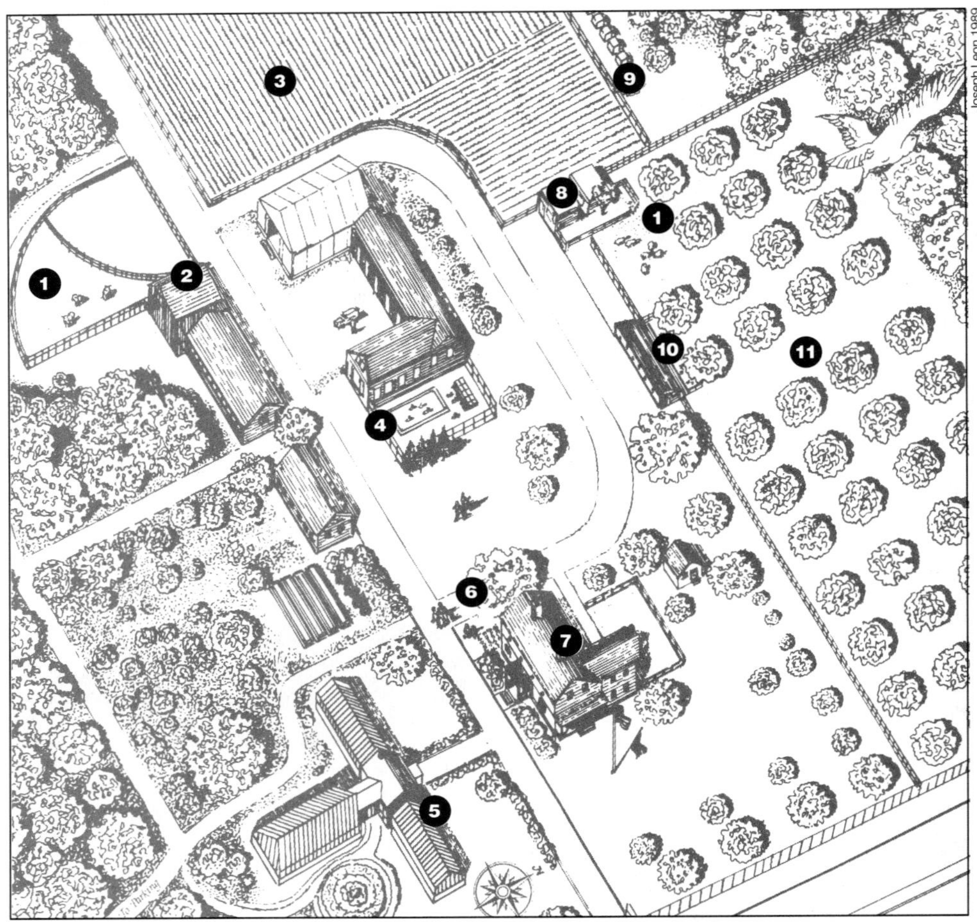

1 Sheep Pastures
2 Cowbarn
3 Planting Fields
4 Duck Pond
5 Greenhouse
6 Herb Garden
7 Farmhouse
8 Cow Shed
9 Bee Hives
10 Chicken Coop
11 Orchard

be "excess land," residents formed a coalition to save it from development.

Special events at the farm include agricultural and craft fairs, Native American powwows, apple festivals and antique car shows. In addition to providing tours of the farmhouse, the museum offers a variety of special events and educational programs.

GENERAL INFORMATION

Hours Grounds: Mon–Fri 9 am–5 pm, throughout the year; April–Dec: farm grounds and museum open Sat, Sun 12–5 pm
Admission Free; small fee for school groups
Giftshop Farm-related toys, T-shirts, souvenirs
Disability Access Fully accessible
Directions Subway: E or F to Kew Gardens–Union Turnpike, transfer to Q46 bus; Bus: Q46 to Little Neck Pkwy, then walk three blocks north
Parking On public streets

Queens Museum of Art

The New York City Building
Flushing Meadows–Corona Park
Queens, NY 11368
718-592-5555

Located in the New York City Building—one of the major structures surviving from the 1939 World's Fair—the Queens Museum of Art presents an ambitious program of exhibitions on loan from other institutions and selections from its own permanent collection. The primary focus is on 20th-century art. Exhibitions have included "Keith Haring," works from the artist's estate; "Across the Pacific: Contemporary Korean Art"; and "Ante America" (Regarding America), works by several Native American and Latin American artists.

The permanent collection includes an archive of memorabilia from both World's Fairs, and 19th- and 20th-century works relating to New York City by numerous artists, including Reginald Marsh and Bruce Davidson. The museum features the famous Panorama of the City of New York, a 15,000-square-foot model of the five boroughs featuring detailed models of thousands of buildings. Various educational workshops, docent-led tours, film screenings, lectures and performances are also offered. Nearby, visitors will find the New York Hall of Science (see separate entry), Shea Stadium and the 120-foot Unisphere, the huge steel globe that is a remnant of the 1964 World's Fair.

GENERAL INFORMATION

Hours Tues–Fri 10 am–5 pm; Sat, Sun 12–5 pm; closed Mon
Admission Suggested contribution: adults $3, students and seniors $1.50, children under 5 free
Giftshop Books, catalogs, and reproductions relating to exhibits and a fine selection of children's merchandise
Library Institutional archives accessible through registrar only
Disability Access Fully accessible; parking available
Directions Subway: 7 to Willets Point–Shea Stadium, walk to Unisphere then go right; Bus: B58 to 108th St
Parking On-site lot
Landmark Status New York City Landmark
City-owned, privately operated

Queens Zoo–Wildlife Conservation Center

NYZS/Wildlife Conservation Society
53-51 111th Street
(at 54th Avenue)
Flushing Meadows Park
Flushing, NY 11415
718-271-7761

The Queens Zoo is a tribute to indigenous North American fauna. It is home to about 250 animals of some 40 species. A recent four-year, $16 million renovation has totally reconfigured the zoo, giving it more naturalistic wildlife environments. The center perimeter is a pathway that blends into adjacent Flushing Meadows –Corona Park. Off this pathway the visitor is led into pockets of wild habitats ranging from the Great American Plains to the rocky California coast and Northeastern Forest.

Ducks, geese, herons and egrets occupy the enlarged marsh. The geodesic aviary—designed by Buckminster Fuller for the 1964 World's Fair—is home to a variety of birds, including the cattle egret, black-billed magpie, wild turkey and several species of ducks. The sandhill crane has a special new exhibition area, as do the mountain lion and bobcat. Roosevelt elk, coyote, sea lion, American bison, prairie dog and black bear exhibits are other points of interest. In the separate domestic animal area, youngsters can meet and touch animals such as horses, sheep, goats and rabbits.

The Queens Zoo is managed by New York Zoological Society/The Wildlife Conservation Society, which operates the Bronx Zoo, the Central Park Zoo, the Prospect Park Zoo, the New York Aquarium and the St. Catherines Wildlife Conservation Center, Georgia.

. INFORMATION

... April–Oct: Mon–Fri 10 am–5 pm; Sat, Sun 10 am–5:30 pm; Nov–March: 10 am–4:30 pm daily
Admission Adults $2.50; seniors $1.25; children 3–12, 50¢; children under 3 free
Giftshop Books, T-shirts, toys, souvenirs
Food Service Cafeteria on premises
Disability Access Fully accessible; parking available
Directions Subway: 7 to 111th St; Bus: Q58 to 111th St
Parking Adjacent lot, on 111th St between 54th and 55th Aves; also at nearby New York Hall of Science

City-owned, privately operated by New York Zoological Society/The Wildlife Conservation Society

Queensborough Community College Art Gallery

Queensborough Community College of the City University of New York
222-05 56th Avenue
Bayside, NY 11364

718-631-6396

The Queensborough Community College Art Gallery mounts about eight exhibitions a year. Notable among them have been "American Women Artists: The 20th Century," featuring works by Louise Nevelson, Georgia O'Keeffe and others; "Latino Influences in American Art," featuring the work of Jasper Johns, Frank Stella and others; and "Black Photographers: 1840–1940." In addition, the work of faculty, students and other local artists is regularly shown. Exhibitions are frequently planned in conjunction with other campus events.

The gallery's permanent collection contains over 1,200 works and is strongest in American modernism since 1950; artists represented include Roy Lichtenstein, Sol Le Witt and Josef Albers.

The gallery is located on a rolling 34-acre campus, formerly the site of a golf course. The gallery was started in 1966 to provide an exhibiting venue for faculty and students. In 1981 it moved to renovated and expanded spaces in the Oakland Building, the oldest structure on campus.

GENERAL INFORMATION

Hours Mon–Wed, Fri 9 am–5 pm; Thurs 9 am–9 pm; closed weekends
Admission Free
Food Service Cafeteria, Mon–Fri 8 am–3 pm; closed weekends
Library Exhibition-catalog collection
Disability Access Fully accessible
Directions Bus: Q27 to 56th Ave and Springfield Blvd
Parking On-site lot

Socrates Sculpture Park

Broadway at Vernon Boulevard
Long Island City, NY 11106

718-956-1819

Socrates Sculpture Park is the principal site for the exhibition of large sculpture in New York City. Set on a small inlet of the East River, the 4.5-acre park consists of a large central open space encircled by rock gardens, specially built walls, gravel walkways, areas of wild grasses and boulders lining the shore. The sculpture, placed at strategic points, has the dramatic city skyline as a backdrop.

Sculptors exhibiting at the park have included Mark di Suvero, Alice Aycock, Richard Serra and others. Many sculptures have been specially created to be experienced within the park's unique spaces.

Socrates Sculpture Park, which opened in 1986, was founded thanks to the collaborative efforts of Mark di Suvero, Isamu Noguchi and local community leaders. Noguchi's own museum is only a few blocks away (see separate entry). The park is located in Long Island City, which has become a center for the arts as more artists establish studios there.

GENERAL INFORMATION

Hours 10 am–sunset daily
Admission Free
Giftshop Exhibition catalogs and T-shirts for sale in office
Disability Access Fully accessible
Directions Subway: N to Broadway (Queens), then walk eight blocks to East River; Bus: Q103 to Broadway; Q104 to Vernon Blvd
Parking On-site lot and public streets

City-owned, privately operated

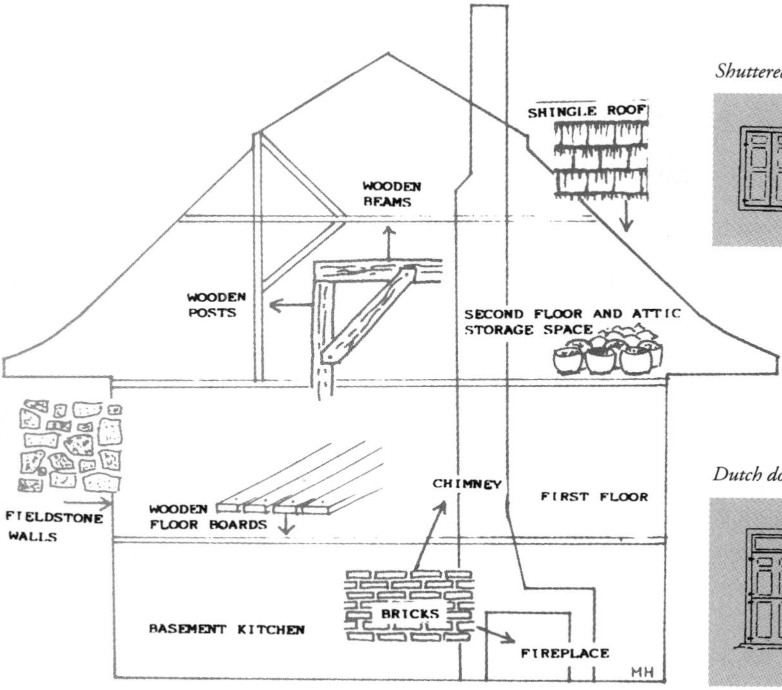

Shuttered window

Dutch doors

Vander Ende–Onderdonk House

Greater Ridgewood
Historical Society
18-20 Flushing Avenue
(at Onderdonk Avenue)
Ridgewood, NY 11385

718-456-1776

The Vander Ende–Onderdonk House is the oldest Dutch-American farmhouse in New York City. Its notable architectural features include heavy fieldstone walls, a wooden-shingle gambrel roof and large brick chimneys. The interior is mainly exposed post-and-beam construction with wooden floors. There are double Dutch doors and numerous small, shuttered windows. In the cellar stands an old fireplace that was once used for the kitchen. On display inside the house are objects found during excavations conducted in the 1970s and 1980s, as well as architectural and historical exhibits.

The house was built by Paulus Vander Ende, a Dutch farmer, about 1709. The smaller wooden wing was erected much later. In the early 1800s, the house was purchased by the Onderdonk family. After the last Onderdonk moved out, successive owners used the house as a livery stable, speakeasy, office and, most recently, as a factory for parts for the Apollo space program. The Greater Ridgewood Historical Society was formed to save the house, which was nearly destroyed by fire in 1975. It opened to the public in 1982.

GENERAL INFORMATION

Hours Sat 2–4:30 pm or by appointment
Admission Adults $2, children $1
Giftshop Colonial memorabilia such as soap, candles, replicas of 18th century money and historic flags
Library Extensive genealogical materials and titles on local and regional history; open Tues–Thurs 9:30 am–4:30 pm
Disability Access Limited wheelchair access
Directions Subway: L to Jefferson St, then walk five blocks north along Flushing Ave; Bus: Q54 to Flushing and Metropolitan Aves; B57 to Flushing and Onderdonk Aves
Parking On-site lot
Landmark Status National Register of Historic Places, New York City Landmark

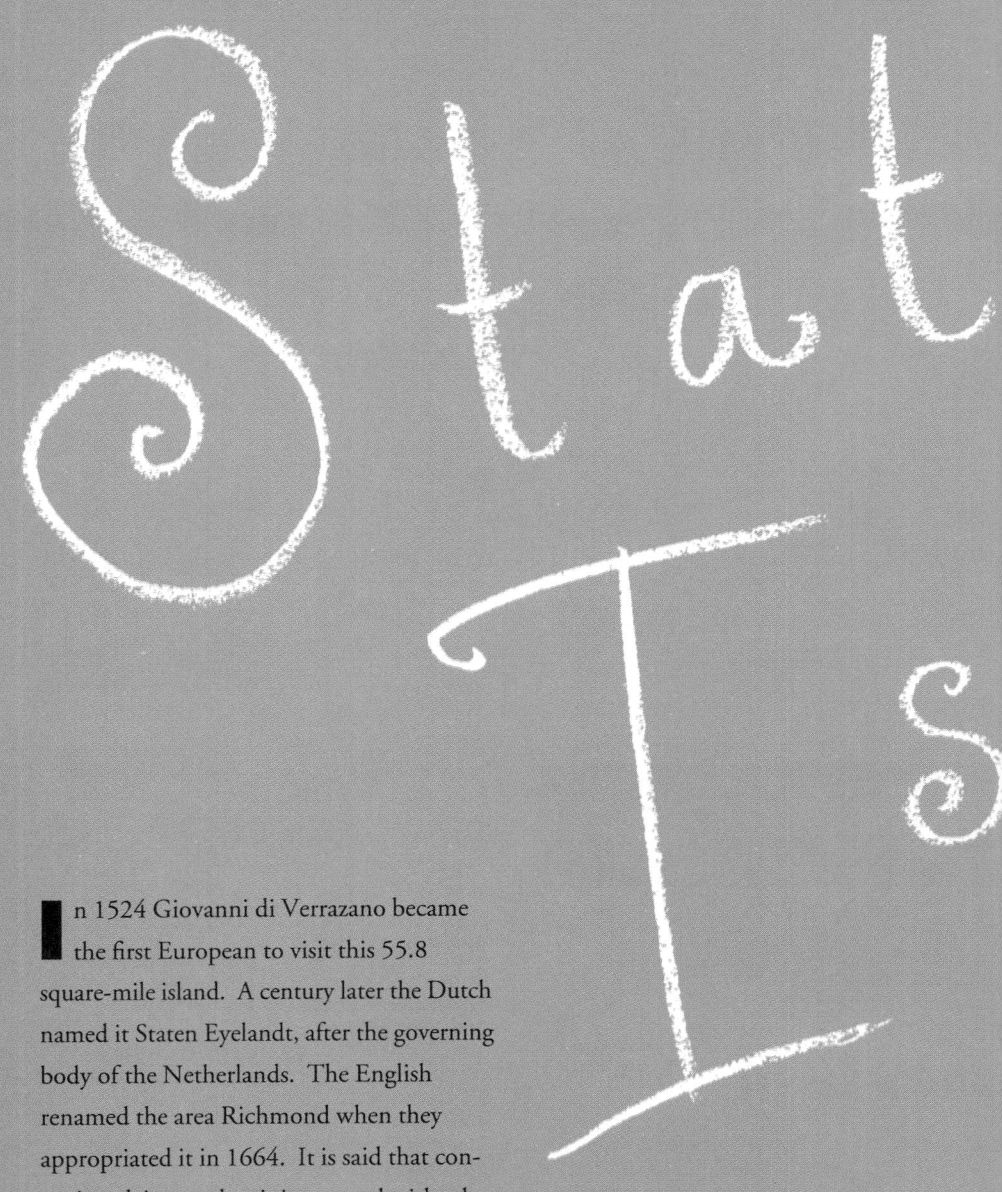

In 1524 Giovanni di Verrazano became the first European to visit this 55.8 square-mile island. A century later the Dutch named it Staten Eyelandt, after the governing body of the Netherlands. The English renamed the area Richmond when they appropriated it in 1664. It is said that contesting claims to dominion over the island between lords from New York and New Jersey were settled by a contest. The winner would be the claimant whose emissary could circumnavigate the island in less than 24 hours. Captain Christopher Billop, representing New York, succeeded in 1687.

While in fact much closer to New Jersey, Staten Island's 349,000 residents are connected to Brooklyn by the Verrazano-Narrows Bridge and to Manhattan by the famous five-mile ferry ride. The single largest physical feature of Staten Island is the Greenbelt, a 2,500-acre expanse of woodlands, wetlands

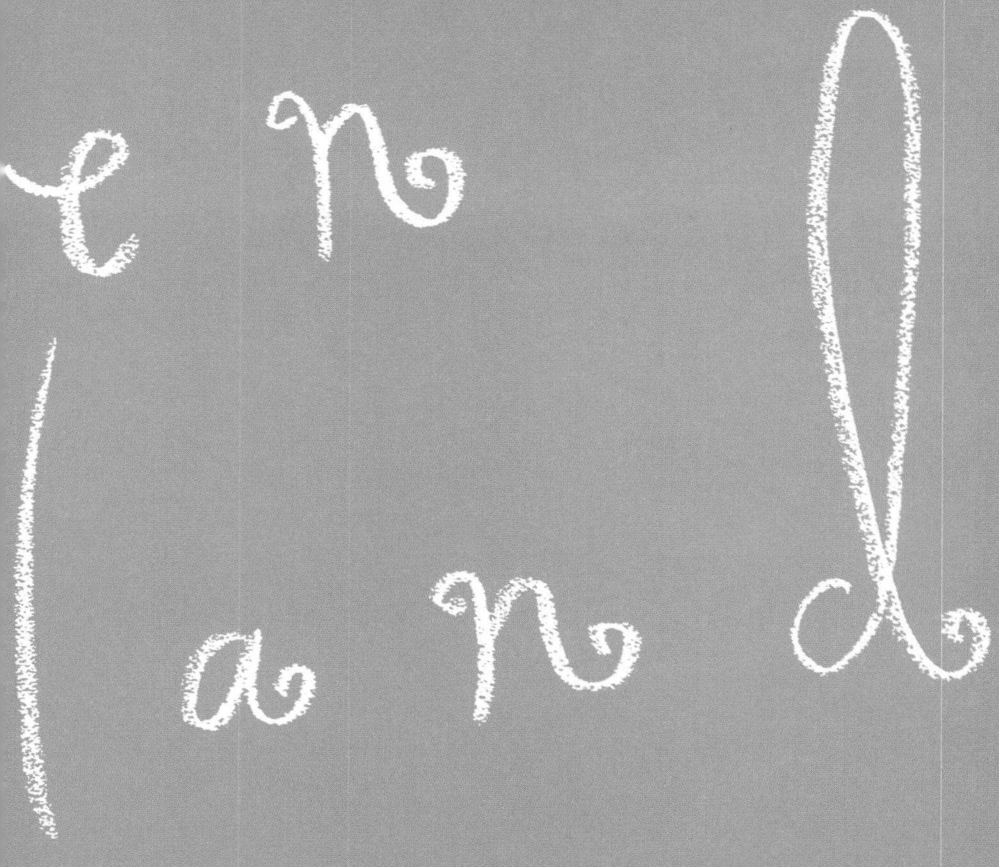

and open fields that stretches through the middle of the borough. Surrounded by developed areas, it is a habitat for native wildlife and a resting place for migratory birds. The Greenbelt encompasses a number of separate parks and wild spaces, including Willowbrook Park, Latourette Park, Deer Park and the Great Swamp at Farm Colony (see Parks Appendix, page 212, for further information).

The borough is the birthplace of Alice Austen, pioneer woman photographer, and Cornelius Vanderbilt, financier and railroad magnate, among others. Physical remnants like Conference House bespeak a rich Colonial past when events in Staten Island had implications for the whole of America. Twentieth-century creations, such as Snug Harbor Cultural Center and the Staten Island Institute of Arts and Sciences, ensure that this colorful history is understood today, just as they seek to enrich the lives of residents and visitors through a varied schedule of cultural activities.

Staten Island

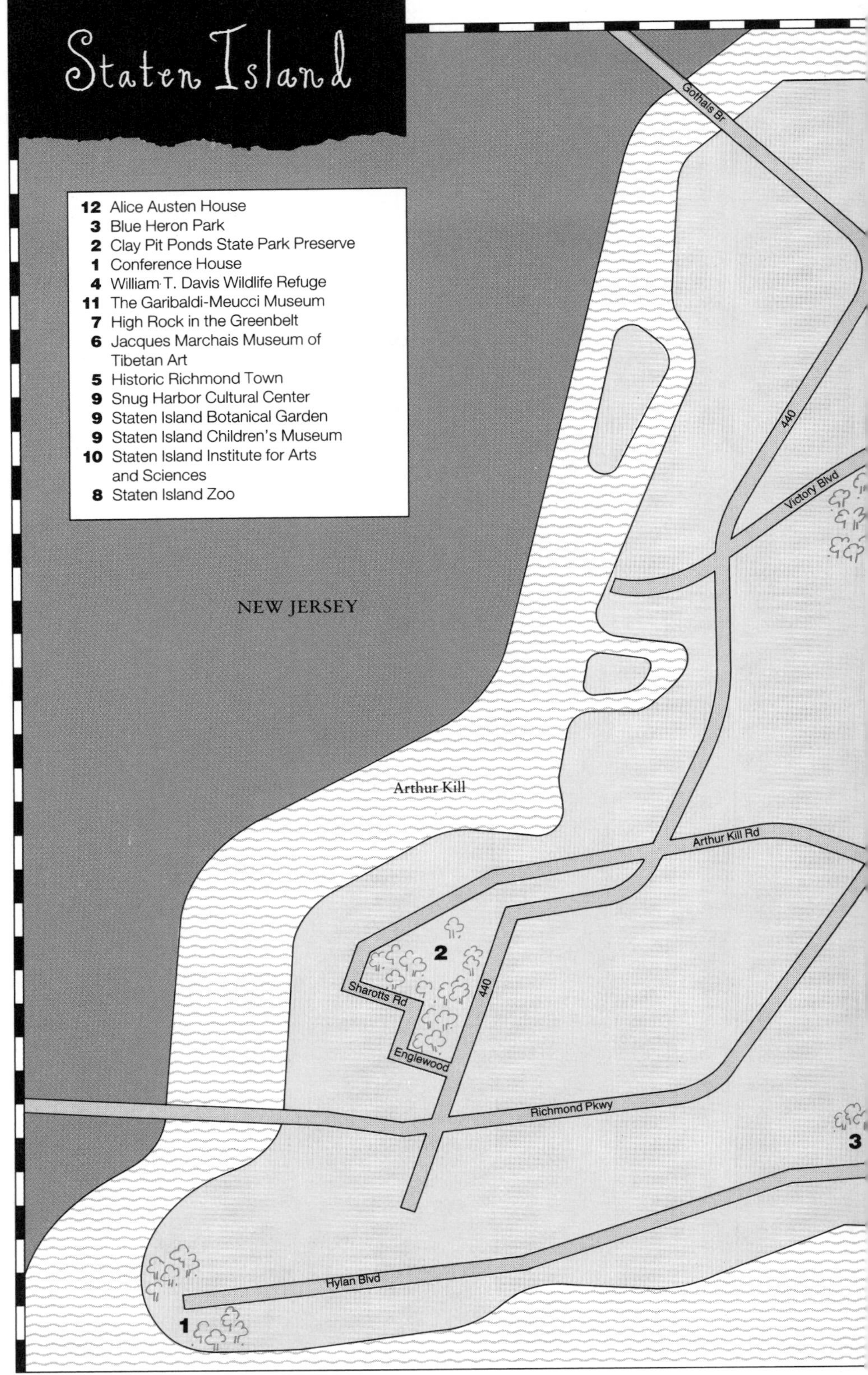
12 Alice Austen House
3 Blue Heron Park
2 Clay Pit Ponds State Park Preserve
1 Conference House
4 William T. Davis Wildlife Refuge
11 The Garibaldi-Meucci Museum
7 High Rock in the Greenbelt
6 Jacques Marchais Museum of Tibetan Art
5 Historic Richmond Town
9 Snug Harbor Cultural Center
9 Staten Island Botanical Garden
9 Staten Island Children's Museum
10 Staten Island Institute for Arts and Sciences
8 Staten Island Zoo
NEW JERSEY
Gothals Br
440
Victory Blvd
Arthur Kill
Arthur Kill Rd
Sharotts Rd
Englewood
Richmond Pkwy
Hylan Blvd
1
2
3

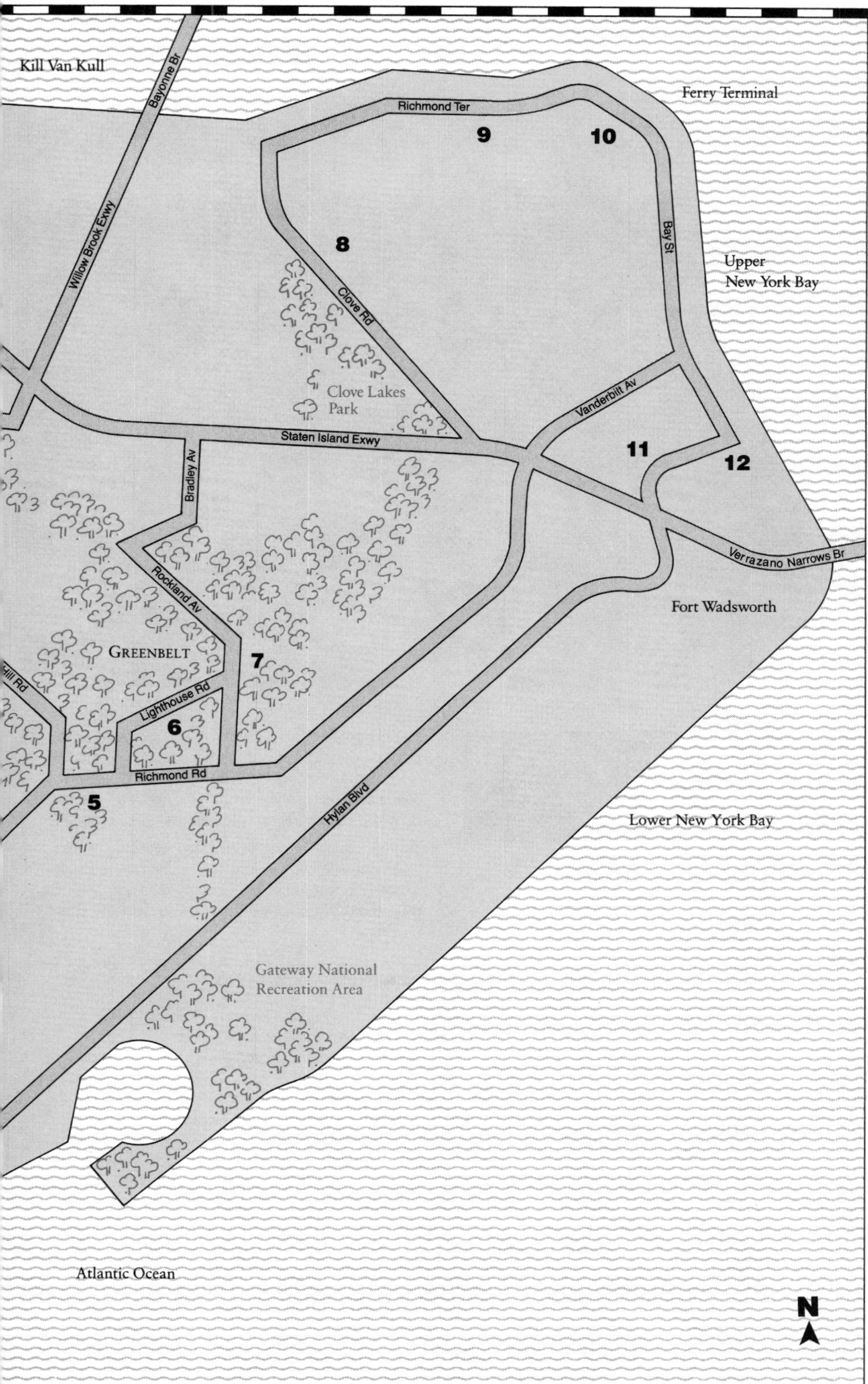
Kill Van Kull
Bayonne Br
Ferry Terminal
Richmond Ter
9
10
Willow Brook Exwy
8
Bay St
Upper
New York Bay
Clove Rd
Clove Lakes
Park
Vanderbilt Av
Staten Island Exwy
11
12
Bradley Av
Verrazano Narrows Br
Rockland Av
Fort Wadsworth
GREENBELT
7
Hill Rd
Lighthouse Rd
6
Richmond Rd
5
Hylan Blvd
Lower New York Bay
Gateway National
Recreation Area
Atlantic Ocean
N

Alice Austen, 1899

Alice Austen House

2 Hylan Boulevard
Staten Island, NY 10305

718-816-4506

This elegant vine-covered gingerbread cottage surrounded by a Victorian garden was home for almost 80 years to Alice Austen (1866–1952), the pioneer woman photographer. The house is nestled within ample lawns that slope down to meet the Verrazano Narrows, the entrance to New York Harbor. From this vantage point you can see Manhattan, the Statue of Liberty and the Verrazano-Narrows Bridge.

Containing many architectural and landscaping delights, the Alice Austen House today serves as a repository for the photographer's work. In addition to its permanent exhibition of Austen's photographs, there are regular shows related to her work and the work of associated 19th- and 20th-century artists. Original Austen family furnishings, heirlooms and decorative arts of the period offer a glimpse into the social milieu Austen documented throughout her life. The PBS documentary "Alice's World" is shown regularly, and lectures, antique fairs and community picnics are held at the house.

The original structure, one of the city's oldest, was a small one-and-a-half-story farmhouse built in the 1690s. Austen's grandfather bought it in 1844, expanded it, gave it a Gothic Revival facade and named it Clear Comfort.

GENERAL INFORMATION

Hours Thurs–Sun 12–5 pm; closed Mon-Wed
Admission Suggested donation $2
Giftshop Books, postcards, Victorian-style decorative objects, etc.
Food Service Seasonal concession stand
Disability Access Limited wheelchair access
Directions Subway: From Manhattan: N or R to Whitehall St–South Ferry; 1/9 to South Ferry; 4 or 5 to Bowling Green; then take Staten Island Ferry to bus; Bus: S51 from ferry terminal to Hylan Blvd
Parking On public streets
Landmark Status National Register of Historic Places, New York City Landmark

City-owned, privately operated

Blue Heron Park

48 Poillon Avenue (between Amboy Road and Hylan Boulevard)
Staten Island, NY 10312
718-967-3542

This 155-acre park on the southern tip of Staten Island is one of New York City's newest public spaces. Within Blue Heron Park, visitors will discover streams, woodlands, ponds and meadows. In spring, blue herons and egrets feed in the shallows while muskrats and spring peepers break the surface of Spring Pond; spring is also a good time to observe wildfowl pause along their migratory routes. In summer, the meadows are alive with purple gerardia, goldenrod, Turk's cap lilies and other flora. Fall triggers a vibrant display of foliage and the intense renewal of migratory activity. And then there is winter at Blue Heron Park with its stark, raw beauty.

Activities led by volunteer naturalists are held throughout the year. Wildflower, fungus and geology walks, pond studies and photography sessions are just a few of the family activities offered.

GENERAL INFORMATION

Hours Dawn to dusk daily
Admission Free
Disability Access None
Directions Subway: From Manhattan: N or R to Whitehall St–South Ferry; 1/9 to South Ferry; 4 or 5 to Bowling Green; then take Staten Island Ferry to bus; Bus: S78 from ferry terminal to Poillon Ave; or Staten Island Rapid Transit (SIRT) to town of Annadale, walk to Poillon Ave
Parking On public streets

City-owned, privately operated

Clay Pit Ponds State Park Preserve

83 Nielsen Avenue
Staten Island, NY 10309
718-967-1976

Two hundred and fifty acres of wetlands, fields, sandy barrens, spring-fed streams and woodlands can be found on the quiet southwestern shore of Staten Island. Clay Pit Ponds, named after a clay-mining operation once on the site, was designated New York City's first State Park Preserve in 1980. The area is rich in plant and animal life, including white oak and sorghum, raccoons, screech owls and box turtles. Guided nature walks, pond ecology, bird-watching, tree and wildflower identification and children's programs are offered throughout the year. Also provided are nature-related arts and crafts, gardening, beekeeping, evening campfires and seasonal festivals. There are trails for hiking, and horseback riding is permitted for those keeping a mount in nearby commercial stables.

GENERAL INFORMATION

Hours Dawn to dusk daily
Admission Free
Disability Access Limited access; restrooms, observation deck available. Call for reservations/information
Directions Subway: From Manhattan: N or R to Whitehall St–South Ferry; 1/9 to South Ferry; 4 or 5 to Bowling Green; then take Staten Island Ferry to bus; Bus: S113 from ferry terminal to Sharrotts Rd
Parking On-site lot

The Conference House

7455 Hylan Boulevard
Staten Island, NY 10307
718-984-2086

Constructed in 1680, the Conference House was originally a customs station where British tax collectors could spot incoming ships, appraise their cargo and levy taxes. Sited at the southernmost shore of Staten Island, the building commands a view of the Arthur Kill and the Raritan River.

Domestic American artifacts spanning 300 years make up the collection at the Conference House. Visitors may roam through the house, which includes a formal dining room, master and children's bedrooms and study. Each room is maintained in period style. Individual and group tours are available.

The Greenbelt

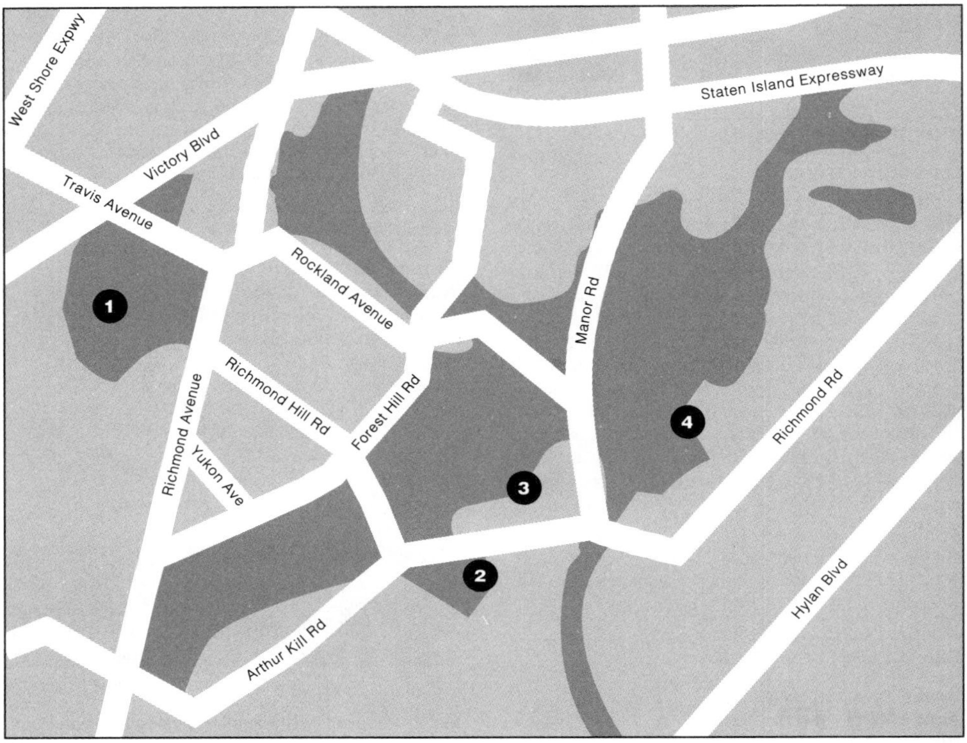

The Conference House derives its name from a famous meeting in 1776 when British forces and rebellious American leaders convened to negotiate an end to the Revolutionary War. Among those attending were Benjamin Franklin and John Adams. The Conference House Association was founded in 1925 to manage the renovation and upkeep of the historic house.

GENERAL INFORMATION

Hours March–Dec: Wed–Sun 1–4 pm; closed Mon, Tues
Admission Adults $2, seniors and children under 12, $1
Giftshop Historical souvenirs and toys
Disability Access None
Directions Subway: From Manhattan: N or R to Whitehall St–South Ferry; 1/9 to South Ferry; 4 or 5 to Bowling Green; then take Staten Island Ferry to bus; Bus: S78 from ferry terminal to Hylan Boulevard
Parking On public streets
Landmark Status National Register of Historic Places, New York City Landmark
City-owned, privately operated

1 William T. Davis Wildlife Refuge
2 Jacques Marchais Museum of Tibetan Art
3 Historic Richmond Town
4 High Rock Park in the Greenbelt

William T. Davis Wildlife Refuge

Travis and Richmond Avenues
Staten Island, NY 10304

718-667-2165
The Greenbelt

The William T. Davis Wildlife Refuge bears the name of one of Staten Island's most prominent naturalists. The wide variety of habitats found within this 260-acre refuge make the park an ideal wildlife preserve. The refuge consists of a patchwork of tidal marshland, freshwater wetlands, woodlands and open areas vital to migrating and native species. There is a meandering trail visitors can take to view mammals, reptiles, amphibians and birds in their natural surroundings. Established in 1933 by the Staten Island Institute of Arts and Sciences (see separate entry), the refuge was the first wildlife sanctuary in New York City.

GENERAL INFORMATION

Hours Dawn to dusk daily
Admission Free
Disability Access Limited access
Directions Subway: From Manhattan: N or R to Whitehall St–South Ferry; 1/9 to South Ferry; 4 or 5 to Bowling Green; then take Staten Island Ferry to bus; Bus: S92 or S62 from ferry terminal to Travis Ave
Parking On-site lot

City-owned, privately operated

Symbol Key

 *Institutional Giftshop*

 *On-Site Food Services*

 *On-Site Library or Archive*

 *Full Accessibility*

 *On-Site Parking*

 *National Register of Historic Places and/or New York City Landmark*

The Garibaldi-Meucci Museum

420 Tompkins Avenue
(at Chestnut Street)
Rosebank
Staten Island, NY 10305

718-442-1608

During the 1850s two remarkable Italians, Giuseppe Garibaldi and Antonio Meucci, shared a humble white clapboard farmhouse on Staten Island. This building now houses the Garibaldi-Meucci Museum, a tribute to their lives and historical contributions. Meucci is best known as the inventor of the telephone prototype, which he developed when Alexander Graham Bell was two years old. Garibaldi lived in the house for about four years before returning to Italy to lead his volunteer legions to the victories that established the modern Italian nation.

The museum houses photographs, letters, memorabilia and medals of Garibaldi, as well as Meucci's death mask and a schematic of his *teletrofono*. There is an extensive collection of military artifacts, including period rifles and uniforms, and a giant cauldron used for melting wax. This was used by the two men to manufacture candles, the trade that sustained them through their years of poverty in America.

GENERAL INFORMATION

Hours Tues–Fri 10 am–5 pm; Sat, Sun 1–5 pm; closed Mon
Admission Free
Library Library of the Risorgimento contains volumes on Italian cultural and military history, open by appointment only
Disability Access Fully accessible
Directions Subway: From Manhattan: N or R to Whitehall St–South Ferry; 1/9 to South Ferry; 4 or 5 to Bowling Green; then take Staten Island Ferry to bus; Bus: S52, S78, S79 from ferry terminal
Parking On public streets
Landmark Status National Register of Historic Places, New York City Landmark

High Rock Park in the Greenbelt

200 Nevada Avenue
Staten Island, NY 10306
718-667-2165

High Rock Park in the Greenbelt consists of 90 acres of hardwood forest, swamp and glacial ponds, and three unique gardens, each housing special plant species. It is the habitat for much native plant and animal life, and visitors come from throughout the region to walk its wilderness trails. Established in 1965 to protect native forest from residential development, High Rock Park has grown into one of the most important environmental education centers in America.

Each year, the center teaches thousands of local schoolchildren about environmentally sound practices; there are also sophisticated ecology field trips for college students and workshops for teachers. High Rock Park has been designated a National Environmental Education Landmark by the U.S. Department of the Interior. Its Discovery Room, located in the Visitors Center, offers a variety of challenging exhibits, and a teacher resource area for environmental education is available for interested educators and students.

GENERAL INFORMATION

Hours Visitors Center: 9 am–5 pm daily
Admission Free
Giftshop Nature-related gift items in Visitors Center
Food Service Picnic facilities in nearby Willowbrook Park
Library Environmental resource library at Visitors Center, open by appointment only
Disability Access Limited access
Directions Subway: From Manhattan: N or R to Whitehall St–South Ferry; 1/9 to South Ferry; 4 or 5 to Bowling Green; then take Staten Island Ferry;
Bus: S74 from ferry terminal to Rockland Ave and Richmond Rd, walk on Rockland to Nevada Ave, then up Nevada Ave to entrance
Parking On-site lot
City-owned, privately operated

Historic Richmond Town

441 Clarke Avenue
Staten Island, NY 10306
718-351-1611

Located on 100 acres in the center of Staten Island, Historic Richmond Town is New York City's only restored village. It features 27 original structures dating from the late 17th to early 20th centuries. The buildings range in style from Gothic and Greek Revival to simpler structures with Dutch and Flemish influences.

Period exhibits of Dutch furnishings, antique toys, horse-drawn coaches, costumes and memorabilia give the visitor a glimpse of Staten Island's colonial beginnings. Costumed people reenact the daily tasks of early Staten Island householders, farmers, merchants and tradesmen. There are demonstrations of harness-making, traditional country carpentry, food preparation, tinsmithing and wool processing.

In 1856 the Staten Island Historical Society began collecting many of the items now on display at Richmond Town. In 1922 it merged with the Staten Island Antiquarian Society and purchased the Billiou-Stillwell-Perine House, the second-oldest building in New York City. In 1934 the old County Clerk's and Surrogate's Office—in use from 1848 to 1920—was opened as a museum to display the permanent collection. During the 1950s and 1980's several buildings were restored by the society and the City of New York.

GENERAL INFORMATION

Hours Jan–March: Wed–Fri 1–5 pm; closed Sat–Tues
April–June: Wed–Sun 1–5 pm; closed Mon, Tues
July–Aug: Wed–Fri 10 am–5 pm; Sat, Sun 1–5 pm; closed Mon, Tues
Sept–Dec: Wed–Sun 1–5 pm; closed Mon, Tues
Admission Adults $4; seniors, students, children 6-18, $2.50; children under 6 free
Giftshop Books, postcards, toys, historic souvenirs and reproductions by local artisans
Food Service Refreshments in Bennet House; picnic grounds outside
Library Extensive Staten Island archives, open by appointment only
Disability Access Limited access; call ahead for assistance
Directions Subway: From Manhattan: N or R to Whitehall St–South Ferry; 1/9 to South Ferry; 4 or 5 to Bowling Green; then take Staten Island Ferry to bus;
Bus: S74 from ferry terminal
Parking On-site lot
Landmark Status National Register of Historic Places, New York City Landmark
City-owned, privately operated

Jacques Marchais Museum of Tibetan Art

338 Lighthouse Avenue 718-987-3500
Staten Island, NY 10306

This museum was founded in 1945 by Jacques Marchais, the professional name of Mrs. Jacqueline Klauber, to promote study and research in the art and literature of Tibet. Marchais spent more than 20 years amassing this unique collection of Tibetan art, which started with gifts from her seagoing great-grandfather. The collection includes 17th- to 19th-century bronzes, ritual objects, paintings and painted silk *thangkas* from Tibet, as well as notable examples of the art of China, Japan, Nepal and Mongolia.

The museum and library, designed by Marchais, were modeled after a Tibetan monastery or *gumpa*. The main exhibition area is an exact replica of the interior of a Tibetan temple (a Tibetan Cloisters of sorts). Terraced gardens, a lily pond and a fine view over the bay to Sandy Hook provide a meditative retreat for the visitor.

Buddha, Kamakura Japan, in the sculpture garden, Jacques Marchais Museum of Tibetan Art.

In addition to the permanent display, exhibits relating to Tibetan art and culture change every two to four months. The museum is located in a residential neighborhood near Staten Island's Greenbelt.

GENERAL INFORMATION

Hours April to Nov: Wed–Sun 1–5 pm; closed Mon, Tues, Dec–March: by appointment only
Admission Adults $3, seniors $2.50, children $1
Giftshop Various items from Asia
Disability Access Special resources available for blind and visually impaired visitors; no wheelchair access
Directions Subway: From Manhattan: N or R to Whitehall St–South Ferry; 1/9 to South Ferry; 4 or 5 to Bowling Green; then take Staten Island Ferry to bus; Bus: S74 from ferry terminal to Lighthouse Ave
Parking On public streets

Snug Harbor Cultural Center

1000 Richmond Terrace 718-448-2500
Staten Island, NY 10301

  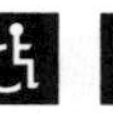  

Snug Harbor is Staten Island's principal cultural center. At an historic 83-acre site, Snug Harbor staff is restoring and adapting buildings for a variety of visual and performing arts programs. The main buildings of Snug Harbor comprise one of the nation's greatest groupings of Greek Revival architecture, surrounded by other structures built in the Italianate, Beaux-Arts and Second Empire styles.

The Newhouse Center for Contemporary Art exhibits the work of emerging and mid-career artists throughout the year; the work displayed is in all media, including painting, sculpture, photography, installations and crafts. Concerts and performances are held in Veterans Memorial Hall and outdoors in the South Meadow and gazebo areas. In summer, free family outdoor performances feature popular and ethnic music, dance, juggling, clowning and puppetry events.

Several cultural institutions make their home at Snug Harbor. These include the Staten Island Botanical Garden and the Staten Island Children's Museum (see separate entries), plus the Art Lab School, the Staten Island Civic Theatre and the Staten Island Children's Theatre. Snug Harbor offers an impressive range of educational programs for pre-kindergarten to high school students as well as adults.

Snug Harbor Cultural Center

Sailors' Snug Harbor was founded as a retirement home for seamen. In 1833 thirty-seven former sailors arrived at the facility on Staten Island's north shore and it grew over the years into a self-sufficient farming community for thousands of seamen. By the 1960s, however, with the number of retiring seamen declining, the large facility was no longer practical. Snug Harbor residents were moved to North Carolina. In 1973 the City of New York purchased the property and began plans for its conversion into a cultural center. This undertaking represents the largest architectural preservation project of its kind in the country.

GENERAL INFORMATION

Hours Newhouse Center for Contemporary Art: Wed-Sun 12–5 pm
Admission Grounds: free; Newhouse Center: suggested contribution $2
Giftshop Jewelry, cards, posters, books and souvenirs
Food Service Melville's Cafe offers entrees, sandwiches and snacks
Disability Access Fully accessible; restrooms and parking available
Directions Subway: From Manhattan: N or R to Whitehall St–South Ferry; 1/9 to South Ferry; 4 or 5 to Bowling Green; then take Staten Island Ferry to bus; Bus: S40 from ferry terminal to Snug Harbor
Parking On-site lot
Landmark Status National Register of Historic Places, New York City Landmark

City-owned, privately operated

Staten Island Botanical Garden

1000 Richmond Terrace
at Snug Harbor Cultural Center
Staten Island, NY 10301

718-273-8200

Within the Snug Harbor Cultural Center (see previous entry) lies a small sanctuary of cultivated land, the Staten Island Botanical Garden. It is the borough's only public garden. Since opening in 1977, the garden's English perennial border has become one of the largest in the New York area. Inside the greenhouse, exotic blossoms change with the seasons. Rolling lawns are dotted with specimen trees and bordered by woodlands. The Staten Island Botanical Garden has a new sensory garden for the handicapped and an old-style rose garden. In the Reception Hall are exhibitions on horticulture, such as "Mechanical Gardens," a view of America's forgotten mechanical relics in natural surroundings, and shows concentrating on the work of artists interested in the natural environment.

GENERAL INFORMATION

Hours 8 am–6 pm daily
Admission Free
Giftshop Handmade horticulture-related jewelry and decorative items in Garden Cottage shop
Food Service Cafeteria with vending machines: open Wed-Fri 12–2:30 pm; Sat, Sun 11 am–5 pm
Disability Access Fully accessible; special garden for visually impaired
Directions Subway: From Manhattan: N or R to Whitehall St–South Ferry; 1/9 to South Ferry; 4 or 5 to Bowling Green; then take Staten Island Ferry to bus; Bus: S40 from ferry terminal to Snug Harbor
Parking On-site lot
Landmark Status National Register of Historic Places, New York City Landmark

City-owned, privately operated

Staten Island Children's Museum

1000 Richmond Terrace, Building M
at Snug Harbor Cultural Center
Staten Island, NY 10301
718-448-6555

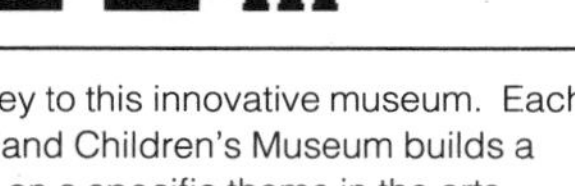

Interaction is the key to this innovative museum. Each year, the Staten Island Children's Museum builds a new exhibit based on a specific theme in the arts, humanities or sciences, creating environments that engage multiple senses.

Bugs and Other Insects, for instance, lets children visit the miniature, teeming world of insects and includes a crawl-in, child-size ant home. It's News to Me teaches youngsters about journalism and helps them develop critical thinking skills about news gathering, editing and transmitting. Wonder Water is an exploration of the life-sustaining properties of water and how to maintain it in our environment. The museum has also sponsored

Snug Harbor Cultural Center

1. Newhouse Center for Contemporary Art
2. Future exhibition space of the Staten Island Institute of Arts and Sciences
3. Staten Island Children's Museum
4. Staten Island Botanical Garden

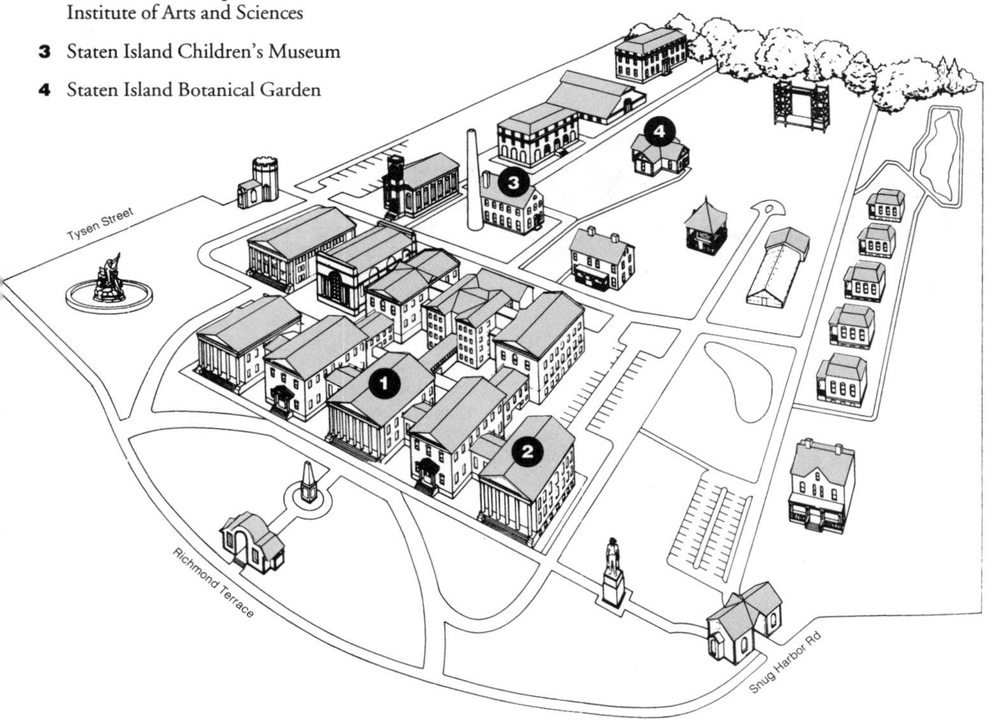

Tysen Street
Richmond Terrace
Snug Harbor Rd

Once Upon an Island, a show of four decades of Staten Island history, and Soundtracks, with unusual features like a topographic "sound map" and "seasonal sound windows."

In 1974 a group of Staten Island parents began organizing the museum, eventually housing it in a storefront. In 1986 the museum opened a new facility in a three-story Italianate structure at the Snug Harbor Cultural Center (see separate entry). It features a main atrium crossed by bridges and stairways, and other devices intended to make moving through the building an interesting experience. The newly converted building has 20,000 square feet of gallery space, a multi-purpose theater and an arts and crafts workshop.

GENERAL INFORMATION

Hours July–Aug: Tues–Sun 10 am–5 pm; closed Mon Sept–June: Tues–Sun 12–5 pm; closed Mon
Admission $3, children under 2 free
Giftshop Books, toys, souvenirs; open Tues–Fri 11 am–3 pm; Sat, Sun 12–4:45 pm
Food Service Vending machines with snacks and beverages
Disability Access Fully accessible; parking and restrooms available
Directions Subway: From Manhattan: N or R to Whitehall St–South Ferry; 1/9 to South Ferry; 4 or 5 to Bowling Green; then take Staten Island Ferry to bus; Bus: S40 from ferry terminal to Snug Harbor
Parking On-site lot
Landmark Status National Register of Historic Places, New York City Landmark
City-owned, privately operated

Staten Island Institute of Arts and Sciences

75 Stuyvesant Place (at 50th Street) Staten Island, NY 10301 — 718-727-1135

The Staten Island Institute of Arts and Sciences, founded in 1881, is one of the oldest cultural organizations in New York City. Dedicated to the heritage of Staten Island, the institute's exhibitions and programs focus on the relationship between art, science and history.

The institute's three-story red brick building is located just a few blocks from the Staten Island ferry terminal. Twelve exhibitions a year are mounted in three galleries. Exhibits have included "Kills, Creeks and Coves: Maritime Influences on Staten Island," "Lizard Tales: Reptiles and Amphibians of Staten Island" and "Good Vibrations: An Introduction to String Instruments."

V. Amessé

Cicadas, Insect Collection, Staten Island Institute of Arts and Sciences

The institute has an extraordinary insect collection with half a million specimens, with particular strength in cicadas and beetles. The herbarium contains 25,000 mounted plant specimens, with the flora of the northeastern United States especially well represented. There are also 8,000 geological specimens, 2,000 bird eggs and several thousand exotic seashells in the science collection.

Beginning in 1905, the institute began to collect and exhibit art as well as science and history. The art holdings are an eclectic mix that includes examples of Italian Renaissance art; African, Asian and Native American works; European and Asian clothing from the 16th to the 20th centuries; and important pieces of 18th- and 19th-century American, European and Asian furniture. The decorative arts collection is strong in American and European china, glass and silver from the 18th to the 20th centuries. These holdings and numerous traveling exhibitions created by other museums are regularly displayed.

GENERAL INFORMATION

Hours Mon–Sat 9 am–5 pm; Sun 1–5 pm
Admission Suggested contribution: adults $2.50, students and seniors $1.50
Giftshop Gifts, books relating to Staten Island and the institute's collections
Library 65,000 books and periodicals in natural history, art and history; also the 5,500-title Environmental Education Library
Disability Access Limited access, call for details
Directions Subway: From Manhattan: N or R to Whitehall St–South Ferry; 1/9 to South Ferry; 4 or 5 to Bowling Green; then take Staten Island Ferry
Parking On-site lot
City-owned, privately operated

Staten Island Zoo

614 Broadway — 718-442-3100
Staten Island, NY 10310

This small urban zoo, on eight acres of manicured lawns known as Barrett Park, contains a menagerie of 422 animals representing 196 species—from monkeys and bears to wolves, badgers, otters and prairie dogs. The zoo is especially well known for its collection of reptiles and the largest captive community of vampire bats in the country. The Staten Island Zoo has an aquarium containing 46 species, and a children's zoo where youngsters can feed tame animals and participate in other educational activities.

The land on which the zoo is situated was willed to the City of New York by Mrs. Edward E. Hardin and reconstructed into a zoological park in the 1930s through the Work Projects Administration. Opening in 1936, it was the first educational zoo in the nation. It has maintained this focus over the years by offering outreach programs to students, seniors and others. A pony barn and a hospital for zoo residents are new additions to the complex.

GENERAL INFORMATION

Hours 10 am–4:45 pm daily
Admission Adults $3, children 3–11, $2; children under 3 free
Giftshop Zoovenir Shop has both food and gifts
Food Service Fast-food counter, tables throughout zoo
Library Zoological reference materials, open by appointment only
Disability Access Fully accessible; restrooms available
Directions Subway: From Manhattan: N or R to Whitehall St–South Ferry; 1/9 to South Ferry; 4 or 5 to Bowling Green; then take Staten Island Ferry to bus; Bus: S48 from ferry terminal to Forest Ave and Broadway; S53 from Brooklyn to Broadway entrance of zoo
Parking On-site lot
City-owned, privately operated

V. Amessé

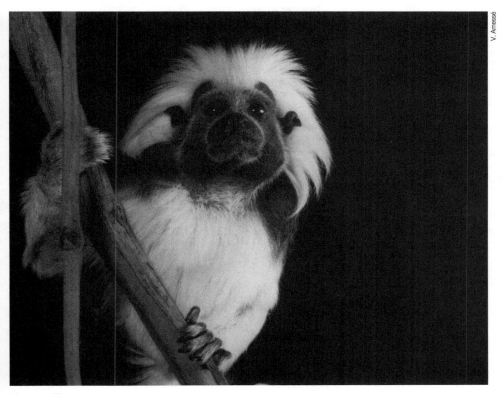

Cottontop Tamarin

Other Cultural Attractions

GENERAL INFORMATION

What follows are listings of selected theaters (on Broadway and off), music and dance venues, cinemas and galleries that—because of their commercial nature or infrequent public offerings—were not included in the body of this guidebook. They represent, however, an important aspect of the New York cultural scene and are included here for the reader's information.

Ads and schedules in The Daily News, New York Newsday, The New York Post, The New York Times, The Amsterdam News, El Diario, New York magazine, The New Yorker, The Village Voice and Museums New York are also the source of information about current attractions.

Half-price tickets for music and dance events can be purchased on the day of performance at:

Bryant Park Music and Dance Ticket Booth
42nd St and Sixth Avenue
Hours: Tues–Sun 12–2 pm, 3–7 pm. Call 212-382-2323 for listings of ticket availability.

THEATER

Call the Broadway Line: 212-563-2929 to purchase tickets or hear information about Broadway or Off Broadway shows. The League of American Theaters and Producers makes this service available free of charge.

Call the TDF Arts Information Phone Line (New York City On Stage): 212-768-1818 for information about current theater, dance and musical offerings throughout New York City. The Theatre Development Fund makes this telephone service available free of charge.

Half-price tickets can be purchased on the day of the performance at TDF's **tkts** booths at the following locations:

tkts—Times Square Theater Center
47th St and Broadway
Hours: Mon–Sat evening tickets 3–8 pm; Wed, Sat matinee tickets, 10 am–2 pm; Sun matinee and evening tickets, noon to closing.

tkts—Lower Manhattan Theater Center
Mezzanine, 2 World Trade Center
Hours: Mon–Fri tickets 11 am–5:30 pm. A limited number of matinee and Sunday tickets are sold one day prior to performance date. Saturday hours are 11 am–3:30 pm. Off Broadway tickets are sold 11 am–1 pm.

Broadway Theaters

Ambassador Theatre
219 West 49th St
212-239-6200

Brooks Atkinson Theatre
256 West 47th St
212-719-4099

Ethel Barrymore Theatre
243 West 47th St
212-239-6200

Vivian Beaumont Theatre
150 West 65th St
212-239-6200

Martin Beck Theatre
302 West 45th St
212-239-6200

Belasco Theatre
111 West 44th St
212-239-6200

Booth Theatre
222 West 45th St
212-239-6200

Broadhurst Theatre
235 West 44th St
212-239-6200

Broadway Theatre
53rd St and Broadway
212-239-6200

Circle in the Square
1633 Broadway at 50th St
212-239-6200

Cort Theatre
138 West 48th St
212-239-6200

Criterion Center
1530 Broadway
212-764-7903

Gershwin Theatre
222 West 51st St
212-586-6510

John Golden Theatre
252 West 45th St
212-239-6200

Helen Hayes Theatre
240 West 44th St
212-944-9450

Imperial Theatre
249 West 45th St
212-239-6200

Walter Kerr Theatre
219 West 48th St
212-239-6200

Longacre Theatre
220 West 48th St
212-239-6200

Lunt-Fontanne Theatre
205 West 46th St
212-575-9200

Lyceum Theatre
(National Actors Theatre)
149 West 45th St
212-239-6200

Majestic Theatre
247 West 44th St
212-239-6200

Marquis Theatre
1535 Broadway
212-382-0100

Minskoff Theatre
200 West 45th St
212-869-0550

Music Box Theatre
239 West 45th St
212-239-6200

Nederlander Theatre
208 West 41st St
212-921-8000

Eugene O'Neill Theatre
230 West 49th St
212-239-6200

Palace Theatre
1564 Broadway at 47th Street
212-730-8200

Plymouth Theatre
236 West 45th St
212-239-6200

Richard Rodgers Theatre
226 West 46th St
212-221-1211

Royale Theatre
242 West 45th St
212-239-6200

St. James Theatre
246 West 44th St
212-239-6200

Shubert Theatre
225 West 44th St
212-239-6200

Neil Simon Theatre
250 West 52nd St
212-757-8646

Virginia Theatre
245 West 52nd St
212-239-6200

Winter Garden Theatre
1634 Broadway at 51st St
212-239-6200

Off Broadway Theaters and Companies

Actors Playhouse
100 Seventh Ave South
212-691-6226

American Place Theatre
111 West 46th St
212-840-3074

Judith Anderson Theater
422 West 42nd St
212-886-1889

Astor Place Theatre
434 Lafayette St
212-254-4370

Cherry Lane Theatre
38 Commerce St
212-989-2020

Circle in the Square/Downtown
159 Bleecker St
212-254-6330

Circle Repertory Co.
99 Seventh Ave South
212-924-7100

Harold Clurman Theatre
412 West 42nd St
212-594-2370

Douglas Fairbanks Theatre
432 West 42nd St
212-239-4321

John Houseman Theatre
450 West 42nd St
212-967-9077

Lamb's Theatre Co.
130 West 44th St
212-997-1780

Lucille Lortel Theatre
121 Christopher St
212-924-8782

Manhattan Theatre Club
131 West 55th St
212-581-7907

Minetta Lane Theatre
18 Minetta Lane
212-420-8000

NY Theatre Workshop
Perry St Theater
31 Perry St
212-279-4200

Orpheum Theater
126 Second Ave at 8th St
212-477-2477

Playhouse 91
316 East 91st St
212-831-2000

Playwrights Horizons
416 West 42nd St
212-279-4200

Promenade Theatre
Broadway at 76th St
212-580-1313

Provincetown Playhouse
133 Macdougal St
212-477-5048

Puerto Rican Traveling Theatre
304 West 47th St
212-354-1293

Ridiculous Theatrical Co.
1 Sheridan Sq
212-691-2271

Roundabout Theatre Co.
1530 Broadway at 44th St
212-719-9393

Second Stage
Broadway at 76th St
212-873-6103

Sullivan Street Playhouse
181 Sullivan St
212-674-3838

Theatre East
211 East 60th St
212-838-9090

Village Gate/Top of the Gate
160 Bleecker St
212-475-5120

Off Off Broadway Theaters and Companies

Aboutface Theatre Co.
442 West 42nd St
212-268-9638

AMAS Repertory Theatre
1 East 104th St
212-534-6080

American Ensemble Co.
101 Murray St
212-571-7594

American Theatre of Actors
314 West 54th St
212-581-3044

A/NY Theatre Co.
48 East 80th St
212-969-0146

Argonaut Repertory Theater
555 East 90th St
212-369-8890

Blue Heron Theatre
555 East 90th St
212-787-0422

City Lights Youth Theatre
130 West 56th Street
212-262-0200

Colony Theater
152 West 71st St
212-595-0355

Courtyard Playhouse
39 Grove St
212-765-9540

CSC Repertory/Classic Stage Co.
136 East 13th St
212-677-4210

Cubiculo
414 West 51st St
212-265-2138

Elysium Theater Co.
204 East 6th St
212-713-5478

Ensemble Studio Theatre
549 West 52nd St
212-247-3405

Greeks and Co.
Pelican Studios
750 Eighth Ave
212-730-2030

Heights Players
26 Willow Place
Brooklyn
718-237-2752

Billie Holiday Theatre
1368 Fulton St
Brooklyn
718-636-0918

HOME for Contemporary Theatre & Art
145 Sixth Ave
212-647-0202

Independent Theatre Co.
99 Stanton St
212-353-3088

Interart Theatre
549 West 52nd St
212-246-1050

Jewish Repertory Theatre
1395 Lexington Ave
212-415-5550

Latin American Theatre Ensemble
172 East 104th St
212-410-4582

Little People's Theatre Co.
39 Grove St
212-765-9540

Manhattan Class Co.
120 West 28th St
212-727-7722

Minor Latham Playhouse
Barnard Campus
117th St and Broadway
212-854-2079

Music-Theatre Group
29 Bethune St
423 West 46th St
212-924-3108

Musical Theatre Works
440 Lafayette St
212-677-0040

New Dramatists
424 West 44th St
212-757-6960

New York Children's Theatre
250 West 65th St
212-496-8009

Ohio Theater
66 Wooster St
212-966-4844

Open Eye: New Stagings
Henry Lindenbaum Center
270 West 89th St
212-769-4143

Pan Asian Repertory Theatre
St. Clement's Church
423 West 46th St
212-245-2660

Paper Moon Players
459 Avenue P
Brooklyn
718-375-8515

Pearl Theatre Co.
125 West 22nd St
212-645-7708

Perry Street Theatre
31 Perry St
212-691-2509

Playwrights' Preview Productions
Mazur Theater in the Asphalt Green
555 East 90th St
212-996-7287

Primary Stages Co.
William Redfield Theatre
354 West 45th St
212-333-7471

Project III Ensemble
Ohio Theatre
66 Wooster St
212-966-4844

Pulse Ensemble Theatre
870 Sixth Ave
212-695-1596

Qwirk Productions
William Redfield Theatre
354 West 45th St
212-595-5673

Repertorio Español
Gramercy Arts Theatre
138 East 27th St
212-889-2850

Riverside Shakespeare Co.
Playhouse 91
316 East 91st St
212-831-2000

Paul Robeson Theatre
40 Greene Ave
Brooklyn
718-783-9794

St. Peter's Church
54th St and Lexington Ave
212-688-6022

Salt & Pepper Mime/New Ensemble Actors Theatre Co.
218 West 64th St
212-262-4989

Seventh Sign Theatre Co.
Good Shepherd Faith Church
152 West 66th St
212-749-4725

Sidewalks of New York
40 West 27th St
212-481-3077

SoHo Repertory Theatre
46 Walker St
212-941-8632

Staten Island Shakespearian Theatre
460 Brielle Ave
Staten Island
718-816-2606

TADA!
120 West 28th St
212-627-1732

Ten Ten Players
Park Avenue Christian Church
1010 Park Ave at 85th St
212-879-7669

Thalia Spanish Theatre
41-17 Greenpoint Ave
Sunnyside, Queens
718-729-3880

Theater 22
54 West 22nd St
212-243-2805

Theatre for the New City
155 First Ave
212-254-1109

Theatre Off Park
224 Waverly Place
212-627-2556

Theatre-Studio
750 Eighth Ave
212-719-0500

Theatreworks/USA
Promenade Theatre
76th St and Broadway
212-677-5959

Thirteenth Street Playhouse
50 West 13th St
212-675-6677

Tiny Mythic Theatre Co.
45 Sixth Ave
212-647-0252

TRG Repertory Company
311 West 43rd St
212-246-5877

Triangle Theatre Co.
Church of the Holy Trinity
316 East 88th St
212-860-7245

Villar-Hauser Theatre Co.
Greenwich Street Theatre
547 Greenwich St
212-627-8631

Vineyard Theatre
108 East 15th St and
109 East 26th St
212-353-3874

Vorten Theatre Co.
Sanford Meisner Theatre
164 Eleventh Ave
212-206-1764

Westbeth Theater
151 Bank St
212-741-0391

Westside Repertory Theatre
252 West 81st St
212-874-7290

Wings Theatre Co.
154 Christopher St
212-627-2961

Wooster Group
Performing Garage
33 Wooster St
212-966-3651

WOW Cafe
59-61 East 4th St
212-460-8067

WPA Theatre
519 West 23rd St
212-206-0523

Writers Theatre
145 West 46th St
212-869-9770

York Theatre Co.
Church of the Heavenly Rest
2 East 90th St
212-534-5366

DANCE

Mary Anthony Dance Studio & Theatre
736 Broadway
212-674-8191

Brooklyn Academy of Music
see page 31

City Center Theater
see page 77

Merce Cunningham Studio
55 Bethune St
212-691-9751

Dance Space
622 Broadway
212-777-8067

Dance Theater Workshop
see page 85

Dia Center for the Arts
see page 87

Florence Gould Hall at French Institute/Alliance Française
see page 96

Free Range Arts
250 West 26th St
212-691-4551

Gowanus Arts Exchange
see page 36

Intimate Space Dance Theatre
135 West 14th St
212-929-4019

Joyce Theater
see page 113

Long Island University School of the Arts
University Plaza
Brooklyn
718-488-1051

Metropolitan Opera House
Lincoln Center
see page 121

Movement Research
179 Varick St
212-691-5788

Mulberry Street Theatre
see page 128

New York State Theater
Lincoln Center
see page 122

Pace Downtown Theater
see page 150

Performing Garage
33 Wooster St
212-966-3651

Peridance Studio Theatre
132 Fourth Ave
212-505-0886

P.S. 122
see page 149

Riverside Church
120th St and Riverside Dr
212-864-2929

Spina Loft
115 Prince St
212-674-8885

Tisch School of the Arts
New York University
see page 146

University Theatre
35 West 4th St
212-998-5278

Winter Garden
see page 170

Woodpeckers Tap Dance Center & InterArts Space
170 Mercer St
212-219-8284

MUSIC

This appendix represents a judicious selection of some of New York City's most popular clubs and smaller concert halls. It has been designed simply, to help the reader find his or her way amid an overwhelming number of alternatives.

One further note: New York City offers a wealth of religious music (choral, gospel, etc.). Some religious centers advertise to the general public. Consult the listings mentioned under the theater appendix above, especially during the holiday season, for performance times and locations.

Abbracciament
2200 Rockaway Pkwy
Brooklyn (jazz)
718-251-5517

Algonquin
Oak Room
59 West 44th St (cabaret)
212-840-6800

Apollo Theater
253 West 125th St
(various, popular)
212-749-5838

Ballroom
253 West 28th St (cabaret)
212-244-3005

Beekman Bar and Books
889 First Ave at 50th St (jazz)
212-980-9314

Birdland
2745 Broadway at 105th St (jazz)
212-749-2228

Blue Angel
321 West 44th St (cabaret)
212-262-3333

Blue Note
131 West 3rd St (jazz)
212-475-8592

Bottom Line
15 West 4th St (various, popular)
212-228-6300

Cajun
129 Eighth Ave (jazz)
212-691-6174

CAMI Hall
165 West 57th St (classical)
212-397-6900

Carlyle Hotel
35 East 76th St (cabaret)
212-744-1600

Continental Club
17 Irving Place at 15th St
(various, popular)
212-533-0210

Copacabana
617 West 57th St
212-582-2672

Danny's Skylight Room
346 West 46th St (cabaret)
212-265-8133

Del's Down Under
266 West 47th St (cabaret)
212-719-4179

Don't Tell Mama
343 West 46th St (cabaret)
212-757-0788

Duplex
61 Christopher St (cabaret)
212-255-5438

Fat Tuesday's
190 Third Ave (jazz)
212-533-7900

Hudson Bar and Books
636 Hudson St (jazz)
212-229-2642

Kaptain Banana
101 Greene St (cabaret)
212-343-9000

Knickerbocker Bar and Grill
33 University Place (jazz)
212-228-8490

Knitting Factory
47 East Houston St (various, popular)
212-219-3055

La Cave on First
1125 First Ave at 62nd St (cabaret)
212-759-4011

Limelight
47 West 20th St (various, popular)
212-807-7850

Lone Star Roadhouse
240 West 52nd St (various, popular)
212-245-2950

Manny's Car Wash
1558 Third Ave at 87th St
(various, popular)
212-369-2583

Steve McGraw's
158 West 72nd St (cabaret)
212-595-7400

Michael's Pub
211 East 55th St (cabaret)
212-758-2272

Paramount
Madison Square Garden
(various, popular)
212-465-6741

The Rainbow Room
30 Rockefeller Plaza (cabaret)
212-632-5100

Rock 'n' Roll Cafe
149 Bleecker St (various, popular)
212-677-7630

Russian Tea Room
150 West 57th St (cabaret)
212-265-0947

St. Peter's Church
54th St and Lexington Ave (jazz)
212-935-2200

S.O.B.'s
204 Varick St (various, popular)
212-243-4940

Spotlight
107 MacDougal St (various, popular)
212-254-8683

Studio 54
254 West 54th St (various, popular),
212-541-8900

Supper Club
240 West 47th St (cabaret)
212-921-1940

Sweetwater's
170 Amsterdam Ave (jazz, Latin)
212-873-4100

Swing Street Café
253 East 52nd St (jazz), 212-754-4817

Tavern On The Green
Central Park West at 67th St (jazz)
212-873-3200

Time Cafe
380 Lafayette St (jazz)
212-533-7000

Tramps Cafe
45 West 21st St (various, popular)
212-727-7788

Village Gate
160 Bleecker St (jazz)
212-475-5120

Village Vanguard
178 Seventh Ave South (jazz)
212-255-4037

Visiones
125 MacDougal St (jazz)
212-673-5576

West End Gate
2911 Broadway (jazz)
212-666-8687

Wetlands
161 Hudson St (various, popular)
212-966-4225

Yardbird Suite
35 Cooper Sq (jazz)
212-228-5800

YWCA
610 Lexington Ave (jazz)
212-755-4500

FILM & VIDEO

Film Revival Houses, Film Libraries, Etc.

American Museum of the Moving Image
see page 174

The American Museum of Natural History
see page 56

Angelika 57
225 West 57th St
212-586-1900

Angelika Film Center
18 West Houston St
212-995-2000

Anthology Film Archives
see page 59

Cinema Village
22 East 12th St
212-924-3363

Film Forum
209 West Houston St
212-727-8110

Film Society of Lincoln Center
Walter Reade Theater
Lincoln Center
see page 122

French Institute/Alliance Française
see page 96

Goethe House—The German Cultural Center
see page 99

Japan Society
see page 111

Korean Cultural Center
see page 116

Museum of Modern Art
Roy and Niuta Titus Theaters
see page 132

Joseph Papp Public Theater
425 Lafayette St
212-598-7171
see page 142

Spanish Institute
see page 160

Symphony Space
see page 163

Thalia Cinema
250 West 95th St
212-316-4962

Theater 80 St. Marks
80 St. Marks Place
212-254-7400

Village East Cinemas
181-187 Second Ave at 12th St
212-529-6799

Whitney Museum of American Art
see page 169

GALLERIES

Every form of art, ancient and modern, is on exhibit somewhere in New York City. No other city on earth offers such a profusion of artistic expression. Most of the commercial galleries listed below welcome the public. They therefore represent, collectively, the city's largest free museum. You will find almost all of them concentrated in three areas of Manhattan: Tribeca/SoHo/ Greenwich Village, 57th Street/Fifth Avenue and the Upper East Side/ Madison Avenue.

Tribeca/SoHo/ Greenwich Village

Brooke Alexander
59 Wooster St
212-925-4338

Art in General
79 Walker St
212-219-0473

Pamela Auchincloss
558 Broadway
212-966-7753

Josh Baer
476 Broome St
212-431-4774

David Beitzel
102 Prince St
212-219-2863

Berman-Daferner
568 Broadway, #103
212-226-8330

Mary Boone
417 West Broadway
212-431-1818

J. Cacciola
125 Wooster St
212-966-9177

Leo Castelli
420 West Broadway
212-431-5160

Cavin-Morris
560 Broadway
212-226-3768

Condeso/Lawler
524 Broadway
212-219-1283

Paula Cooper
149-155 Wooster St
212-674-0766

Charles Cowles
420 West Broadway
212-925-3500

E.M. Donahue
560 Broadway
212-226-1111

F.D.R. Gallery
670 Broadway
212-777-3051

Fawbush
76 Grand St
212-274-0660

Gagosian
136 Wooster St
212-228-2828

Sandra Gering
476 Broome St
212-226-8195

John Gibson
568 Broadway
212-925-1192

Barbara Gladstone
99 Greene St
212-431-3334

Jay Gorney Modern Art
100 Greene St
212-966-4480

Granary Books Gallery
568 Broadway
212-226-5462

Stephen Haller
560 Broadway
212-219-2500

Elizabeth Harris
524 Broadway
212-941-9895

Penine Hart
457 Broome St
212-226-2761

Helander
594 Broadway
212-966-9797

Hirschl & Adler Modern
420 West Broadway
212-966-6211

Nancy Hoffman
429 West Broadway
212-966-6676

Images
580 Broadway
212-219-8484

Michael Ingbar Gallery of Architectural Art
568 Broadway
212-334-1100

Interart Center
167 Spring St
212-431-7500

June Kelly
591 Broadway
212-226-1660

Nicole Klagsbrun
51 Greene St
212-925-5157

Lennon, Weinberg
580 Broadway
212-941-0012

M-13/Howard Scott
72 Greene St
212-925-3007

Curt Marcus
578 Broadway
212-226-3200

Lawrence Markey
55 Vandam St
212-627-4446

Robert Morrison
59 Thompson St
212-274-9059

P.P.O.W.
532 Broadway
212-941-8642

Joan Prats
568 Broadway
212-219-0510

Max Protetch
560 Broadway
212-966-5454

Julie Saul
560 Broadway
212-431-0747

Tony Shafrazi Gallery
119 Wooster St
212-274-9300

Sonnabend
420 West Broadway
212-966-6160

Sperone Westwater
121 and 142 Greene St
212-431-3685

Stark
594 Broadway
212-925-4484

Stux
163 Mercer St
212-219-0010

Edward Thorp
103 Prince St
212-431-6880

Thread Waxing Space
476 Broadway
212-966-9520

Jack Tilton
47–49 Greene St
212-941-1775

Michael Walls
156 Wooster St
212-982-9800

John Weber
142 Greene St
212-966-6115

Jan Weiss
68 Laight St
212-925-7313

Willow
470 Broome St
212-941-5743

57th Street/Fifth Avenue

Rachel Adler
41 East 57th St
212-308-0511

Associated American Artists
20 West 57th St
212-399-5510

Babcock
724 Fifth Ave
212-767-1857

Paolo Baldacci
41 East 57th St
212-826-4210

Baron/Boisante
50 West 57th St
212-581-9191

Blum Helman
20 West 57th St
212-245-2888

Grace Borgenicht
724 Fifth Ave
212-247-2111

Garth Clark
24 West 57th St
212-246-2205

Tibor De Nagy
41 West 57th St
212-421-3780

Terry Dintenfass
50 West 57th St
212-581-2268

Andre Emmerich
41 East 57th St
212-752-0124

Fischbach
24 West 57th St
212-759-2345

Fitch-Febvrel
5 East 57th St
212-688-8522

Forum
745 Fifth Ave
212-355-4545

Galerie Lelong
20 West 57th St
212-315-0470

Sidney Janis
110 West 57th St
212-586-0110

Kennedy
40 West 57th St
212-541-9600

Jan Krugier
41 East 57th St
212-755-7288

Littlejohn/Sternau
41 East 57th St
212-980-2323

Long Fine Art
24 West 57th St
212-397-2001

Marlborough
40 West 57th St
212-541-4900

Barbara Mathes
41 East 57th St
212-752-5135

Midtown Payson
745 Fifth Ave
212-758-1900

Robert Miller
41 East 57th St
212-980-5454

O'Hara
41 East 57th St
212-355-3330

Pace Gallery
32 East 57th St
212-421-3292

Reggiani Light Gallery
800A Fifth Ave
212-421-0400

Michael Rosenfield
24 West 57th St
212-247-0082

Mary Ryan
24 West 57th St
212-397-0669

Schmidt Bingham
41 East 57th St
212-888-1122

Susan Sheehan
41 East 57th St
212-888-4220

Tatistcheff & Co.
50 West 57th St
212-664-0907

Zabriskie
724 Fifth Ave
212-307-7430

Upper East Side/ Madison Avenue

Acquavella
18 East 79th St
212-734-6300

CDS
76 East 79th St
212-772-9555

Cohen
1018 Madison Ave
212-628-0303

Eastlake
1078 Madison Ave
212-772-8810

Elysium Arts
28 East 78th St
212-628-3828

David Findlay
984 Madison Ave
212-249-2909

M. Knoedler & Co.
19 East 70th St
212-794-0550

Kouros
23 East 73rd St
212-288-5888

Matthew Marks
1018 Madison Ave
212-861-9455

Victoria Munroe Fine Art
9 East 84th St
212-249-5480

Perls Gallery
1016 Madison Ave
212-472-3200

Salander-O'Reilly
20 East 79th St
212-879-6606

Sindin
956 Madison Ave
212-288-7902

Spanierman Gallery
50 East 78th St
212-879-7085

L.J. Wender Fine Chinese Paintings
3 East 80th St
212-734-3460

Parks Appendix

CITY OPERATED

New York City possesses some of the most beautiful urban parks in the world. Taking up an impressive 13 percent of the city's land area—26,369 acres—New York's city-run parks include five zoos, six beaches, 13 golf courses, 45 indoor and outdoor swimming pools, 522 tennis courts, 700 playing fields and 872 playgrounds. To truly experience New York City, you must visit its parks!

Disability Access Information

For questions or accommodations for you or your group, call the Parks Hot Line 1-800-834-3832 or the Parks Telecommunications Device for the Deaf (TDD) 1-800-281-5722.

Major City Parks

For information about New York City's major parks or to find out how to make a donation:

Central Park
Manhattan
see page 70: 212-360-8236 or
212-794-6564 (recorded events line)

Flushing Meadows Corona Park
Queens
718-760-6561

Forest Park
Queens
718-235-0815

The Greenbelt
Staten Island
718-667-2165

Prospect Park
Brooklyn
see page 41: 718-965-8951 or
718-788-0055 (recorded events line)

Riverside Park
Manhattan
212-408-0264
79th Street Boat Basin
212-496-2105

Van Cortlandt Park/Pelham Bay
The Bronx
718-430-1890

Free Nature Walks

The Urban Park Rangers conduct nature walks and craft workshops for adults and children in city parks. Rangers also offer programs for schools and other groups.

Central Office
212-360-2774

The Bronx
718-430-1832

Brooklyn
718-287-3400

Manhattan
212-427-4040

Queens
718-699-4204

Staten Island
718-667-6042

Special Events

The Department of Parks and Recreation conducts special events throughout the year. For information on upcoming events, call 212-360-3456. To organize a special event call:

The Bronx
718-430-1848

Brooklyn
718-965-8913

Citywide
212-360-8126

Manhattan
212-408-0226

Queens
718-520-5941

Staten Island
718-390-8023

STATE OPERATED

Bayswater State Park
Queens
212-387-0271

Clay Pit Ponds State Park Preserve
Staten Island
see page 193: 718-967-1976

Roberto Clemente State Park
The Bronx
718-299-8750

Empire-Fulton Ferry State Park
Brooklyn
718-858-4708

Riverbank State Park
Manhattan
212-694-3600

FEDERALLY OPERATED

Gateway National Recreation Area
Brooklyn
718-338-3338

Castle Clinton National Monument
Manhattan
see page 68: 212-344-7220

Statue of Liberty National Monument and Ellis Island
see Ellis Island, page 90; Statue of Liberty, page 161: 212-363-3200

Federal Hall National Memorial
Manhattan
see page 92: 212-264-8711

General Grant National Memorial
Manhattan
see entry, page 98: 212-666-1640

Hamilton Grange National Memorial
Manhattan
212-283-5154

Alphabetical Index

by page number

86 Aaron Davis Hall
52 ACA Exhibition Space
52 Abigail Adams Smith House Museum
53 African Arts Cultural Center
123 Alice Tully Hall (Chamber Music Society of Lincoln Center)
176 Alley Pond Environmental Center
53 Alternative Museum
54 American Academy of Arts and Letters
54 American Craft Museum
55 American Indian Community House
55 American Institute of Graphic Arts
56 American Museum of Natural History
176 American Museum of the Moving Image
58 American Numismatic Society
58 Americas Society
59 Anthology Film Archives
177 Anthropology Museum of the People of New York
59 Aperture Foundation/Burden Gallery
29 New York Aquarium/Aquarium for Wildlife Conservation
60 Archives of American Art-Smithsonian Institution
61 Art Students League Gallery
82 Arthur Ross Architecture Gallery, see Columbia University
61 Artists Space
170 Arts and Events Program, see Wintergarden
28 Arts at St. Ann's
62 Asia Society
62 Asian American Arts Centre
194 Alice Austen House
63 Austrian Cultural Institute
120 Avery Fisher Hall (New York Philharmonic)
80 Avery Hall, see Columbia University
30 BACA/The Brooklyn Arts Council Downtown
64 Bard Graduate Center for Studies in the Decorative Arts
30 Bargemusic
14 Bartow-Pell Mansion Museum
65 Baruch College/Sidney Mishkin Gallery
119 Vivian Beaumont Theater (Lincoln Center Theater Company)
65 Black Fashion Museum
194 Blue Heron Park
178 Bowne House
20 New York Botanical Garden
146 Broadway Windows, see New York University
15 Bronx Museum of the Arts
15 Bronx River Art Center and Gallery
16 Bronx Zoo–Wildlife Conservation Park
31 Brooklyn Academy of Music
32 Brooklyn Botanic Garden
33 Brooklyn Center for the Performing Arts
34 Brooklyn Children's Museum
34 Brooklyn Historical Society
35 Brooklyn Museum
59 Burden Gallery, see Aperture Foundation
82 Butler Library Exhibition Space, see Columbia University
66 Caribbean Cultural Center
66 Carnegie Hall-Weill Recital Hall
145 Casa Italiana Zerilli-Marimo, see New York University
68 Castillo Cultural Center
68 Castle Clinton National Monument
68 Cathedral of St. John the Divine
36 Center for Art and Culture of Bedford-Stuyvesant
69 Center for Book Arts
146 Center for Music Performance, see NYU
70 Central Park
72 Central Park Zoo–Wildlife Conservation Center
123 Chamber Music Society of Lincoln Center, see Alice Tully Hall
74 Charas
74 Children's Museum of Manhattan
75 Children's Museum of the Native American
75 China Institute in America
76 Chinatown History Museum
179 Chung Cheng Art Gallery
77 Cinque Gallery
77 City Center
195 Clay Pit Ponds State Park Preserve
78 Clocktower Gallery
78 Cloisters (Metropolitan Museum of Art)
177 Colden Center for the Performing Arts
80 Columbia University
83 Con Edison Energy Museum
196 Conference House
83 Cooper Union Gallery
84 Cooper-Hewitt National Museum of Design
85 Dance Theater Workshop
86 Aaron Davis Hall
196 William T. Davis Wildlife Refuge
143 Delacorte Theater, see NewYork Shakespeare Festival
86 Dia Center for the Arts
87 Dixon Place
88 Downtown Art Co.
88 Drawing Center
89 Dyckman House Museum
82 East Asian Library, see Columbia University
21 Edgar Allan Poe Cottage
89 Educational Alliance
145 80 Washington Square East Galleries, see New York University
124 Elaine Kaufman Cultural Center, Merkin Concert Hall
90 Ellis Island Immigration Museum
129 El Museo del Barrio
110 Elsa Mott Ives Gallery
189 Vander Ende-Onderdonk House
91 Equitable Center and Gallery
91 Exit Art-The First World
92 Fashion Institute of Technology Galleries
92 Federal Hall National Memorial
122 Film Society of Lincoln Center, see Walter Reade Theater
120 Avery Fisher Hall (New York Philharmonic)
180 Flushing Town Hall-Flushing Council on Culture and the Arts
17 Focal Point Gallery
94 Forbes Magazine Galleries
94 14 Sculptors Gallery
95 Franklin Furnace Archive
95 Fraunces Tavern Museum
96 French Institute/Alliance Française
97 Frick Collection
146 Gallatin at La Mama Project, see New York University
98 Gallery 62
98 Gallery 1199
197 Garibaldi-Meucci Museum
98 General Grant National Memorial
99 Goethe House New York–German Cultural Center
100 Governor's Room at City Hall
36 Gowanus Arts Exchange
100 Gracie Mansion
101 Grand Central Art Galleries
102 Greenwich House Pottery
145 Grey Art Gallery and Study Center, see New York University

102 Grolier Club
102 Solomon R. Guggenheim Museum
104 Guggenheim Museum SoHo
104 Guinness World of Records Exhibition
17 Hall of Fame for Great Americans
37 Harbor Defense Museum at Fort Hamilton
56 Hayden Planetarium, see American Museum of Natural History
105 Henry Street Settlement
198 High Rock Park in the Greenbelt
106 Hispanic Society of America
196 Historic Richmond Town
82 Horace Mann Theatre, see Columbia University
106 Horticultural Society of New York
180 Langston Hughes Library and Cultural Center
114 Hunter College Auditorium, see Sylvia and Danny Kaye Playhouse
107 IBM Gallery of Science and Art
107 INTAR/Hispanic American Arts Center
108 International Center of Photography
109 Intrepid Sea-Air-Space Museum
110 Irish Arts Center
184 Isamu Noguchi Garden Museum
110 Elsa Mott Ives Gallery
199 Jacques Marchais Museum of Tibetan Art
181 Jamaica Arts Center
111 Japan Society
111 Jewish Museum
112 Joseph Gallery
142 Joseph Papp Public Theater, see NewYork Shakespeare Festival
113 Joyce Theater
18 Judaica Museum of the Hebrew Home for the Aged at Riverdale
114 Kampo Cultural and Multi-Media Center
82 Kathryn Bache Miller Theatre, see Columbia University
124 Elaine Kaufman Cultural Center, see Merkin Concert Hall
114 Sylvia and Danny Kaye Playhouse (Hunter College)
115 Kenkeleba House
181 King Manor Museum
182 Kingsland Homestead
115 Kitchen
116 Korean Cultural Service
116 Kosciuszko Foundation
38 Kurdish Library and Museum
145 La Maison Française, see New York University
117 La Mama E.T.C.
178 Langston Hughes Library and Cultural Center
82 Minor Latham Playhouse, see Columbia University
38 Lefferts Homestead
18 Lehman Center for the Performing Arts and Lehman College Art Gallery
118 Lincoln Center for the Performing Arts
119 Lincoln Center Theater Company, see Vivian Beaumont and Mitzi E. Newhouse Theaters
19 Longwood Arts Gallery
80 Low Memorial Library, see Columbia University
124 Lower East Side Tenement Museum
82 Macy Gallery, see Columbia University
82 Horace Mann Theatre, see Columbia University
77 Manhattan Theatre Club, see City Center
199 Jacques Marchais Museum of Tibetan Art
124 Merkin Concert Hall
125 Metropolitan Museum of Art
120 Metropolitan Opera House
127 Midtown Y Photography Gallery
82 Kathryn Bache Miller Theatre, see Columbia University
82 Minor Latham Playhouse, see Columbia University
80 Miriam and Ira D. Wallach Art Gallery, see Columbia University
65 Sidney Mishkin Gallery, see Baruch College
119 Mitzi E. Newhouse Theater (Lincoln Center Theater Company)
152 Pierpont Morgan Library
127 Morris-Jumel Mansion
128 Mulberry Street Theater
128 Municipal Archives of New York City
129 El Museo del Barrio
130 Museum for African Art
130 Museum of American Financial History
131 Museum of American Folk Art
131 Museum of American Illustration
132 Museum of Modern Art
134 Museum of Television and Radio
132 Museum of the American Piano
135 Museum of the City of New York
136 National Academy of Design
137 National Museum of the American Indian
138 New Museum of Contemporary Art
138 New York Academy of Science
29 New York Aquarium/Aquarium for Wildlife Conservation
20 New York Botanical Garden
121 New York City Ballet, see New York State Theater
139 New York City Fire Museum
121 New York City Opera, see New York State Theater
39 New York Experimental Glass Workshop
183 New York Hall of Science
139 New York Public Library
141 New York Public Library for the Performing Arts
142 New York School of Interior Design Gallery
142 New York Shakespeare Festival
121 New York State Theater (New York City Ballet, New York City Opera)
143 New York Studio School Gallery
40 New York Transit Museum
144 New York University
147 New-York Historical Society
New York Zoological Society/ The Wildlife Conservation Society, see Bronx Zoo, Central Park Zoo, New York Aquarium, Queens Zoo
119 Mitzi E. Newhouse Theater (Lincoln Center Theater Company)
153 Nicholas Roerich Museum
147 Nikon House
148 92nd St Y
184 Isamu Noguchi Garden Museum
21 North Wind Undersea Institute
146 NYU Creative Writing Program, see New York University
149 Old Merchant's House
150 Pace Downtown Theater at Schimmel Center for the Arts
150 PaineWebber Art Gallery
142 Joseph Papp Public Theater, see New York Shakespeare Festival
51 Park Avenue Atrium
151 Pen and Brush
152 Pierpont Morgan Library
43 Pieter Claesen Wyckoff House Museum
21 Edgar Allan Poe Cottage
152 Police Academy Museum
82 Postcrypt Arts Underground, see Columbia University
153 Pratt Manhattan Gallery
41 Prospect Park
184 P.S. 1 Museum
149 P.S. 122
185 Queens Botanical Garden
185 Queens County Farm Museum
187 Queens Museum of Art
187 Queens Zoo–Wildlife Conservation Center
188 Queensborough Community College Art Gallery
81 Rare Books and Manuscripts Library, see Columbia University

122 Walter Reade Theater (Film Society of Lincoln Center)
153 Nicholas Roerich Museum
154 Theodore Roosevelt Birthplace
82 Arthur Ross Architecture Gallery, see Columbia University
42 Rotunda Gallery
154 Roulette
28 St. Ann and the Holy Trinity, see Arts at St. Ann's
160 St. Mark's Church In-the-Bowery
155 Salmagundi Club
42 Schafler Gallery
82 Schapiro Theatre, see Columbia University
50 Schimmel Center for the Arts, see Pace Downtown Theater
156 Schomburg Center for Research in Black Culture (New York Public Library)
146 School of Education, Dance and Dance Education Program, see New York University
146 School of Education Program in Educational Theater, see New York University
157 Sculpture Center
158 Seagram Gallery
65 Sidney Mishkin Gallery, see Baruch College
52 Abigail Adams Smith House Museum
199 Snug Harbor Cultural Center
188 Socrates Sculpture Park
102 Solomon R. Guggenheim Museum
158 South Street Seaport Museum
82 Southern Asian Institute Reading Room, see Columbia University
160 Spanish Institute
200 Staten Island Botanical Garden
201 Staten Island Children's Museum
202 Staten Island Institute of Arts and Sciences
203 Staten Island Zoo
161 Statue of Liberty
162 Studio Museum in Harlem
82 Sulzberger Parlor, see Columbia University
162 Swiss Institute
114 Sylvia and Danny Kaye Playhouse (Hunter College)
163 Symphony Space
164 Synchronicity Space
164 Taller Boricua Gallery
82 Teatro Piccolo (Casa Italiana), see Columbia University
154 Theodore Roosevelt Birthplace
146 Tisch School of the Arts Dance Program, see New York University
146 Tisch School of the Arts Graduate Acting Program, see New York University
146 Tisch School of the Arts Photograpy Galleries, see New York University
146 Tisch School of the Arts Undergraduate Drama Program, see New York University
164 Town Hall
165 Tribeca Performing Arts Center
166 Trinity Church Museum
123 Alice Tully Hall (Chamber Music Society of Lincoln Center)
167 Ukrainian Museum
167 Urban Center
22 Valentine-Varian House
22 Van Cortlandt House Museum
189 Vander Ende-Onderdonk House
168 Visual Arts Museum
119 Vivian Beaumont Theater (Lincoln Center Theater Company)
80 Miriam and Ira D. Wallach Art Gallery, see Columbia University
122 Walter Reade Theater (Film Society of Lincoln Center)
23 Wave Hill
66 Weill Recital Hall, see Carnegie Hall
168 White Columns
169 Whitney Museum of American Art
196 William T. Davis Wildlife Refuge
170 Winter Garden (Arts and Events)
43 Pieter Claesen Wyckoff House Museum
171 Yeshiva University Museum
171 YIVO Institute for Jewish Research

Subject Index

by page number

BOTANICAL GARDENS/ ENVIRONMENTAL

176 Alley Pond Environmental Center
194 Blue Heron Park
32 Brooklyn Botanic Garden
70 Central Park
195 Clay Pit Ponds State Park Preserve
196 William T. Davis Wildlife Refuge
198 High Rock Park in the Greenbelt
106 Horticultural Society of New York
20 New York Botanical Garden
21 North Wind Undersea Institute
41 Prospect Park
185 Queens Botanical Garden
185 Queens County Farm Museum
200 Staten Island Botanical Garden

DANCE

31 Brooklyn Academy of Music
33 Brooklyn Center for the Performing Arts
77 City Center
179 Colden Center for the Performing Arts
85 Dance Theater Workshop
86 Aaron Davis Hall for the Performing Arts
86 Dia Center for the Arts
89 Educational Alliance
36 Gowanus Arts Exchange
111 Japan Society
113 Joyce Theater
114 Sylvia and Danny Kaye Playhouse
115 Kitchen Center
116 Korean Cultural Service
18 Lehman Center for the Performing Arts
118 Lincoln Center for the Performing Arts
120 Metropolitan Opera House
128 Mulberry Street Theater
121 New York State Theater
149 P.S. 122 (Performance Space 122)
160 St. Mark's Church in-the-Bowery
165 Tribeca Performing Arts Center
170 Winter Garden

HISTORIC STRUCTURES

52 Abigail Adams Smith House Museum
194 Alice Austen House
28 Arts at St. Ann's
14 Bartow-Pell Mansion Museum
178 Bowne House
68 Castle Clinton National Monument
196 Conference House
89 Dyckman House Museum
90 Ellis Island Immigration Museum
92 Federal Hall National Monument
180 Flushing Town Hall
95 Fraunces Tavern Museum
197 Garibaldi-Meucci Museum
100 Governor's Room at City Hall
100 Gracie Mansion
98 General Grant National Memorial
37 Harbor Defense Museum at Fort Hamilton
198 Historic Richmond Town
109 Intrepid Sea Air Space Museum
181 King Manor Museum
182 Kingsland Homestead
38 Lefferts Homestead
124 Lower East Side Tenement Museum
127 Morris-Jumel Mansion
149 Old Merchant's House
21 Edgar Allan Poe Cottage
199 Snug Harbor Cultural Center
158 South Street Seaport Museum
161 Statue of Liberty National Monument
154 Theodore Roosevelt Birthplace
166 Trinity Museum at Trinity Church
22 Valentine-Varian House/ Museum of Bronx History
22 Van Cortlandt House Museum
189 Vander Ende-Onderdonk House
23 Wave Hill
43 Pieter Claesen Wyckoff House Museum

LIBRARIES/LITERARY ARTS

54 American Academy of Arts and Letters
28 Arts at St. Ann's
74 Charas, Inc.
83 Cooper Union
96 French Institute/Alliance Française
97 Frick Collection
102 Grolier Club
106 Hispanic Society of America
180 Langston Hughes Community Library and Cultural Center
38 Kurdish Library and Museum
82 Kathryn Bache Miller Theatre, Columbia Univ.
152 Pierpont Morgan Library
128 Municipal Archives of New York City
139 New York Public Library
141 New York Public Library for the Performing Arts
147 New-York Historical Society
148 92nd Street Y
81 Rare Books & Manuscripts Library, Columbia Univ.
153 Nicholas Roerich Museum
160 St. Mark's Church in-the-Bowery
156 Schomburg Center for Research in Black Culture
163 Symphony Space
164 Synchronicity Space

MUSEUMS/GALLERIES

Art

52 ACA Exhibition Space
53 African Arts Cultural Center
53 Alternative Museum
54 American Craft Museum
55 American Indian Community House
55 American Institute of Graphic Arts
58 American Numismatic Society
58 Americas Society
59 Aperture Foundation/ Burden Gallery
71 Arsenal, Central Park
60 Archives of American Art-Smithsonian Institution
61 Art Students League of New York Gallery
61 Artists Space
62 Asia Society
62 Asian American Arts Centre
63 Austrian Cultural Institute
80 Avery Hall, Columbia Univ.

30 BACA/The Brooklyn Arts Council
64 Bard Graduate Center for Studies in the Decorative Arts
65 Baruch College/ Sidney Mishkin Gallery
65 Black Fashion Museum
15 Bronx Museum of the Arts
15 Bronx River Art Center and Gallery
34 Brooklyn Historical Society
35 Brooklyn Museum
66 Caribbean Cultural Center
145 Casa Italiana Zerilli-Marimo, New York Univ.
68 Cathedral of St. John the Divine
36 Center for Art and Culture of Bedford-Stuyvesant
69 Center for Book Arts
75 China Institute in America
76 Chinatown History Museum
179 Chung-Cheng Art Gallery
77 Cinque Gallery
78 Clocktower Gallery
78 Cloisters
83 Cooper Union
84 Cooper-Hewitt Museum
86 Dia Center for the Arts
88 Drawing Center
89 Educational Alliance
145 80 Washington Square East Galleries, New York Univ.
91 Equitable Center and Gallery
91 Exit Art/The First World
92 Fashion Institute of Technology
180 Flushing Town Hall
17 Focal Point Gallery
94 Forbes Magazine Galleries
94 14 Sculptors Gallery
95 Franklin Furnace Archive
97 Frick Collection
98 Gallery 62
98 Gallery 1199
99 Goethe House New York–German Cultural Center
101 Grand Central Art Galleries
102 Greenwich House Pottery
145 Grey Art Gallery and Study Center, New York Univ.
102 Solomon R. Guggenheim Museum
104 Guggenheim Museum SoHo
17 Hall of Fame for Great American
105 Henry Street Settlement
106 Hispanic Society of America
180 Langston Hughes Community Library and Cultural Center
107 IBM Gallery of Science and Art
107 INTAR Hispanic American Arts Center
110 Elsa Mott Ives Gallery
181 Jamaica Arts Center
111 Japan Society
111 Jewish Museum
112 Joseph Gallery
18 Judaica Museum
114 Kampo Cultural and Multi-Media Center
115 Kenkeleba House New York
115 Kitchen Center
116 Korean Cultural Service
116 Kosciuszko Foundation
145 La Maison Française, New York Univ.
18 Lehman College Art Gallery
19 Longwood Arts Gallery at P.S. 39
80 Low Memorial Library, Columbia Univ.
199 Jacques Marchais Museum of Tibetan Art
125 Metropolitan Museum of Art
152 Pierpont Morgan Library
129 El Museo del Barrio
130 Museum for African Art
131 Museum of American Folk Art
131 Museum of American Illustration
132 Museum of Modern Art
135 Museum of the City of New York
136 National Academy of Design
137 National Museum of the American Indian
138 New Museum of Contemporary Art
39 New York Experimental Glass Workshop
139 New York Public Library
141 New York Public Library for the Performing Arts
142 New York School of Interior Design Gallery
143 New York Studio School Gallery
147 New-York Historical Society
184 Isamu Noguchi Garden Museum
150 PaineWebber Art Gallery
151 Park Avenue Atrium
151 Pen and Brush
82 Postcrypt Arts Underground
184 P.S. 1 Museum
149 P.S. 122 (Performance Space 122)
153 Pratt Manhattan Gallery
187 Queens Museum of Art
188 Queensborough Community College Art Gallery
153 Nicholas Roerich Museum
42 Rotunda Gallery
155 Salmagundi Club
42 Schafler Gallery
156 Schomburg Center for Research in Black Culture
157 Sculpture Center Gallery
157 Seagram Gallery
199 Snug Harbor Cultural Center
188 Socrates Sculpture Park
158 South Street Seaport Museum
160 Spanish Institute
202 Staten Island Institute of Arts and Sciences
162 Studio Museum in Harlem
162 Swiss Institute
164 Taller Boricua Gallery
166 Trinity Museum at Trinity Church
167 Ukrainian Museum
167 Urban Center Galleries
22 Valentine-Varian House/ Museum of Bronx History
168 Visual Arts Museum
80 Miriam & Ira D. Wallach Gallery, Columbia Univ.
23 Wave Hill
168 White Columns
169 Whitney Museum of American Art
170 Winter Garden
171 Yeshiva University Museum
171 YIVO Institute for Jewish Research

Children

71 Belvedere Castle, Central Park
34 Brooklyn Children's Museum
74 Children's Museum of Manhattan
75 Children's Museum of the Native American
201 Staten Island Children's Museum

Science/Technology

56 American Museum of Natural History
58 American Numismatic Society
177 Anthropology Museum of the People of New York
69 Center for Book Arts
83 Con Edison Energy Museum
107 IBM Gallery of Science and Art
109 Intrepid Sea Air Space Museum
138 New York Academy of Sciences
183 New York Hall of Science
40 New York Transit Museum
158 South Street Seaport Museum
202 Staten Island Institute of Arts and Sciences

MUSIC

28 Arts at St. Ann's
63 Austrian Cultural Institute
30 Bargemusic
31 Brooklyn Academy of Music
33 Brooklyn Center for the Performing Arts
66 Caribbean Cultural Center
66 Carnegie Hall
68 Cathedral of St. John the Divine
179 Colden Center for the Performing Arts
86 Aaron Davis Hall for the Performing Arts
89 Educational Alliance
120 Avery Fisher Hall
180 Flushing Town Hall
114 Sylvia and Danny Kaye Playhouse
115 Kitchen Center
18 Lehman Center for the Performing Arts
118 Lincoln Center for the Performing Arts
124 Merkin Concert Hall
82 Kathryn Bache Miller Theatre, Columbia Univ.
148 92nd Street Y
150 Pace Downtown Theater
82 Postcrypt Arts Underground
153 Nicholas Roerich Museum
154 Roulette
199 Snug Harbor Cultural Center
163 Symphony Space
164 Town Hall
165 Tribeca Performing Arts Center
123 Alice Tully Hall
23 Wave Hill
170 Winter Garden

OPERA

31 Brooklyn Academy of Music
179 Colden Center for the Performing Arts
96 French Institute/ Alliance Française
114 Sylvia and Danny Kaye Playhouse
118 Lincoln Center for the Performing Arts
124 Merkin Concert Hall
120 Metropolitan Opera House
82 Kathryn Bache Miller Theatre, Columbia Univ.
121 New York State Theater
148 92nd Street Y
165 Tribeca Performing Arts Center

PHOTOGRAPHY/FILM/VIDEO

176 American Museum of the Moving Image
59 Anthology Film Archives
59 Aperture Foundation/ Burden Gallery
194 Alice Austen House
63 Austrian Cultural Institute
80 Avery Hall
30 BACA/The Brooklyn Arts Council
74 Charas, Inc.
83 Cooper Union
86 Aaron Davis Hall for the Performing Arts
90 Ellis Island Immigration Museum
96 French Institute/ Alliance Française
99 Goethe House New York–German Cultural Center
180 Langston Hughes Community Library and Cultural Center
108 International Center of Photograpy
115 Kitchen Center
116 Korean Cultural Service
127 Midtown Y Photography Gallery
129 El Museo del Barrio
132 Museum of Modern Art
134 The Museum of Television and Radio
147 Nikon House
146 Photography Galleries, New York Univ.
122 Walter Reade Theater, Lincoln Center
163 Symphony Space
169 Whitney Museum of American Art

THEATER

55 American Indian Community House
119 Vivian Beaumont Theater, Lincoln Center
31 Brooklyn Academy of Music
68 Castillo Cultural Center
74 Charas, Inc.
77 City Center
179 Colden Center for the Performing Arts
142 Delacorte Theater, New York Shakespeare Festival
87 Dixon Place
88 Downtown Art Co.
180 Flushing Town Hall
36 Gowanus Arts Exchange
146 Graduate Acting Program, New York Univ.
105 Henry Street Settlement
180 Langston Hughes Community Library and Cultural Center
107 INTAR Hispanic American Arts Center
110 Irish Arts Center
111 Japan Society
114 Sylvia and Danny Kaye Playhouse
115 Kitchen Center
116 Korean Cultural Service
117 La Mama E.T.C.
142 New York Shakespeare Festival
119 Mitzi E. Newhouse Theater, Lincoln Center
150 Pace Downtown Theater
142 Joseph Papp Public Theater, New York Shakespeare Festival
149 P.S. 122 (Performance Space 122)
199 Snug Harbor Cultural Center
160 St. Mark's Church in-the-Bowery
164 Town Hall
165 Tribeca Performing Arts Center

ZOOS

29 Aquarium for Wildlife Conservation
16 Bronx Zoo–Wildlife Conservation Park
72 Central Park Zoo–Wildlife Conservation Center
41 Prospect Park Zoo–Wildlife Conservation Center
187 Queens Zoo–Wildlife Conservation Center
203 Staten Island Zoo

Acknowledgments

The **NEW YORK CITY CULTURE CATALOG** was conceived of by Patricia Jones, former Executive Vice President of the Alliance for the Arts (originally known as the Cultural Assistance Center). Much of the research was supervised by Pat Jones, who remains a member of the board of the Alliance.

Paul Gottlieb, President and Publisher of Harry N. Abrams, Inc., remained faithfully committed to this book during its long gestation. We are very grateful for his support and the cooperation of the gifted staff at Abrams, especially Margaret Rennolds Chace, the project manager; Kate Norment, our editor; Gertrud Brehme, Production Manager; Samuel Antupit, Vice President, Art and Design; and Toula Ballas for her encouragement.

We thank each of the 238 organizations featured in this book, which could not have been produced without their cooperation in providing information and pictures.

Other organizations and individuals offered extraordinary advice and assistance, including: the Bronx Tourism Council, the Historic House Trust of New York City, New York City Department of Cultural Affairs, New York City Department of Parks and Recreation, New York City Landmarks Preservation Commission, New York State Council on the Arts, New York State Office of Parks, Recreation and Historic Preservation, the Theatre Development Fund, and the U.S. Department of the Interior.

We are grateful to Kitty Carlisle Hart, both for her introductory words and for the support of the New York State Council on the Arts, of which she is the valiant chairperson; to Stephanie French and Karen Brosius of Philip Morris for their generous support; to Jonathan Tisch of Loews Hotels for his support and guidance; and to Joan Davidson and the staff of The J.M. Kaplan Fund, which patiently encouraged this project with both funds and advice.

For the staff of the Alliance, this book was a labor of love, the heaviest burden of which was carried by Sarah Peterson. Francine Goldenhar generously contributed her knowledge at an early stage of the book's preparation. And, finally, we were fortunate in having the services of Bill Beavers, a writer with extensive knowledge of the arts and a just sense of language.

The design firm of Patterson Wood transformed words on a page into an accessible visual format. We are grateful to Peg Patterson, Caroline Kavanagh, Michael Graziolo and Jeff Kryvicky for their creative ideas, attention to detail and unflagging commitment to this project.

This project was aided and guided at crucial moments by the board of the Alliance, especially by our Chairman, Robert H. Montgomery, Jr., a man as remarkable for his modesty as for his wisdom, and by Betty Prashker, a dependable source of editorial direction.

The **NEW YORK CITY CULTURE CATALOG** is dedicated to Robert F. Wagner, Jr., former member of the board of the Alliance for the Arts and a great citizen of New York City, whose untimely death occurred shortly before the book's completion. Bobby Wagner knew more about New York than anyone we know, and he would have loved a book that opened so many of its treasures, large and small, to so many people.

Randall Bourscheidt
President
Alliance for the Arts

Additional Books About New York

Access for All: A Guide for People with Disabilities
Hospital Audiences, New York: Hospital Audiences, and WCBS 88 Radio, 1992.

American Institute of Architects Guide to New York City
Willensky, Elliot, and White, Norval. New York: Harcourt Brace, 1988.

Applause: New York Guide to the Performing Arts
Carter, Gladys (ed.). New York: Applause Book Publishers, 1991.

Art Walks in New York
Harrison, Marina, and Rosenfeld, Lucy (eds.). New York: Michael Kesend Publishing, 1991.

Birnbaum's New York
Birnbaum, Stephen, and Birnbaum-Mayes, Alexandra. New York: Harper Perennial, 1992.

Blue Guide, New York
Von Pressentin-Wright, Carol. New York: W.W. Norton, 1991.

Changing New York: The Architectural Scene
Gray, Christopher. New York: Dover, 1992.

Chinatown: Portrait of a Closed Society
Kinkead, Gwen. New York: Harper Collins, 1992.

The City Observed: New York, A Guide to the Architecture of Manhattan
Goldberger, Paul and Dunlap, David W. (photography). New York: Vintage Books, 1979.

The Greenwich Village Guide
McDarrah, Patrick and McDarrah, Fred. New York: A Capella Books, 1992.

Greenwich Village and How It Got That Way
Miller, Terry. New York: Crown, 1990.

Guide to New York City Landmarks
Dolkart, Andrew. New York: New York Landmarks Preservation Commission, 1993.

Historic Houses in New York City Parks
City of New York Parks and Recreation. New York: The Historic House Trust of New York City and City of New York Parks and Recreation, 1992.

It Happened in Brooklyn
Katz-Frommer, Myrna, and Katz, Harvey. New York: Harcourt Brace, 1991.

Kids Culture Catalog
Alliance for the Arts. New York: Alliance for the Arts, 1987.

The Landmarks of New York
Diamonstein, Barbaralee. New York: Harry N. Abrams, Inc., 1993.

Manhattan's Outdoor Sculpture
Gayle, Margot, and Cohen, Michelle. New York: Art Commission of the City of New York and the Municipal Art Society.

Manhattan Up Close: District to District. Street by Street
New York: Passport Books, 1992.

Maximum City: The Biography of New York
Pye, Michael. London: Sinclair-Stevenson, 1991.

Monuments and Masterpieces, Histories and Views of Public Sculpture in New York City.
Martin Reynolds, Donald. New York: Macmillan, 1988.

Museums in New York
McDarrah, Fred W. and Mc Darrah, Gloria S. New York: St. Martins Press, 1990.

New York City Museums
Ross, Betty. Washington, DC: Globe Peuot Press, 1991.

New York: A Guide to the Metropolis
Wolfe, Gerard. New York: Mcgraw-Hill, Inc., 1994.

New York on Stage
Rodriguez, Eve (ed.). New York: Theatre Development Fund, 1991.

New York Theatre Sourcebook
Lawliss, Chuck. New York: Simon & Schuster, 1990.

New York Walks–The 92nd Street Y
Plotch, Batia. New York: Henry Holt, 1992.

New York's Best-Kept Secrets
Michaelson, Mike. New York: Passport Books, 1993.

On Broadway: A Journey Uptown Over Time
Dunlap, David W. New York: Rizzoli, 1990.

722 Miles: The Building of the Subways and How They Transformed New York
Hood, Clifton. New York: Simon & Schuster, 1993.

SoHo, The Artist in the City
Simpson, Charles. Chicago: University of Chicago Press, 1981.

Upper West Side Story: A History and Guide
Salwen, Peter. New York: Abbeville Press, 1989.

NOTES

NOTES

NOTES

NOTES